In Precarious Battle

In Precarious Battle

Labour Broking in the South African Post Office

David Dickinson

UNIVERSITY OF KWAZULU-NATAL PRESS

Published in 2021 by University of KwaZulu-Natal Press
Private Bag X01
Scottsville, 3201
Pietermaritzburg
South Africa
Email: books@ukzn.ac.za
Website: www.ukznpress.co.za

© 2021 David Dickinson

All rights reserved. No part of this publication may be reproduced or transmitted in any form or by electrical or mechanical means, including information storage and retrieval systems, without prior permission in writing from the publishers.

ISBN: 978 1 86914 468 5
e-ISBN: 978 1 86914 469 2

Project manager: Sally Hines
Editing: Karin Pampallis and Sally Hines
Layout: Patricia Comrie
Proofreader: Catherine Munro
Indexer: Judith Shier
Cover design: Marise Bauer, M Design
Cover photograph: Tshidiso Selialia, DEPACU shop steward and Mabarete member, 2014 (photo: David Dickinson)

Printed and bound in South Africa by XMD Books (Pty) Ltd

Contents

Preface	vii
Acronyms and Abbreviations	x
1 Introduction	1
2 Precarious South Africa	10
3 The Long Road to Legislation	30
4 SAPO and Labour Brokers	45
5 Postmen	57
6 A Divided Class	71
7 A Divided Union	80
8 A Constitutional Crusade	102
9 To Stand and Fight	121
10 Three Times a Failure: Organising Casuals	138
11 We Are the Union Ourselves!	149
12 The Long Tactics of Labour Broking	174
13 The Mabarete Strike I: Striking and Scabbing	199
14 The Mabarete Strike II: Invisible Violence	215
15 The Mabarete Strike III: Manifest Fear	238
16 Above and Below the *Lex*: Insurgent Unionism and Technologies of Struggle, 2011–2014	251
17 Conclusion: Permanent Battle	278
Notes	285
References	307
Index	323

Preface

A book is a collective endeavour and this one is no exception. As I outline in the introductory chapter, the research for this book began, unintentionally, in the township of Katlehong, south-east of Johannesburg. Many thanks to my Katlehong friends and, in particular, to Maja Mokhutsoane whose varied contributions run, acknowledged and unacknowledged, throughout this book.

While researching this book and beyond, I have remained alongside the Democratic Postal and Communications Union, but my sincere thanks go to all those who assisted me, irrespective of where their loyalties now lie in the communication sector's fractured labour landscape. The slogan *Unity is strength!* is easily uttered but hard to achieve. South Africans are divided in many ways and each division makes us weaker. This book tells the story of how precariously employed workers triumphed over labour broking in the South African Post Office (SAPO). Labour broking is but one form of precarious employment that entrenches exploitation and divisions in societies across the world. However, the book also illustrates divisions within labour as well as the way in which one precarious employment practice can morph into another. There is nothing new to exploitation or to how divided workforces permit it to continue in ever-changing form. The book's title nods to John Steinbeck's *In Dubious Battle*, a novel centred on the resistance of migrant fruit pickers to exploitation in 1930s' California. Steinbeck saw his description of a violent strike symbolising 'man's eternal, bitter warfare with himself' (McParland 2016: 44). While my writing does not match Steinbeck's prose, if the book assists in any way to address exploitation and the divisions that pit us against each other, then it will have been worth writing.

My initial reporting and analysis on labour broking in SAPO appeared as a working paper for the Society, Work and Development Institute at the University of the Witwatersrand. Articles published in the *Journal of Southern African Studies* and the *Review of African Political Economy* provided further opportunity to develop arguments and perspectives. So, too, did presentations at the Wits Institute for Social and Economic Research, the 2015 and 2017 South African Sociological Association congresses and elsewhere. The book's first draft was written during a six-month sabbatical, partly funded by the Anderson-Capelli Fund, at the QwaQwa campus of the University of the Free State; my thanks to colleagues there and to the residents of Sehlajaneng village for welcoming me among them.

Two anonymous reviewers for UKZN Press made helpful comments, including pointing out that the manuscript was too long. I turned to Karin Pampallis for assistance, and my thanks to her for excellent editing. Funding for the research came from my university research publication fund, ad hoc grants from the Wits Faculty of Humanities and, when these ran short, from my own resources.

It would be impossible to explain the individual contributions of the many people who assisted in one way or another, and would probably in some cases be unwise. So, many thanks to everybody and in particular: Lesenyeho Bass, Kodisang Bokaba, Thabiso Bopape, Keith Breckenridge, Aaron Buthelezi, Tracey Calmeyer, Gavin Capps, Caphus Chauke, Moraba Choshi, Jackie Cock, Dawood Dada, Owen Dakama, Kenneth Diane, Bheki Dlamini, Anthea Edwards, Weizmann Hamilton, Nkele Jele, Charles John, Hans Kgodu, Jerry Kgodu, Samuel Khanye, Eric Khumalo, Maureen Kirori, Jonathan Klaaren, Samuel Kobo, Siphiwe Kubheka, Albert Lebago, Lefa Lenka, Moeketsi 'MP' Lepheane, Dipuo Letsai, Wanga Linda, Carmen Ludwig, Jabulani Mabena, Andile Mabitzela, Mkwabe Mabulane, Ian Macun, Grey Magaiza, Jaqueline Maja, Makalo Makale, Jonas Makaung, Marcus Makhura, Stembiso Makulukulu, Solly Malepe, Bonita Mashishi, Sam Matiki, Ernest Mazibuko, Sibusiso Mbele, Jared McDonald, Toto Mlaza, Sarah Modise, Desmond Moeketsi, Zoleka Moeng, Tshidiso Mofokeng, Peter Mofula, Phuti Mokgethle, Maja Mokhutsoane, Justice Mokoena, Papiki Mokoena, Tutu Mokoena, David 'City'

Mulaudzi, Nanakie Moroti, Alfred Mosito, Ernest 'Tovey' Montoedi, Mmalokoalo Motha, Ronnie Motoling, Mathapelo Mphuti, Moloko Mpolobosho, Russel Mutavhatsindi, Nelson Ndlangamandla, Freddy Nkela, Alfred Ntshengedzeni, Bongani Nxumalo, Palesa Papi, Charles Petersen, Malandela Radebe, George Ramagaga, Gibson Ramotsi, Sello Ramokgopa, Prince Rampoti, Mashudu Ratshifheti, Rob Rees, Carin Runciman, Xoliseka Santi, Mametlwe Sebei, Ighsaan Schroeder, Ben Scully, Lerato Seema, Tshidiso Selialia, Shitas Selota, Themba Sibiya, Sibusiso Simelane, Vusumuzi Thango, Jan Theron, Phutas Tseki, Seun Tshabalala, Tsu Tsotsetsi, Wouda Venter, Sifiso Vilikazi, Karl von Holdt, Eddie Webster and Sipho 'Levy' Zwane.

Acronyms and Abbreviations

AMCU	Association of Mineworkers and Construction Union
ANC	African National Congress
ANCYL	African National Congress Youth League
APC	African People's Convention
BCEA	Basic Conditions of Employment Act
BEE	Black Economic Empowerment
BUSA	Business Unity South Africa
CCMA	Commission for Conciliation, Mediation and Arbitration
COSATU	Congress of South African Trade Unions
COSAWU	Commercial, Services and Allied Workers Union
CWAO	Casual Workers Advice Office
CWU	Communication Workers Union
DA	Democratic Alliance
DEPACU	Democratic Postal and Communications Union
DSM	Democratic Socialist Movement
GDP	gross domestic product
GEAR	Growth, Employment and Redistribution
HR	human resources
IICUSA	Intelligent Information and Communications Union of South Africa
ILO	International Labour Organization
LBWC	Labour Broker Workers Committee
LEWUSA	Labour Equity General Workers Union of South Africa
LRA	Labour Relations Act

MCP	Mail Collection Point
NACAWU	National Communications and Allied Workers Union
NEDLAC	National Economic Development and Labour Council
NGO	non-governmental organisation
NUM	National Union of Mineworkers
NUMSA	National Union of Metalworkers of South Africa
PNL	Pos en Telekommunikasie Unie
POTWA	Post Office and Telecommunications Workers Association
PPTE	Permanent Part-Time Employee
PSIRA	Private Securities Industry Regulatory Authority
SABC	South African Broadcasting Corporation
SACP	South African Communist Party
SAF	South Africa Foundation
SAGWAWTU	South African Gaming, Waitron and Admin Workers Trade Union
SAIRR	South African Institute of Race Relations
SAPAWU	South African Postal and Allied Workers Union
SAPO	South African Post Office
SAPS	South African Police Service
SAPWU	South African Postal Workers Union (later SAPAWU)
SATAWU	South African Transport and Allied Workers Union
SER	standard employment relationship
SRC	student representative council
T&L	T&L Appointments
TAS	TAS Appointments and Management Services
TES	temporary employment services
UIF	Unemployment Insurance Fund
UNISA	University of South Africa
VUT	Vaal University of Technology
WASP	Workers and Socialist Party
YCL	Young Communist League

1

Introduction

In Precarious Battle tells how labour broking was confronted and defeated in the South African Post Office (SAPO). Labour broking has, for good reason, become synonymous with worker exploitation. In 2011, at the height of SAPO's use of labour brokers, a third of its workforce consisted of labour broker employees or 'casuals'. I use the term casuals since it was the term used by the workers themselves. They were, however, not casual in the sense of being employed temporarily for several days, weeks or months. These casuals worked for SAPO alongside directly employed, or 'permanent', workers for years. Beyond their employment contracts, the critical difference between permanents and casuals was the salary: casuals received a quarter of the pay that the permanents received.

Labour broking 'externalises' the employment relationship from the company. SAPO casuals worked as postmen and mail handlers under the management of Post Office supervisors but were the employees of a labour broking company.

Chapter 2 describes the triangular employment relationship created by labour broking. However, what should be underlined immediately is the longevity of these arrangements. The legislation that regulates labour broking, the Labour Relations Act (LRA), does not use the term labour broking, but rather refers to temporary employment services. The statutory term suggests that such services provide workers to cover for absences by company employees or a temporary increase in its order books. Labour brokers do indeed fulfil this function, and some labour brokers began as placement agencies. Although labour brokers do meet genuinely needed, temporary labour needs, their key business evolved into the provision of cheap and compliant labour far beyond any flexibility requirements. The focus of this book is not temporary placements but the provision by labour brokers of workers on a long-term basis, sometimes for over a decade. There was nothing temporary about these placements. Indeed, the oxymorons 'permanent casual' or 'permanent temp[orary]' better describes the situation.

The struggle to end labour broking brings into relief key post-apartheid social fractures. In particular, it exposes how the vision of an egalitarian society based on the constitutional values of dignity, rights and freedom has been subverted by a scramble for personal advancement. This undermining of social transformation has taken place in the shadows, often disguised by *ubuntu* rhetoric.[1] The Post Office, traditionally focused on serving the white minority, was mandated by the post-1994 democratic government to advance social development. The organisation made significant strides in this direction. However, it did so on the backs of thousands of casuals who were all but invisible within an organisation that trumpeted good governance and social responsibility in report after annual report.

When placed in context, the struggle against labour broking documented in this book is a reaction to the subversion of laws promoting social justice. Loopholes in the LRA were used to create instruments of labour supply that perpetuated inequality through the re-creation of a two-tier labour market, based not on race but on the contractual form of employment.

It took time for the casuals in SAPO to realise that they were trapped by their contracts, but when this dawned what emerged was the mobilisation of extra-constitutional self-help in the form of intimidation and violence. It was with this that they broke their chains; and this response raises the morally taut question of what responses are legitimate when the law is deployed to defeat social justice.

To understand why SAPO casuals used physical violence we need to recognise how the labour broking system perpetuated structural violence against them (Galtung 1969). Labour broking was upheld in SAPO by a range of social actors. As well as narrating resistance to labour broking in the Post Office, this book looks at how it entered SAPO, who benefited and the roles they played in maintaining this system of labour exploitation.

On 1 January 2015, amendments to the LRA regulating, inter alia, labour broking contracts came into effect. As is made clear in the explanatory memorandum to the parliamentary bill, the intention was that labour broker employees placed with a client company for more than three months would be 'deemed' a permanent employee of the client.[2] Further, they must be employed on the same terms and conditions as other employees doing equivalent work. If the amended legislation had fulfilled its intended purpose, the struggles of the SAPO casuals would be largely of historical interest. However, just as labour broking originally emerged via loopholes in the post-apartheid LRA, various forms of precarious labour are being continued and adapted post the 2015 LRA amendments. The meaning of 'deemed' was contested in a protracted legal battle, resolved only in July 2018 with a Constitutional Court (2018) ruling. The legal uncertainty delayed use of the amended legislation and provided labour brokers the opportunity to restructure their business models. What continues, under different names and in different forms, is the business of providing precarious workers.

The end of apartheid brought a dramatic rupture in South Africa's legal framework. More important than bald claims to the progressiveness of the country's Constitution is how the new legal order impacts people's lives. The idea of 'transformative constitutionalism' suggests a society that is being systematically and progressively reformed with the advance of political, social and economic rights (Davis and Klare 2010). The new industrial relations system, enabled through the LRA and other legislation, was an important component of this agenda of transformative constitutionalism. Yet, the story of casual workers in SAPO illustrates how the quest for precarious labour is without end. And so, too, is resistance. Systems of structural violence and resistance to them have one striking parallel. Both operate without rigid boundaries between constitutional and extra-constitutional forms or, as described later in this book, above and below the *lex*.

In Precarious Battle focuses on labour broking in one South African organisation. Yet, the supply of precarious labour takes many forms in every country on earth. The book illustrates but one example of a much wider battle.

Researching struggle

The research for this book began in Katlehong Township as I saw the labour broking system through the eyes of postmen friends. I listened and kept notes with increasing interest as I learned more about their working lives and their participation in the struggles described in this book. As it happened, my friends were participants in the 2009 strike called by the Communication Workers Union (CWU), as well as both the mid-2011 and Mabarete strikes. I first expanded my contact with SAPO casual workers beyond my group of township friends when I joined a meeting of striking workers in July 2011. Thereafter, I sporadically attended a range of their activities. It was only in November 2013, however, that I requested permission to interview leaders of the organisation with a view to writing a history of the Mabarete. This was granted during a long Saturday afternoon in Soweto spent with the then united leadership of the Mabarete's Top 9 and former officials of the South African Postal and Allied Workers Union (SAPAWU).

After applying for ethical permission for the research from the Human Research Ethics Committee at the University of the Witwatersrand, I started interviewing in February 2014. Eventually, I interviewed eight of the Top 9 leaders, along with others within the Mabarete who had played varied leadership roles. I also interviewed a number of individuals in SAPO, political parties, trade unions, academics, a former SAPO board member, and the director of the Germiston-based Casual Workers Advice Office (CWAO); all of them provided different perspectives on events. In total, I conducted 65 formal interviews with 46 individuals. Additionally, I held a group discussion with five SAPO supervisors on their experiences of the casuals' strikes.

As well as formally interviewing key leaders of the Mabarete and the Democratic Postal and Communications Union, I spent time with the organisation during two industrial disputes in 2014. This opened up a wealth of research avenues, including short, informal interviews with rank-and-file Mabarete members at various locations. As well as providing a wider range of perspectives on earlier strikes, participant observation gave me a better understanding of how the strategies and tactics, described in interviews, were carried out on the ground.

It was important to understand the work of a postman. Without this it would be difficult to understand how labour broking operated in SAPO. And, since the Mabarete strike in particular was about stopping postmen from working, it was also important to understand the work of postal delivery. I learned a great deal from ongoing discussions with postmen about their work, which I supplemented by working informally as a postman: sorting mail and going out on delivery.

Written documents, along with my field notes, provided important references. Two worker leaders provided me with their handwritten minutes of workers committee meetings, along with other material. I was also given access to documents held by the CWAO. Additionally, the Commission for Conciliation, Mediation and Arbitration (CCMA) provided me with a database of cases involving SAPO and TAS Appointments and Management Services (TAS), the largest labour broker in Gauteng between 2008 and 2012. Labour Court files for four interdicts applied for by SAPO, as well as the Vaal Workers Committee's own application to the Labour Court in 2011, provided information, including the contemporary perspectives of SAPO management and labour brokers during strikes. Additional written sources included SAPO's annual reports, its Employment Equity Reports (obtained from the Department of Labour), the *South African Labour Bulletin*, and various newspaper/media accounts of events. All these assisted in triangulating the accounts given to me in formal and informal interviews.

Any research project has limits and there are three perspectives that I failed to secure. It would have been very informative to interview Clyde Mervin of CWU, but I had published a working paper that was critical of CWU and he was not interested in talking to me. It would have been insightful to talk to E.T. Mpai about the Mabarete's visit to his home in 2012. Through an intermediator I spoke to him and he agreed to be interviewed, but then stopped taking my calls. Finally, I made strenuous efforts to interview labour brokers and in particular TAS's owner, Colleen Ramaphakela. I eventually spoke to her husband. He said he would pass my message on, but I never heard back. These interviews, and undoubtedly others, would have added to the depth of the book if they had taken place.

Outline of the book

The following two chapters focus on labour broking in South Africa and the long campaign for legislative regulation. Chapter 2 introduces key features of South Africa's urbanscape through an early morning train journey from township to town in Gauteng Province. The chapter explores how precarious work undermines dignity and challenges personal status. It concludes by exploring how class is being reconstructed by precarious work that traps many into perpetual poverty while providing others with opportunities for success. Chapter 3 explores how post-apartheid legalisation provided a mechanism for companies to procure cheap workers. The opportunity arose via a loophole in the 1995 LRA, and the chapter examines the long campaign, led by the Congress of South African Trade Unions (COSATU), to ban labour broking; this campaign ended with the 2015 amendments to the LRA, which sought to regulate the practice.

The next four chapters focus on labour broking in SAPO, on the business of the Post Office, the working lives of postmen, and the impact that labour broking had on workers and unions. Chapter 4 describes how labour broking was brought into SAPO to cut costs and then mushroomed to one-third of the organisation's workforce. It explains how labour brokers operated and the terms and conditions under which casuals were employed. We then turn our attention to some of the individuals caught in SAPO's labour broking regime. Chapter 5 follows three postmen on their daily rounds. The chapter illustrates how the mail system functions, including delivering letters door to door. Such work is not without its difficulties, and some of these are narrated in the chapter. Chapter 6 surveys how the precarious legal status of casuals made them vulnerable in the workplace. SAPO management took advantage of this vulnerability, though the exploitation was hidden from public view behind a veneer of corporate respectability. It was not, however, only management and labour brokers who exploited the casuals but also a section of their own class: the permanent workers. The forms of this division are explored along with the bitterness that it engendered. Permanent workers in SAPO were represented by the COSATU-aligned Communication Workers Union. CWU had an iron grip on SAPO, and for many years was the company's only union. Chapter 7 explores how the union campaigned nationally to ban labour brokers while allowing them to enter and expand in SAPO. Internally, CWU was split over the issues of casuals, but the faction championing their cause was defeated in an internal power struggle. The chapter outlines how CWU's complicity with labour broking was ultimately a disastrous strategy for the union.

Chapters 8 to 15 describe the struggle against labour brokers in SAPO. Casuals initially used legal and constitutional methods in attempts to address their situation. These focused on improving their position, without challenging their status as labour broker employees. In Chapter 8, particular emphasis is placed on the tenacious but unsuccessful attempts by the Vaal Workers Committee to use the CCMA and the Labour Court to challenge their terms and conditions of employment. Chapter 9 looks at how casual workers started to mobilise outside of union structures, initially in individual workplaces and then through area-based workers committees across Gauteng. The chapter also explores why it was postmen rather than casuals in the sorting hubs, and why it was men rather than women, who led the struggle to end labour broking. Alongside the emergence of workers committees, three attempts were made by unions to assist casual workers. This focused on gaining legal recognition with labour broking companies. These endeavours, described in Chapter 10, were made by organisations with different ideological approaches. However, all three were ultimately defeated by the industrial relations system that they relied upon to advance the casuals' cause. The first major strike of casual workers was initiated by the Tembisa Workers Committee in mid-2011, and is described in Chapter 11. The wildcat strike halted mail delivery for several weeks across the East Rand, the Vaal and elsewhere. The strike was a decisive break with past attempts to work within the industrial relations system. Strikers declared that they 'were the union themselves' and developed 'technologies of struggle' that were to prove critical in ending SAPO's labour broking. However, the strike was crushed by a Labour Court interdict that declared it illegal and saw leaders facing jail for contempt of court. Chapter 12 breaks the narrative of rising resistance to labour broking in SAPO to ask why labour broking lasted so long. It is argued that the system's longevity cannot be explained by focusing on labour brokers alone, but rather through understanding a confederacy of actors, which include the labour broking companies, SAPO management, line managers and even the CWU and permanent workers. I describe the tactics used by the labour brokers, which, in a mirror image of the casuals' technologies of struggle, operated above and below the *lex*. The Mabarete strike, which ended labour broking, is covered over three chapters. Chapter 13 introduces the strike that was initiated by the West Rand Workers Committee six months after the mid-2011 or Tembisa strike. It explains how a small group of men (and a handful of women) – a now mythologised band of 294, the Mabarete – were on strike for over four months. This chapter explores the complexities of striking outside of the industrial relations system, with fragmented organisation, intense interpersonal rivalries and competing strategies. It looks at the difficult choices made by casuals with few resources as to whether they should strike or scab, and the consequences of those choices. Chapter 14 explores how the impact of the strike rested on the Mabarete's ability to disrupt the operations of the Post Office through the application of violence. Avoiding the courts (a lesson learned from the mid-2011 strike), the Mabarete hunted working postmen. Those caught were punished with increasingly severe beatings. The result was that delivery all but stopped in Gauteng townships where the Mabarete were able to operate relatively freely. Yet, given the location of this disruptive action, the chapter concludes that this technology of struggle, while effective in preventing mail delivery, remained all but invisible. While the hunting of postmen in the townships was ignored by SAPO, Chapter 15 explains how it established the Mabarete's reputation. When they then paid a 'home visit' to a senior SAPO manager, the balance of forces tipped and negotiations commenced. At this point, the Mabarete turned to a group of union officials working for SAPAWU (a union established in a break-away from CWU) to assist them. Because CWU was not party to these negotiations, the settlement was not put to paper. Verbally, it was agreed that the Mabarete (and eventually all casuals) would be hired, initially as SAPO-employed temporary workers and then converted to permanents. The Mabarete returned victorious to their depots in April 2012.

Ending the story with the victory of the Mabarete would finish the book on a high note. However, the final two chapters are reflections, essentially an exploration of how South African industrial relations do not correspond to the prescribed constitutional system. Chapter 16 examines the messy aftermath to the Mabarete strike. It demonstrates the disastrous long-term results of SAPO's use of labour brokers. It also shows how class struggle is waged in South Africa – not the comfortable narrative framed by constitutional rights and labour legislation but rather with intimidation and violence that is embedded deep in the fabric of society; how those who do not, in practice, have the equality outlined in the country's Constitution struggle above and below the *lex*. Chapter 17 closes the book by attempting a wider reflection on what the precarious battle of the SAPO casuals tells us about South Africa and systems of exploitation. It reflects on the tragedy of labour broking in the Post Office. It looks at how short-term gain created misery for those trapped in the labour broking system, how the Constitution failed casual workers, and the trajectory that the struggle against labour broking subsequently took. The chapter concludes with an evaluation of how the contractual arrangements of labour broking, and other forms of precarious employment, whether in South Africa or elsewhere, facilitate the exploitation of some for the benefit of others. It also demonstrates how struggles do not end, but instead reconfigure the terrain of social conflict.

2

Precarious South Africa

South Africa from the Metrorail
Extremes of wealth and poverty are enabled by the separation of rich and poor. Yet, since the poor labour for the rich, their separation is incomplete. South Africa, shaped by its colonial and apartheid past, is among the world's most unequal societies. This is an account of inequality, exclusion and struggle in Gauteng, South Africa, post-1994. Post-*Uhuru*.

Gauteng is the smallest of South Africa's nine provinces, less than 2 per cent of the country's land mass, but it has the largest population: more than 13 million people in 2015, around 25 per cent of the nation's total. Much of its 18 000 square kilometres is urban. It embraces the cities of Johannesburg and Pretoria, numerous smaller towns, leafy suburbs, office blocks, industrial zones, sprawling townships and informal settlements of tightly packed *mekhukhu* (shacks). The population is racially and ethnically diverse. The 2011 census records five of South Africa's eleven official languages spoken at home by just over 10 per cent of the population: isiZulu, English, Afrikaans, Sepedi and Sesotho. On the streets, however, the lingua franca is a bubbling argot that mixes, mashes and makes language in more flavours than you will find in an ice-cream parlour.

This population grows daily as a result of centripetal economic forces, since the province accounts for one-third of gross domestic product (GDP). Migration from other provinces and from across South Africa's borders swell the population. Migrants and residents work in factories, warehouses, malls, restaurants, schools, universities, hospitals, government departments and financial institutions, or in myriad services provided by private companies, parastatals and non-governmental organisations (NGOs). Alongside this is an informal economy operating from street stalls, *spaza* shops (corner stores), bakkies (pickup trucks), backyards, garages and kitchens that retail goods and services on the cheap and on the side. Further into the shadows of the grey economy, are illegal electricity connections, *fongkong* (fake) goods, afterhours drinking, corrupt officials and back-door purchases of *dulas* (stolen goods).

The residents of Gauteng live and work in this metropolis stretching almost 100 kilometres from the province's northern to southern border. With few exceptions, they live apart, divided by race and by income into their respective suburbs, townships and informal settlements. But they are connected for the purpose of work. Those who labour for others travel on buses, minibus ('black' taxis), privately owned cars whose owners subsidise running expenses with paying passengers, and the Metrorail. The rush-hour traffic that chokes the freeways is studded with BMW and Mercedes-Benz sedans: de rigueur models for those riding atop South Africa's inequality. Apart from the prestigious Gautrain that links Pretoria, Johannesburg, the affluent northern suburbs and O.R. Tambo International Airport, the rich use private cars (without paying passengers), metered taxis or Uber hails. Few have ever used a public bus, even fewer a black taxi, almost none the Metrorail.

The Metrorail in the province has eleven lines and more than 200 stations that reach across the urbanised core of Gauteng. There are three major hubs in the network where commuters change lines: Johannesburg's Park Station, Pretoria and Germiston, the last a small, run-down industrial town on the East Rand.[1] Travelling by Metrorail is not fast, nor comfortable, nor reliable, nor safe. But it is cheap. Its primary function is to transport those who live in the townships to work and back again. Generally, it is the cheapest option for those with tight budgets. Minibus taxis are not comfortable either; however they ply any route for which there are passengers; you'll get to your destination quicker, but it will cost you more.

Jerry lives in Tsietsi in the south of Katlehong Township. By the time he reaches the Kwesine Station, the end of the Katlehong Metrorail line, he has walked for a good half hour. He works at the Boksburg postal depot, which means he first rides the train to Germiston. The 30 or so kilometres of track will take as many minutes on a good day.

There, he will change trains for a fifteen-minute ride to Boksburg Station, where another ten minutes of walking completes his commute. As long as there are no delays, and he makes the change at Germiston without a hitch, it's a one-and-a-half hour journey. If he went by taxi, it would be quicker and there would be almost no walking. But the monthly fares would come to R420 (in 2011 prices).[2] A lift to Boksburg from a neighbour would be even more convenient, but it would cost him R550. A monthly rail pass for the train is just R160. That is still a sizeable chunk of his monthly salary, which rarely hits R2 000, and he is tempted to ride *mangober* (without a ticket), but having to change trains at Germiston makes that difficult.

Kwesine Station towers above the surrounding township. Even though it is the terminus, the station buildings stand on tall concrete pillars that straddle the track. Jerry climbs a long flight of steps strewn with litter and makes his way through a windswept hall with broken windows and grey walls to show his monthly pass at the turnstiles before climbing down another flight of stairs to reach the platform that runs underneath the station buildings. There he joins Tshepiso.

Tshepiso has made his way onto the platform via a well-worn footpath that passes through a gap in the surrounding fence. He works at the Germiston Depot and a monthly pass would be just R120, but, as he is quick to explain, that amounts to a case of beer every month. He prefers to ride *mangober* and save his money. There is a security guard at the end of the platform, but she is not interested in the *mangobers* who clamber up onto the platform and make their way to join the waiting commuters. The guard is there to protect the train drivers, many of whom are white, from attacks by angry commuters should the train be delayed. The *mangobers* must rather watch for the squads of inspectors who every now and again board and sweep the trains along the line.

Despite the early hour there is a jovial mood on the platform. People greet loudly, especially if it is a Friday and there is the weekend coming. There are informal stalls on the platform. A woman is selling *makwenya* (fat cakes, fritters) from a twenty-litre tub, along with sliced polony for those who did not have time to eat before leaving home.[3] A one-armed man sells single sweets and 'loose draw' (single cigarettes), which he has laid out on upturned cardboard boxes. When the train pulls in, it is almost empty. The few passengers who alight have been on night shift; some wear their security guard uniforms. The train stands for a few minutes before starting back to Germiston. The carriages have rows of yellow plastic seats running along the sides; otherwise it is standing room.

Carriages are appropriated for different uses. On the Kwesine-Germiston routes, the first carriage is where the *zol* (cannabis cigarette) smokers, typically men in their twenties and thirties, congregate. This is a fun carriage to ride in, but not a respectable one. Should young women enter in haste so as not to miss the train, they will not stay long, but exit squealing in embarrassment amid proffered joints and offers of seats. Other carriages are regularly appropriated for church services where women, for the most part, will sing, clap and *rera* (preach/prophesy). Always there are hawkers, making their way up and down the train, and in the afternoon entertainers who will perform for a few minutes before passing a hat around.

The Metrorail is a moving world: inside is the *kasi* (township). What is outside the carriages tells us much about South Africa. There are four stations before we leave Katlehong. A few schoolchildren board and alight; in term-time college students board in numbers. But otherwise it is workers who join the train. All, bar the occasional Coloured person, are African.[4] The carriages are crowded as we leave the *kasi* and pass the reed beds of the *vlei* (marshy ground) that separates Katlehong from the outskirts of Germiston. Those standing at the carriage doors can watch the crowded taxis and cars streaming out of the township along the road that runs parallel to the railway. Coming back into the township, at breakneck speed, ignoring traffic lights, are empty taxis rushing to pick up more fares in the frantic morning rush to work.

After this transition from township to town, from African space to white space, we first reach Wadeville Station. Workers stream off the train to their factory work. After the industrial area comes Germiston Lake Station. It is in a residential suburb. Fewer people alight. They are nearly all women. They work 'kitchening' – domestic workers for the white employers who still dominate these older suburbs.[5]

There are another two suburban stops before President Station. This is the stop for students attending Ekurhuleni West College. It is also one stop before Germiston, where people are heading to jobs in shops and offices of the town, yet crowds alight whether the college is open or not. Those without tickets alight here and walk a few extra blocks rather than negotiate the turnstiles of Germiston Station. An eccentric hawker greets those who alight: 'Welcome to President Station! Welcome to the Station of *Mangobers*! Welcome Kings and Queens of *Mangobers*! Welcome!' People laugh and buy the airtime, *simba* (crisps), *disweets* and loose draws that he sells.

On the journey home, the mood is subdued; people are tired. Only the hawkers, with the energy of necessity, are still busy manoeuvring their way through the crowded carriages while calling out the price of their goods. Those with seats are nodding off. When the train reaches Kwesine Station nobody uses the stairs. Ticket or no ticket, customers and *mangobers* alike shun the steep station steps. Even middle-aged women scramble onto the tracks to take the quickest routes home.

Those catching early morning trains at Kwesine Station are drawn from the reservoirs of labour that reside in the province's townships and informal settlements. Left behind, still in the warmth of their beds, is the balance: a reserve army of labour – the unemployed.

When they do rise, they must strive to keep boredom at bay. Without money, this is no easy task. The Unemployment Insurance Fund pays for eight months, after which there is no support, unless they qualify for a disability, old age or child support grant.[6] In a country where the expanded definition of unemployment has remained in the 30 per cent range for years, long-term unemployment is part of township life. It takes experience to pass the time. An inexperienced *lehaepharama* (one who sits at home) will complete what there is to be done too quickly and will then be punished with hours of unbroken boredom.[7] While Tshepiso and Jerry are travelling to work, Mampho is asleep in the backyard room of the family house. He has not worked since failing Grade 11 for the second time, three years ago. He will wake up at around nine and watch soapies till noon. Then he washes, dresses and eats leftovers from the family meal of the previous night. He might do some washing; otherwise, he will snooze the afternoon away.

Around four, the streets start to liven up as people return from work. If Mampho is lucky, someone will want to relax after work with a beer and will welcome his company; otherwise he might club together with other *mahaeparama* to buy *zol*. Then it is back to watching TV till late. He will likely wake in the early hours of the morning unable to sleep. He will lie in the dark, thinking about what he cannot afford but wants: a smartphone, a fridge, DSTV, branded clothes and a swanky car. He is the *moreki* (buyer) and he is king. Boredom would be far, far away in such a world. Eventually, he slips back to sleep, to wake later for the cycle to start afresh.

Mampho will scramble if there is the opportunity to work, but not all jobs are the same. Teachers, nurses, policemen and others with middle-class work are at the top of the township's occupational hierarchy. Below them are those in permanent blue-collar employment, and under them are the casuals who labour in one or other form of precarious employment. And at the bottom are the unemployed. If Mampho gets a job, the chances are close to certain that he will be at the precarious end of the pile: it will be faded T-shirts, not fast cars.

Labour broking: A triangular employment relationship

Labour brokers, defined as temporary employment services (TES) in current legislation, provide labour to clients. Clients may be private or public (state-owned) companies, national government departments or municipal authorities. Outside South Africa, the terms labour-hire firms and temporary employment services are used for labour brokers, whilst user, user enterprise and host enterprise is used for the client (Benjamin 2013). Globally, the term agency worker is used to describe the employee in the triangular relationship. In South Africa, the term casual is widely used to describe the workers in this form of employment, although, as already noted, this is misleading in that it fails to capture how labour broking, in practice, involves permanent placement. Where placements are of an extended duration, the term permanent casual is often used. In this book, I use the following terminology: 'labour broker' or simply 'broker'; the 'client' or 'client company'; and 'casual', 'casual worker', 'permanent casual' (where appropriate) or 'labour broker employee'. For those employed directly by companies, I use the term 'permanent' or 'permanent employee'.

Labour broking creates a triangular employment relationship of broker, client and casual worker, as illustrated in Figure 2.1. The client

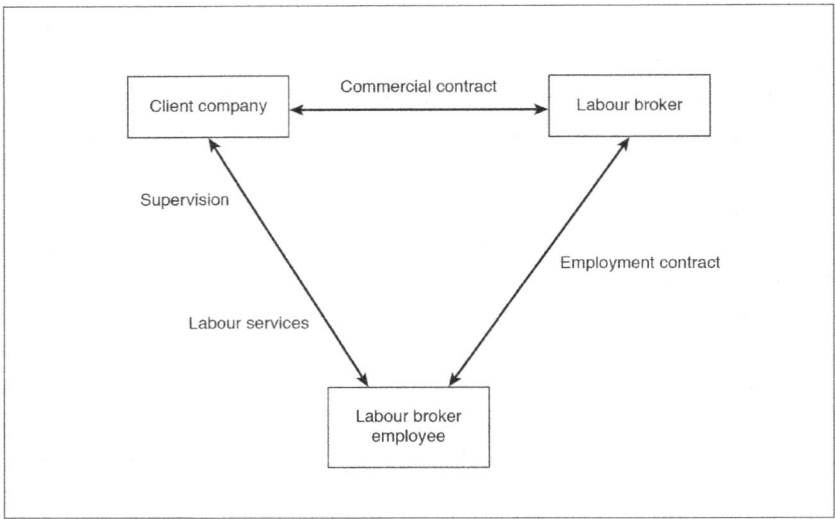

Figure 2.1 The triangular employment relationship.

company has a commercial contract with the labour broker (to provide labour). The labour broker enters into an employment contract with its employee, the casual who works at the client company and under their supervision.

The triangular employment relationship deviates from the standard employment relationship (SER); the latter is typically permanent, full-time, direct employment by an employer. While labour broker employees are atypical workers, there are many possible forms of atypical employment. Paul Benjamin (2006) outlines how atypical employment is created: casualisation, the use of temporary or part-time contracts; externalisation, employment regulated by a commercial contract in a triangular employment relationship (such as but not restricted to labour broking); and informalisation, where work is unregulated (the informal economy). A key feature of the triangular employment relationship is the generally vulnerable or precarious position of the casual worker compared to the typical permanent employee, manifest by limited employment security, low wages and few, if any, employment benefits such as pension provision.

Labour broking is a form of externalisation, in which there is no direct employment relationship between a worker and the company or organisation to which they provide labour. Rather, this employment relationship is externalised to a third party, here a labour broker. Other forms of externalisation include outsourcing (in which supervision is also externalised), subcontracting, franchising and contract farming (Theron 2015). Externalisation does not exclude the co-presence of casualisation, as, for example, when a labour broker employee works part-time for the client; nor does it exclude informalisation as when, for example, the labour broker is a member of the 'bakkie brigade' (about which more shortly).

As well as locating labour broking within the wider field of atypical and generally precarious employment, we also need to recognise that, in practice, the use of labour brokers is often more complex than indicated by the simple triangular model. This is because client companies typically contract with more than one labour broker and also have their own permanent employees, as illustrated in Figure 2.2.

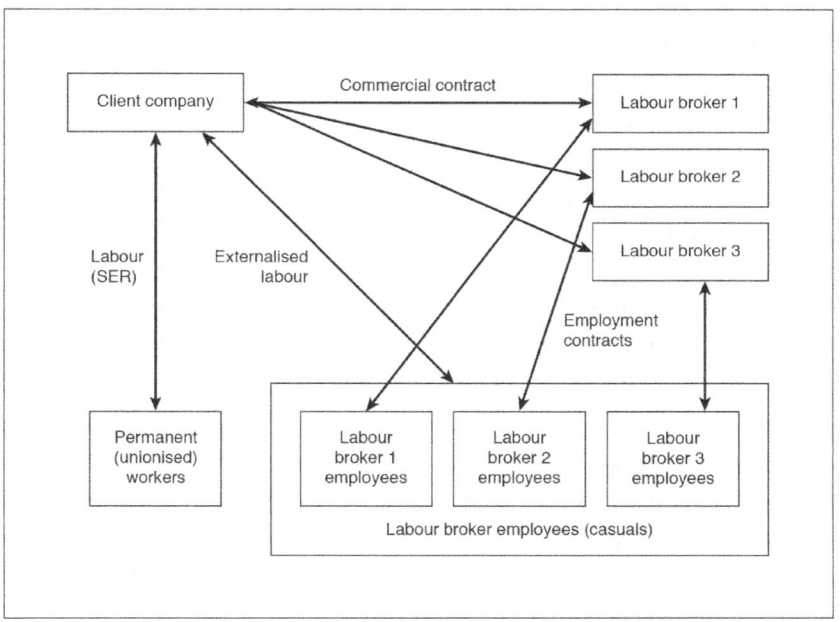

Figure 2.2 The expanded triangular employment relationship.

Figure 2.2 allows us to grasp three important features of labour broking. First, the use of more than one labour broker by the client company intensifies competition between labour brokers. This competition for market share of the client company's labour requirement sees labour brokers seeking to offer better value propositions to the client company than is offered by rival labour brokers. Second, the use of multiple labour brokers by one client means that casuals working for the client do not constitute a single workforce. This fragmentation among brokers has, as we will see in later chapters, implication for union organisation and recognition. It also means that terms and conditions of casuals' employment may vary. Third, since the triangular employment relationship is often accompanied by the client's employment of permanent workers, there is a division between permanent and casual workers, based on their respective employment contracts. This manifests in different levels of security and conditions of employment. Permanent workers are much more likely to be unionised than casuals, for reasons that will become apparent in later chapters, and less likely to be fragmented because they share one employer, the client company.

Labour brokers: The big, the BEE and the bakkie brigade

Although the law only makes provision for a single category of temporary employment services or labour brokers, in practice the labour broking industry is far from homogeneous. Industry representatives put forward the dichotomy of responsible, lawful brokers, on the one hand, and the 'bakkie brigade', on the other hand: unscrupulous cowboys who ignore the rules and exploit workers.[8] This binary picture serves the interests of the larger industry players, but it is misleading. The labour broking industry constitutes a range of organisations that stretch from multinational companies to gang masters. Importantly, the different categories, shown in Table 2.1, are often interlinked.

What this spectrum of forms reveals is that larger companies have an interest in and often control smaller, wholly owned or joint-venture companies that operate head-to-head with independent, often black-owned, independent labour brokers. This is sometimes to pursue Black Economic Empowerment (BEE) business but it also allows greater flexibility over business practices.

Table 2.1 Categories of labour brokers.

Category	Features and examples
Large, established companies	Ranging from multinational to national or regional companies, typically publicly listed. Many established for several decades, they frequently emphasise placement of more skilled employees. General practice is to operate within labour legislation. For example, Workforce Holdings (2017), a JSE-listed company, operates across southern Africa with over 1 100 permanent staff and some 32 000 weekly paid temporary contract workers.
Subsidiary companies and BEE partnerships/fronts of large established companies	Large companies frequently establish subsidiary companies or partner with otherwise independent labour brokers. This allows them to focus on a range of different market segments. It also allows them to obtain business that requires BEE credentials. Subsidiary companies also have more flexibility than their parent companies in adhering or not to labour legislation.
Independent labour broker companies	Generally, these are private companies, ranging from well-established organisations with a national footprint to small start-up operations with a single office. They are typically entrepreneur-driven, often assisted by having BEE credentials. Sometimes they are almost entirely dependent on a single client.
The 'bakkie brigade'	Small-scale labour brokers using a bakkie to transport workers; typically they operate without any business premises (Benjamin 2012, 2013).
Informal recruiters	Companies, including farms, may request workers to bring other workers for seasonal or otherwise fluctuating work (Benjamin 2012). In this situation, they can act as gang masters responsible for payment (generally taking a percentage). They draw on personal networks, sometimes extending into neighbouring countries, to recruit.

The use of casuals in the South African Post Office (SAPO), explored in Chapter 4, was by any measure exploitative. Yet, the companies supplying labour to SAPO were not the bakkie brigade. Rather, they were either subsidiary companies or independent brokers with BEE credentials. Thus, Adcorp, a JSE-listed company with a market capitalisation of R1.5 billion, is one of the largest labour brokers in the county (Fin24 2017). Quest Staffing Solutions, which provided labour to SAPO, is a subsidiary company of Adcorp. Marula Staffing was established by Kelly (itself part of the Adcorp group) to obtain BEE business with SAPO (Dickinson 2015a). A major competitor for SAPO business for these subsidiary companies was TAS Appointments and Management Services, which relied entirely on SAPO business (Dickinson 2015a). TAS was run by a South African black woman entrepreneur, Colleen Ramaphakela, who will feature in subsequent chapters. This insight into the industry suggests that responding to exploitation by labour broker employees is not as simple as squeezing out the bakkie brigade.

Until the amendments of 2015, much of the policy debate over labour broking focused on labour law and the legal loophole over the lack of joint and several liability of the client and labour broker for dismissal. This meant that casuals could be fired at the request of the client company and the labour broker could justify this as a necessary commercial decision. This hobbled casuals' ability to challenge the labour broker or the client company for whom they worked. If the client was challenged, they could point to the fact that the casual was not their employee. If the labour broker was challenged, they could say that the commercial contract on which the casual's employment was dependent had been terminated. The lack of joint and several liability meant that neither could be held responsible. The real reason for the dismissal would slip away and any appeal to the Commission for Conciliation, Mediation and Arbitration (CCMA) for reinstatement was difficult (Benjamin 2014). In short, when casuals are contractually detached from the organisation they work for, they are unable to access formal labour rights (Benjamin 2006).

A vulnerable workforce is hard to organise. An unorganised workforce is not in a position to make demands that it can back up with action. Kally Forrest (2015) puts it bluntly: 'Labour brokers' profitability depends on preventing unionisation.' However, as we will see in Chapter 12, the legal loophole in the Labour Relations Act (LRA), while real enough, was far from the only way in which labour brokers and client companies prevented casuals from organising or engaging in collective bargaining.

A two-tier labour market

South Africa's post-1994 industrial relations system was supposed to be comprehensive and inclusive: everybody would be on one level playing field. Key to this was a voluntarist approach: the law would provide a framework, but it was workers (organised into unions) and employers (organised into federations) who would work out between them, through collective bargaining, the terms and conditions of employment.

Collective bargaining embraces not just negotiations but also the dispute process, including strike action. Much as a strike may appear to be a breakdown in relationships, within a voluntarist industrial relations system it is but a step in the process that is sometimes necessary to reach agreement. This step allows the two sides to understand their respective power and come to a realisation of what can be won and what must be conceded. Since strikes impact economic output, industrial relations systems are designed to minimise them. Under South Africa's LRA, in return for strikers' employment security, unions are required to follow a dispute process, which attempts to reach agreement through conciliation, mediation and cooling-off periods facilitated by the CCMA. Only if the CCMA commissioner assigned to the dispute believes that agreement is unreachable, will he or she issue a 'strike certificate'. A strike is then 'protected'. Those engaged in a protected strike will not receive wages – the 'no work, no pay' principle – but they are entitled to return to their jobs at the conclusion of the strike. Not only does this process minimise disputes becoming strikes, but it also institutionalises conflict to achieve agreement.

However, only around 32 per cent of formal workers' salaries are negotiated between organised labour and organised employer (Stats SA 2015). In the words of Shane Godfrey, Jan Theron and Margareet Visser, 'the scheme for collective bargaining in the new LRA has not worked' (2007: xv). A crucial reason, they go on to argue, has been the failure to anticipate the changing nature of the labour market, particularly the growth of atypical employment.

Karl von Holdt and Edward Webster (2008) outline how different forms of atypical work constitute increasing levels of insecurity radiating out from the relatively secure core formal workforce of employees with permanent, full-time work. In this scheme, outside the core is a workforce of temporary, part-time and externalised workers (including domestic and agricultural workers). And beyond this is a periphery made up of, first, the informal economy, and beyond that the outer circle of greatest insecurity: unemployment. Our focus is on casuals, one form of externalised workers in Von Holdt and Webster's concentric scheme – those employed, typically full-time, within formal companies but without the security or salary of permanent workers.

Such a dual or two-tier labour market operating within the formal economy was not the intention of the African National Congress (ANC) government when it overhauled the industrial relations system. Their response to such a proposal illustrates the point. In February 1996, the South Africa Foundation (SAF) released a document entitled *Growth for All: An Economic Strategy for South Africa*. It was a critique of the labour market framework then under construction. The SAF represents big business, but the document's arguments spoke up for small entrepreneurs, unemployed workers and young people about to enter the labour market. It critiqued the social democratic labour market model, which it believed the new government was following, as unaffordable. Rather, the SAF (1996: 100) recommended a two-tier labour market in which the existing privileges of workers would remain while new entrants would join a vibrant 'free-entry labour-intensive tier in the formal sector' with more limited rights. The Foundation acknowledged that this was not ideal, but it was practical: 'On the whole [it is] . . . far better to have a formal sector job than to be in the informal sector or without any job at all' (SAF 1996: 104). This second tier would create jobs, initially in the second tier, but, in time, it was suggested hopefully, who knows?

It was not well received. The ANC's National Executive Committee led the outrage:

> *Growth for All* runs the risk of pushing our country backwards . . . The suggestion to create a 'two-tier' labour market, in which people employed under such conditions will not have basic human rights is to say the least an affront on democracy and a fundamental departure from any principles of justice . . . This proposal would mark the return of institutionalising black

workers once more in a cheap labour system under the disguise of a 'second tier' labour market . . . we cannot associate ourselves with it (ANC 1996).

But it was exactly such a two-tier labour market that subsequently emerged, indeed one little different from that put forward in *Growth for All*.

Externalisation of employment, such as labour broking, is a global phenomenon driven by companies seeking greater profits and by state-funded bodies balancing constrained budgets in line with currently dominant neoliberal economic practices (Vosko, MacDonald and Campbell 2009; Standing 2011; Lee and Kofman 2012; Barrientos 2013). However, beyond this blanket explanation, the creation of South Africa's two-tier labour market has emerged through myriad processes, each with variations and differences.

In South Africa, the shift of economic policy from the Keynesian Reconstruction and Development Plan to the market-focused Growth, Employment and Redistribution (GEAR) policy, with its core foci on fiscal discipline and open markets, was critical in the rise of labour broking and other forms of externalisation. The ANC lashed out at the SAF's proposed two-tier labour market, yet GEAR appeared just four months after *Growth for All* was published. It was a surprise. There were vociferous complaints, notably from the ANC's Tripartite Alliance partners, the Congress of South African Trade Unions and the South African Communist Party. Both complained, but knuckled under. The SAF, prudently, made no comment.

There was now tension between neoliberal pressures resulting in an intensification of market forces, unleashed by macro-economic policy and union-friendly policies entrenched in law. The result, perhaps not surprisingly, has been a furtive proliferation of atypical employment (Benjamin 2006; Theron 2010). This has happened in different ways in different sectors, and with varied outcomes.

Atypical work: Different sectors, different routes
In the case of SAPO, the rise of labour broking was a result of the new government mandating state-owned enterprises to advance development without burdening state coffers. The Post Office managed

to do that for a while, with profits recorded between 2005 and 2012. This achievement was, however, underpinned by freezing the recruitment of permanent employees and the use of labour brokers.

Other sections of the public sector have also made use of labour broking, outsourcing and other alternatives to a permanent workforce. Most public universities have outsourced cleaning, maintenance, catering, ground staff and other functions. Given that each institution is governed by its own council, these processes have been independently initiated, but the common factor has been decreasing state funding and increasing enrolment targets set by government. Outsourcing 'non-core' activities provided a way for university councils to help balance budgets.

Municipalities have also made use of outsourcing. Johannesburg privatised municipal services in 1997. As Franco Barchiesi explains, 'The Gauteng provincial government intervened [in the financial crisis of the municipalities] by halting new capital investment, imposing a three-year freeze on permanent employment, and requiring a municipal restructuring based on "public-private partnership" agreements that would reconfigure services as independent business units' (2007: 60).

In the retail sector, Bridget Kenny and Edward Webster (1998) outline how supermarket chains have increasingly made use of atypical workers in their stores. Here the trigger has been intense competition between a few large companies in a sector with thin profit margins. Kenny and Webster also describe how mining made widespread use of subcontractors. Long used for specialised functions, such as shaft sinking, they have been increasingly used for core mining work. This has been driven by factors that include declining profits when the price of minerals has fallen, and the need to maintain profit levels for shareholders. By 2011, one-third of the country's 65 000 platinum miners were estimated to be subcontracted, at an average of 60 per cent of the cost of employing a permanent miner (Makgetla and Levin 2016).

These cases illustrate how different forms of atypical work have been established in response to various pressures within the formal sector, both public and private (see also Jordhus-Lier 2013; Wilderman 2015).

Full, half and quarter loaves

Atypical employment allows for greater labour flexibility, most obviously through part-time and limited-duration contracts. The Post Office has to deal with fluctuations in the amount of mail it carries. There is the end-of-year peak in the run-up to Christmas. There is also a spike in mail volumes around the third week of the month, when companies and municipalities mail statements and invoices. Fluctuations in volumes require labour flexibility in some form, but that is not what the growth in labour broking in SAPO was about. Rather, it was primarily about providing workers, on a permanent basis, at a fraction of the cost.

The creation of a second tier of worker is, according to a well-rehearsed mantra, a case of half a loaf being better than no loaf. This argument echoes the SAF's position in *Growth for All*. It was about young workers getting their foot on the first rung of the employment ladder. It would be nice to be able to pay more, but it was also better to have an entry-level wage than nothing.

In SAPO, it was not half a loaf, but a quarter. Nevertheless, the principle is the same: better something than nothing. That is obviously true if measured in rands and cents. But it was not true with regard to what the jobs were; it was not entry-level opportunities that were created but long-term positions. Neither is the mantra true when held to other measures such as dignity.

Section 10 of the South African Constitution states: 'Everyone has inherent dignity and the right to have their dignity respected and protected' (RSA 1996: Preamble). But since dignity is measured in the township (and elsewhere) by, above all else, money, Section 10 cannot float freely in a detached world of rhetorical rights; it must be rooted in the lives of those for whom it claims to speak. There is a meme that makes the point well. It is funny, cruel and telling. The list of names women give their men, based on the monthly income, goes like this:[9]

R1 000 – R3 000	*Motho wa Modimo* (Poor Thing)[10]
R3 000 – R7 000	*Ka lebitso* (By their first name, i.e., without any title indicating respect)
R7 000 – R10 000	Babe

R10 000 – R13 000	My Love
R13 000 – R16 000	My Man
R16 000 – R19 000	Hubby
R19 000 – R22 000	*Ka lebitso la ngwana* (By their child's name, e.g., *Ntate wa Themba*: Themba's father)
R22 000 and above	*Ntate wa Ntlung* (Father of the House)

Told in jest, but all the truer for it, the meme underlines that it is money that commands respect. You can cut a loaf and it is still bread, but you cannot cut dignity. Getting a quarter loaf, while working for the Post Office, gave a *Motho wa Modimo*'s inferior social status an additional indignity. People know, or at least think they know, that SAPO employment is government employment – a source of envy, not of pity. According to the meme, a postman should, at least, be called 'Babe' at home. But, actually you're a *Motho wa Modimo*, which means you have to explain that you are a postman, but, to your shame, you are not earning a postman's salary.

A crisis of reproduction?

Precarious employment, in its varied forms, divides the working class – decent work for permanent employees and work of a lower standard for precarious workers. Edward Webster, Deborah Budlender and Mark Orkin (2015) have put forward a nine-variable index for measuring the 'decent work deficit'. Such indexes provide a benchmark for empirical research and guide debate over policy. They also provide a platform for critiques over the best variables to include and how these should be measured.

Indexes like this represent an *etic* approach to the problem: what those who are not in precarious employment see as problematic about precarious work. Some of the variables put forward by Webster, Budlender and Orkin overlap with what precarious workers themselves see as the problem, their *emic* understanding. 'Skills reproduction security' – the opportunity to gain skills for vocational advancement – fits squarely into a progressive agenda in which there are career paths for workers. But it is one that has usually been stripped out from workers' own expectations. Generally, such ambitions are filtered out during secondary schooling, along with unrealistic hopes for dream jobs. Now, more realistically, their prospects of something better lie not in individual career progress, but in making what they have got work better for them.

Over one variable in particular, both *etic* and *emic* perspectives converge – that of income. Yet, the emphasis placed on this differs. The *etic* perspective seeks to measure whether what is paid is sufficient to support workers and their dependants. This provides plenty of scope for discussion on what this means in terms of minimum and living wages. The *emic* perspective starts from the view that it is not enough.

The concept of social exclusion, as a result of relative poverty, gets us closer to the *emic* perspective. It captures some of the outcomes of inequality, but it does not get to grips with the belief that wages are never enough and that one can only dream of meeting all one's responsibilities and aspirations on a salary. This insatiability is usually passed over in academic discourse. Rather, the focus is on the bare essentials, more or less generously defined. Minimum wages, like calculations for social grants, tend towards the absolute minimum: what is needed for an adequate diet, fuel, clothing and so on. The idea of a living wage can move beyond this, taking into account that lives amount to more than calorie intake and protection from the elements. You would struggle, however, to find calculations of a living wage taking into account that the recipients want to advance their social status, to be better than they are now. But that is what people want and what they strive to achieve.

What the *etic* perspective's focus on need does is raise the question of social reproduction; how societies and groups raise the next generation and whether it will have an equal, better or worse starting point than their parents. Ching Kwan Lee and Yelizavetta Kofman (2012) ask whether precarious employment creates not only a crisis of job quality, but also a crisis of social reproduction. That is, are those in precarious work able to reproduce the next generation of workers that will replace them? This approach shifts concern from the individual worker's salary to the long-term interests of everybody. Extended slightly, the argument moves our focus from short-term gain for some to long-term stability for society.

Whether such arguments are likely to be taken to heart is another matter. An important question is: for whom is precarious work a crisis? For precarious workers, every day, except perhaps pay day, is a crisis. The crises of the everyday are about juggling money and dignity, about managing to get through each day. It is the hard scrabble of living on not enough that reproduces precarious labour.

Class decompression, creation and division

The South African Constitution provides a framework for a social order based on the legal equality of all citizens and, based on this, the means by which social tensions and disputes can be resolved without violence (Brown 2015). This was a response to the legacy of apartheid and colonialism, which had divided society through discriminatory practices. Much as the Constitution is about order, it is also about ordering change. However, as Von Holdt points out, the constitutional settlement represented a dramatic political shift, but left 'socio-economic inequality intact and open to further struggle' (2013: 593). Specifically, he points to the decompression of the liberated black population. Even as it remained disadvantaged in competition with whites' hold on capital, education and skills, the African population was differentiating in ways that opened up internal conflicts between those who remained disadvantaged in the new South Africa and those who were able to take advantage of the new order to advance their position.

Among more rapidly mobile blacks, an emerging black petty bourgeoisie, including the owners of labour-broking start-ups, struggled to gain traction within an economy dominated by white capital. Among those left behind by their upwardly mobile brothers and sisters were the working poor, including labour brokers' employees. On the one side were black entrepreneurs scrambling to succeed and on the other side were black workers scrabbling to survive.

As Jan Theron outlines, labour broking, outsourcing and other forms of externalisation broaden South African capital's class base by providing opportunities for an intermediate layer to enrich itself, 'typically at the expense of the most vulnerable section of the working class, namely those who lack skills. It is of course politically preferable in the South African context that these intermediaries be Black' (2009: 182).

Despite withdrawing from the policy battlefield, the SAF's suggestions came to fruition: opportunities for entrepreneurs were created on the back of the second-tier labour market. True, there were differences to the picture presented by the SAF: it was not only BEE start-ups who were able to benefit from the new market in cheap labour provision, but also established white-owned companies, increasingly integrated into the international labour agency industry. The racial inequalities of apartheid have been shifting to inequalities based on employment contracts.

3

The Long Road to Legislation

In the shadow of the high road

Labour broking, and other forms of precarious work, grew in the shadow of South Africa's planned post-1994 high road of economic development. The new industrial relations framework, anchored around the 1995 Labour Relations Act (LRA), was pro-labour, but it was also strategic. It sought to drive the private sector into a skills-intensive, high-value, export-oriented and competitive trajectory – one that would provide decent work. It was an ambitious strategy and it had to contend with a low starting point: the apartheid economic model of profitability based on cheap black labour. International isolation had permitted healthy profits even in poorly run, low-productivity industries. One objective of the new legislation was to block a 'race to the bottom', in which profits were maintained through cheap labour. Rather, companies would be forced to improve their game. They would have to compete in an increasingly opened South African economy using a skilled and engaged workforce; wages were to be taken out of competition.

The country's economic advantage was to come from the 'regulated flexibility' outlined in the International Labour Organization's (ILO's) 1996 country report, *Restructuring the Labour Market: The South African Challenge* (Standing, Sender and Weeks 1996). The Skills Development Act of 1998 was intended to support this strategy; an earmarked training levy on the payroll would cajole companies to upskill their employees.[1] Despite the likelihood that a high-skill, high-wage approach would raise capital intensity, it was hoped that a growing domestic market and increased exports would see a net increase in job creation, and decent jobs to boot.

There were some attempts to pick up the baton of regulated flexibility (Von Holdt 2003; Dickinson 2005; Venter and Levy 2011). But such initiatives were swimming against the tide. The stronger response was to scout for weaknesses in the new labour legislation, allowing companies to continue on the low road of cheap labour – in other words, to keep labour costs as the focus of competitive advantage. An initial foray in this regard was the contrived conversion of employees into 'independent contractors'. These schemes were, in effect, processes of outsourcing. Employees were set up with nominally independent companies and retitled as contractors, but, in reality, they continued to work for the company. This wheeze was painted in bright empowerment colours, but, in practice, it allowed labour legislation to be bypassed by disguising the true employment relationship. A prominent example of this was companies turning delivery drivers into owner-drivers, supposedly independent business people, except that they were not actually independent and ended up worse off than when they were employees (Poplak et al. 2015). In 2002, amendments to labour laws blocked this loophole in the legislation. Whether someone was an independent contractor or employee would be determined by the actual relationship between them, not what the contract stated.

The rise of labour broking was far more successful in bypassing the proposed new labour regime. Companies' workforces were separated into permanent employees, who remained within the industrial relations framework, and a range of casual workers, including labour broker employees, who were shuffled outside the reach of the new labour laws.

Red flags
The dangers that these strategies presented to organised labour were apparent soon after the 1995 Labour Relations Act came into law. In early 1996, the Congress of South African Trade Unions (COSATU) established the September Commission; its task was to investigate the 'changed political and economic conditions in South Africa and assess whether COSATU's policies and strategies were appropriate'. The report, published in August 1997, devoted a chapter to organising new sectors and layers of workers (COSATU 1997). It found that 'in

many strongly organised sectors, there are increasing trends to create categories of employment which place workers in a weaker relationship to management . . . This is a strategy to divide workers into permanent, more skilled "insiders" and vulnerable, insecure and less skilled "outsiders"' (COSATU 1997: Chapter 7). Pointing to the dangers this posed, the report went on to outline how, should 'COSATU affiliates fail to organise or defend the growing layers of "flexible" workers . . . [created by] . . . sub-contracting, casualising, labour-brokering . . . they will undermine the unions' bargaining position, weakening the unions and undermining labour standards' (COSATU 1997: Chapter 7). It would, the report believed, threaten a 're-emergence of apartheid employment strategies in a new form' (COSATU 1997: Chapter 7). The alternative approach was for COSATU, and its affiliates, 'to prevent "flexibility" from undermining workers' rights and organisation' (COSATU 1997: Chapter 7).

Not long after the September Commission, in 1998, Wits University academics Bridget Kenny and Edward Webster published an article, 'Eroding the Core', which provided two case studies, in mining and retail. The paper detailed how the National Union of Mineworkers (NUM) had made limited efforts to stem subcontracting in mining, while the South African Commercial, Catering and Allied Workers Union, like the NUM a COSATU affiliate, was similarly doing little to prevent increasing non-standard employment in retail. The article was an appeal for the unions to look to their own interests. It stressed that this re-segmentation of the labour market would come to threaten the standards of core, permanent workers, on which union membership was based.

The Department of Labour, custodian of labour legislation and the industrial relations framework that it creates, was also aware of the problem. Guy Mhone, then chief director of Labour Market Policy at the Department, outlined how 'atypical forms of employment raise a number of policy concerns that need to be addressed . . .' (1998: 210).

Key among these was labour broking, in which a company provides labour to a second, client company. This practice had first been legally regulated by the 1983 LRA amendments. In the 1995 LRA, in what was now Section 198 of the legislation, the term labour broking changed to temporary employment services (TES), reflecting the understanding of what these companies did: provide short-term placements. However, the Act did not make labour brokers and the client to whom they provided labour jointly and severally liable for breaches of the LRA. This was a gap in the defences of labour that those seeking cheap labour were able to enter. Once in the gap, they worked hard to keep it open.

The long road
In September 2003, at its 8th National Congress, COSATU sought to close up this breaching of the industrial relations system. It resolved that 'all casual workers must be employed permanently, directly by the employer and not through labour brokers . . .' (COSATU 2003: Resolution 2). COSATU was, in effect, calling for labour brokers to be banned. They never got it. And what they did get was a long time coming.

It started out promisingly enough. In 2003, the Department of Labour commissioned research on the changing nature of work. The anticipation was that it would feed into the upcoming April 2004 general election.[2] It would make its way into the ANC's manifesto, and since the ANC was going to win the election . . . well, the rest could be worked out. The interim (and only) report of the process was finalised in March 2004 and what appeared in the ANC's manifesto for the April elections was what often appears at the end of research reports: a promise to 'conduct research into the full impact of casualisation of labour and outsourcing, and devise ways of dealing with their negative impact on workers and the economy as a whole' (ANC 2004). As often with recommendations for more research, not much happened. The report was presented to the Minister of Labour who referred it to the National Economic Development and Labour Council (NEDLAC), a tripartite structure that is mandated to debate labour legislation before it is read in parliament.[3] There it entered into a deep sleep.

There was a brief stirring in mid-2006; the COSATU congress was again approaching. In July, the then Minister of Labour, Membathisi Mdladlana, made a speech at the 19th Annual Labour Law Conference, outlining that:

> In light of the burgeoning practice of using atypical workers who find it difficult to exercise their rights, I am of the view that the labour law should cushion and mitigate the adverse nature of atypical forms of employment and lack of protection for these workers. Just as a new born baby who is vulnerable and needs protection from the mother, so too will these vulnerable workers receive the adequate protection and guarantees from the government in their pursuit for decent work (Mdladlana 2006).

COSATU's 9th Congress was held in September that year. Again, and in more detail, the organisation outlined its concerns over labour broking and other attempts 'by certain companies to avoid the obligations of law by casualising the employment relationship' (COSATU 2006). In December 2007, the ANC held its 52nd National Conference in Polokwane. It was a moment of high drama regarding ANC politics, with then President Thabo Mbeki defeated by the 'Zunami' of Jacob Zuma, supported by, among others, the COSATU leadership. But not much was said about labour broking. Among almost 30 000 words of conference resolutions, it was noted that substantial progress had been made since 1994 in terms of economic transformation, but that this was an ongoing process and that there still needed to be: 'The progressive realisation of socio-economic rights, through fair labour practices, social security for the poor, universal access to basic services and ongoing programmes to defeat poverty.' That was it.[4]

In 2008, more research was commissioned by the Department of Labour and things again began to stir (Webster et al. 2008). In December, the Namibian High Court confirmed a ban against labour broking, based on the ILO's 1944 Declaration of Philadelphia that labour is not a commodity. The Namibian ban was later repealed, but it emboldened those in South Africa opposed to the practice. At this point, it was estimated that there were 6 000 labour brokers employing some 500 000 people in a R26-billion industry (Palmer 2009). This was a fivefold increase since the ILO's 1996 report on the South African labour market, which estimated that 100 000 workers were being placed by agencies (Standing, Sender and Weeks 1996). The

Minister of Labour was applauded by COSATU when he promised that there would be a ban on labour brokers, once the ANC won the 2009 national elections. Whether the minister actually said he would ban labour brokers was later to become a matter of contention, but it was clear that the practice was under threat. The ANC's (2009) election manifesto stated: 'In order to avoid exploitation of workers and ensure decent work for all workers as well as to protect the employment relationship, [the ANC will] introduce laws to regulate contract work, subcontracting and out-sourcing, address the problem of labour broking and prohibit certain abusive practices.'

Labour broking: Slavery or opportunity?

Opinions over labour broking are divided. On the one side, it is seen as slavery, on the other it is portrayed as creating employment opportunities, particularly for young people. There is clearly a need for temporary workers in a range of situations, and agencies – whether called TES, labour brokers, placement agencies or whatever – provide a way of meeting this need in an efficient way. Their role is to match the workers on their databases with the temporary labour needs of companies.

The argument that labour brokers/TES create employment does not stand up to scrutiny, unless it is combined with their ability to lower real labour costs, which, in turn, encourages more labour-intensive forms of economic activity. This argument aside, labour brokers do not create employment but rather shift the legal status of workers from one form to another. Indeed, as externalised employment has become increasingly common, this has become practically the only route through which employment can be secured at lower skills levels of the labour market. Thus, the claim that labour brokers provide job opportunities, especially for young people, is true but not in the way it claims to do. In the past, township youth found work typically through family members and neighbours working in companies who would alert them that the company was recruiting. Companies now recruit via labour brokers, which effectively hold a monopoly on low-skilled employment.

However, labour brokers placing young people into the labour market serves a useful purpose. High unemployment among young people is a major concern in South Africa. Just as the American 'temp industry' was initially legitimised as 'women's work, suitable for white, middle-class housewives with a little extra time on their hands' (Hatton 2011: 21) to minimise resistance from organised labour, so too the argument over assisting young people is used to counter the negative image of the labour broking industry.

But these arguments for labour broking all skirt around the fact that the bulk of the business is not to provide short-term placements, but to place vulnerable and cheap workers in companies on a long-term basis while maintaining an externalised employment format (Davies 2013; Eichhorst et al. 2013). Look no further than the 8 000 labour broker employees in the South African Post Office (SAPO), which this book is based upon.[5]

One tactic that labour brokers and their apologists use to parry this fundamental criticism is that there are good and bad labour brokers. The good labour brokers keep the law and provide decent employment; the bad labour brokers are unregulated and exploit workers. A quick look at the ownership structure of many labour broking companies puts paid to any idea that this represents reality. Some of the labour broking companies operating in SAPO were ultimately owned by the biggest corporate players in the labour broking industry: the very ones that advance the argument that they are the good brokers who should not be judged by the activities of the bad.

Still on the road
In April 2009, the ANC won the national elections, receiving just under 66 per cent of the poll. In May, Minister Mdladlana was confident that draft amendments to labour legislation would be ready by 2010, and in August the Parliamentary Portfolio Committee on Labour held hearings in parliament on labour broking (News24 2009). COSATU's submission outlined, 'Labour broking is tantamount to slavery, as it amounts to the trading of human beings as commodities' (COSATU et al. 2009). As well as being an election year, 2009 was also the year of COSATU's 10th Congress. The union federation met in September. Resolutions on labour broking noted, 'Government in the post-election period is adopting a softer approach to labour broking by seeking to

regulate this activity as opposed to the outright banning of labour broking as trumpeted by the Minister of Labour, prior to the elections' (NUM et al. 2009).

In October, the Portfolio Committee held public hearings on labour broking around the country. Some were raucous events. In Germiston on the East Rand, the Democratic Alliance (DA) and the Congress of the People walked out, claiming that 'participants wearing COSATU T-shirts waved sticks and threw empty bottles and tin cans at participants with whom they did not agree' (Louw, Madisha and Ollis 2009). Sizwe Mchunu, the DA leader in KwaZulu-Natal (where the next scheduled hearing was to be held) protested that it was a done deal: 'They have already taken a decision that labour brokers should be banned' (Mail & Guardian 2009a).

The DA's Shadow Minister of Finance, Dion George, also weighed in; the research conducted by the Department of Labour was the wrong kind. It 'did not focus specifically on the fiscal, financial and economic effects of banning labour brokers . . .' (George 2009). The Treasury conceded, in response to a parliamentary question from the DA, that it had not conducted any such research. Furthermore, it could only do so with a more reliable data set.

With the matter framed along party lines, Minister Mdladlana, his spokesperson asserted, 'was very passionate about the abolishment of labour brokers . . . So far we have tabled a submission to NEDLAC . . .' (Majova 2009). NEDLAC, it seemed, was still slumbering. In November, the minister complained in a speech that the organisation had spent five years discussing the matter but was still claiming that it was being rushed. The minister asserted that 'we are going to govern. So be prepared, be prepared for drama' (Mail & Guardian 2009b).

In February 2010, the then director general of the Department of Labour, Jimmy Manyi, said that a copy of the necessary legislative amendments had been prepared. However, with the elections out of the way, the ANC's resolve over labour broking seemed to be weakening. COSATU declared concern over President Zuma's lack of action on labour broking. The organisation noted that his State of the Nation Address had 'said nothing on the creation of decent work, the spread of casualisation of labour and the scourge of labour broking, and nothing to explain how he intends to implement the 2009 manifest commitment to ... introduce laws to ... address the problem of labour broking and prohibit certain abusive practices' (COSATU 2010).

In March, the minister got into a pickle over what was going to happen about labour broking. His spokesperson denied that the minister had ever used the word 'ban'. The DA had a field day. 'What nonsense!' it cried. Not only had he said he would ban labour brokers, he had also called for them to be 'stamped out', a 'criminal activity', 'abusive' and 'against the Constitution' (Ollis 2010).

At the end of October, Mdladlana's long stint as Minister of Labour came to an end when he was replaced by Mildred Oliphant. The legislative reforms that her predecessor had developed were gazetted in December.[6] Whether labour brokers were banned or not was not clear. Section 198 of the LRA, the section on TES (that is, labour brokers), was repealed in its entirety. It would no longer exist. Ergo, neither would the labour brokers. But they had not been banned.[7]

Instead, and elsewhere in the amendments, it was proposed that employment would be legally defined by 'direct supervision'. In other words, if a labour broker placed somebody, they would become the client's employee.[8] As Paul Benjamin (2014) has outlined, this was not really going to solve the problem and would likely be unconstitutional (since it would prevent labour brokers pursuing their trade, a right guaranteed under Section 22 of the Constitution). Additionally, there were likely to be unintended and negative consequences that would leave many workers worse off. These problems were summarised in a Regulatory Impact Assessment requested by the Cabinet and commissioned by the Department of Labour (Benjamin, Bhorat and Van der Westhuizen 2010; Botes 2014).[9] The proposed amendments were at a dead end and were withdrawn in early 2011.

In July that year, Minister Oliphant (2011) reported that negotiations in NEDLAC over new amendments to the legislation were 'going well'. At this point, the National Association of Bargaining Councils had, in 2010, come up with the improbably precise number of 979 539 labour broker employees in the country. Rounding this indicates a figure twice that put forward a couple of years earlier

(Anderson 2011). This is a phenomenal rate of growth, though who knows if the 2008 figure of half a million was correct? In the absence of government statistics that capture atypical forms of employment, a problem not limited to South Africa, the available data involves some guesswork, a few assumptions and any biases from whoever is counting (Countouris et al. 2016). The use of labour brokers was undoubtedly growing, so an increase would be expected, but additionally both sides in this now-heated debate were happy to see research conjure large numbers. For those against labour broking, a big number demonstrated how many workers were in bondage. Those defending the practice, pointed to how many jobs would be lost if labour broking ended.[10] At its zenith, this statistical arms race reached a figure of close to three million, a statistic produced by COSATU's (2012b) research unit, the National Labour and Economic Development Institute.

The bigger the number, the more that was at stake. NEDLAC was no longer the site of slumber, but a combat zone. Since legislation was now inevitable, the key battle was over the new law's teeth. This focused on how long it would be before a casual, placed with a client, was legally deemed to be a permanent. If that period was long enough, labour brokers would remain in business; they would just have to put up with the inconvenience of working out some rotation or renewal of contracts to keep their current business model in place. If the period was short enough, labour brokers would, in effect, be banned. All that would remain of the sector's activity would be to act as 'placement agencies', providing suitable candidates to companies looking to hire. Business was arguing for a longer period, COSATU and other union federations for a shorter one, and no compromise could be agreed (Benjamin 2014: 137). The proposed amendments to the LRA were eventually gazetted without the benefit of a final report from NEDLAC, which was in effect bypassed (BUSA 2012). The bill specified a six-month period for casuals to become permanents, a position between the camps of business and labour.

On 22 March 2012, the second attempt at legislation on labour broking was published in the *Government Gazette*. The legislation's introduction followed a demonstration organised by COSATU and the National Council of Trade Unions, a union federation unaligned to the ANC, on 7 March. The protest combined a call for the banning of labour brokers and scrapping of e-tolls on Gauteng's highways. The marches, organised across the country but particularly impressive in Johannesburg, were a sign of an increasingly strained relationship between the ANC and COSATU. Miffed, Zuma pointed out that although they were calling for a ban, they, along with the third Tripartite Alliance partner, the South African Communist Party, had adopted the ANC's 2009 manifesto that promised regulation, not banning, of labour brokers (Mail & Guardian 2012).

To interpolate the main subject of this book into the narrative, it was at this point, with reform still plodding towards the goal of legislation, that the de facto end of labour broking in SAPO was achieved. The striking Mabarete had joined the March protest, making something of a media splash as they alone fingered their company for using labour brokers with placards and by wearing SAPO bibs. The Mabarete strike was concluded at the beginning of April 2012, with an agreement to end labour broking in the organisation.

At its congress that September, the federation made its views on labour broking clear: 'We want labour brokers banned now!' (COSATU 2012a). The matter was now in the parliamentary process where the key battleground was the Portfolio Committee on Labour, which had the matter on its agenda in June 2013. However, COSATU could look to its Alliance partner in parliament. In a statement, Business Unity South Africa (BUSA) accused ANC MPs, who were in the majority on the committee, of pushing to limit temporary employment services to zero months: a ban by any other name. Any change to the draft legislation would, BUSA argued, 'make a mockery of NEDLAC negotiations', which had been, the statement noted, going on for more than three years (Ensor 2013). The statement neglected to mention that the matter was first brought to NEDLAC almost ten years earlier, nor that NEDLAC had never been able to reach agreement.

In the end, the Portfolio Committee's ANC majority cut the six-month placement period of the draft legislation to three months, although the DA members of the committee argued for twelve months, and it was in this form that the bill was sent for its second reading in the National Assembly on 20 June 2013. The DA's objections, particularly over the three-month period, were pushed aside, and the bill approved.[11] The National Council of Provinces, South Africa's second chamber, approved the bill in October 2013. Thereafter it was sent to the Presidency, where it sat for almost a year. The Labour Relations Amendment Act (6 of 2014) was finally signed by President Zuma on 15 August 2014 and proclaimed into law on 1 January 2015.

Bumbling and stumbling that serves a purpose
Reaching the terminus of this legislative road did at least save COSATU having to crank up yet further its rhetorical broadsides against labour broking at its 2015 Congress. The regulation of labour brokers through amendments to the LRA was long coming. COSATU, the largest and most powerful union federation in the country, had made it clear at its 2003 Congress that there was no place for labour brokers. COSATU was in an alliance with the ruling ANC, and COSATU was critical in mobilising the electorate to vote for the ANC.

There had been dancing on the tables in NEDLAC when agreement had been reached over the 1995 LRA. Proponents of South Africa's post-apartheid labour legislation envisaged a legally undivided workforce, unionised along sectoral lines and able to partner with employers to provided regulated flexibility in return for dignified work. Yet, Section 198 of the LRA created, in ways that were never anticipated by the negotiators, an opening for the business of selling labour and the circumvention of this ideal. The opening included opportunities for an emerging black entrepreneurial class, who, alongside international firms and established local white capital, seized their chance and established themselves as labour brokers.

Incompetence and inertia are always at play in any process of legislative reform, and they were certainly displayed on the slow road to the 2015 LRA amendments. However, the bumbling and the stumbling along the legislative road allowed a parallel *sub rosa* industrial relations system to replace the apartheid cheap labour system. It was always going to be impossible for business, given its near pariah post-apartheid position, to openly argue for a cheap labour supply. As the South Africa Foundation foray into labour market options in 1996 illustrates, some things are better done and not said. In this context, the bumbling and the stumbling are effective weapons of the strong. They are obstacles on the reform road and they hinder progress. They delay change and they blunt confrontation while maintaining the status quo. In this case, it meant maintaining cheap labour based not on racial categories but on a contractual move.

In Chapter 12, we look at the 'long tactics' of labour broking that can be seen as another series of impediments thrown up to defend the system of contractually precarious labour; one that differs from the legislative road in that it was fought away from public scrutiny and which aimed not to delay the passing of legal reforms but to stymie effective worker organisation.

The dragon

But was not COSATU (and other union federations) there to organise workers? Yes and no. Rhetorically it was fighting for the working class; in practice, it fought harder for part of it: permanent employees. True, COSATU ran a high-profile campaign with the demand that labour broking be banned. In December 2010, COSATU's then general secretary, Zwelinzima Vavi, had called on workers to prepare 'for the mother of all battles', which would be waged against labour brokers in 2011. 'We are,' he said, 'only interested in one thing: do not regulate labour brokers, but we must ban them' (Mail & Guardian 2010). But, it is always important to look behind the rhetoric. As President Zuma pointed out when angered by criticism in 2012, COSATU's call for a ban contradicted its endorsement of the ANC's 2009 manifesto promise to regulate labour broking.

Much as COSATU's September Commission had raised the need to organise vulnerable workers, it had also pointed to white-collar workers, particularly in the public sector: civil servants, teachers, health professionals and so on. Over labour brokers, there was a lot of noise; over white-collar public servants, there was action. During the next two decades the profile of COSATU membership shifted from blue-collar private-sector workers, the industrial working class, to white-collar public-sector workers who increasingly became part of an emerging black middle class.

At the federation level, membership growth in the public sector defused the problem of precarious employment: the organisation could grow without dealing with the issue. Of course, as the use of labour broking continued to increase, it began to present COSATU with a problem, one that could no longer be masked by growing membership in other segments of the workforce. COSATU was becoming all but irrelevant to precarious workers – a class fraction that would, as it grew, undercut the wages and benefits of the federation's core membership.

Adcorp's chief executive, Richard Pike (2012), pointed out in his Annual Report, that COSATU sought, through its call for a ban on labour broking, 'to slay the dragon they helped to create'. Pike's point was that COSATU's victory in obtaining the pro-labour 1995 LRA had seen employers find ways around the 'labour problem' it had created. But it was more complex than that. What has to be explained is why COSATU let the dragon grow inside workplaces that its own affiliates organised.

What is true at the level of the federation is not reflected at the level of COSATU's individual affiliates. Given the federation's 'One Industry, One Union' policy, individual affiliates were rarely balancing a loss of blue-collar workers to labour broking (or outsourcing) with recruitment of white-collar workers. Each COSATU affiliate faced the growth of precarious labour within its area of organisation. And, by extension, they were affected by the degree to which holding back labour broking depended on the strength, commitment and strategy of each union (interview, Tseki). If COSATU was, by 2012, attempting to slay a dragon, it was one that had grown in the cantons of its affiliates.

Each economic sector, public and private, has its own dynamics in regard to the use of labour brokers or other precarious labour systems. But one dynamic that labour broking introduced within the territory of each individual COSATU affiliate (or any other union) was the division between permanent and casual workers. As Kenny and Webster pointed out clearly enough in 1998, this was setting up one group of workers against another. Crudely put, savings on the wage bill from employing casuals through a labour broker was a resource for unions to negotiate increased salaries for permanent workers, who made up their membership base. What follows in subsequent chapters is the case of labour brokers in SAPO, at the time the exclusive domain of COSATU's affiliate, the Communication Workers Union (CWU). The dynamics of how the labour-broking dragon hatched and grew in the Post Office is the subject of the following chapter; how labour broking divided the Post Office's workforce into permanent and casual workers is the focus of Chapter 5; and how CWU rode the dragon is discussed in Chapter 6.

4

SAPO and Labour Brokers

The post office
Post offices around the world provide a range of services. Key services are the delivery of mail (letters and parcels) as well as a range of further 'retail' services, including financial services. Through the International Postal Union, mail delivery is global. A fundamental advantage of post offices is their extensive 'footprint' – they are in a position to deliver everywhere and their extensive retail network makes them physically accessible on a scale that other organisations are unable to match.

This 'universal service' that post offices can offer has its downside. Maintaining services in areas where transaction volumes are low, such as in sparsely populated areas, is expensive and incurs losses. A national pricing system, such as a standard postage rate, results in some users subsidising others. Should rival companies focus on the profitable, high-volume areas of activity, such as mail delivery in urban areas, the post office will be left with only loss-making activities. Unless some form of protection or subsidy is in place, universal service provision will then collapse, leaving parts of the country without services. This is undesirable for a number of reasons: it excludes sections of the population from communication channels, exacerbates geographic inequalities, deepens social exclusion, undermines existing economic activities, and restricts social and economic development.

This problem is usually resolved by governments providing post offices with a monopoly in return for an agreed standard of universal service. Thus, the legal barring of companies from delivering mail (variously defined by size and weight) allows post offices to charge a national standard tariff for mail delivery. This amounts to a cross-subsidisation, in which profits generated in some areas, typically urban, subsidises the service in others, typically rural, keeping a national system operating. Depending on circumstance, this may still require direct state subsidisation, depending on the tariffs permitted and the efficiency of post office operations.

The growth of new communication technologies has resulted in further challenges to post offices. This is not new, though it is intensifying dramatically. The development of landline telephone systems and then fax machines provided alternative communication systems alongside mail delivery. Typically, post offices, as custodians of national communication, developed telephone systems, which were later separated from mail delivery. In South Africa, this occurred in 1991 when the South African Post Office (SAPO) and Telkom were separated; they became state-owned enterprises under the then Department of Posts and Telecommunications (Telkom 1991). The development of email and other means of transmitting documents meant the virtual death of the personal letter. However, the letter as a form of commercial communication remains important, and in urban areas profitable. This is especially so where Internet penetration remains limited, such as in many South African townships and in suburbs with older populations.

Hardly surprisingly, the pre-1994 post office in South Africa mirrored the racist nature of society at the time. While providing a universal service, the quality of services provided was biased towards whites. The organisation itself was also racially structured with an exclusive white management, differential pay, and de facto racial separation of employees' canteens and other amenities well into the 1990s (interviews, Radebe; Von Holdt). At the same time, Tutu Mokoena (interview) recalled the post office as a disciplined organisation: postmen would line up to have their uniforms inspected before going out to deliver mail.

As part of the public service until 1991, post office workers were not permitted to join unions. Despite this ban, the Post Office and Telecommunications Workers Association (POTWA) was established in September 1986 (interview, Von Holdt). Organising primarily African workers, it almost immediately staged several national strikes, some of which resulted in mass dismissals; key grievances driving these strikes were racial discrimination and wage disparities (Markham 1987). With the creation of SAPO in 1991, POTWA's concerns extended to privatisation and possible retrenchments (Zikalala 1993; Collins and Ginsburg 1996).

In 1996, POTWA merged with two other unions: the Post Office Employees Association, based primarily in the Western Cape and organising Coloured workers, and the South African Post Telecommunication Employees Association, organising primarily Indian workers. Together, they formed the Communication Workers Union (CWU). Another union, the largely white Pos en Telekommunikasie Unie (PNL) had a significant presence in the Post Office, but was squeezed out by a 30 per cent plus one criterion for union recognition, which CWU was the only union able to meet (interview, Petersen).[1] Having knocked out any opposition, CWU then negotiated an agency shop agreement, in which all employees of SAPO had to pay a monthly fee to the union whether they chose to take up membership or not. CWU thus held a monopoly of representation within SAPO.[2] This lasted until 2012 when the South African Postal Workers Union (SAPWU),[3] formed by a break-away from CWU in 2009, was also recognised by SAPO.[4]

Although SAPO has not, to date, been privatised and remains a state-owned company,[5] its creation was part of a drive for commercialisation of what was a loss-making operation. The post-apartheid government charged state-owned enterprises with a dual mandate: first, to roll out infrastructure that would support development goals and address discrepancies of the past, and, second, to do this without burdening state finances with the need for subsidisation. For the Post Office, the situation that needed to be addressed was:

> An apartheid legacy which is characterized by inequality in access to postal services, particularly... in the former black communities, rural areas and the former TBVC areas;[6] and a monopoly mentality which has translated into poor customer service and an unhealthy reliance... on an external government subsidy (Ministry for Posts, Telecommunications and Broadcasting 1997: 9).

The Post Office's key role in development was the establishment of 'points of service' (retail post office facilities) and the provision and servicing of physical addresses across the country. Previously, the luxury of door-to-door mail delivery had been focused on the white population, and many households, especially those in mushrooming informal settlements, did not have an address – something that severely limited their ability to get credit or access services.

Mail delivery
Mail delivery is the largest section of the Post Office, accounting for some 67 per cent of revenue in the 2010/2011 financial year.[7] Much of it is generated from corporate clients, such as banks, municipalities, stores selling on credit, and other companies providing paid-for services, for example, DSTV and distance education institutions such as the University of South Africa.

Mail delivery operates on a 'hub-and-spoke' principle in which mail is sorted into increasingly precise locations. Letters are first collected and taken to sorting hubs where 'mail handlers' sort it by postal code. Larger hubs, such as Witspos in the South of Johannesburg, send sorted mail to smaller hubs, such as Germiston on the East Rand and Krugersdorp on the West Rand, were it is further sorted for delivery to depots.

Postal depots have between 10 and 50 postmen, and sometimes women.[8] Each postman is responsible for a 'walk' or delivery area. If the depot has a Mail Collection Point – cluster post boxes from which individuals pick up their letters – this mail is sorted by a separate group of workers, often women. Mail for door-to-door delivery is sorted to the walk level in the hub to which the depot is linked. The postman sorts the mail for his walk into a 'press', a large set of metal cabinets with shelves and dividers to create a unique slot for each address on the walk. Above each shelf are strips with the street names and numbers (or in the case of townships and informal settlements simply numbers) that guide the postman as he is sorting. Miss-sorts from the hub that belong to other walks in the depot are exchanged. Letters that should have gone to another depot are returned to the hub for resorting. The strips organise the press into the route that the postman will take on the walk. In other words, the layout of the letters in the press mirrors the postman's physical route. Once the postman has sorted the letters, he bundles them using rubber bands and, keeping these bundles in order, goes out to deliver. Walks are covered by bike, foot or sometimes motorbike.[9] If the mail has been sorted correctly, the order of the letters in the bundles will match the postman's route; if it is has not been accurately sorted, he will end up cursing as he goes unnecessarily backwards and forwards to ensure all letters are delivered. SAPO's 'clear flow' principle dictates that mail that arrives at a depot should be delivered that day. If the postman comes back with undelivered letters, the supervisor will have something to say.

Large walks, especially when there are high volumes of mail, require 'dump sacks' because the mail is too much to be carried in the postman's bag or in the box fixed to the front of the bicycle. These sacks of mail are dropped off by the depot's driver or supervisor at locations on the walks where the postman will pick them up to continue delivery.[10] Undeliverable mail must be returned to the depot and affixed with an appropriately completed 'Return to Sender' sticker, before being returned to the hub for its return journey. Postmen are generally rotated around the depot's walks so that, over time, they know all the walks and can 'cover' if someone is absent. In this case, walks are usually split between two or more postmen who have adjacent walks to that of the absentee. Rotating walks among the depot's postmen also helps to even the workload. Some walks are bigger than others, despite periodic resizing exercises, and those that are closer to the depot involve less travel time.

Apparent success on the back of labour broking

The Post Office made extensive progress in fulfilling its post-apartheid mandate as a state-owned enterprise. Under a predominantly black management team, it created addresses for twelve million households nationwide (Manyatshe n.d.: Slide 34). The initial strategy had been to use 'address boxes' to service newly enumerated areas, as a means to control costs (interview, Von Holdt).[11] However, these were not popular and represented a second-class form of delivery in comparison to door-to-door deliveries (Ministry for Posts, Telecommunications and Broadcasting 1997: 28). It was door-to-door delivery that was subsequently expanded, particularly to the growing urban peripheries. Yet, SAPO was able to turn around its finances from a R1-billion annual loss in the late 1990s to profits (excluding once-off income and government subsidy) starting in the 2004/2005 financial year (the first time the organisation had ever been in the black) to 2011/2012 of between R471 million and R22 million. Most of the profit generated came from mail delivery. The major loss-making component of the organisation has been its retail arm, burdened with high overheads and low transaction volumes (SAPO 2015: 13.)

This was a considerable achievement, but it did not last. The financial viability of the organisation was achieved with unremitting emphasis on cutting costs. A major mechanism to contain expenses was the use of labour brokers. The result was an expansion of SAPO's mail delivery workforce, even as the number of permanent employees was decreased. At its height, the labour broking system was saving the Post Office approximately R380 million a year in salaries.[12] In addition, SAPO's overall labour costs were reduced by not having to provide employee benefits such as pensions and medical aid contributions that had been negotiated for permanent employees. Despite optimism that SAPO was now in a 'growth and sustainability era' (SAPO n.d.), by 2012/2013 the organisation was once again in the red, and facing an industrial relations crisis of unprecedented scale that stemmed directly from its use of labour brokers.

The need for labour flexibility

Although the use of labour brokers on a massive scale was driven by the desire to cut costs and meet budget targets, mail delivery (and other post office services) involves fluctuating workloads, for which some form of labour flexibility is necessary. There is a peak in deliveries around the third week of the month, when companies send out statements and municipalities their bills. There is also a seasonal peak prior to Christmas. The need for labour flexibility is most acute in the upstream mail sorting stages: higher mail volumes require more people working in the hubs.[13]

Prior to 1996, SAPO had catered for fluctuating volumes with its own part-time and temporary workforce. The part-time category – Permanent Part-Time Employee (PPTE) – was used extensively in retail, often for women workers who also had family commitments. The temporary category, S32 (named after the form used by applicants) catered for short-term employment. In both cases, pay was on a pro-rata basis. That meant that S32s would actually earn more in the hand than the permanent employees they worked alongside as there were no deductions for the benefits that permanents were entitled to, such as pensions. Around 1996, SAPO started to make use of placement agencies, primarily the established companies of Kelly, Quest and Transman, to fill vacancies and meet peaks in work flow. The move was, in part, a response to industrial action by S32s, who had demanded permanent status. A strike at the Germiston Hub by some 130 S32s in 1996 had a racial dimension. Previously, few Africans had been employed in the Post Office; now Africans were being employed in this position, but without permanent contracts. The striking S32s were not union members and the strike was unprotected, but CWU had been aware that it was coming and swiftly moved in to mediate an agreement. The strikers were made permanent and the agreement extended to S32s in other hubs (interview, Mputhi).

The arrival of labour brokers

Around 2000, the use of placement agencies to provide temporary labour began to morph into the provision of 'permanent casuals'. The key factor in this change was the 1999 moratorium placed on entry-level appointments (interviews, John; Tutu Mokoena; Petersen; Radebe). This was a key component in the board-initiated cost-cutting campaign extended throughout the organisation. It also followed a restructuring exercise that had created, at least on paper, supernumerary positions that were to be reallocated as suitable vacancies occurred. At the same time, there had been a centralising of power within the organisation. Any exception to the moratorium had to be signed off by the chief executive officer (interview, Petersen). It was also enforced by the introduction of a performance management system, in which mangers needed to meet savings targets to receive bonuses (interview,

Mputhi). It is not clear if the moratorium was ever lifted, but, if it was, it was only after the labour broking system was already an embedded part of SAPO's labour force.

Over the next decade or so, various factors accelerated the replacement of permanent workers with casuals in positions such as postmen and mail handlers. Traditionally, depot workforces had included supplementary postmen or 'subs' who would cover for those on leave or sick. When this post, which had been allocated on the basis of one sub for ten walks, was cut, subs were given the walk of postmen who, through dismissal, retirement, death or resignation, had left the organisation. This then resulted in the problem of how absences were to be covered. The so-called Sparkling Waters agreement between CWU and SAPO provided that permanent employees would be allocated three hours of overtime for each walk or part walk that they covered.[14] It was a good deal for workers and reflected the power of CWU at the time, and the cosy relationship it had with the Post Office's Human Resources Department, staffed in the main by ex-CWU office-bearers. The expense of the Sparkling Waters agreement made the employment of labour broker employees the preferred solution for covering for absent postmen and served to introduce managers to the convenience and economy of such workers.

Another factor in the uptake of casuals was a change to pension rules in 2005, which encouraged many permanent SAPO employees to take voluntary severance packages (interview, Petersen). Given the ongoing moratorium on permanent positions, the resulting vacancies accelerated the use of labour brokers, whose benefits were now evident.

The value of labour brokers

Labour brokers provide flexible labour. Employees could be called to the hubs at a few hours' notice if volumes started to peak, something made possible with the widespread ownership of cell phones. Zoleka Moeng (interview), for example, recalled that she would wait at home in case there was a call from Marula, the labour broker she was registered with as a mail handler. It could come any time up till 10 a.m. to tell her that she was needed for a 1 p.m. to 9 p.m. shift.

The labour provided by brokers was not only flexible, but also cheap. Unlike the old S32s and PPTEs, casuals provided by labour brokers did exactly the same job as the permanents of the Post Office whom they worked alongside, but were paid less. Considerably less. In rounded 2011 figures, a permanent SAPO postman received R8 000 a month, plus a range of benefits, including a thirteenth cheque, pension contributions and medical aid; a casual postman received R2 000 and no benefits. SAPO paid a monthly placement fee to labour brokers, but even taking this into account it was, as one Post Office manager explained, 'Three for the price of one!' Just the ticket for managers trying to meet performance management targets that stressed cost-cutting.

As well as being flexible and cheap, casuals were also vulnerable and, therefore, compliant; getting rid of somebody simply required picking up the phone and calling their labour broker, who would provide a replacement (interview, Petersen). Unlike the S32s of the 1990s, they were not easily able to organise and force their way into permanent positions. How this was achieved, for over a decade, is explored in Chapter 12. But, for now, small wonder that labour broking in SAPO took off in a big way, far beyond what was needed for operational flexibility. By 2011, almost a third of its 23 000-strong workforce were casual workers. In depots, casuals outnumbered permanents.

The beneficiaries

There were not many people, apart from the casuals themselves, who did not benefit from the use of labour brokers in SAPO. Managers met their cost-reduction targets and labour brokers got business. A critical factor in getting that business was Black Economic Empowerment (BEE) requirements. The result was a shift from the established placement agencies that had provided labour in the late 1990s to new start-up companies owned by emerging black business men and women, as well as front companies set up by companies that were otherwise unable to compete on BEE criteria. Kelly, for example, established Marula Staffing and Workforce Management, companies that were BEE compliant and which were both major suppliers of labour to SAPO (South Gauteng High Court 2010; Mataboge 2013).

At least 24 labour brokers supplied labour to SAPO from 2001 to 2012, amounting to payments of R2 735 942 000 (Madonsela

2016). Established companies and their subsidiaries or fronts took the lion's share. Transman, Kelly and its subsidiaries, and Adcorp's Quest subsidiary together took R1.5 billion, some 54 per cent of SAPO's total spend on labour brokers.[15] There was, however, also room at the trough for the start-up companies. Key among these was TAS Appointments and Management Services (TAS), established in 2006 when T&L labour brokers, which had been providing labour to SAPO for several years, split into two: TAS and T&T Appointments.[16] TAS was the dominant labour broker operating in SAPO's Wits Mail Delivery Region.[17] It received a total of R381 million from SAPO. TAS was wholly owned and run by Colleen Ramaphakela. In a 2011 interview with the *Voice of Hope* magazine, Ramaphakela explained, 'The recruitment industry was predominantly white and . . . the government had already introduced BEE programmes . . . in order to enhance the economic participation of black people. I'd say that I'm blessed to have been one of the few women who managed to seize the moment' (Shilubana 2011: 10).

Seizing the moment meant cultivating relationships with those who decided who got business. While the moratorium on recruitment of permanent workers was monitored by head office, the appointment of labour broker employees became increasingly decentralised. The decision as to which of the competing labour brokers would fill a vacancy was in the hands of depot supervisors and their area managers (interview, Mputhi). If you wanted business, you needed to keep in with them. Labour brokers held Christmas parties, to which managers and supervisors were invited (interview, Mputhi).

Among those interviewed it was common cause that securing business involved more than throwing parties. Kickbacks are, however, hard to prove. The Public Protector's report that investigated the use of labour brokers in SAPO drew a blank in this regard, noting: 'I was also advised by the Special Investigating Unit [also conducting an investigation into SAPO] that due to the lapse of time and the non-availability of records/data it was also not able to identify the specific role-players and to investigate possible collusion between such role-players and the labour brokers' (Madonsela 2016: 68). The Special Investigating Unit's (2017) investigation did, however, reveal corruption elsewhere in SAPO's operations and went on to make seven disciplinary recommendations, three criminal referrals and one civil matter. The civil matter concerned the lease taken on a new head office for SAPO, costing R493 million over ten years, in which close to R11 million in bribes were identified (SIU 2017: 43).

The competition between labour brokers was intensified when SAPO dropped long-term contracts with brokers in favour of paying for the labour provided on a month-by-month basis. In a letter to Marula Staffing on 31 May 2005, the Supply Chain Management department of SAPO stated that the contract between them had expired, but that SAPO 'would like to continue using your services on the same terms and conditions, on a month-to-month basis . . . this arrangement will remain in force until otherwise decided on by one or both parties'.[18] In other words, the use of Marula's placements could be terminated at a month's notice. Just to be sure that Marula understood where things stood, the letter went on to note that SAPO 'retains the right to make use of . . . other recruitment service providers'.

SAPO even went as far as to set standard rates that it would pay to labour brokers for placements and what they must pay these workers. This prevented casuals from switching between brokers to take advantage of marginal pay differences that had earlier existed between brokers. It also meant that price was taken out of the competition between brokers competing for SAPO business. Labour brokers had to find other ways, beyond parties and kickbacks, to compete for the business and keep their own costs down. This was done through ensuring a compliant workforce, a process described in Chapter 12.

A compliant workforce was to the benefit of supervisors on the shop floor. It was also beneficial for permanent SAPO employees who, as described in Chapter 6, often treated the casuals as the 'donkeys of the depots', allowing them to lighten their own workload. Permanents also benefited in terms of wages since a section of the workforce was all but removed from the collective bargaining process. This made it easier for CWU to secure salary increases and other benefits for its members during negotiations.

The disappeared

The presentation of the triangular employment relationship of labour broking (and outsourcing) on lecture hall blackboards suggests an orderly employment relationship. In reality, the system has to be worked into a shape that must configure to the company structure and a range of interests located within it. The system that emerges has gone through mediations, in which different stakeholders take their cut.

It was the casual workers who were bled. Like most victims of structural violence, for the system to continue it was helpful that they remain invisible. Although the lack of joint and several liability for client and labour broker over dismissal in the 1996 Labour Relations Act had provided an important means to keep casuals in their place, other labour legislation did take them into consideration. Thus, the Employment Equity Act of 1998 states clearly that for the purpose of equity reporting, workers placed by temporary employment services for three months or more are employees of the client company (RSA 1998a: Section 57). SAPO, which only started to submit employment equity reports in 2008, did not follow this statutory requirement. What its reports showed was a gradually declining number of permanent employees, the continued effect of the moratorium on appointments, along with under 1 000 non-permanent employees. By 2011/2012, some 8 000 labour broker employees, a third of its actual workforce, had statistically disappeared from the company's employment equity and annual reports. They were to appear, dramatically increasing the company's reported workforce, when labour broking was ended in 2012.

But there were other ways in which their presence could be ascertained. As permanent workers were replaced by casuals, this was captured within managerial information systems as 'unfunded posts'. By 2011, this number was approximately 5 000. You did not need an MBA to ask how the organisation was managing to operate with 5 000 vacant positions. People knew well enough; it was just that nobody wanted to say.

Eventually, the Post Office casual workers made themselves visible.

5

Postmen

The work of a postman straddles the depots where mail is sorted and the streets where it is delivered. Like all jobs, being a postman has its ups, downs, opportunities and risks. Some of the downsides are compensated for at the end of the month, though whether sufficiently is contested.

Thabo: Sorting not sorted
Thabo was sorting mail at his press.[1] Some walks are bigger than others. Some have heavier volumes. It depends on those living in the area and, of course, the time of the month. Thabo knew every walk of the depot, all 35 of them. He had either rotated through them during his thirteen years at the depot or covered them when others were on leave. One thing he hated was backtracking on his walk for a misplaced letter, so he would rather focus on sorting the mail without mistakes. When he found mis-sorted mail in the crates that came from the hub, he would tut-tut at the sloppy approach; they did not care about making work for other people. Sometimes, there would be scores of mis-sorts. Some he would have to take to other presses; he knew every address for the depot. He took pride when other postmen asked him about one that they were not sure about; '*Hana, 47 Rose-a-kres. Ke 32 kapa 33?*' ('Tell me, 47 Roseacres Street. It's [Walk] 32 or 33?'). Mis-sorts that did not belong in the depot would go back to the hub. A few, Thabo could understand, but sometimes it seemed the mail handlers in the hubs, sorting mail to the walk level, hardly had their eyes open.

Thabo was employed by TAS Appointments and Management Services (TAS). It had not started that way. He had joined the South African Post Office (SAPO) in 1998, aged 28, as an S32 – the casual category in the days before labour brokers, directly employed by the Post Office but on a casual basis. It was a good job; although only a temporary worker he was paid at the pro-rata rate for a permanent employee. He had started as a 'sub', in the industry lingo; someone who covered the walks for those on leave. And if he was not needed in his own depot, he would be sent to a depot that was short of postmen. With overtime, and without deductions for benefits, he could pull in R4 000 some months. Even without overtime, he would clear R3 000. That changed in 2001 when he ceased to be an employee of the Post Office and was transferred to T&L Appointments. His first salary as a T&L employee came in at R1 200 for the month. It was unexpected; he had been told that things would not change. But he was trapped; his wife was pregnant with their second child. When he remonstrated with his supervisor, she had told him that she only needed to ring his new employer and they would fire him. The choice, she said, was his. In 2002, his employer changed; he became an employee of TAS. But it was not until 2004 that he had a contract. Not that he ever knew what was in his contract. He had signed the document in front of his employer and never saw it again.

At the end of the month, other people went home with a smile on their faces, but nobody saw Thabo's teeth. Any attempt to remonstrate met the same response: all the supervisor had to do was pick up the phone. Thabo had filled out a Communication Workers Union (CWU) membership form and given it to the CWU shop steward in the depot. In fact, he had handed over several, but his dues were never deducted. CWU, it seemed, had no need of him. Until it came to a strike. Along with other casuals, he had been a foot soldier in CWU's battles. A strike's power is shown by filling the street: the more militant the mob, the better. The bosses, and anybody thinking about working, must know that you mean business. The bosses must know they must talk nicely to the union leaders. Thabo only realised much later that they had been fighting the battles of the permanents, not their own. It the 2009 strike, Clyde Mervin had told them at a boisterous rally outside the Post Office headquarters in Pretoria that they would all be permanent. He had never seen Mervin after that day, so had not been able to ask why he was still a casual worker. What the strike achieved was an increased salary for permanents. But for all the shouting on the streets, those strikes had been 'soft'. They had lasted as long as the permanents' funds had held out. Those funds were depleted by drinking. When the party was over, it was back to work. The casuals were left high and dry.

He had come close to being a permanent. Before the labour broking system really took hold, there had been a trickle of conversions. Once his name had been on the list for conversion, but his area manager had scratched it to make way for a relative. Giving up on CWU, he and others had run through a string of unions, hoping each time that they would be able to help. There had always been hope, along with a few months of collecting subscriptions for the union by hand, and then things had stalled. It always seemed that they needed to do something to help whoever was supposed to be helping them.

He had all but given up. Now he nursed regrets. Regret that he had hung on so long, hoping to be made permanent. Then there was a particular mistake that he regretted more than any other. It was his mistake, but he also blamed the SAPO area manager, Richard Radebe. In 2004, he had responded to a call for applications from the municipal council. He had sent in his CV. They had called him to offer him a job, but it was only a six-month contract. There was the possibility that the post would be made permanent, but it was not guaranteed. This was just after a meeting where Radebe had stressed the folly of the casuals leaving SAPO. As usual, this had been in response to their constant complaints whenever a meeting was held. Permanent status was, he suggested, just around the corner. Much as they might be unhappy, Radebe acknowledged, they should not throw away the opportunity that was coming. If they left, they would be starting at the bottom of the ladder again.

Thabo had told the woman from the municipality that he had a job. He was okay. He was sorted. But really, he was gambling. And his gamble flopped. Later, he regretted listening to Radebe. He had a friend who took up one of the municipal jobs that he had turned down. After the six-month contract, he had been made permanent and was now far ahead of Thabo. His friend had a car, a house . . . Thabo's regret was a bitter pill.

Thabo kept on sorting. It took about six crates of letters to fill his press. Of course, the press was not entirely full; some people got many letters, some people got little more than a monthly municipal statement. But with six crates sorted into the press, there was enough for a full walk. Now he bundled the letters that he took from the press. When his hand could hold no more, he fastened the bundle with one of the rubber bands that he kept around his wrist. He put the bundle on the floor and prepared the next one, which he placed alongside the first until he had nine, maybe ten bundles. Postmen new to a walk would number the bundles with a pen. Not Thabo; he could tell just by looking at the address on the first letter where the bundle belonged in the sequence of the walk. The first five bundles went into the plastic basket at the front of his bike, and the remainder into a 'dump sack' that the depot driver would drop off for him to pick up halfway around the walk.

Modise's delivery
Modise had finished his sorting by 10 a.m. It was time for breakfast: two large *makwenya* from the woman who ran a stall on the pavement across the road. He added a slice of polony to upgrade his meal, and two 'long' (single cigarettes) bought from the Zimbabwean next to the *makwenya* stall. Back in the depot he joined the other casuals, and sat apart from the permanent workers who had their own arrangements over tea.

The postmen heaved the heavy, clumsy bikes out of the depot. These bikes were built to last and not for the weak, nor the fainthearted. There were no gears to assist with hills and braking was by means of the chain: you locked the back wheel by jamming your feet firmly on the pedals. To make matters more difficult, the front box, weighted with bundles, could swing the front wheel around at the slightest shift of equilibrium and you had to keep tight hold of the handlebars, especially when the road was rough.

And they're off! A flotilla of mounted postmen streamed out of the depot with the benefit of an initial downhill slope. They gradually separated from each other as they dispersed to their different walks. Modise pedalled to the start of Walk 25, a good twenty minutes away at the extremities of the depot's delivery area. Walks were supposed to be rotated each year, but that only really applied to the casuals. The few permanents still left in the depot long dominated the cushy walks close to the depot. He cycled out of town.

When the uphill steepened, he let the bike come to a halt and pushed it until the ground levelled again. Walk 25 consisted of suburban bungalows and the occasional block of flats. The high street where the walk started was struggling; more shops were boarded than trading. Other than forgotten essentials, people in this long-established suburb had cars and shopped elsewhere. Off the high street, in the tree-lined avenues, the houses varied. Most were neat and well kept, a few needed painting; one or two were run-down to an extent that they worried the neighbours. One section was boomed off and there was a security guard checking who went in and out. There were gardeners who watered the lawns and kept the grass cut short. This was where Modise would get his best Christmas boxes come December.

Away from the boomed estate, the tree-lined suburban streets had a jaunty air expressed, in particular, by their post boxes. Post boxes were an outlet for a little fun. Perhaps it sat atop a chain welded rigid into a spiral, perhaps, for a smile, a box shaped as a gigantic boot on a garden wall.

But for Modise, the aesthetics of the post box was not the point. There were other factors of much higher priority. Could he ride his bicycle up to the box or must he dismount, balance the unwieldy bike at the curb and walk to the box? Could he slip letters into it, or could the owner not work out that standard 10.5-centimetre letters would not slide into a 9-centimetre slot? Must he cram each letter, one by one, into the inadequate slot?

Mr and Mrs Potgieter's letters had to be forced through the box's ridiculously stupid, far too small slot. It was not just the Potgieter's box that he had to deal with. What about the Greylings' further up the street? They had a flower bed in front of their low precast concrete wall. Their gardener planted the flowers that Mrs Greyling bought at the nursery. They brightened up the street. They looked nice. But the box was set back from the wall and the pretty flowers prevented Modise riding his bike to the box. Instead, he had to prop his bike up and stretch over the flowers. If he stood on the flowers, he knew there would be a complaint phoned to the depot.

And the boxes that were choked with drop-and-knock newspapers wedged in tight? To get the mail in the box Modise had to yank out the rain-swollen, sun-beached, rolled-up pieces of letterbox-constipating trash. It was tempting to throw what he extracted onto the pavement. He was a postman; he was not a letterbox caretaker.

Modise finished the street but instead of riding to the next, he pulled up out of sight of the last barking dog. There was a grass verge and a concrete palisade fence of a school playing field. No longer provoked by his presence, the dogs' barking gradually hushed. He propped up his bike, found a spot to sit and took out the *long* he had bought earlier. He had planned to smoke it when he had finished his walk, but he changed his mind. He would smoke it now. His purchases were fake fags costing a quarter of the real thing and they had little kick. The trick was to work out the filter and pull hard. Then you felt something. He still had the match from the Zimbabwean since he had lit his first from a borrowed cigarette in the depot. Now, carefully striking the match on the concrete fence, he cupped his hands to shield the flame and leaned in. He drew in deep, then held his breath to boost the hit before slowly exhaling and preparing for another draw.

Modise was enjoying the break. The sun was shining; he was relaxing. In truth, it was nice being a postman. He liked coming into town every day; it beat sitting in the township. And he liked being out and about. Once out on the streets he was his own boss: deciding how fast to work, when to take a break, when to push on. Plus, people liked postmen. Sometimes, they would give him something *feela* (just for the sake of it). He was not counting Christmas when he would get something from pretty much everybody, even if he had to ring the bell and wish them a Happy Christmas! If it was a hot day, he might get a cool drink. 'Mr Postman!' somebody would shout, 'Wait, I've got something for you!' Then they would go into the house to fetch whatever it was. Some people were lonely and wanted to chat. Some people wanted a postman they could trust; perhaps they had something important coming in the post.

Modise liked to think of himself as a good postman. He could list the ways he was a good postman. He had not once dumped mail. When he realised that a letter contained bank notes he would make a point of pushing it fully in the mail box so that it could not be pulled back out. Once, when covering a walk, he had found a bundle of mail, still bound with rubber bands in the lobby of a block of flats. The regular postman was cutting corners. He had opened the bundle and put the letters into the correct boxes for the twenty or so flats in the complex. When the regular postman came back, he made a point of telling him that he should do his own work and not expect others to cover. Next time, he told himself, he would report such an incident to the supervisor.

He was a good postman, and on balance it was a good job. The real problem was that he was a casual and not permanent. He could not manage on R2 000 or so a month. That became obvious on pay day. Pay night really; the SMS notification that his pay was in his bank account usually came in the early hours of the morning. The transaction was conveyed on his cell phone with a *ting!* A happy sound. But what happened next was dispiriting. No sooner had the happy '*ting!*' rung out than it was '*ting! ting! ting!*' More transactions. He knew what *they* were: stop orders. One after the other his creditors would take their cut. The chorus of *tings!* had always been depressing but now they were capsizing him. There was next to nothing left for him after the night's plunder. Being a permanent would solve everything. He would be buying what he wanted, when he wanted, with cash not credit.

Thapelo's canine encounter

Thapelo had come to Gauteng more than ten years previously with high hopes. Home was a village in Limpopo. He had arrived with a friend, Tumi. They had rented a shack together in a backyard. To begin with, it had been hard. Now and then they had picked up day jobs, waiting at a busy junction along with other hopefuls. At the time, the going rate was R50, cash in hand, for a day's labouring. If one of them was hired, they bought a 2-kilogram bag of maize meal, fish oil for cooking, onions, tomatoes and *maotwana* (chicken feet), and went to bed with full stomachs.

Then, with the help of a relative, he had trained as a security guard. With a PSIRA Level C certificate,[2] he had got a job with a security company working at the access control gate of an engineering company. It paid R2 000 a month, and it meant twelve-hour shifts, five days (or nights) on and three days off. Weekends and public holidays did not disrupt the cycle, which was only broken once 49 weeks were completed. Then there were three weeks annual leave, before the cycle started for another 49 weeks.

He had applied for work with TAS, which he had found out about through a friend who attended the same Zion Christian Church branch. He had been called three days after the interview and told to report to Boksburg the following morning. He was out delivering mail that afternoon. There had been no bike for him and he had gone out on foot. He got hopelessly lost. He was still out when it got dark. Finally, the supervisor had come looking for him. He still had mail in his bag. He went out the next morning to finish the round.

The monthly salary depended on how much mail was delivered. The casuals were paid by the amount of mail. Before they set out, they had to weigh the bundles of mail. If the supervisor was not around, Thapelo would add a kilogram to the weight displayed on the scale. Exactly a kilogram. Or exactly two, if it was displaying 6 kilograms something. Six and eight looked very similar in digital display. He kept the three figures after the decimal point unchanged. Should the supervisor make a spot check, the discrepancy could be put down to an innocent mistake. Sometimes, it was hard to read the display in the dim light of the depot and through the grime and grease on the screen. But even with a few extra kilograms his salary never reached R2 000. Usually it would fluctuate between R1 600 and R1 800 – less than he had been earning as a security guard. But he stuck with the job. He was glad to be rid of the night shifts that he had come to dread.

Like every casual, he was hoping that he would be made permanent. If that happened he was planning to put money aside and set up a small business. He would buy stock in town and get one of his younger brothers to run the shop while he was working. He had a stand back in Limpopo, allocated by the local chief. What he did not have was money to build a house on the stand. And he needed to get married, which was all but impossible with the money he earned. He and Palesa already had two children, but until he could pay *lobola* (bride wealth) and until he could show that he could support her, she remained living with her parents. In truth, he had almost nothing to show for his ten years in Gauteng. He was running backwards.

Thapelo thought a lot about the dogs he encountered on his walks. In this he was not alone. All postmen worry about dogs. All postmen have stories. Some have scars. With few exceptions, postmen and dogs are enemies in a war of asymmetric reasoning: postmen must deliver the mail, dogs must defend their territory. It is a war without end. Most confrontations take place over fences and walls that are high enough to keep the parties apart, but sometimes not.

Most dogs in the suburbs, Thapelo had long concluded, are disturbed in the head. Dogs in the townships, or back in his village, were not disturbed. They knew their place. If you raised your hand, the dog ran. Township dogs knew that a raised hand meant a stone was about to be thrown. They knew a stone hurt. They knew to run. Not suburb dogs. As far as Thapelo could see, dogs in the suburbs were never disciplined. You could raise your hand, but it would only provoke them to bark more. They were spoiled. They could do what they wanted. They had rights.

Thapelo placed dogs into categories. Thapelo's first category was small dogs that yapped, and jumped, and ran around in circles. They were disturbed, irritating, but not a problem. Bigger dogs were a problem. Grade I Disturbed big dogs were probably nice dogs, if you were not a postman reaching over the fence trying to cram letters into a post box. But if you were the postman, then they thought your hand belonged in their mouth.

Then there were Grade II Disturbed big dogs. When these dogs sprinted for your hand, the matter did not end when you got your body safely back street-side. The Grade II dog's attack was only arrested when it threw itself at the gate in a paroxysm of fury. The dog had become sound and teeth and fury. And people expected postmen to put their hands over the man-dog frontier of safety. No chance! thought Thapelo. If there was a big dog (Grade II Disturbed), he felt entitled to wedge the mail in the gate. It could get wet if it rained. Blame your dog. Blame yourself. He was going to keep his hands intact.

No. 42 Venus Street had all three categories of dog: a Yap dog, a Grade I Disturbed dog that barked but did not do much else, and a Grade II Disturbed dog – a blue American Pitbull – that threw itself at the side gate when Thapelo climbed up the steep steps to the box that was built into a pillar. That meant Grade II dog and Thapelo ended up almost face to face. Grade II dog was on his hind legs barking right in Thapelo's face, fangs exposed, slobber spraying out, as Thapelo stuffed letters into the post box. The Yap dog was trying to bark through the fence and turn around at the same time; Grade I dog was joining in the barking but was keeping its distance from Grade II dog. 'Just be calm,' Thapelo told himself. A dog's fury was one thing behind a tall gate. It was another thing when the lock clicked and the gate swung outward. As it had just done.

'Shit!' Neither Thapelo nor Grade II dog had expected that to happen. They had been through this ritualised rage many times and the gate had always remained firm. In truth, that state of affairs had suited them both. Today things were different. For a fraction of a second, after the gate swung open, the dog remained upright. Thapelo's first thought was that it was going to wrap its huge teeth-lined mouth around his face. But as the gate swung open, Grade II dog, his front feet no longer supported, dropped down. Thapelo, without turning, was already backing down the steps. He knew not to turn his back on a dog; then it would bite. He needed to get to his bike, which he could use as a shield to keep the dog at bay long enough for the owner to emerge. But he lost his balance on the third step and fell backwards. He managed to keep his head from hitting the tarmac and he broke his fall instinctively by thrusting his hands out behind him. He felt the sharp sting of road grit bite into his hands. There was also a deeper, sharper pain that he felt in his left hand. But there was no time to give it any attention. He was scared. He was about to be mauled. The dog was going to take advantage of his vulnerability. It was going to rip his flesh off. It was going to lock its jaws onto his leg. It was going to rip his throat open. The Grade I dog was going to join in.

Grade II dog bounded down the steps after him. But with a stroke of luck Thapelo clipped his bicycle as he fell, and it started to fall, spilling bundles of letters from the front box. It blocked the direct route between Grade II's mouth and Thapelo. It gave Thapelo a moment. He swung his body and kicked out wildly to the left of the spinning front wheel, right in the dog's path.

The dog lurched forward a couple of times, but held back from attacking. Perhaps it was uncertain now that it was outside of familiar territory. Thapelo was able to scramble up. He was on his feet now, but he still had to get the bike between him and the dog. He started with a diversionary tactic, stooping to pick up one of the spilled bundles of letters. He advanced on the dog, his arm raised high with the bundle in it. The dog held its ground, barking furiously. Thapelo hurled the bundle with as much force as he could. It was a direct hit! The dog yelped and retreated, but only for a moment. Then it was back, more fury and teeth than before. It was not intimidated. But Thapelo had won a few second and he grabbed the bike with both hands, ignoring the stabbing pain is his left. His right hand gripped the seat, his left the handlebar. He managed to get the bike between himself and the dog.

It was a letter-strewn suburban arena: man versus dog. To the dog, the bike was much like the gate. It knew what to do: it hurled itself at the bike-cum-gate. Thapelo braced against the weight of the dog and held on grimly even though pains were shooting up from his left wrist. He was not going to let go of his shield. Instead, he was trying to swing the basket onto the dog, hoping to knock it hard. But all he achieved was the dog locking his jaws onto the wheel. There was a hiss as the air escaped from the punctured tire. At least the other dogs were staying put. It was just this Grade II bastard he had to beat. He was shouting and screaming. 'Somebody! Come out! Somebody!' He hoped his voice would be heard above the wild barking that was normal at 42 Venus Street when the postman came to deliver.

He was tired by the time the domestic worker came out of the house. Her first reaction was fear that she was in trouble: she knew that she was the last person through the gate that morning. But she phoned Mrs van der Merwe who was at work. And Mrs van der Merwe phoned her neighbour, a pensioner, but who was still spritely. He was a reliable neighbour, though this was asking a lot. He was also nervous about the dog, but he was calm and talked quietly to the dog. 'Good dog! Go inside, go inside. Good dog!' He pointed to the open gate.

Thapelo was able to back off, bike still firmly gripped, and Grade II dog took the chance to get back into familiar territory. The old man jumped forward and, keeping his hand high, swung the gate closed again. The dog was inside.

It was over. Thapelo's heart was beating fast. His voice was hoarse. The pain in his hand was now stabbing every time he tried to grip something. The ballpoint pen that was in his pocket was sticking out of his trousers; in the tussle it had somehow forced through the fabric. He manoeuvred it back into his pocket with his right hand. He found his phone, which had fallen onto the street.

There was a call to the owner via the domestic worker's phone. Once it was clear that nobody had been bitten, Mrs van der Merwe was relieved. She said she would look into the gate. The domestic worker brought ice for Thapelo's wrist, which she passed through the fence. She was also apologising. She said that there must be something wrong with the gate. She knew she closed it properly.

There were letters everywhere, some covered in boot marks. Thapelo collected them up and dumped them in the basket. He phoned Bongani, his supervisor, but there was no transport available, so he started to wheel the bike, front tire flat as a pancake, back to the depot, pushing with his right hand, using his left only to steady the handlebars.

Thabo's temptation

It had not the first time Thabo had been approached while delivering. There would be greetings, a clumsy conversation, and then whoever it was - usually, Thabo noted, a Nigerian (a term covering any West African) - would talk about how they could help each other. Thabo would try to get away before the punchline, which was, invariably, if he could give them the letters marked 'Private & Confidential', especially those coming from abroad, there would be a generous reward. How much was never specified, but it would be a lot. It was, however, always made clear that the Nigerian was just the conduit; other people would be making use of the letters.

Thabo would explain how two postmen in his depot had been dismissed and he could not afford to lose his job. He could not help. Such casual approaches were rarely too persistent and could be shrugged off. But this latest approach had been more difficult to refuse. It had not come from Nigerians but from people who spoke his own language; they were also from the Free State, practically homeboys. They had met in a tavern, watching the match on a Saturday afternoon. At some point, he had said he was a postman and one of the two men had asked for his number.

A few days later, he got a call from a number he did not know. It was Lefa. It took Thabo a while to remember, but Lefa reminded him about the game and that being from the Free State they both favoured Free State Stars. 'Ntate,' Lefa had used the respectful term of address; he had a friend who he wanted to introduce to Thabo. Out of politeness Thabo had agreed and the next Saturday Lefa had come with his friend Lehlohonolo. Lehlohonolo drove an Audi, which he had parked in front of the tavern where they had agreed to meet. Lefa bought the first round, Lehlohonolo the second. Lefa had already bought the third before the second was finished. The conversation came around to Thabo's work. Lehlohonolo could see a way to help Thabo. What he was looking for were store cards. They went through a list: Jet, Edgars, Ackermans – all clothing stores that offered credit accounts. Thabo knew the branding that each store used on its envelopes and he knew that you could feel if it had a card inside. Lehlohonolo explained that he knew somebody who could use the cards. Thabo was not to worry about the intended card owner; if they never got the card they would not be held responsible for the R2 000 initial credit. Lehlohonolo did not explain the rest, but Thabo could work it out. Somebody would go to store and max the card's credit limit to buy clothes. Somebody else would then sell the clothes 'back door'. There would be a story about why they were so cheap, which would not be believed but nor would it be challenged.

Thabo was wondering how much he would get for each card misdelivered, but he was also thinking about the risk. Lehlohonolo had anticipated this. He had a suggestion: Thabo should not take cards from his own walk, but from others. It was easy enough, Lehlohonolo explained. Just walk through the depot and keep your eyes open. He explained that he could not disclose exactly how much Thabo would get for each card; it would depend on 'the market' but, it might be R100, perhaps more.

Thabo said he would think about it. He thought about the thirteen years he had worked for the Post Office. He thought about how they had lied to him when he was handed over to the labour broker. He thought about how his supervisor had told him he was a phone call away from losing his job. He thought about how CWU had used him to fight for the permanents. He thought about how he had been fooled into missing an opportunity to better himself. He thought about the string of unions that had all failed him. He thought about the shame he felt when explaining that although he was a postman he actually worked for a labour broker. He thought about the lies he told to his children when they asked for something. And he thought about what he could do with R100 for a letter. It could, Thabo thought, be a way of getting what he should be getting. It would mean he could stand tall and proud.

Homeward bound
When Thapelo got back to the depot Bongani was out. No one was sure where. When he rang, Bongani said he would be back in half an hour. Thapelo should wait; he would have to fill in an incident form. An hour later Bongani returned. Thapelo's wrist was now swollen, but Bongani thought it would be better in the morning. He made a concession, though, telling Thapelo that he would get someone to help him fix the bike.

By the time Modise got back to his depot he had the solution to his problems. On the way to the station he dropped into the crowded Top Bet shop and put down R20 on Crazy Numbers. He was bound to win. He would, he as good as knew, be collecting R200 tomorrow and that would be just the start.

Thabo went home with two letters marked Private & Confidential in his pocket.

6

A Divided Class

Two workforces

Labour broking created two workforces within the South African Post Office (SAPO). Most casuals placed by labour brokers worked in its sorting hubs and depots. They worked under SAPO supervisors and alongside permanent employees. The first of the 'General Terms and Conditions of Employment' of Temporary Appointments and Management Services (TAS) outlined: 'TAS carries on the business of providing temporary services (assigning temps)...' (TAS n.d.). Condition 16 referred to a permanent placement fee should a temp be offered permanent employment by the client. In reality, however, placements were perpetual. Casuals did exactly the same work as permanents, some for over a decade. Casuals held *de jure* temporary employment status, but their situation was of de facto permanence.

Not only did casuals do the same work as permanent SAPO employees, they also shared social space outside the workplace. In Mail Delivery, both permanent and casual workers were overwhelmingly African.[1] Apartheid had divided workforces by race, a division that extended beyond the workplace to the communities from which they hailed. But here the legacy of apartheid meant that permanents and casuals lived together; they came from the same townships, sometimes from the same streets.

Yet, it was insisted that they – casuals or agents or any other term used to *other* them – were different. Labour brokers T&L Appointments outlined in a memo, 'You are being employed by us and as our employees you don't qualify to compare yourselves and your contracts to that of the employees of the client' (T&L n.d.).[2] This difference had very real effects. It was most obvious in the terms and conditions of employment. However, the contractual difference permeated the social relationships of workplace order, creating an intra-class division. Workers were divided in subjective as well as objective terms, with tensions that extended beyond the workplace.

Different treatment

The most obvious objective difference between permanent employees and casuals was pay. A permanent worker's monthly take-home pay, in 2011 figures, was R8 000, approximately four times what the casual worker received.[3] The difference was huge. It meant that casual workers could do little more than get through the month, even if they budgeted wisely and spent prudently. Caphus Chauke, a postman in Soweto who hailed from Limpopo Province and was employed by TAS, explained: '[Our salary was] not real money. If I had a funeral [of a relative] at home, I could not afford to go to home; that money was too small. I had children at school, but I could not afford the fees.[4] All of those things I couldn't afford' (interview, Chauke).

Casual workers might be able to put food on the table, but not much else. They were, in effect, socially disabled; beyond the basics of survival their resources did not stretch to societal necessities: to travel to family funerals or provide for their child's education. Lacking a pension fund meant there was nothing better to look forward to when they eventually stopped working. They would retire with little more than the clothes on their backs. They were not going to starve to death; the country's social security system would see to that. But they would be no better off, in fact worse. In 2011 figures, they would receive R1 140 a month old-age pension, and they might well be under pressure to share that with family members who had nothing at all.

Permanent workers, earning R8 000 a month, struggled to meet some commitments they felt were important. But they could at least look forward to their birthday. As a government employee, they would receive a thirteenth cheque that month. The annual windfall could be used to make a large purchase. Another windfall was an annual bonus payment of R5 000 negotiated by the Communication Workers Union (CWU) in 2005 as the company was moving into the black (on the back of casual workers). There was also an agreement for CWU and management to jointly work on a performance-based 'gain-sharing' scheme. The actual scheme was never finalised but the payments were nevertheless made: in 2006 the amount was settled through arbitration at R4 000 (SAPO 2006). By 2009, CWU was demanding that it be raised to R7 000 (Roberts 2009a).[5] But more significant than these negotiated cherries, was the provident fund contributions that accrued month by month and medical aid that allowed permanents to access private health care.

By comparison, the perks handed out by the labour brokers were derisible and a source of shame: not something you could brag about. For example, in 2002, T&L employees received a Christmas hamper. It was remembered by recipients for its limited contents. Moraba Choshi, a postman in Tembisa, recalled how Colleen Ramaphakela (then a partner in T&L) had come to the depot while they were out delivering and left the hampers with the supervisor. 'When we open those things, inside we get a small [packet of] rice, a small jelly . . . everything was small . . . we took those boxes because we have suffered a lot, but we suffered more when we check those things . . . the small size . . . Ah! I still remember those things. I was so embarrassed . . .' (interview, Choshi).

Another Christmas it was a R100 Checkers supermarket voucher, the meanness of which was raised in several interviews.

The way in which casuals' salaries were calculated gave rise to tensions. Permanents got their salary irrespective of the volume of mail, as stipulated in collective bargaining agreements. If volumes were high, it meant overtime. If it was slack, they could knock off early. As supposedly temporary placements, casuals were paid by the hour. However, since work can be stretched, especially out on the walks where surveillance is difficult, ways to allocate claimable hours to mail volumes were necessary. These methods included standard times for walks, weighing mail, and the number of letters sorted and/or delivered.[6] Depot supervisors were responsible for managing these proxy time measures. Their calculations would be submitted to SAPO's human resources department for payment to the labour broker. The calculations were often contested at the depot level. Supervisors under pressure to contain costs would seek to minimise the hours billed. Casuals would attempt to push up their hours, either through negotiation or fraud, since more hours meant more pay.

Uniforms were another point of conflict. Permanents were issued with uniforms, including wet-weather gear. Casuals got nothing. When casuals asked for uniforms, the labour brokers pointed out that it was not their responsibility. As always, it came down to who would be paying. In the end, SAPO issued bibs that casuals could fix over their clothes to identify themselves as postmen. The bibs served to entrench the difference between casuals and permanents. Furthermore, the bibs resembled *mathandakitchen*, or kitchen aprons, and were an affront to male workers.

But it was perhaps the smallest difference in terms and conditions of service between permanents and casuals that hurt the most – the tea allowance. SAPO gave depots a tea allowance based on the number of employees – permanent employees, obviously, as the casuals did not count. It was not much: R15 per month per person, later increased to R20. When there were only permanents in the depots, it had been straightforward; tea, sugar and milk powder would be bought for the morning break. But with increasing numbers of casuals, the tea allowance would not pour far enough. With a few exceptions, discussed in Chapter 7, permanents asserted ownership of the allowance and brewed for themselves.

The sum of differences between casuals and permanents equalled workers of different worth. That was not, of course, the company's position, as the following extract from SAPO's 2012 Annual Report makes clear. The passage illustrates the gulf between workplace realities and corporate-speak, which are common enough, but are here all the more jarring given that SAPO had already entered a period of industrial chaos, was close to bankruptcy and facing technological irrelevance.

> While our employees remain the biggest differentiator from our competition, there is a need to describe the mix of our employee offerings, be it through the benefits we offer, the actual workplace and [the] ways of working in the organisation. There is a dire need to package our value proposition in a way that appeals to current and potential employees. An employee

value proposition is therefore an important attractor and retainer of sought-after talent. As part of the value proposition, the SA Post Office will continue to nurture talent though appropriate talent management strategies and will systematically improve the working environment so that everyone experiences it as the best place to work. While the SA Post Office's business strategy provides the direction for its efforts, it is the people in the company who will seal the success of the organisation. Recent successes are the result of the outstanding commitment and focus of employees at different levels of the organisation (SAPO 2012: 69).

Hyperbole and naivety aside, the passage works if by 'everyone' the writer meant 'permanents', as is confirmed by a table in the report (SAPO 2012: 69). The Annual Report goes on to outline the value proposition that SAPO offered 'everyone'. This included skills development courses, a range of study bursaries, health and wellness programmes, and corporate citizenship projects that staff were encouraged to support two days per year (working days, not their own time). Nice. Shame about the casuals, though.

But if SAPO managers weighed the worth of the two workforces so differently, they were not the only ones constructing the discrepancy.

The donkeys of the depots

The casuals' second-class status rested on their inferior terms and conditions of employment; it was maintained with their vulnerability. CWU organised permanent employees. The casuals were, to begin with, neither represented nor organised, an issue explored in the next chapter. Although it was cost-cutting, driven at board level, that initially brought labour brokers into SAPO, on a day-to-day basis both supervisors and permanents were in a position to mitigate being squeezed by squeezing the casuals.

Casuals were most vulnerable when they were first placed by the broker. They did not know if they would be kept on and they did not know the ropes. Jabulani Mabena, a TAS casual in the Springs Depot on the East Rand, was sent out to deliver on his first afternoon. He got lost. He had been sent out on foot as bicycles were reserved for permanents. He got home past 9 p.m. Themba Sibiya, employed at the Edenvale Depot, also on the East Rand, had a similar induction. They were the donkeys of the depot; when there were walks that needed to be split because someone was absent, it was the casuals who were called to help (interview, Sibiya).

Mabena's experience of split walks was similar to that of Sibiya. Sometimes the split walk that they were expected to help cover was far away from their own walk. They were supposed to be transported between the two areas using the depot van, but that did not always happen. They were not priority, and transport could be allocated elsewhere. If they spoke out or complained, they would hear it directly: 'Who are you? You are just an agent!'

There were also disputes over the hours that supervisors allocated. The paid hours credited to casuals depended on the supervisor's judgement. If Mabena rushed a walk to beat the rain one day, that was taken as the standard. As casuals, they were the last to get dump sacks delivered.[7] That meant working late, especially when the volumes were high. The permanents would be home by the time the casuals got back to the depot.

Not all supervisors sided with the permanents. Charles John, a depot controller on the West Rand and a CWU office-bearer, was one of a minority of CWU office-bearers who championed the casuals. He recalled how casual workers were discriminated against by management, the union and the permanent workers. He found the latter particularly disappointing, the 'wrong mentality' for permanent workers to take against other workers.

When appointed as depot controller, bicycles had only been available for the permanents; casuals delivered on foot. John allocated bicycles based on travel distance and walk size. He also used the tea allowance to buy for everybody. There were some complaints from some permanents, but he stood his ground. He shamed the permanents who complained by insisting that the casuals were their 'brothers'. Perhaps, he pointed out, if they ended up at the same *mosebetsi* (ceremony-cum-gathering) in the township they would need to introduce the casual. They would introduce them as a co-worker, working in the same company. But when it came to sharing something, they did not want to be brothers (interview, John).

However, few supervisors followed John's lead. Eric Khumalo, a mail handler in the Krugersdorp Hub, where casuals were used extensively on a part-time basis, explained how supervisors favoured permanents. If a permanent wanted to leave early, the supervisor would allocate a casual to finish his work. Casuals in the hub were paid by the hour, so to be allocated somebody else's work meant more pay, but they resented the practice. Sure, they were getting money for the hours they worked, but the permanent was getting money to knock off. Should they refuse, the supervisor would not call them for a couple of weeks, just to show who was in charge.

However, permanents did not require the supervisor to take advantage of casuals. Permanents' superior salaries meant that they could pay casuals to cover their walks. This could be between R50 and R100 a walk depending on its size and the generosity of the permanent. It allowed permanents to go home early after sorting if they had something they wanted to do. Casuals were, in effect, auxiliaries to the permanents.

It was also possible for permanents to make money from the casuals through short-term loans. SAPO employees are paid on the 25th of the month; labour broker employees were paid at the end of the month (and sometimes later). In the interval, one group of workers was flush, the other broke. Of course, as workmates it was possible for one to help the other with an interest-free loan to tide them over till the end of the month. That sometimes happened, but permanents also stepped into the gap as *mashonisas* (informal lenders) charging interest (interviews, Ramagaga; Papiki Mokoena).

Byoung-Hoon Lee and Stephen Frenkel (2004), in their study of contract and permanent workers in a Korean car manufacturing plant, draw on the psychological concept of 'moral exclusion'. Moral exclusion allows a group to justify its privileges by labelling the other group as morally inferior. Casual workers in SAPO recalled how permanent workers referred to them as being on a government job opportunity project: they were not real postmen. George Ramagaga (interview), a postman in the Vaal, explained that the permanents treated them 'like you are nothing'. Maintaining this difference was psychologically important for permanent workers working alongside casuals. Establishing different moral categories enabled permanents to justify their privileges. Those privileges, in turn, confirmed their superiority. Denying casuals the use of 'their' bicycles was not only about making their own lives easier, it also denied casuals the props necessary to confer full status as postmen. The lack of uniforms served a similar purpose. Permanents were, of course, not responsible for issuing uniforms, but if a casual got hold of an item of SAPO uniform, permanents would complain: casuals were not entitled to wear SAPO uniform; they were not employed by the company.

Used by everybody, owned by nobody

The creation of a bifurcated workforce within one workplace, created by externalising part of the labour force through labour broking or other contractual means, has been described by Kally Forrest (2015) as a combination of Michael Burawoy's (1985) hegemonic and despotic workplace regimes. In other words, the loyalty of some workers is secured through concessions and consent while the compliance of others is maintained through fear and discipline. As Gibson Ramotsi, a postman in the East Rand township of Katlehong, explained, there might, as required by law, be posters summarising key labour legislation on the walls of the depots, but that didn't mean that the law applied to everyone equally (interview, IICUSA office-bearers). What casual workers began to see was that nobody was on their side, but that everyone was using them. Russel Mutavhatsindi (2009), a Soweto-based postman and a leader of the West Rand casuals, described how the casuals were 'slaves used by everybody, but owned by nobody'.

Conclusion

This chapter has explored how SAPO's casual workforce was exploited, including by their own class. Their precarious legal status was critical to this vulnerability in the workplace. Casuals' vulnerability, as second-class workers, was exploited not only by SAPO management and the labour broking companies. Their vulnerability was also exploited and therefore deepened, by others: supervisors, permanent SAPO employees and, as we will see in the next chapter, the only union operating in the Post Office. In different ways, all these actors benefited from the casuals' cheap labour. At times they were in competition and sometimes in conflict with each other, but those conflicts could be mitigated through their combined exploitation of casuals.

This book is about how casuals came to fight their own battles. By necessity they had to fight on many fronts, but consciousness takes time to develop. Early struggles were not against the giants that they were to later confront, but over issues of equality on the shop floor. In the Krugersdorp Hub, one of the first demands that the casuals formulated was that permanent workers should work their full shifts; casuals should not be expected to finish their work for them (interview, Khumalo).

At the Sebokeng Depot in the Vaal, Papiki Mokoena (interview) led a 'dump sack war'. The walks in Sebokeng Township are large, and the largest were given to casuals. When volumes were high, the biggest walks could require four or five dump sacks. These were left in boxes located inside people's yards for safety. If volumes were high, sorting took longer and those with the largest walks might not set out to deliver until 2 p.m. The depot driver, a permanent employee, would drop off the dump sacks and go off duty. Postmen now had to deliver all the mail or risk disciplinary action if the mail was left out overnight. The supervisor was happy with the driver not being available to pick up undelivered mail; it meant clearflow every day, and that was good for his bonus.[8] In the end, Mokoena organised a collective knock-off; everybody knocked off at 5 p.m., finished or not. The supervisor backed down. It was, initially, small struggles waged and small victories achieved by casuals. Sometimes these struggles ended in frustration, as being palmed off with bibs when they asked for uniforms. Yet, each struggle helped bring clarity to their situation – clarity over just who benefited from their exploitation and who must therefore be counted among their enemies.

7

A Divided Union

Introduction: Tensions

The Communication Workers Union (CWU), established in 1996, dominated SAPO's industrial relations until 2012. The zenith of the union's power in SAPO came in 2008. At that time, the union had 11 000 members, 75 per cent of the company's bargaining unit (Labour Court 2009b).[1] There was no other union in the South African Post Office (SAPO) to challenge them and employees who opted not to join had to pay an agency fee equal to the membership subscription, since it negotiated on behalf of everyone in the bargaining unit. The agency fee was, however, value for money: CWU negotiated a good deal. Over the twelve months of the 2008/2009 agreement, inflation ran at around 7 per cent, but the union's negotiators came away with 10.75 per cent. They did not even need to strike. The truth was that they had management eating out of their hands.

Actually, in many respects, CWU *was* management. Almost everyone in the first three rungs of management in the mail delivery section - supervisors, depot controllers and area controllers - were CWU members. This was not surprising since the bargaining unit extended to SAPO's C5 level (that of area controller). CWU was negotiating for them. And frequently the human resources (HR) managers on the other side of the table were former comrades from the union.

Four years later, the union was down to just over 4 000 members and competing for members with three other unions (CCMA 2012; see also Chapter 16). This collapse resulted from fissures within the union, present though not yet apparent in 2008. The deepest of these fissures was over the increasing number of casual workers who remained outside the bargaining unit and CWU's membership. Indeed, as employees of the labour brokers and not SAPO, they did not pay the agency fee to CWU. Nor, of course, did they benefit from any agreement that CWU negotiated.

There was a gaping chasm between CWU's high-profile involvement in the national campaign by the Congress of South African Trade Unions (COSATU) to ban labour broking and the steady march of labour brokers into the de facto SAPO workforce. While it was easy to stand united over the national campaign to ban the 'slavery' of labour broking, responding to brokers in their own backyard was not so easy. The issue of casuals was of strategic importance for the position of the union in the company. However, conflict over how the union should respond crystallised around whether the union should represent casuals in disciplinary hearings. The different approaches taken by CWU office-bearers over this question fed into a power struggle between various leadership factions for control of the union.

Yet, the division within the union over labour brokers within the company was not the most immediate challenge to CWU's monopoly within SAPO. This came from a break-away of permanent, often more skilled employees, in the form of the South African Postal and Allied Workers Union (SAPAWU). The emergence of SAPAWU and the long, ultimately unsuccessful, rearguard action that CWU waged against this rival union was one of several factors that diverted CWU's attention, along with that of their SAPO HR partners, from the more potent and disruptive force that organised casuals were to become.

This chapter explores the tensions within CWU over their approach to casual workers within SAPO. These are well illustrated by events at the Edenvale Depot, beginning on 10 June 2008 when Florida Mbageni argued with her supervisor.

Two hats, one face

The Edenvale Postal Depot serves a suburban area east of Johannesburg. As well as some twenty walks to which deliveries are made, the depot has mail boxes, referred to as Mail Collection Points (MCPs), where people pick up their mail. In 2008, there were some 30-odd people working at the depot, either as postmen or in the MCP section. The depot was managed by a supervisor and a depot controller who reported to the SAPO area manager. The majority of workers were casual; two or three were employed by Marula and the rest by TAS Appointments and Management Services (TAS). Most of the postmen who delivered mail and the women who worked in the MCP section came from the nearby townships of Tembisa and Ivory Park, a few kilometres to the north. Florida, who worked in the MCP section, was a TAS casual. As previously noted, 'casual' is a term describing employment status and not length of service. Of nineteen TAS labour broker employees in Edenvale in 2008, two, including Florida, had worked there for six years, five for five years, another five for four years, three for three years, three more for two years and one under a year. Around that time, it was rumoured that three casual positions were in line for conversion. Florida claimed that the argument arose when the supervisor demanded a 'cool drink' (bribe) for help in converting her to permanent status.[2]

The Edenvale supervisor reported Florida to the depot controller, Mike Mabaso. Like the supervisor, Mabaso was a Post Office employee, but in the event of a disciplinary problem with a TAS casual it was TAS that would deal with the matter. When TAS was informed that Florida was arguing with the supervisor, it was decided that she would be transferred to the Alberton Postal Depot, some 30 kilometres away, beginning from 1 July. Florida refused to sign the transfer letter that TAS's Michael Motlokoa sent her. At stake for her was the possibility of securing one of the three permanent positions because she was one of the longest-serving casuals at the depot. Come 1 July Florida continued to come to work as usual, at Edenvale. The same thing happened the next day.

Mabaso had a problem on his hands. He called TAS. He also called his superior, the Post Office's area controller, Mr Mervin. Both came to the depot and the next day Florida reported for duty 30 kilometres away at the Alberton Depot. But the problem was not settled. Indeed, it was set to get worse.

On 9 August, Motlokoa, along with another TAS manager, met with Florida in Alberton and informed her that there was to be a disciplinary hearing over her behaviour. The charge sheet listed: gross insubordination; being rude to management; failure to take instruction; breach of contract; bringing the company's name into disrepute; and being absent from work without permission. New to Alberton Depot, Florida was isolated. But she had not been forgotten; the next day Edenvale Depot came to a standstill. Exactly what happened was later disputed. But Mabaso called Mervin to inform him there was a strike; the workers were *toyi-toying* and the two CWU shop stewards who represented SAPO's permanent employees were in the thick of it. The strike was about Florida's banishment to Alberton. It was also directed at the supervisor who had caused the problem and who was deeply unpopular in the depot.[3]

Mervin faxed Mabaso a letter that he could distribute to the workforce instructing them to return to work and said that he would come as soon as he could. James van den Berg, SAPO's employee relations manager, who had also been alerted to the problem, got hold of Freddie Marutha, a CWU full-time shop steward, who arrived at Edenvale around 11.30 that morning. He found Mervin together with Van den Berg. Mervin had attempted to address the *toyi-toying* workers but they had refused to let him speak. Mervin told Marutha that he was willing to talk to the strikers and resolve the problem of Florida's transfer. He also pointed out, however, that if a meeting was to be held that day it would be impossible for the postmen to complete their delivery rounds. He suggested that he return the following day in order to resolve the matter. After Marutha conveyed this message to the strikers, the disruption subsided and work resumed.

However, this apparent resolution of the matter quickly fell apart. Nothing came of Mervin's promise, as TAS proceeded with its disciplinary hearing against Florida and additionally instituted a disciplinary hearing for its eighteen Edenvale employees. The disciplinary hearing for the latter was held in Sebokeng, some 90 kilometres from Tembisa where most of them lived, presumably to minimise the dangers of protest. Their request to be represented by the one of the CWU shop stewards was refused on the grounds that they must be represented by a co-worker who must, following the contractual logic of labour broking, be a TAS employee and, in this situation, one of the accused given that the entire TAS component of the Edenvale workforce had been charged. The chairperson of the hearing, Neal Lakey, group human resources manager for the Moloko Group, which included TAS,[4] focused on the eighteen employees' participation in what he termed a 'partial, illegal strike' that had resulted, he found, in both the company's code of conduct and the Postal Act being violated.[5] All eighteen workers were dismissed with immediate effect. Florida's hearing, also chaired by Lakey, was held in Alberton and she, too, was dismissed.[6]

On the surface, these events read fairly straightforwardly. Admittedly, the two cases – that of Florida's transfer and the Edenvale 18's solidarity actions – are intertwined and sometimes convoluted. Even the protagonists got confused at times, with documents transposing dates between the two cases. Also up for interpretation is what exactly took place in the Edenvale Depot on 10 July 2008. At the time, it looked very much like a wildcat strike. Yet, by the time Marutha was giving evidence at the Commission for Conciliation, Mediation and Arbitration's (CCMA's) hearing and attempting to save the eighteen workers' jobs,[7] it had not been a strike at all. The workers had been merely waiting for Mervin, the SAPO manager, to come and address their concern.

Whether strike or stoppage, the situation could be read as one that CWU, in the form of Marutha, had helped to calm. The two hot-headed shop stewards in the depot had been called into line. A plan to resolve the problem had been agreed between SAPO management, represented by Mervin, and the union, represented by Marutha. Marutha had used his credibility as a CWU office-bearer to inform the strikers, or waiting workers (depending on whether you were arguing that a strike had occurred or not), of the agreement. Work had then resumed. Of course, after that, things had gone pear-shaped, but that could be put down to TAS acting on its own initiative and SAPO (Mervin) washing their hands of the matter and giving TAS free rein once the crisis had been averted.

Freddie Marutha, as we will see, was a champion of the casual workers within SAPO. As a full-time CWU shop steward, he was independent of SAPO. As a previous SAPO supervisor, he could use his operational knowledge to see a sensible solution and, as in this case, try to shield the most vulnerable workers from dismissal. He was part of the group within CWU that believed that casuals should be organised by the union. He was also popular with permanent workers, especially on the East Rand, and was a strong contender for the chair of CWU's Gauteng Provincial Executive Committee, one of the most powerful positions in the union and one that brings national office within striking distance.

Now pay attention, there is a punchline coming: the person that Marutha would have to unseat to become the chair of CWU's Provincial Executive Committee was Clyde Mervin, the SAPO area controller. Below the apparently reasonable solution that Marutha and Mervin worked out that morning lay deep tensions.

That Mervin ran CWU's Gauteng Province was not a secret, though the fact never once appeared in the testimony provided in the disciplinary hearings and subsequent CCMA arbitrations. As one of the fired TAS employees put it in the CCMA arbitration, 'all of us, of the Post Office [permanents], and Marula [the second labour broker in the Edenvale Depot] staff and TAS were all working for Clyde [Mervin] . . .' Of course, people are capable of switching hats, but for the casual workers in SAPO, Clyde Mervin the SAPO manager and Clyde Mervin the CWU unionist looked like one and the same person.

'Come September!' – CWU and collective bargaining

Despite the complexity of the relationship between CWU and the increasing number of casuals in SAPO, the situation vis-à-vis collective bargaining is clear: CWU promised to help casuals, but in practice did nothing.[8] As the only union recognised in the Post Office, CWU negotiated with management on behalf of its members. Its members did not include casuals, who were legally employed by one of the labour broking companies with which CWU had no recognition agreements.

However, in August 2005, CWU negotiated a clause regarding the conversion of casuals. In fact, the clause covered the conversion to permanent positions not only of casuals but also of Permanent Part-Time Employees (PPTEs) and S32s. The latter were the Post Office's own contract workers; they were employed as needed and were paid by SAPO at the same rate as the permanent workers employed at the same grade. In Mail Delivery, S32s had been transferred over to the labour brokers but some still remained in other departments. The agreement specified a hierarchy of the order in which conversions were to be prioritised: first PPTES, second S32s and third casuals. The conversions were linked to re-deployment of workers as part of ongoing restructuring within the organisation. The end of October 2005 was set as the deadline for completing the conversion process. But this deadline was pushed back. Eventually, the agreed process would be rolled over in six subsequent annual agreements and never implemented (Dickinson 2015a).

Conversions did take place, but the beneficiaries of this policy were mainly PPTEs and S32s. There were more casuals being employed at the bottom of the hierarchy than were being appointed into permanent positions at the top, so the number of casuals increased. All that came their way were promises that their time was coming: Come September, when the annual agreement was typically finalised, they would be permanents. Eventually, 'Come September!' was used by casuals to mock CWU's failure to assist them.

Working groups were established to deal with the conversion issue but because the process was never completed it kept returning, as unfinished business, to the annual negotiations. For CWU negotiators it became embarrassing, especially for a union that was taking a high-profile role in the national campaign to ban labour brokers.

The CWU was deeply split over its actual (if not public) approach to casuals in SAPO. However, clearly casuals were at the bottom of the union's priorities. For a number of years, CWU put forward a demand for casuals to receive a salary increase equivalent to that which they were negotiating. Technically, that was not a demand they were entitled to make; they were not in negotiations with the casuals' employers. Practically, however, SAPO set the rate that labour brokers could claim for casual workers. Not that the nuances mattered. This demand would always disappear as the negotiations proceeded and never once made it to the final agreement. The logic of dropping this demand was obvious: negotiating for the casuals decreased what could be gained for the union's membership. Unsurprisingly, many casual workers started to see CWU as 'indirectly oppressing' them.

Only in September 2011 did CWU declare a dispute with SAPO over appointing labour broker employees into permanent positions. This was after the storm had broken and CWU saw the danger that thousands of casual workers, repeatedly let down by the union, represented. CWU's letter demanded, among its ten points, 'All contracts between SAPO and all Labour Broker companies must be abolished with immediate effect.' SAPO was given five days to respond to the demands (Mogane 2011). It was tough talk, but signified little. By 2011, CWU had lost the casuals.

The A-Team: CWU and casuals in disciplinary hearings

While the account of CWU's response to casualisation in SAPO may be clear when told through the history of collective bargaining agreements, that is not the case when it comes to representation of casuals in disciplinary hearings. The bread-and-butter work of representing workers at company disciplinary hearings and, if the workers are dismissed, at subsequent appeals to the CCMA and Labour Court, is often overlooked. In contrast to the dramatic, public and collective nature of industrial action, representation takes place largely away from the public eye. It does not look or smell like class struggle. Yet, while lacking heroics, it is an important part of unions' day-to-day work. Disciplinaries may involve one person, such as Florida Mbageni's case; sometimes larger groups, as with the eighteen Edenvale TAS employees. However, the aggregated impact of disciplinary hearings is significant.

The Employment Equity reports that large South African companies must file with the Department of Labour require information on disciplinary action.[9] The accuracy of Employment Equity reports can be questioned. Nevertheless, the statistics indicate that disciplinary action is far from unusual. Between 2007 and 2012, SAPO's Employment Equity reports were filed on approximately 16 000 permanents and a small number of its own temporary employees. The number of disciplinary cases reported fluctuated between 6 per cent and 10.2 per cent of the workforce annually.[10] Of these cases, between 7.6 per cent and 37.7 per cent resulted in dismissal from the company. The combined result of these two statistics saw between 0.7 per cent and 2.3 per cent of SAPO's (permanent) workforce dismissed annually over this period as a result of disciplinary charges.[11]

Thus, disciplinary action represents a significant threat to workers. So, having somebody to represent you, especially somebody who knows what they are doing, is no small thing. All the more so if you have limited education, almost no knowledge of legal procedures, struggle to decipher the legal language of charge sheets and are up against company managers with legal training. Internal disciplinary hearings preclude lawyers, but you may be represented by a colleague or, as a member of a company-recognised union, by a union official or office-bearer. A union worth its salt will train shop stewards on disciplinary procedures and ensure they know the company regulations backwards. Should a member be found guilty at a company hearing and dismissed, the union will represent them at the CCMA, arguing for reinstatement. Of course, not all unions are worth their salt, but some representation is better than flying solo in a storm and union representation provides an important insurance policy for workers. A union that defends its members commands a premium that translates into loyalty and a willingness to pay monthly fees to the union.[12]

Although CWU failed to organise casuals in SAPO, there were union office-bearers who believed that they should be organised. This was based on both moral and strategic grounds. The group, who styled themselves as the A-Team, saw themselves in the tradition of the Post Office and Telecommunications Workers Association (POTWA), CWU's historic root: fighting for all workers, 'not fighting with CVs in their hands'.[13] Moreover, the increasing number of casuals meant that strikes would only be effective with their support, meaning they had to be organised. Since CWU had no recognition agreement with the labour brokers, casuals were not members and, consequently, it was not entitled to represent them in disciplinaries. That did not stop the A-Team from trying though. A good unionist will always push the boundaries.

In the Edenvale 18 case, Neal Lakey successfully prevented CWU shop stewards from representing the TAS employees at their disciplinary hearing. Other workers were more successful. Peter Mofula, a CWU branch office-bearer in the Vaal, made it his business to represent casuals. Union policy was that only members should be represented,[14] but when it came to casuals he disagreed. He recognised the strategic importance of recruiting casuals, and he could also see that they were getting a rough deal. It was, he recalled, the 'Wild West'; casual workers could be dismissed on the spot at the request of a supervisor. He would get the casual worker to fill in a backdated CWU membership form and tough his way into the hearing as the 'member's' representative (interview, Mofula).

With casual workers knocking on CWU's door for help, the A-Team, working with Mathapelo Mphuti, the union's second deputy president between 2007 and 2011, attempted to represent casuals at disciplinaries and, if unsuccessful there, at the CCMA (interviews, Lepheane; Mofula; Tutu Mokoena; Mphuti). The A-Team included Peter Mofula, Freddie Marutha whom we have already met, Moeketsi 'MP' Lepheane, a CWU office-bearer about whom we will hear more, and Charles Kwata, a veteran unionist from POTWA.[15] Between June 2008 and August 2010, A-Team members represented TAS casuals at the CCMA on at least nine occasions.[16] However, this became increasingly difficult as TAS challenged their right to represent casuals. The point that TAS kept making was that dismissed casuals were not members of CWU and therefore CWU had no *locus standi*, that is no legal standing to act on their behalf at the CCMA hearing.

On 7 October 2009, eleven TAS employees at the Springs Postal Depot left work early to attend the Department of Labour's hearing into labour broking held in Germiston. At a disciplinary hearing held on 5 November, chaired by Neal Lakey, an attempt by a CWU office-bearer to represent the workers failed. Being unable to prove *locus standi*, the office-bearer was 'excused from the proceedings' by Lakey. All eleven workers were dismissed. Lepheane took the case to the CCMA. However, it was only at the third set-down date that it went ahead. On the first two occasions TAS successfully challenged CWU's *locus standi* and the matter was postponed to allow the union to prove that the eleven were their members. It was a case of third time lucky; on 5 May 2010 the CCMA commissioner allowed CWU to represent them on the basis of completed membership application forms. The commissioner found that the dismissals were unfair and gave an arbitration award ordering reinstatement of nine of the eleven with five months' back pay.[17] TAS, however, appealed to the Labour Court over the standing granted to CWU by the commissioner.[18]

As we will see in Chapter 10, there was an attempt, driven by Lepheane, for CWU to negotiate a recognition agreement with TAS. The result indicated that TAS had no intention of signing any agreement. The A-Team concluded that labour brokers knew that SAPO had their backs on this: once casuals were unionised, it would be the end of the dual labour market (interview, Mphuti). However, fighting for the casuals was difficult not only because of resistance from the SAPO-backed labour brokers, but also because the A-Team were up against other CWU office-bearers opposed to bringing casuals into the union.

Corruption and distractions

The frustrations of the A-Team with CWU's reluctance to organise casuals is understandable. In addition to moral concerns, there was the money. A union depends on its members' monthly stop orders to pay salaries, rent, phones, transport and other bills. Every time a casual replaced a permanent worker, it meant one less monthly subscription.

There was also the power that comes with numbers. Casuals as employees of the labour broking companies were not counted in the SAPO bargaining unit. Although fewer permanents and more casuals did not impact on CWU's representation in percentage terms (since the bargaining unit shrank each time a casual replaced a permanent), the same could not be said about CWU's power when it came to a strike. Ultimately, a union's institutional power rests on its ability to strike. A union that cannot mount a strike carries little at the negotiating table. And why would casuals join a CWU strike? If CWU called a strike, it would be for permanents. It would not be the casuals' concern: they would 'push work' as normal and, likely, CWU's strike would fail.

So, why then did CWU, the A-Team excepted, not organise casuals within SAPO? There is no single answer to the question. However, prominent among the reasons that can be put forward are corruption, distractions and power struggles.

Corruption is hard to prove, but the relationships that labour brokers forged to secure business within SAPO extended beyond management. CWU office-bearers were recipients of tickets for soccer matches and jazz festivals, courtesy of labour brokers. The relationship between these union office-bearers and labour brokers was, as Lepheane (interview) put it, 'not in the open'.

There were also distractions. In early 2009, a break-away union, the South African Postal Workers Union (SAPWU) was established by dissident CWU office-bearers. (It later became the South African Postal and Allied Workers Union, SAPAWU.) Their recruitment focus was permanent SAPO employees, and it targeted those in higher positions who felt that CWU was not addressing their concerns adequately. CWU's strike of 2009, described below, brought a flood of members to the new union. SAPAWU was a threat to CWU and over the coming years CWU fought tooth and nail to keep its rival from being recognised within the Post Office. This rearguard action included making resignation from the CWU difficult[19] and reaching an agreement with SAPO to raise the threshold for union recognition from 30 to 40 per cent of the bargaining unit (Labour Court 2011c). Without recognition, the new union could not use stop orders to collect its members' subscriptions. However, CWU was unable to maintain its monopoly position within SAPO. By late 2011, an independent audit of union membership in SAPO found that SAPAWU's membership, in a bargaining unit still restricted to permanent employees, had overtaken that of CWU (Ntsaluba 2011). SAPAWU was recognised by SAPO in February 2013. The four-year battle against SAPAWU absorbed a huge amount of CWU's energy and diverted attention from what, at least until mid-2011, was the less immediate danger to the union of casuals inside SAPO but outside CWU.

Power struggles and double-footing

As a rival organisation, SAPAWU represented a direct threat to CWU. At the same time, however, the casuals' cause became part of CWU's internal conflict. The A-Team championed the casuals; Clyde Mervin and those around him had kept them at arm's length. Both groups were competing for control of the union. If casuals were organised by CWU, they would be voting in leadership elections. It was clear which side they would favour. What had been a strategic challenge to the union became a matter of survival for the factions.

While CWU office-bearers slugged it out over who was to run the union, the casuals were breaking away. This separation happened unevenly. The Tembisa Committee was the first to break away from CWU. The leadership of the West Rand casuals remained in contact with sympathetic CWU office-bearers for much longer. Nor was the parting of ways smooth. Disenchantment with CWU would spike if there had been a betrayal, but then recede to the point where CWU could again call in support from the casuals by talking up their issues. It was a stormy relationship. CWU and casuals were bound together by their shared space and integrated labour. But casuals realised that being recognised by CWU was not the only possible organisational route for them. As Chapter 10 outlines, other unions attempted to organise them, even if the casuals' most successful form of organisation turned out to be a syndicalist-type network structure, albeit one with cankerous relationships between the half-dozen committees. Between affiliation with unions and the casuals acting for themselves, there was a period during which committees 'double-footed'. Double-footing allowed the committees to hedge their bets. They worked with unions, but in parallel reached an independent understanding of their struggle against labour broking, including the realisation that unions were not going to assist.

This double-footing could take the form of a long embrace; the West Rand double-footed with CWU the longest, only losing faith when they had embarked on a path that made reconciliation all but impossible. Double-footing could be a swift and passionate tryst, a surge of enthusiasm for a new union, or even the flame with CWU rekindled. Despite mobilisation attempts by the South African Gaming, Waitron and Admin Workers Trade Union (SAGWAWTU) in August 2009 (outlined in Chapter 10), casuals flocked to support the national postal strike that CWU had called, promising the end of labour broking. Kodisang Bokaba (interview), the SAGWAWTU organiser, counselled casuals against joining the strike, reminding them that CWU had failed them in the past. But he was left talking to himself as casuals rushed to join the strike.

CWU's 2009 strike

For casuals, CWU's 2009 national strike was a disaster. They came out in support of the strike but came away empty-handed. Permanents, on the other hand, got a 7 per cent pay increase, well above inflation, and a resolution to the long-standing 'salary anomalies' dispute. The combined effect of these two gains saw salary increases for some permanents of between 16 and 22 per cent (CWU 2009). The strike revealed that casuals were now necessary to make a strike in SAPO effective. The participation of casuals was critical for the 'street theatre' of South Africa's industrial disputes, in which striking and demonstration are entwined. Yet, despite their participation on the streets, casuals remained all but invisible within the strike negotiations and the subsequent court case. That the casuals came away without anything was, for many, final proof that CWU cared nothing for them. The strike also revealed increased tensions within CWU's leadership.

When CWU obtained a strike certificate from the CCMA and called for a national strike starting 20 August, there was no guarantee that the casuals would come out in support. The East Rand was with SAGWAWTU and, although the West Rand had remained largely aloof from this initiative, they were already sceptical about CWU and what it would do for them. At a West Rand Workers Committee meeting in July 2009, the minutes recorded, 'As the committee we decided not to [go] with CWU but to use them to our advantage. As they say, keep your friend close and your enemy closer.'[20] Russel Mutavhatsindi, a leader on the West Rand, was on his annual leave when the strike started. He was called by CWU office-bearers and agreed to help mobilise casuals for the strike. In the end, East and West Rand, Pretoria, Vaal and other casuals' committees in Gauteng rallied to the cause. Their hope was that the strike would make them permanents.

It is true that the promise of permanency was made. It was made many times. Interviewees recalled Clyde Mervin addressing rallies during the strike and promising that CWU's victory would be their victory; with the strike won they would return to work as permanents. The strike was, however, not about converting casuals to permanents. In April 2009, a long-running dispute over 'salary anomalies' between CWU and SAPO reached the CCMA. The issue concerned different wages paid to permanent employees in the same job grades. This went back a long way; for CWU it was an 'apartheid wage gap'.

While this dispute was still under mediation, CWU had presented its demands for the 2009/2010 annual negotiations to SAPO. These included the annual salary increase and the rolled-over agreement that casuals be converted to permanent positions. These demands were merged into the CCMA mediation over salary anomalies. When mediation failed, the CCMA issued a strike certificate, protecting the jobs of those who went on strike. CWU then served SAPO with the required 48 hours' notice for a protected strike starting on 20 August.

To win the strike, CWU needed to stop the mail. And to do that, it needed the casuals to participate. It was critical that they did not 'push the work' and it was necessary – as the youngest, most militant workers, with the most to gain – that they joined the marches and pickets that would gird the strike. The casuals rose to the occasion. Mail delivery came to a halt and the streets hummed.

Away from the streets, negotiations took place. The CWU team was led by its general secretary, Gallant Roberts, and included Mathapelo Mphuti, the union's second deputy president who had assisted the A-Team members who had represented casuals. On 28 August, with the assistance of the CCMA, an agreement was reached between CWU and SAPO management. Or at least it appeared so. There was the 7 per cent pay increase, an R83.5-million allocation to address the salary anomalies, and there was the issue of labour brokers. The clause on labour brokers had three sections. The first was an agreement that the union and the company would take their cue from 'the broader debate between labour, government and business'. The second was a reiteration of the 2005 clause to 'engage on the conversion of current labour brokers into permanent positions . . .' The third was a commitment from the company to ensure that labour brokers in SAPO met employment conditions required by the Basic Conditions of Employment Act (SAPO and CWU 2009). In short, if you were a casual, you were still a casual.

The CWU leadership felt, however, that it had got as much as it could and was calling off the strike. A letter sent out by Gallant Roberts (2009b) to CWU provincial offices on 28 August outlined the consensus that had been reached on salary anomalies and the salary increase. Everybody was thanked and members were called on to resume work on Monday, 31 August. The agreement itself, the letter outlined, would be circulated to CWU's provincial structures 'in order [that] members be given a report on the consensus reached'. The agreement would be signed after these report-backs were completed. SAPO sent its own 'Touching Base Communication' to employees. In the memo, entitled 'Final Update on Protected Strike: End of Strike Action', there was a specific mention of the Security and Investigations Unit for managing the process. 'Even at times when the crowd was hurling abusive comments, non-striking Sapoans [SAPO employees] maintained their professionalism . . .' (SAPO 2009). It had been, as one interviewed striker recalled, in the context of South African disputes, a 'soft strike' (interview, Diane).

The situation was, however, about to harden. The casual workers who had supported the strike, and who were not Sapoans but had been expecting to become so, were not happy. There were feedback meetings, in line with the general secretary's letter, on Monday, 31 August. In Gauteng, these meetings degenerated into chaos. Ernest 'Tovey' Montoedi (interview), a postman at the Vereeniging Depot, recalled how the CWU office-bearers sent to explain the agreement to a mass meeting in the Vaal were shouted down by angry casual workers. The permanents were inclined to accept but held their tongues, seeing the fury of the casuals. While they were milling around after the collapse of the meeting, there was a call from casual leaders in the West Rand. They intended to continue the strike. Strikers were to assemble at CWU's Gauteng provincial office in central Johannesburg the next day.

It was the same at other meeting across Gauteng. The casuals were not going back. They started to pull out those who had gone back to work and the tempo of the strike escalated. It was no longer insults being hurled at those working, but stones (Labour Court 2009b). CWU had called the casuals onto the streets; getting them back was not so easy.

At CWU's provincial office, Clyde Mervin, the provincial chairperson, pointed them to the national office in Gandhi Square, central Johannesburg (interview, Montoedi). It was, they were told, the national CWU leadership that was responsible for calling off the strike. When Mathapelo Mphuti attempted to address the strikers gathered in Gandhi Square, the anger of casuals was boiling over. She was held responsible for CWU selling them out and a section of the crowed assaulted her, kicking her while she was on the ground. Numerous interviewees pointed to Clyde Mervin as the person responsible for Mphuti's beating. He had, they alleged, tipped off Gallant Roberts, the union's general secretary and chief negotiator, leaving Mphuti in the firing line.[21] Behind the scenes he told casuals that it was Mphuti who had signed the agreement. One account put Mervin in Gandhi Square, brushing his finger across his mouth as Mphuti attempted to address the angry crowd, signalling that her explanations were lies.

Mphuti was pulled to safety, bruised and shaken, but without serious injury. It was the end of her career in CWU; once a rising star in the union, she was not even nominated for a position at the union's 2011 national congress (interview, Mphuti). The media covered the meeting and the assault on Mphuti in Gandhi Square (Seale 2009). On hearing what had happened, Joe Chauke, the president of CWU, had called Lepheane, the Gauteng provincial secretary, to assist. Lepheane (interview) asked Chauke where the Gauteng chairperson, Mervin, was. Chauke's response was that it was the chairperson who was the cause of the problem. Lepheane addressed the strikers, first in Gandhi Square and the following day at Witspos, telling them that the strike would continue (Pongoma 2009). CWU now sought to walk back from its agreement to end the strike.

With the return to work unravelling, SAPO made an urgent application to the Labour Court to interdict the strike on 2 September. There was an initial hearing the following day. The organisation's affidavit outlined the strike, negotiations, agreement and subsequent strike continuation. Among several instances of intimidation documented was an SMS to 'Mr Clyde Mervin, an employee of the company'. The text of the SMS was quoted verbatim: 'Yes! Clyde may be now you are happy that Mathapelo was attacked by workers. Marutha is sick because of u! What goes around comes around! [C]heck, before they die u will be buried . . .'

Mervin was presented to the court as a company employee, but the text of the SMS actually referred to his stance as a union leader over casuals. As we saw earlier, Mervin moved easily between his positions as a manager and unionist. The reference to Mathapelo Mphuti has already been explained. The reference to Freddie Marutha, Mervin's likely challenger for the Gauteng Province chair, related to the long and debilitating illness to which Marutha was to eventually succumb. On perhaps a dozen occasions, ranging from formal interviews to casual conversations, Mervin was fingered, sometime obliquely but often directly, as responsible for Marutha's illness. All accounts cited poison, although the type of poison varied between the straightforward and 'African poison' (witchcraft). Indeed, Marutha himself was reported to have warned people never to leave food or drink unattended in the provincial office. Even a cup of tea – if you left it on your desk when you went out, just for a moment, you would be wise not to drink it when you came back (interview, Mphuti). There were songs composed by casuals that linked Mervin to Marutha's fate.[22]

CWU was caught between the Labour Court on the one side and still-striking casuals on the other. It attempted to escape the dilemma by arguing that there had never been an agreement. They pointed to the fact that the agreement had not been signed. This was true, but it cut little ice with the judge. What was important was not signatures but whether 'the objective facts and the circumstances of this case support the contention that an agreement was reached . . .' (Labour Court 2009b). The court concluded that this was the case. A *rule nisi* (suspended order) was granted on 3 September, which required the respondents to return on 11 September to argue against the order that the strike had ended and that further industrial action was unlawful and unprotected. On 11 September the order was confirmed, though by that time the strike was over. The first court order had been enough to bring the strike's *bittereinders* (bitter-enders) to heel, even if their presence, and their cause, had never formed part of the legal arguments.

A noise at the door

After the strike of 2009 and Marutha's death, it was Lepheane who picked up the SAPO casuals' baton within CWU. Lepheane worked for Telkom, but had been released on a full-time basis for union work. As CWU's Gauteng secretary he would get calls from COSATU's head office: 'Secretary, what is going on? Your people are in our office . . . They say they are being treated bad' (interview, Lepheane). This was casual workers marching on COSATU in an effort to highlight their plight. Of course, they were not CWU members, but they worked in SAPO and CWU was responsible, under COSATU's 'One Industry, One Union' policy, for organising workers in the telecommunications sector. Zwelinzima Vavi, then COSATU general secretary, was, Lepheane explained, 'not a happy man'. The protests outside COSATU House were embarrassing, indicating that CWU was not doing its job.

Lepheane would tell whoever was phoning to send the workers to him and he would find out what the problem was. When they got to his office, the first thing he noticed was their clothing.

> When these people arrive, you see that point number one is [their clothing]. If these people come to work like this, what does the employer say? They didn't have uniform, their shirts were torn, some of their shirts were washed [till they had] lost their colour . . . and you started to sympathise with these people now (interview, Lepheane).

When he asked them what they wanted, 'they said all that they want is to be permanent and be treated equally like the employees of the Post Office because they do the same job'. He then proposed a plan to deal with this 'noise at the door'. He would devote 40 per cent of his time to organising the casuals in SAPO, even though it was not his company. He could see the threat that unorganised casuals represented for the union, and the potential that organised casuals had for internal CWU politics (interview, Lepheane).

His attempt to integrate casual worker representatives into CWU structures was unsuccessful, however. He initiated a system where SAPO depots and hubs sent two representatives to CWU's Gauteng monthly shop stewards council meetings. One, the official shop steward, would be representing permanents; the other would be a casual worker. For some time, casuals from West Rand and Vaal depots sent representatives to these meetings, but that did not mean that their issues were addressed. The meetings were for CWU shop stewards, including those in Telkom. Meeting agendas started with Telkom issues, then COSATU campaigns, then the Post Office. Last on the agenda would be casuals' concerns (interviews, Tutu Mokoena; Lepheane). Even getting these onto the end of the agenda was a struggle. CWU shop stewards would tell Lepheane, 'we elected you; you are not elected by labour broker [employees]'. In the end he met separately with the casuals, even though that meant meeting 'under trees' on Saturday afternoons. As he explained, 'I could not take these things [of the casuals] anymore into organisational meetings because they [permanent shop stewards] didn't want to hear about it. It was wasting their time. I was bringing people [into the meeting] that are going to steal their jobs and blah, blah, blah' (interview, Lepheane).

Seeking a way of representing casuals, Lepheane went down the same route as Kodisang Bokaba on the East Rand just a year before – attempting to negotiate recognition agreements with the labour brokers. He got further than Bokaba, but still did not make it to the final stretch. On 29 April 2010, Lepheane wrote to TAS outlining that CWU had 'a substantial number of members that will qualify us to secure comprehensive rights' and proposed a meeting (Lepheane 2010). At the meeting, he presented a list of 217 SAPO casuals employed by TAS.[23] Several meetings took place, with TAS countering the demand for organisational rights with a range of objections: who, for example, would pay the casuals' salaries when they attended CWU meetings? TAS, Lepheane was informed, was a small company and would not be able to cover such expenses.[24] Despite these objections, Lepheane drew up a recognition agreement. TAS then stopped meeting with him. Lepheane took the matter to the CCMA. The case was set for 26 August 2010. TAS pitched and it was agreed that the two parties would meet within fourteen days and endeavour to conclude a collective agreement. This did not happen and Lepheane was back in the CCMA for an arbitration hearing. This time TAS did not pitch. The commissioner ruled in CWU's favour; TAS must grant organisational rights outlined in Sections 11 to 16 of the Labour Relations Act to the union within fourteen days. These included the right to hold meetings, the election of shop stewards and the company processing stop orders deducting union subscriptions from members' salaries. They would also be in a position to bargain.

It was, however, a pyrrhic victory; TAS never granted the rights and Lepheane was not around to follow up. Working with the casuals had become increasingly difficult. The provincial executive, chaired by Clyde Mervin, had instructed that no union funds could be used for this purpose. One afternoon, Lepheane was confronted in his office by two CWU office-bearers. He was told he must stop working with the casuals and that he was not to meet with them. The argument turned into a fight, two against one. After that, he pulled back from working with the casuals. The final showdown was at CWU's 2011 congress. Lepheane went head to head with Mervin for the first deputy president position. Mervin won.[25]

CWU: From solidarity to social closure

Writing about COSATU, the union federation to which CWU belonged, Sakhela Buhlungu (2010) has argued that the organisation gained influence but lost power in the transition from apartheid to democracy: a 'paradox of victory'. Buhlungu outlines how the federation gained influence through its alliance with the ruling party, something that delivered a raft of labour laws that, at least on paper, created a labour-friendly industrial relations system. It lost power as its internal structures ossified and, frequently, became corrupted. Importantly, the foundation of its power, the membership base, has increasing become alienated from the union's leadership.

The trajectory of CWU illustrates Buhlungu's argument, although, as with all examples, there are variations, complexities, contradictions and nuances that are not visible at higher, aggregated levels of abstraction. Telling the story of CWU and the casuals through rolled-over agreements points to cynical abandonment. Told through the lens of individual office-bearers, the story is not so simple: there was contestation within the union over casuals. In the end, however, it is who wins that matters, and those championing the casuals lost.

The result was a union that shifted from principles of solidarity that it had previously espoused, for example, its historic fight against racial discrimination in SAPO. Instead, it followed what Frank Parkin theorises as Weberian social closure in which 'social collectivities seek to maximise rewards by restricting access to rewards and opportunities to a limited circle of eligibles' (1974: 3). The demarcation of a limited circle can use almost any characteristic; in this case it was the employment contract of workers, and it trumped the union's history of racial and worker solidarity. As with practically all acts of self-benefit, this social closure around those with permanent positions was concealed with moral rhetoric: the strident call to ban labour brokers.

8

A Constitutional Crusade

Introduction: The workers committees

With the Communication Workers Union (CWU) failing to stem labour broking in the South African Post Office (SAPO), casual workers started to create their own organisations. From the mid-2000s, casual workers in Gauteng initiated groups that coalesced, faltered, divided and re-formed. CWU's 2009 strike, which left casuals out in the cold, boosted those arguing for independent mobilisation. The committees that emerged were liminal organisations without resources or formal status. Some were assisted by CWU office-bearers who chose to swim against the tide of CWU's compliance, at least until routed at the union's 2011 congress. But the committees' strength lay in personal contact between casuals rather than affiliation with formal organisations. These connections were established at work and in the townships where the casuals lived. Relatively stable committees emerged in Pretoria, the West Rand/Soweto, the Far West Rand, the Vaal, Tembisa/East Rand and the 'Far East Rand' (all of the East Rand minus the six depots that made up the Tembisa/East Rand Committee) (Dickinson 2015a).[1] Nevertheless, even the life of these committees was uneven and sporadic; large areas of the province never established groups on more than a fleeting basis.

Casuals' meetings were held on township football fields, public parks, car parks and wasteland. Meeting minutes, if they were kept at all, were handwritten in old desk diaries to be read out at the following meeting. Some groups appointed office-bearers; others selected the meeting chairperson from whomever was present that day. If funds were needed, those attending would have to 'pop out' whatever was required. Some of these groups called themselves 'casuals' committees' and others 'workers committees';[2] some did not even have a name. Yet, despite disadvantages, the workers committees pursued myriad avenues to remedy their status as second-class workers.

This chapter outlines how the workers committees pursued multiple channels of redress within the constitutional framework of post-apartheid South Africa. It does this through surveying the range of initiatives pursued by different Gauteng workers committees and through a case study of the Vaal Workers Committee's endeavours, which were to reach the Labour Court. Such an account is important; it helps explain and contextualise the extra-constitutional methods of struggle that were employed later.

Exploring every avenue
The casuals ventured down many avenues of redress within South Africa's constitutional landscape. Some were attempted several times. Attempts to seek recognition from labour brokers, explored in Chapter 10, is one example of how initiatives were duplicated, each time with essentially the same outcome. These duplications point to the limited coordination between workers committees. Looking back on events, Thabiso Bopape (interview), a postman at Ennerdale Depot south of Soweto and who emerged as a key leader in the Mabarete strike, explained how the Gauteng committees had been working in 'silos'. Each committee pushed strategies favoured by influential group members; these were voluntary groups and things happened when somebody took the initiative. But because there was limited coordination between groups, activists might not be aware that what they were attempting had already been tried elsewhere.

This silo effect could be replicated even within a single committee; different activists might explore different prospects. In theory, any developments would be reported back to meetings of the workers committee, but sometimes it did not even get that far. Tovey Montoedi (interview) recalled going with his co-worker and friend Samuel Khayne to the Vaal office of the South African Communist Party (SACP). They went because the SACP was 'the vanguard of the working class'. Montoedi and Khayne were hoping that their case would be thrust to the front of the class struggle that the SACP championed. But when they got to the office things did not proceed along the lines they were hoping.

The woman from the SACP whom they met told them that they needed to take up the matter with CWU. It was, she reminded them, the COSATU-aligned union responsible for SAPO. They told her that CWU was not doing anything to help them. The woman, however, knew a senior CWU leader. She rang him up there and then. He had taken her call and told her that CWU was fighting to end labour broking. And that was where things ended. Montoedi and Khayne were disappointed; they had thought that the SACP might do 'something big'. If something had come from the initiative, they would have taken it to the committee meeting. But their visit had been 'just a disappointment' and, embarrassed at their initial hopes, they stayed mum (interview, Montoedi). They were not the only ones to approach the SACP. In the end, nothing came of these various, uncoordinated approaches – just as nothing came of many other initiatives.

A constitutional cornucopia of rights
The post-apartheid industrial relations system provided a comprehensive system of rights for all workers. As the section in the Bill of Rights on Labour Rights, states:

1. Everyone has the right to fair labour practices.
2. Every worker has the right:
    (a) to form and join a trade union;
    (b) to participate in the activities and programmes of a trade union; and
    (c) to strike . . . (RSA 1996: Section 23).

This seems straightforward enough: you have the right to fair labour practices and you have the right to join a union that will look after your interests, if necessary through protected strikes. However, as we saw in the previous chapter, it was not so straightforward. The only union recognised by SAPO (until 2013) was CWU, and its approach to the casuals was deeply ambiguous. Casuals approached other unions, but the results were no different (see Chapter 10).

It was not only unions, though, that casuals turned to in seeking to end their entrapment as casuals within SAPO. Table 8.1 summarises the many and varied initiatives that were undertaken within South Africa's constitutional framework.

Table 8.1   Organisations approached and strategies attempted by SAPO casual workers in Gauteng.

Attempts to get assistance from registered unions • Communication Workers Union (CWU), from the introduction of labour broking • South African Gaming, Waitron and Admin Workers Trade Union (SAGWAWTU), in 2009 • Labour Equity General Workers Union of South Africa (LEWUSA), *circa* 2010 • Commercial, Services and Allied Workers Union (COSAWU), 2010-2011 • COSATU (2008-2012) • South African Postal Workers Union (SAPWU, later SAPAWU), 2012
Attempt to register their own casual workers union The National Communications and Allied Workers Union (NACAWU) was an initiative by the Vaal Committee. Registration was declined by the Department of Labour in 2011.
Attempts by unions to get recognition with labour brokers • SAGWAWTU, 2009 • COSAWU, 2010-2011 • MP Lepheane, CWU office-bearer in the Wits Region, 2010-2011
Attempts to negotiate as workers committees • Attempts to negotiate directly with the Post Office, from 2005 • Attempts to negotiate with labour brokers, particularly TAS, 2008-2010
Protected strikes • One, unsuccessful protected strike took place in the Vaal area in early 2009 with the assistance of Vaal University of Technology (VUT) staff and students.
Private legal assistance • The Vaal Committee engaged a private lawyer, circa 2005.
Advice centres • The Germiston-based Casual Workers Advice Office (CWAO), 2011 onwards
South African industrial relations institutions • Minister/Department of Labour, resulted in a ministerial enquiry in the Vaal, 2007 • Commission for Conciliation, Mediation and Arbitration (CCMA), various actions from 2009 • Labour Court, various cases from 2010-2011

Table 8.1 (*continued*)

Political parties and organisations
• African People's Convention (APC), 2009 and 2012
• South African Communist Party (SACP), various attempts from 2009
• Young Communist League (YCL), 2010
• African National Congress (ANC), 2010
• Democratic Socialist Movement (DSM), 2010-2011
• African National Congress Youth League (ANCYL), 2011

Media coverage
• Lesedi FM, Vaal, *circa* 2004
• *Vaal Weekly*, 2008
• *The Tembisan*, 2011
• Soweto TV, 2012
• Jozi FM, 2012

Attempts to get official bodies to intervene/adjudicate
• Department of Labour public hearings on labour broking, 2009
• Gauteng Premier, 2012
• Minister of Communications, 2012
• The Public Protector, 2012

Three different unions, or parts of them, attempted to organise casuals and bring the casuals into the industrial relations system. COSATU, the ANC-aligned union federation, was also approached directly on several occasions. Their response was to refer delegations of casuals back to CWU. Admittedly, behind the scenes there was annoyance on the part of COSATU and embarrassment on the part of CWU when this happened (interviews, Lepheane; Tseki). But that was not seen by the casuals. In the words of Thabiso Bopape (interview), 'COSATU was USELESS in capital letters'.

The South African Constitution gives workers the right not only to join a union but to establish one. The Vaal Workers Committee attempted to do this in 2011. Engaging with the CCMA and then the Labour Court led them to the conclusion that they needed to be formally constituted as a union if they were to be taken seriously. So, they applied to the Department of Labour for registration of the National Communications and Allied Workers Union (NACAWU). This involved considerable effort on the part of the Vaal Committee.

They drew up a 27-page constitution for the union (which bore a great deal of resemblance to CWU's 2008 constitution, but little resemblance to how they actually operated). They also stepped up their efforts at minute-taking, rented a small room in an Internet café, which provided an address for their letterhead, produced membership application forms, and opened a bank account to which hand-collected subscriptions of R20 a month could be deposited as proof of a membership base. It all came to nothing as the Department of Labour rejected their application a few months later.[3]

In South Africa, the right to strike is constitutional and is not dependent on being a member of a registered union. But, in practice, it is hard to secure a CCMA strike certificate and the protection it provides without the union's certificate of registration. A copy of a union's certificate routinely forms part of any dispute referral to the CCMA.[4] But, as we saw with the case of the fired Springs Depot casuals who were represented by CWU, there could be flexibility. In the Springs case, it was third time lucky, with the commissioner of the day accepting backdated membership forms. The one protected strike mounted by casual workers was also the result of luck at the CCMA. It was the Vaal Workers Committee that pulled this off, with assistance from a number of volunteers, including Toto Molaza (interview), a lecturer in labour relations at the Vaal University of Technology (VUT).

The Vaal Committee obtained a strike certificate in early 2009 against TAS Appointments and Management Services (TAS) when attempts to initiate talks over wages failed.[5] The strike, however, was a flop. The involvement of outsiders was used by Post Office supervisors and TAS managers alike to undermine support. Those that did strike mounted pickets outside Vaal depots and retail outlets, but that did not stop permanent postmen and casuals who elected to continue working from delivering mail. Given that this was a protected strike, strikers were guaranteed their jobs at the end of it, but it was 'no work, no pay'. Mail was still being delivered while their pay cheques were shrinking by the day. The strike ended without concessions. Failure of the only protected strike by SAPO casual workers was a lesson in the futility of following a constitutional path.

Legal advice outside of unions was also pursued. The SAPO casual workers were hardly in a position to pay hefty legal fees. Generally, the closest a casual worker, or any worker for that matter, gets to an attorney is a legal aid lawyer. Bazil Hlekiso (interview), a postman in the Sebokeng Depot, and chair of the Vaal Workers Committee, recalled how they had gone to an attorney in Vanderbijlpark around 2004 after T&L Appointments (from which TAS later emerged) had told them that their wages would not be increasing since SAPO had frozen the brokers' fee for placed casuals. At that point there was not even a workers committee; it was the casuals at the depot who had together collected R475 for the lawyer to open a file. They had not bothered with CWU because the union 'was not working for us. At all.' The lawyer had contacted T&L a couple of times and then presented the casuals with a bill for almost R9 000, which they never paid.

The Casual Workers Advice Office (CWAO) in Germiston was a better source of assistance, and *mahala* (free) to boot. Ighsaan Schroeder, founder of the centre, met SAPO casuals in November 2011, a month after CWAO had first opened its doors. His assessment was that the casuals were subject to too much advice from too many quarters. Instead of offering yet another direction, CWAO provided meeting facilities, printed leaflets, typed up a letter requesting free travel on the Metrorail, and helped the casuals research the labour broker companies operating in SAPO (interview, Schroeder). Otherwise, CWAO let the casuals run their own campaign.

Several political parties were approached. Some gave assistance in the form of meeting venues and support for protest marches. Mostly, they referred the casuals back to CWU or to other unions.

An essential part of constitutional democracy is a free press. In theory, a public spotlight can illuminate injustice and catalyse change. There were attempts by casuals to highlight their situation in the media. Around 2003 or 2004, casual workers in Vanderbijlpark Mail Centre in the Vaal contacted Lesedi FM. A journalist came to talk to them. They laid out their grievances. They listed broken promises. The journalist said that he would follow the matter up, but nothing happened (interview, Montoedi). It was 2008 before SAPO casuals were in the media again. This time it was the *Vaal Weekly*, a drop-and-knock paper. The journalist, Sonqoba Kunene, reported on workers demonstrating their unhappiness with their R13.40 an hour salary that had been increased by just 67 cents over the previous three years. However, Kunene (2008) could only get one side of the story, explaining to his readers, 'When approached for comment, the employer sent *Vaal Weekly* from pillar to post . . .'

The Vaal workers who spoke to Kunene asked to remain anonymous. This was sensible, given what happened to Marcus Makhura in July 2011 when he spoke to *The Tembisan*, another Gauteng-based drop-and-knock paper. Makhura was a postman at the Birchleigh Depot, one of the six depots that formed the Tembisa or East Rand Workers Committee. The mid-2011 strike had just broken out and Tembisa was its epicentre. Makhura was reported as saying that the striking casuals did not want violence, but wanted the promises made to them honoured. 'We want to be heard; we have been asking them [the labour brokers] questions like when we are going to be registered [as permanents] but they just tell us to wait. We are tired of waiting' (Nemutudi 2011: 5).

When the strike collapsed, Makhura further exposed himself to retribution; he wrote, with two of his co-workers, to the SAPO regional manager, E.T. Mpai, pointing out that the cause of the strike remained unresolved. On 22 August he was given notice by TAS to attend a disciplinary hearing. There were five charges of gross misconduct. One charge related to his request to meet with Mpai, 'to discuss working conditions, without the employer's [TAS's] knowledge or authorisation'. Two charges focused on *The Tembisan* article: first, it had brought the 'company and client's name into disrepute', even though no labour broking company had been named in the article; second, he had failed 'to follow proper procedures and instructions by engaging directly with the client and/or through the media'.[6] Makhura was found guilty of all charges and dismissed, along with two co-workers.

By the time the Mabarete strike of December 2011 to April 2012 was underway, those in leadership positions had little to lose by having their names in the media, since they had already been fired by their respective labour brokers. Nevertheless, they struggled to get coverage. The South African Broadcasting Corporation ignored them completely, something that strikers put down to CWU's influence in the organisation. It was only Soweto TV and Jozi FM that gave them any coverage.

South Africa's constitutional democracy places great emphasis on public participation in the legislative process. Indeed, the Constitution specifies required processes of public input in the development of legislation. That said, the public hearings held around the country to meet this requirement are often perfunctory affairs. However, as we saw in Chapter 2, during the 2009 public hearings on the legislative amendments to the Labour Relations Act over labour broking, raw emotions spilled over. In the end, casual workers showing their anger did not make any difference. The tabled legislation was withdrawn as unworkable in 2011 and only re-tabled, in different form, in March 2012.

Even as wildcat strikes became the order of the day in SAPO from mid-2011, and casuals were engaging in hit-and-run attacks aimed at halting mail delivery, they still sought avenues to raise their grievances with those they thought could help. They used the politics of petitions as an adjunct to the weapons of the weak that they had at their disposal (Scott 1985). It was the latter that worked, but that did not mean they were not petitioning in earnest. They marched to the Minister of Communications, to the Gauteng Premier's Office and to the office of the Public Protector. Their memorandums were accepted with promises of investigation: that is the rule in the politics of petitions. Marchers legitimate the body that they come to petition. It would be rude, not to mention foolish, for those bodies not to acknowledge supplicants. What happens after the petition is handed over is another matter, and nothing came of the casuals' petitions.[7]

Symbolic power

Recent labour scholarship on precarious employment lauds Jennifer Chun's (2009) book *Organizing at the Margins*. Chun describes how marginalised or precarious workers engage in 'classification struggles'. That is, they seek to change their employment status to that of a permanent and so enjoy the benefits of salary and security. Drawing on Pierre Bourdieu's concept of symbolic power, Chun argues that marginal workers can shame employers into addressing their concerns by exposing the conditions of their employment. Her study of university cleaners, in particular, illustrates how marginal workers can improve their positions using symbolic power against their employers.

Winning public support can be an important dimension of social struggles. However, the distinctiveness of Chun's approach is her emphasis on this power resource and how its potency increases inversely to the marginality, or exploitation, of workers. The worse their situation, the greater the symbolic power they can wield. It is an attractive argument, especially for those, including myself, collectively fumbling over what the labour movement should do in the face of rampant neoliberal capitalism. Though, as Chun herself acknowledges, the degree of worker marginalisation is not the only factor affecting the strength of symbolic power. Different organisations have different shame thresholds. But whether an employer's shame threshold is high or low, using symbolic power requires that it first be generated by means of appeals to whomever will listen.[8] It requires a crusade.

The Vaal Committee's constitutional crusade

Of the workers committees, it was the Vaal that got furthest in their constitutional attempts to end labour broking. In terms of organisation, the Vaal consisted of six depots: Mafatsana, Meyerton, Three Rivers, Sebokeng, Sharpeville and Vereeniging, along with the Vanderbijlpark Mail Hub. These were all north of the Vaal River, which marks the border between Gauteng and the Free State Province. The area is a jumble of rustbelt industrial plants, engineering workshops, townships, informal settlements, open veld, grimy town centres, shopping malls and, tucked away from the bustle, tree-lined suburbs.

Some 50 kilometres south of Johannesburg, the Vaal is both an industrial region in its own right and a satellite of the metropolis. Two Metrorail lines link the townships of the Vaal to the city. As well as being the provincial boundary, the Vaal River also separates SAPO's Gauteng Region from the Central Region, which includes not only the Free State but parts of the North West and Western Cape provinces.[9] Unlike the rest of Gauteng with its fractal linguistic map, Sesotho predominates in the Vaal.

There were several waves of activism in the area. There had been isolated acts of protest from 2003. In that year, casuals had complained about their salaries to T&L; the result had been a pay increase. In the winter of 2005, a strike had been triggered by the temporary merger of two Vaal depots: Mafatsana and Sebokeng, while renovations took place. Some 30 casuals, outnumbering the permanent postmen in the two depots, had refused to work. Initially, not being familiar with how strikes are conducted, they had sat in the depot until being forced outside. On the fourth day of the strike they were suspended for three weeks and they were told that disciplinary hearings would be held. These never materialised, however, and when they returned to work it was to a salary increase. They still earned only a fraction of what permanents got, but it had been a success (interview, Hlekiso). After that, however, there were no more easy victories. In following years, complaints and protests were stonewalled. They were told by TAS, the largest labour broker, that the company's contract with SAPO meant that it was impossible to increase salaries.[10]

The Department of Labour

In 2006, Vaal casuals triggered an investigation by the Department of Labour into SAPO's use of labour broking in the Vaal. After the Minister of Labour received a complaint, three Department of Labour officials, TAS management and TAS employees met on 7 March 2007 at the Vanderbijlpark Labour Centre.[11] The casuals had put together an eclectic list of ten complaints. With the exception of one, regarding their contracts, all the complaints were quickly dispatched. The reasons were explained in the Department of Labour's (2007) report.

- Hours of work: The casuals wanted more, but the report explained that their contract specified six hours per day. That didn't violate the Basic Conditions of Employment Act (BCEA).
- Duration of contracts: Casuals wanted permanent employment rather than having contracts constantly renewed, but the report explained that there are two types of contracts: fixed-term and indefinite contracts. If the casuals weren't happy with the contracts they had, they should approach the CCMA as the Labour Relations Act covered the issue of employment contracts. The report went on to point out that this would be pointless since 'labour laws do not specify the duration of the contract'.

- The end-of-year braai: Casuals might want one, but it wasn't in their contract of employment.
- Freedom of association: Contrary to what the casuals claimed, TAS assured the Department of Labour officials that their employees could join any union they wished. The report suggested that the casuals needed to find out from CWU why it was unable to help them, or find another union.
- Basic salaries: The casuals needed to negotiate with TAS over salaries. Should talks deadlock, the matter should be referred to the CCMA.
- Annual bonus: Casuals wanted an annual bonus, as permanents received. Like the braai, there was nothing in their contracts about bonuses. The Department of Labour had no jurisdiction on such matters.
- Leave: TAS explained the basis on which leave was calculated. However, should there be a problem, casuals could approach their nearest [Department of] Labour Centre.
- Late payment of salaries: The problem had been resolved as demonstrated by prompt salary payments the previous month.
- Difference between casuals and permanent staff: The casuals wanted the same terms and conditions as permanent SAPO employees, but the report explained that '[the] Post Office did not employ them but rather outsourced its services to TAS'. The casuals thus needed to negotiate with TAS, their employer, if they wanted better benefits.

The Department of Labour report was a crushing anti-climax for the casuals who had had high hopes for the investigation. The officials running the investigation had failed to see, or chosen not to see, the wood for the trees. Casuals' petitions were often unclearly worded and could, if read out of context, appear risible. But that did not mean they did not have a point: there was a parallel labour market operating within SAPO. Yet, nobody whom they approached took the time to see the bigger picture. Rather, issues were responded to in isolation, on legal and technical grounds and, more often than not, by passing responsibility to somebody else, as the points above illustrate.

Such responses were frequently interpreted by casuals as SAPO, or the labour brokers, bribing the office-bearers or officials in whichever organisation had, for a while, been their beacon of hope. They came to see themselves as trapped in a form of slavery, their masters always one step ahead, blocking every route to freedom.

But there was their tenth complaint: that they did not have copies of their contracts, and this gained some traction. Section 29 of the BCEA requires all employees be given a copy of their 'written particulars of employment' (RSA 1997). On this complaint, the Department of Labour agreed with the casuals. The investigation report stated, 'The employer pleaded guilt [sic] on this one, that it is true that contracts of employer were kept in [TAS's] head office.' Despite this, it had not stopped the Department of Labour officials explaining, on the basis of these contracts that the casuals had never seen, why several of the casuals' complaints were unfounded. Nevertheless, the report noted that this complaint would be resolved: 'The employer rest assured complainants that by Wednesday the 15th March 2007 copies of contracts will be given to all employees' (DoL 2007).

They never did get them. Though, in a twist of fate, this worked out better for the casuals than if TAS's 'rest assured' had been fulfilled. TAS's failure to comply with the one point on which they 'pleaded guilt' was to be the Vaal Committee's ticket to the Labour Court.

At the time, however, the Department of Labour's report was a dispiriting defeat and activism slumped. Typical of workers committees, however, with the underlying problem unresolved, activity once again quickened. In early 2009, there was the previously described protected strike. It also turned out to be a damp squib. CWU's national strike later in the year was an even bigger disappointment for casuals. There was another slump before the next revival.

The CCMA

When the Vaal Workers Committee went to the CCMA in October 2010 they were again on the offensive. This time they were throwing everything they had at the labour brokers. The committee had been reinvigorated with new members. They were still being assisted by Toto Molaza and two of his students at VUT. They provided guidance on dispute procedure and legal assistance.

The casual workers just wanted to find ways of bringing the labour brokers down. They did not really care how it was done. If they could knock out the labour brokers, TAS in particular, then SAPO would, they reasoned, be forced to take them on as permanent workers. One approach was to try to catch TAS out over the Unemployment Insurance Fund (UIF) payments that it was required to deduct from their wages. They individually went to the Department of Labour with their ID books and asked to check on their UIF payment contributions. The result, from the perspective of the workers committee, was disappointing. TAS was up to date with their contributions. No matter; there were other fronts to fight on.

Between late 2010 and early 2011, the Vaal Workers Committee referred three labour brokers to the CCMA: TAS, Autemas Placements and Marula Staffing. In the case of Autemas and Marula, the referrals cited a refusal to bargain. The workers committee had sent letters, by registered mail, to the labour brokers requesting a meeting for the purposes of negotiating a salary increase. When they got no answer, they fired off a referral to the CCMA. The referral of TAS to the CCMA was different. TAS still had not given the casuals their contracts as promised back in 2007 during the Department of Labour investigation. And that is what went down on the CCMA application: TAS was not complying with the BCEA.

The Vereeniging CCMA office set a conciliation hearing between the workers committee and TAS for 9 November 2010 (CCMA 2010b). Four activists of the Vaal Workers Committee attended,[12] but TAS arrived too late. By the time TAS's representatives got to the office, the CCMA commissioner had issued a certificate of non-resolution. The casuals initially thought that they had been issued with a strike certificate (interviews, Papiki Mokoena; Ramagaga). As far as they were concerned, going to the CCMA and winning the case (albeit by default with the employer failing to attend) meant they had the green light to strike. But that was not the case.

Not being given their contracts, as required by the BCEA, created a dispute of rights. Strikes are only permitted when there are disputes of interests. A dispute of rights is a legal matter and is to be settled in court, not through a strike. The Labour Court has jurisdiction over disputes regarding labour legislation, including the BCEA. So the

CCMA commissioner, faced with a no-show from TAS, issued the workers committee with a certificate of non-resolution and a referral to the Labour Court in Johannesburg. The CCMA referral did not specify the complaint about contracts, Section 29 of the BCEA, but rather cited Section 80, the procedure for escalating an unresolved dispute of rights. That turned out to give the workers committee some flexibility when they went to Johannesburg.

The Labour Court

There had been no thought about the Labour Court when they went to the CCMA but, once explained, the opportunity was enthusiastically welcomed. They were scaling new heights and surely they would find justice. A Notice of Motion and other legal documents were duly drawn up. During that process, their scope expanded. Along with TAS's failure to provide them with their contracts, the Notice of Motion requested the court to address another five issues: back pay on pay differentials; compliance with an (unspecified) Sectorial Determination; compliance with the Skills Development Act; compliance with the Code of Good Practice on Key Aspects of HIV/AIDS and Employment; and a requirement for TAS to bargain over a provident fund and a medical aid scheme. Not surprisingly, these newly formulated complaints complicated matters when the committee appeared as plaintiffs in the Labour Court on 2 February 2011.

Workers committee members travelled to Johannesburg on the Metrorail. Hlekiso, chair of the committee, was leading the fight. However, in the courtroom there was confusion when their case was called; three workers simultaneously tried to speak at once to Judge Lagrange (Labour Court 2010d). After Lagrange restored order to his court, Hlekiso asserted himself as the group's spokesperson. He told the judge that they were slaves. The judge sent them to the court's pro bono office for advice.[13] The advice they got was not what they wanted to hear. They were advised to focus on TAS's breach of the BCEA over their contracts. The casuals, of course, did not really want their contracts. They wanted rid of TAS.

When they went back into the courtroom a few minutes later, they at least had the satisfaction of hearing the judge lambasting the Post Office. He complained that he was tired of hearing about problems with the Post Office. But his outburst was a consolation prize. Otherwise, the day was another flop. Beyond his criticism of the Post Office, the workers committee members had struggled to follow the rest of the 'court talk' (interviews, Papiki Mokoena; Ramagaga). In fact, the matter was postponed indefinitely and the applicants had a month to refile papers if the case was not to be closed.

Doggedly, the committee persevered. Much as they had been disappointed with the court's failure to hear them, they tried to follow the advice given. They submitted a revised application. This time their prayers were just two: the contracts and the pay differentials. The application outlined that TAS was in breach of Section 29 of the BCEA for not providing copies of their contracts. The calculations of pay differentials were confused. What they provided as evidence was, in fact, a Post Office document that specified how much it paid labour brokers for the placement of workers and what the labour broker should pay those workers. While this exposed the true nature of the relationship between SAPO and labour brokers, it did not demonstrate the difference between what SAPO and labour broker employees received.

In the end, however, neither of these prayers was heard. By refiling papers, the case was kept in play and a new court date was set for 17 August. But when the date came around, it was the workers committee that was absent. TAS's Group HR manager, Joshua Jabangwe, was there. He claimed that TAS had not been served with the revised papers by the workers committee. Judge Lagrange instructed TAS to make a copy of the casual workers Notice of Motion from the court file and submit their own response for the record (which they failed to do). This was just a precaution should the case be resurrected. He was ordering it to be removed from the roll. For the Vaal workers, it was the end of their constitutional crusade.

Burnout or betrayal?

There are two possible explanations as to why the workers committee failed to show for the 17 August Labour Court hearing.

Between the two hearing dates, a series of strikes by SAPO casual workers erupted across Gauteng, described in Chapter 11. The largest of these strikes, which Vaal casuals joined, was initiated by the Tembisa workers committee in June and continued through most of July. Casuals were on the streets. The strike swept aside other initiatives, including those of the Vaal workers. By early August, the strike had been crushed, largely as a result of a Labour Court interdict granted to the Post Office against the strikers.

Given this, it would not be surprising if the Vaal Committee abandoned their own Labour Court case in the despondency of defeat. Yet, given their evident tenacity, they could have battled on despite the intimidating environment of the courtroom. However, this was not possible, it was explained to me, because they did not know the date when their case would be reheard (interview, Ramagaga). Which brings us to the second explanation.

Betrayal is a leitmotif of struggle.[14] Betrayal conveniently explains failure. It provides a tangible reason as to why hopes are dashed. Concern over the second Labour Court date can be found in the minute book that the Vaal Committee kept as part of its, previously described, attempt to register as NACAWU with the Department of Labour. During its May meetings, there were complaints that Hlekiso, chair of the committee, was not attending and yet it was he who had to find out the date on which they would return to the Labour Court. A date, 26 May, appeared in the minutes but was then dismissed. By early June, Hlekiso, in his absence, was accused of 'playing double standards' by not coming to meetings.[15] Those attending were worried that the case might be struck off the roll. They did not trust the courts. They were convinced that the Post Office had connections with the Labour Court. Something could happen behind the scenes. A judge could be bought.

Hlekiso, it was rumoured, had sold them out for R5 000. One of the VUT students was also suspected; he had been overheard taking calls from TAS. Some suggested that he was using them to get a job with TAS. There were rumours that he was offered a position. In the end, the committee sent Papiki Mokoena to the Labour Court. He returned with the correct date, but there were concerns about missing papers.

As we know, there were papers missing. At the 17 August hearing, TAS claimed that it had not submitted its response because it was never served with the workers committee's revised claim. If TAS's claim was correct, then the case was undermined from within, by negligence or design. That does not explain, however, why nobody from the committee went to court on 17 August: the date is in the minutes of 4 June. Rather, what has become the accepted account is that the case was sabotaged for *Five Stina* (R5 000) and/or for a career start.

Hlekiso, when I interviewed him, told a different story. By the time the final hearing came around, he had already left SAPO and was on a training course, learning to weld. On the day itself, he had a practical test that he could not miss. He stressed that he had not abandoned the cause and as proof offered how he had joined strikers in July 2011 when he was not busy on the training course. He himself had asked members of the committee why nobody else had gone to the Labour Court. Their excuse was, he said, that he had been the front man, with all the information (interview, Hlekiso). Where truth lies regarding the Vaal's August Labour Court hearing is hard to know for sure, other than it marked the end the Vaal's constitutional crusade.

Neither shame nor rights
If things end badly, they are best not repeated. The repeated peaceful efforts of workers committees across Gauteng to get somebody to listen to them all ended, without exception, in failure. By collecting their varied and diverse attempts together in this chapter, I have sought to make an important argument: that the casual workers' turn from petitions to violence should be understood as a response to a failure of South Africa's constitutional democracy. They had a point, but nobody listened. And it was no small point should anyone have bothered to investigate. There were some 8 000 casuals trapped and exploited in a parallel industrial relations system within a state-owned enterprise.

The failure of anyone to hear the casuals and do 'something big' warns us to be cautious over what symbolic power, the shaming of the powerful, can achieve. Jan Theron makes the point well:

> There are of course instances where public pressure has succeeded in forcing even multi-national companies to accept responsibility for labour standards in plants that are not ostensibly theirs. But such campaigns are best reserved for high

profile cases. They do not address the day-to-day problems of workers without voice representation. In any event, even in high profile cases there is no substitute for effective organisation of the workforce (2009: 190-1).

The South African Constitution's bold prose is saturated with noble words: dignity, equality, rights, privileges, benefits, duties, responsibilities, respect, protect, promote. The Constitution is supposed to work for all. But neither shame nor rights, nor both combined, got the casual workers anywhere. As Theron points out, organising is critical and this book now turns to describing how casuals organised. As we will see, the ways in which SAPO casuals organised increasingly moved beyond the constitutional and beyond the law. This was not a straightforward transition. There was no Rubicon, no moment of conversion. There were always competing views within the committees over strategy and individuals changed their minds, sometimes several times. But as the hopes raised by each petition faded, the constitutional road on which they tried to march disintegrated beneath their feet.

9

To Stand and Fight

Without voice

The Communication Workers Union (CWU), for long the only union in the South African Post Office (SAPO), all but ignored casuals, except when they were needed on the streets during a strike. When casuals attempted to raise their voice within SAPO, complaints were bounced between labour brokers and SAPO management. Despite persistent effort, they remained invisible.

Richard Freeman and James Medoff (1984) explain how employees can respond to problems at work. They can leave and find a better job (the 'exit' option), they can grin and bear it,[1] or they can speak out about the problem (the 'voice' option). But for voice to be effective, it must be heard and not ignored. In other words, voice must have authority or power if it is to be a meaningful option. As Freeman and Medoff explain, that is where unions come in: the employer listens to what the union is saying and at least meets demands part way or faces industrial action. The casuals in SAPO did not have a union. Indeed, initially they had no organisation whatsoever. Individually, their voices counted for little: complain too loud and they would be complaining no more, at least not in the workplace.

Casuals also stayed put in SAPO for another reason; they all hoped they would become permanent. A trickle did. But the trickle dried up and the number of casuals increased. Casuals realised that their chance of securing a permanent position were slim – unless they did something.

Voice backed by power comes only with the credible threat of collective action. High-skilled workers, including professionals, back their voice with the control of skills and knowledge that they possess.

This gives them a strong negotiating position that is hard to counter. They may be relatively few in number, but their voice is strong. By contrast, the voice of low-skilled workers depends on numbers. A strike by a handful of workers who can be quickly replaced is not much of a threat. What is needed is collective action. But getting collective action off the ground is not easy.

A bitter pill

Tovey Montoedi (interview) lives in Sebokeng Township in the Vaal. He started working at the Post Office in August 2003. His mother was a domestic worker, his father first a factory worker then a municipal labourer. After completing matric, Montoedi's first job was as a 'garden boy'.[2] He inherited the position from his brother who had got a job at the Sasol petrochemical plant south of the Vaal River. The gardening did not last long; his employer was racist. He had gone home and told his mother he was not going back. Next up was a short stint at Metal Box (now Nampak) in Vanderbijlpark where another brother was working. After that he had the occasional piece job until a sister who had worked at the Post Office since 1994 told him that the labour broker T&L Appointments was recruiting. She explained that, unlike her own post, it was not direct employment with SAPO. But he applied anyway and started working at the Vanderbijlpark Mail Centre.

He started at the extreme end of the labour flexibility spectrum in SAPO. On T&L's books, he was called when mail volumes were high. The rate was the same no matter what days he worked, and he never worked enough hours to reach overtime rates. Fortunately, this only lasted a couple of months. In October, he was called by Mr Mashashane, the T&L manager for the Vaal, asking if he would prefer to be a postman. The call came at 10 a.m. If he wanted the post, he had to be at the mail centre with his identity document by noon. He got there on time and was employed.

SAPO was abandoning its strategy of installing banks of free-standing Mail Collection Points (MCPs) in the area's townships in favour of street delivery. The MCP policy had allowed SAPO to provide large numbers of postal addresses quickly. Each house in the area had been allocated a box. Some had made use of them, but generally they were unpopular. Montoedi and the other newly recruited T&L postmen started by clearing the unclaimed letters that had accumulated in the MCP boxes before they were removed. Once that had been done, they joined the permanent postmen in the Vereeniging Deport to start delivering door to door. Casuals outnumbered permanents. By 2009, there were eleven casuals at the depot, most now employed by TAS Appointments and Management Services (TAS) which had emerged from T&L, and four permanents.

At the end of his first month working full-time his salary was exactly R1 000. He stayed because there were periodic promises that conversions to permanent status would be coming. But Montoedi also stayed because he had to provide. When he started working at the Post Office, he had a three-month-old daughter. Not that he could provide much. His monthly taxi fares swallowed more than a third of his income. He was living at home and felt he had to put something on the table. His girlfriend, the mother of his child, refused to believe that he could not provide more for their child. She knew how much postmen earned.

Why did he not show her his pay slip? *Dihlong* (shame) was the answer. She knew he was a postman, but she did not know he was a casual. She thought he was holding back. No doubt, she suspected that he had a *nyatsi* (woman on the side) taking what should have been for her and the child. The truth was that he did not earn enough to support his child, but he could provide nothing if he left the job. If he became a permanent, he could make things right. But eventually, Montoedi had to swallow a bitter pill. The promises meant nothing: he was going to be a casual forever. That was when he started attending workers committee meetings.

Those who led
Many people led the casuals' struggle. Some led from the beginning; some became leaders later. Some saw the struggle through till the end; others dropped out; still others were taken out. Some became the face of the movement; others led where they worked.

Caphus Chauke (interview) was initially recruited in May 2007 by TAS to work in the Witspos Mail Centre. There were some 300 casuals, employed by three different labour brokers. They had no union. Since his arrival in Gauteng from Limpopo, Chauke had picked up considerable street savvy. He became the casuals' de facto representative. A casual with a problem would talk to him in the canteen during a break. Sometimes he got advice from a CWU shop steward, but gradually he was able to deal with the concerns: late payment, pay slips reflecting incorrect hours or payments, and sexual harassment; the majority of casuals in the mail centres were women. The key to getting things sorted was to understand the managerial hierarchy and who within it was willing to listen. Any influence was based on goodwill. It was always ephemeral: such representatives lacked formal recognition.

It was these local, informal representatives who started to connect with each other and establish workers committees. Once there was a committee, there was something for people to join. Getting such committees started was not easy; nobody was keen to put their head above the parapet. What was to stop somebody reporting back to their supervisor, who would pass the message along, as to who was behind the committee? It was one thing to help resolve problems in the workplace; it was another to organise. It was often unclear who called meetings.

The West Rand casuals initially met in Randfontein, on the far west fringe of Gauteng's urban sprawl, before moving to Thokoza Park in Soweto. Russel Mutavhatsindi (interview), who was to play a key role in the Mabarete strike, went to one of the first meetings and asked who was behind it. He was told not to ask. Chauke heard about the West Rand meetings through rumours and went along. Three meetings went by before he said anything. He watched and he listened. Just as he had worked out who was who in Witspos management, he worked out who was really pushing the committee. He realised there was a network of activists committed to ending labour broking. He lost his fear and started 'preaching': casuals needed to stand together (interview, Chauke).

Fearlessness could cost leaders their jobs. Sometimes they got over-confident and made themselves too visible. They might think they were on the brink of victory and place themselves at the head of what they thought was the final push, only to see the wave of activism crash. Being at the front when you are on the offensive is one thing; it gives a euphoric hit of invincibility. Being at the front when fortunes change is something else; you are on your own and exposed while those you led are pointing fingers and accusing you of being responsible for defeat (interview, Moeketsi).

Most of the time, however, it was just a slog; a seemingly endless, unrewarding slog. As Tovey Montoedi (interview) put it, in the early days of the committees, activists were 'running around like chickens with their heads cut off'. They were trying everything they could think of, but getting nowhere. Not surprisingly, leaders would become disheartened. They would end up fighting among themselves over what should be done. You would get home, Montoedi explained, and you would wonder why you put in so much effort only to be rewarded with criticism, even accusations of betrayal. So, you would drop out of the struggle for a while and others would take over the lead.

The moratorium on recruiting new employees, in favour of using labour brokers, capped CWU's membership. By keeping the casuals at arm's length, the union stopped growing. Without labour broking, those who led the casuals would, as permanent employees, have been the new generation of leaders that CWU could have trained and mentored. Instead, the leadership of CWU was drawn from ageing permanent workers (interview, Mphuti).

Leading with caution

Learning to lead is not easy, especially when there is no structure for you to join and nobody to mentor or advise. The casual leaders had to do what the Post Office and Telecommunications Workers Association had done two or more decades before – build from scratch. In doing so, they drew on a range of organisational experiences and sources of information. Some drew on their responsibilities in church youth groups, some on involvement with street committees in their townships, some from running burial societies, some from sports clubs, and others from positions in school student representative councils (SRCs). Thabiso Bopape (interview) had been involved in a community policing forum in Soweto. He had organised community patrols and helped to initiate the 'orange lumber [jacket] patrols' that had spread across Gauteng townships as communities sought to contain crime.

For many casuals, recruitment by the labour brokers was their first real work, even if it was not a real job. Few had previous experience of unions. Russel Mutavhatsindi (interview) was an exception; his first organising experience was in his school SRC, but he had then worked in a furniture company for four years. The workforce was organised by the South African Commercial, Catering and Allied Workers Union, but Mutavhatsindi saw the union as yellow; the shop steward was being bribed by management to keep things sweet. He tried to bring the National Union of Metalworkers of South Africa into the company. The response was a selective retrenchment of nine of the 50 employees, Mutavhatsindi among them. They took the matter to the Commission for Conciliation, Mediation and Arbitration (CCMA) and won. But they were not taken back; instead they were paid off with compensation. He found another job but was retrenched after again trying to organise the workforce. This time management was sharper; they first laid off fifteen workers before retrenching them, citing a downturn in orders. The company's case held up in the CCMA, though Mutavhatsindi saw it as amounting to the same thing as his first dismissal: preventing independent union organisation.

So, when Mutavhatsindi became involved in the casual workers committee, he was careful. One technique was never giving his own opinions when talking to his supervisor or a manager. Rather, everything he said was something that he had been told; he was just reporting what other people were thinking or saying. The fiction provided a shield. He did the same thing with co-workers; you never knew who was an *impimpi* (informer).

Why postmen?

Both depots and mail centres or hubs made extensive use of labour brokers to procure postmen and mail handlers respectively. But by and large, activists came from the depots where typically there were 20 or 30 people working. This, from the perspective of industrial relations theory, is counter-intuitive since large workplaces are easier to organise than small ones. Certainly, for a union, there are economies of scale in organising large workplaces. But whether organised from within or without, it is harder to mobilise workers in small workplaces because of the intimacy of employment relationships. There are personal connections that bind people together and constrain behaviour. This weakens in larger workplaces; the bonds between worker and management become increasingly tenuous as size increases, until replaced by an 'us and them' perspective.

So, why was it postmen in the depots who took on labour broking rather than mail handlers in the hubs? The attitude of supervisors and depot controllers was one critical factor. A small number of depot supervisors took the casuals' side and helped them organise. Since depots work with only limited management oversight, they were free to assist without risking their own positions. Other supervisors, however, were hostile and intimidated casuals who stepped out of line. In between were gradations of sympathy and hostility to the casuals' cause. If the attitude of supervisors is stripped away, it was true that casuals were more easily organised in larger than smaller depots (interview, Zwane). However, extending that observation would mean that it should have been in the hubs, with workforces of hundreds, where organisation should have been easiest and first to emerge.

A key reason why this was not the case is the different tasks that casuals were required to perform in the two workplaces and their resulting vulnerability. There is a linear relationship between the number of letters a hub has to sort and the hours of labour required. Being able to call in workers at short notice and by the hour is ideal for efficient matching of labour with the work to be done. The sorting process in hubs is also relatively easy to pick up, being based on postal codes.

Thus, the work process in hubs is much more amenable to using generic labour in a flexible manner. Put another way, workers in the hubs build few work-specific skills and can be moved between presses with relative ease. Increasing or decreasing the number of workers depending on volumes saves labour costs and impacts little on productivity. If mail volumes start to climb, you call around. You have casuals waiting at home for a call; they come for the hours that you need them.

The ease with which workers can be plugged into and taken out of sorting in the hubs means there can be more workers on the books than would ever be needed, even at peak volumes. If workers are slow or get bolshie, they do not get work. This form of discipline requires no hearing, and there is no prospect of appeal. You can discipline someone by doing nothing and they cannot prove a thing.

In the depot, it is different. When letters arrive from a hub, the volume obviously does affect the time taken to sort and deliver, but not with the same degree of correspondence as in the hubs. The work in the depots is less generic. The presses, where the final stage of sorting takes place, are organised to reflect the route that the postman will follow. The routes minimise backtracking; they do not follow the logic of street or township house numbers.[3] Someone unfamiliar with the walk will initially find the press bewildering.

How long a postman spends sorting their walk before delivery is influenced by the volume of mail. But pulling in additional workers is much less easy when volumes are high than it is in the hubs. Postmen are typically rotated between walks on an annual basis and required to cover walks when co-workers are absent. As a result, they get to know the different presses/walks in the depot and can be moved between presses. Bringing in additional hands at short notice means they have to confront unfamiliar presses, resulting in slow sorting and likely mistakes. By the time they have mastered the press, the volume peak will have passed.

The second component of the postman's work, delivering door to door, further limits the use of a flexible labour model. The more letters there are to be delivered on any one day the longer the walk will take to complete, but this is not a linear relationship. The hardest day in a postman's month is when the municipal bills are to be delivered. Every single house in the walk is going to have a letter. But even if, on another day, there are far fewer letters to deliver, the postman still has to cycle or walk around every street.

So, the rule of thumb is one walk, one postman. Sometimes they must sweat. Sometimes they can take it easy. But if there is to be delivery, somebody has to cover the walk. Moreover, each walk has to be learned. Postmen build up local knowledge until they can deliver any walk in the depot and still be back at the depot in time to knock off. This knowledge gives postmen control over the work process and prevents them being plugged in and out by the hour.

So when labour brokers started to place casuals in the depots, workplace realities meant that they became de facto permanent workers, even if employed on casual contracts. Fragmenting the work, as was done in the hubs, was difficult in the depots – although it was certainly tried, as we will see.

If postmen started to get bolshie, the supervisor either had to put up with their nonsense or call the labour broker and institute disciplinary proceedings. Disciplining casuals was a lot easier than disciplining permanents, but in the depots it was nowhere near as easy as in the hubs where all a supervisor had to do was *not* pick up the phone. As individual casual workers clocked up year after year of continuous service as postmen, they entrenched themselves, through local knowledge and personal relationships, in a way that was not possible in the hubs. However fragile, this limited their vulnerability and built a platform for mobilisation.

Time wars
The 'one walk, one postman' constraint on the number of full-time workers employed in a depot did not mean, however, that there were not attempts to make the remuneration of casuals flexible. At different times and in different places, casual postmen were being paid by the number of items they delivered, by the size of letters (large or small), by the weight of letters, by the estimated hours allocated to a walk, or by some combination of these.

It was fixing the hours allocated to a walk that constituted the most sustained attempt to reduce the cost of casuals. In this regard, what labour brokers proposed, casual workers opposed. The synthesis that emerged from these opposing agencies was a series of time wars.

The time wars were a precursor to the larger conflict, still to come, over labour broking in SAPO. In resisting the reduction of hours, casuals were not challenging labour broking; rather, they were attempting to maintain already inadequate wages from further erosion. Quinton John was brother to Charles John, a depot controller in Krugersdorp; he was employed by TAS and working as a postman in

Krugersdorp. In 2009, along with seven other casuals, he referred a dispute over hours to the CCMA. They complained, 'At first we were getting eight hours per day. And now they are giving us seven hours per day . . . what we want is to see ourselves having our eight hours back.' The case was withdrawn from the CCMA and the eight hours were restored. This was not, however, the last attempt to cut down on the hours allocated to walks.

The time wars clearly reveal how much of the dirty work of labour broking, here squeezing the hours of low-paid workers, was orchestrated by SAPO managers. Labour brokers billed SAPO for the hours worked by their employees, that is casuals. If there were fewer hours billed because the working day was reduced from eight to seven hours, the casuals got a smaller pay packet at the end of the month, but the labour broking companies also received less. It was not in labour brokers' interests to cut the hours their casuals were paid, but it was in SAPO's interest. SAPO managers would push to lower labour brokers' invoices in order to meet their own cost-containment targets. This is shown by the regionalised and coordinated way in which the time wars were waged. They took place at different times in different SAPO regions of Gauteng. When they erupted, the various labour brokers lowered their hours in unison, coordinated by SAPO managers sitting behind the front line where labour brokers and casuals squared off against each other.

In 2011, the West Rand workers committee fought back and managed to reverse these renewed attempts to cut hours down from eight to seven. These were victories that bolstered their leading position among the casuals' committees in Gauteng. Through such activities, they were learning how to function as a unit in which individuals played different roles for common purpose. They were also learning where to project power. The labour brokers were only the front men of their oppression; it was SAPO they had to reach. They had to work out what would make SAPO squeal. The casuals started to see beyond mail delivery on their walks and depots, and to realise that their walks were part of a much bigger system (interview, Mutavhatsindi).

What they started to think about was the system's vulnerabilities.

But why men?
The casuals' struggle in SAPO was undertaken, outside of Pretoria, overwhelmingly by men. There is an easy explanation for this; the vast majority of postmen are men. And as previously outlined, it was postmen, rather than mail handlers, who largely shouldered the struggle.

The organisation of Pretoria casuals lies beyond the scope of this book, but the differences between them and the other casuals' committees in Gauteng should be noted. Pretoria followed its own struggle trajectory, and was different in various ways. There were woman leaders of the casuals, notably Jaqueline Maja (interview), and the Tshwane Mail Hub was organised, meaning that mail handlers, often women, were involved.

But as for the other Gauteng casuals' committees, it was a very male struggle. When I asked why it had been postmen based in small, scattered depots who took the lead rather than the larger workforces of the hubs or mail centres, they did not provide the socio-technical explanation I have provided. Rather, respondents pointed to the majority of casuals in the mail centres being women. Women accepted hardship. Perhaps, one interviewee suggested, it was their nature. It was men who fought.

The fight had been literal and it was clear to the leadership that the few women who were in their ranks were not cut out for what was required – bringing mail delivery to a halt using violence and the threat of violence. One casual leader from the Tembisa Workers Committee explained to me how women balked at this; they were not up for meting out punishment on scabs nor able to escape should the police arrive. He painted a vivid picture for me; there had been a few women who had come with them in the first days of the Mabarete strike. They had been wearing heels; you cannot run wearing heels.

These explanations reflect the common uber-dominant, working-class African man's view of women's roles in society. The Constitution may declare equality, and gender equality may be omnipresent in policy declarations (including that of unions), but when the chips are down, there is men's work and women's work. A gendered division of responsibilities applies in the domestic sphere, it applies at work and it applies to strikes. The SAPO casuals' strikes was not women's work.[4]

The few women who joined were told to stay at home. They would attend meetings, but otherwise the men got on with the task of striking.

Lerato Seema: A woman among men

Lerato Seema started to work in the MCP section of the Edenvale Depot in 2008.[5] The previous permanent temporary workers, employed by TAS, had staged a wildcat strike (described in Chapter 7). They had been 'chased out' and Seema had been one of those who had come in to take their place. Her work was to sort mail and put it into the lobby boxes for customers to collect. There were nine casual workers, all women, and four permanent employees in the section. For the casuals, the hours of work varied. How much she got at the end of the month depended on the ongoing tussle between the casuals pushing their hours and management restricting hours based on 'volumes'. If she was lucky, she could clear R2 000 on pay day. In a long month – one that was designated as a five-week month for payment purposes by TAS – in which they had managed to stretch their hours, she could made R2 800. Then she was happy – happy because they had pushed the system, not because she was satisfied with what was in her bank account.

None of the casuals in the MCP were happy. The permanents could relax. The casuals were always on notice that they were not really part of the Post Office. Seema recalled how in the depot they were told not to wear uniforms since they were not Post Office employees. At staff meetings, they were told they were not entitled to speak because they were not union members.

Seema stayed put, sorting the mail and holding her tongue. She needed the money. She had a child with her boyfriend, but she was, figuratively speaking, living with African Bank in a backyard room at her mother's place. When she paid off one loan, she was offered another. With the loans, she was able to furnish her room and build a wall around the property, a gift to her mother. On average, she was paying R500 a month to African Bank and there were other debts; if she wanted clothing for her or her child it would be purchased on account. It was the only way to amount to anything. But, even with the self-imposed scrimping that the loans necessitated, she was not getting ahead. She joked, when I interviewed her, that her problems had been resolved on the first December of her employment. Each TAS employees had been given a Christmas bonus: a R100 Checkers voucher.[6]

The Edenvale Depot where Seema worked formed part of the Tembisa Workers Committee. She had gone with other casuals to the hearings in Germiston on labour brokers in 2009 and recalled that there had been members of parliament present. The issue debated that day had been whether labour brokers should be banned or regulated, but she knew that President Jacob Zuma had said they must be banned. Still nothing happened. They were unable to join CWU. A couple of other organisations came to talk to them. They said they understood the casuals' problem. They said they would help, but they just disappeared.

She had been on maternity leave with her second child during the mid-2011 strike that Tembisa initiated, but in early 2012 she had joined what was to become the Mabarete strike, described later in this book. The comrades from the mail delivery section of the depot – that is, postmen – had told them that in the last strike some had stayed at work. This time they were told it was going to be different. Anybody who remained at work would not be beaten. They would be killed.

Seema was afraid and angry at the same time. She compared her monthly salary with the threat of what would happen if she continued working. She thought about what her life amounted to on R2 000 a month. She now had two children. It was not a life she wanted. There is a Zulu proverb, *Uzoyithola kanjani uhleli ekhoneni?* (How will you get what you want if you do nothing?).[7] She decided to join the strike. She was the only casual in the MCP to do so. The others remained at work. The permanents discouraged them from striking, telling them that the strike was illegal and they would lose their jobs.

With the strike underway and the Tembisa depots closed, the strikers had gone to Germiston. She was the only women to go with them. It was mayhem; the strikers were hitting people, there had been police, they had been running and hiding. It was not that she disapproved of what was happening, she knew they had to do something.[8] After that, she had been told to stay at home. It was at the strikers' mass meetings that she realised that she was not the only woman on strike; there were four or five other women, although she never got to know them well.

Alone at home with only occasional contact with the strike, she had been vulnerable. Her supervisor had called to tell her that they were hiring a replacement worker. She would lose her job. He had asked about her children; how would she support them? But she stuck with the strike. As it dragged on, she accepted she had lost her job and started to look for other work.

Mobilisation: Networks, alliances and divisions

If the start of resistance stemmed from individuals realising that they had to stand and fight, the necessary mobilisation was only possible because a network of activists was established across Gauteng. This arose from SAPO's many depots, though it did so in the shadow of CWU. Double-footing, with workers participating in parallel organisations, was one factor that distorted the complex emergence of the casuals' committees. This section looks at some of the dimension of this primary process of mobilisation.

The small number of supervisors who took up the casuals' cause provided critical assistance in establishing this network. This included Charles John who was Alfred Mosito's supervisor in the Krugersdorp Depot. Mosito was to become part of the Mabarete Top 9 leadership. John gave Mosito access to the office phone and arranged for the depot van to take him to other depots; he also arranged to have Mosito's walk covered when he was out on workers committee business (interviews, John; Mosito).

Mobilising, with supervisors' assistance, within the SAPO workplace structure was supplemented by other approaches. Activists made a point of talking to postmen they saw working to find out their depot and if they were employed by a labour broker. If the conversation went well, numbers were exchanged, along with an invitation to attend a workers committee meeting. On at least one occasion, labour brokers themselves facilitated the building of the casuals' network. One December, TAS organised a braai (barbecue) for its East Rand employees at Germiston Lake, which inadvertently provided an opportunity for the casual workers to connect across depots (interview,

Choshi). There was also CWU's Freddie Marutha and Moeketsi Lepheane who both strove to bring activists together (see Chapter 7). Marutha was influential on the East Rand, Lepehane on the West Rand, but both set up meetings that attempted to link casual representatives across Gauteng.

These networking efforts were countered by centrifugal forces of division. Casuals frequently operated in silos rather than as a Gauteng-wide structure. In some cases, that was the result of competition over status. Sometimes the strategies of committees were conflicted. At other times, sensibilities were offended. Within the Vaal, Levy Zwane (interview) explained how the 2005 strike by the Mafatsana and Sebokeng depots had gone ahead without notice to the nascent workers committee. This error of protocol had irritated activists in other depots. Zwane, for example, had found out about the strike from a neighbour; it had been embarrassing. He had tried to drum up support for the strike, but the protocol error gave people an excuse not to get involved. That 'it was their thing' was a frequent explanation from activists that I interviewed about events, which had been central to others' accounts, but about which they knew little.

The relationship between the workers committees was fluid and sometimes tense. The West Rand Committee, based largely in Soweto, initially had strong links with casuals in Pretoria, but these weakened while those with the Vaal Committee strengthened (interview, Bopape). On the East Rand, it was the Tembisa Workers Committee that dominated and their relationship with the far larger, but less comprehensively organised, Far East Rand was complex. It was, however, the relationship between East and West Rand that was most difficult. Simplified, and not withstanding personal friendships that straddled the Rand, there was tension between the Tembisa and Soweto Lines – a reference to the railways that snaked through each township, connecting them to the Metrorail network, but also referencing the very different profiles of the two townships.

On the east side of Johannesburg, the dusty township of Tembisa is one of several reservoirs of the industrial proletariat: Tembisa, Katlehong, Thokoza, Tsakane, Kwa Thema, Daveyton – names with little traction beyond Gauteng. In Tembisa, a handful of activists managed to weld the casuals from six depots into a formidable organisation. They had learned how to organise the hard way; activists Marcus Makhura, Johannes Manamela and Petrus Morenamela had been dismissed. Long before the West Rand Committee, the Tembisa Committee abandoned hope that CWU would end labour broking and accepted that they would have to fight their own battles. Rejecting the union model of elections for office-bearers, they eschewed permanent positions as divisive.[9] Rather, they appointed the chairpersons of meetings on the day.

On the other side of the city is the cosmopolitan township of Soweto, home to two Nobel Laureates and known worldwide. It was the cradle of the revolt against the *boer*, the home of the struggle and, notwithstanding a diverse socio-economic profile, home to a burgeoning African middle class. The casual postmen working in Soweto and outlying areas did not form part of this middle class, but nevertheless they provided the more educated, sharp-thinking and fluent-speaking leadership of the casual workers.[10] When the Soweto Line finally broke with CWU, one of their mocking renditions of the union's acronym was Confused, Weak and Uneducated; Confused, Weak and Useless was another. The workers committees on the West Rand were structured along conventional committee formats with half a dozen office-bearers: chairperson, deputy chairperson and so on, even if meetings sometimes had barely more than six people attending. The Soweto Line was not short of chiefs.

For East Rand activists, the leaders on the West Rand were the Soweto 'clever boys'. They were comrades (indicating that they were on the same side) and their abilities were acknowledged, but this was rarely without also pointing out that, clever as they might be, the West Rand leadership could not mobilise their own depots. This was not entirely true; the West Rand organised a number of one-day strikes and demonstrations. But the slander was not without foundation; some West Rand leaders were the only workers in their depots to stay out during the Mabarete strike.

Who led the Gauteng casuals in the fight against labour broking in SAPO – East or West, Tembisa or Soweto – was a point of contention, sometimes to the point of violence.[11] But both committees knew their fates were linked, and their fundamental differences were about methods not goals. In as much as a compromise was ever found, it was through an analogy: Tembisa was the body, Soweto was the head.

10

Three Times a Failure
Organising Casuals

In total, there were three sustained attempts to establish trade union rights for casual workers in the South African Post Office (SAPO). The first was led by Kodisang Bokaba, using the South African Gaming, Waitron and Admin Workers Trade Union (SAGWAWTU) as a vehicle. The second attempt was led by Moeketsi 'MP' Lepheane, acting on behalf of the Communication Workers Union (CWU), though with considerable opposition from within the union. The third was by the Commercial, Services and Allied Workers Union (COSAWU), but led by the Democratic Socialist Movement (DSM). All three campaigns for recognition followed similar paths: the signing up of casuals to a union using their existing committees and networks to organise; requesting recognition from the labour brokers; and, when this was rebuffed, approaching the Commission for Conciliation, Mediation and Arbitration (CCMA) to seek enforcement.

Sections 11 to 16 of the Labour Relations Act (LRA) outlines a range of rights for unions registered with the Department of Labour. This applies to those with sufficient membership in a company. What sufficient membership means is not specified in the Act, and collective agreements have set this at anything from 10 per cent to 30 per cent or more, of the 'bargaining unit'.[1] Some rights, such as stop order facilities for the union's fees, may be granted at lower thresholds. However, if a union has more than 50 per cent of the bargaining unit as members, then as a 'majority union' the full raft of organisational rights listed in the LRA must be granted. Recognition and the associated organisational rights consolidate a union's organisational power and pave the way for negotiations with the employer.

CWU had been recognised as the only SAPO union since 1996. SAPO's casuals were not, of course, employed by SAPO but by the labour brokers. If they were to obtain organisational rights, the law determined that this must be from the labour brokers. That this split one workforce between multiple employers was not something the law took into consideration. That the casuals worked for SAPO and might want to be SAPO employees was not the point. If they wanted to claim organisational rights, the industrial relations framework channelled them to their labour broker employers.

SAGWAWTU: First to flop

The Tembisa Workers Committee threw in their lot with SAGWAWTU in 2009 after a chance encounter with an African People's Convention (APC) councillor, Moloko Mpolobosho, who lived in Ivory Park, next to Tembisa. The APC emerged in 2007 as a split from the Pan Africanist Congress of Azania, which itself had emerged as a result of a spilt from the African National Congress (ANC) in 1959. Mpolobosho put the Tembisa Workers Committee in touch with Kodisang Bokaba, a member of the APC, a political activist and unionist with a law degree. He took on the casuals' case using SAGWAWTU, a union of convenience in this fight.[2] With its valid Department of Labour registration, it provided access to the CCMA. Bokaba, along with a number of casuals, including Marcus Makhura, a postman at the East Rand Birchleigh Depot, signed up almost 450 Gauteng-based SAPO casual workers in May and June 2009. Reflecting the problem of organising workers employed by labour brokers, the new SAGWAWTU members were employed by five different labour brokers. According to SAGWAWTU membership forms, the vast majority, 82 per cent, were employed by TAS Appointments and Management Services (TAS). Next came Marula Staffing with 11 per cent, while the remaining 7 per cent was split between three other companies – N.T. Ngidi, T&T and ATM/Autemas Placements. Bokaba was on the APC's national executive committee and had hoped that he could use this position to lobby the party's leader, Themba Godi, then chair of the powerful parliamentary Standing Committee on Public Accounts, to talk to the Minister of Communications about the SAPO casuals. In this regard, he was disappointed and came to feel that the APC did little about labour broking beyond a standard token opposition in its publications (interview, Bokaba).[3]

SAGWAWTU first attempted to enforce CWU's, still unimplemented, collective agreement on converting casuals to permanent positions. To do this they approached the CCMA, citing SAPO and TAS as joint respondents. TAS did not pitch at the CCMA but SAPO did and argued that the 2007/2008 collective agreement, on which SAGWAWTU was basing its case, had been superseded. The CCMA instructed SAPO to provide SAGWAWTU with the new agreement. SAPO said it would do and later offered to meet with Bokaba. Here the matter faltered, in part because Bokaba, wary that SAPO and TAS would keep shifting responsibility onto each other, insisted that TAS also attend the meeting.

Changing tack, SAGWAWTU now sought recognition from TAS. With 364 signed-up TAS members, they had a strong case for recognition. TAS was claiming 500 employees (interview, Bokaba). On that basis, they were a majority union in TAS and entitled to full organisational rights prescribed in the Labour Relations Act. They met with Neal Lakey, group human resources manager for the Moloko Group, which included TAS, and unsurprisingly reached no agreement.[4] SAGWAWTU then went to the CCMA in order to enforce these rights.

SAGWAWTU was eventually issued with a strike certificate, allowing its members employed by TAS and working in SAPO to embark on a protected strike to demand TAS recognise the union. Should a strike then achieve SAGWAWTU's recognition, the union could proceed to negotiate with TAS over terms and conditions for TAS employees, with the prospect of moving to another protected strike if there was deadlock. None of that happened, however. CWU's August 2009 national strike, described in Chapter 4, pulled the rug from under Bokaba's feet: casuals had rushed to join the strike only to find their promised conversion squeezed out of the final agreement.

A strike certificate was obtained, but not until 22 September (CCMA 2009a), by which time betrayal in CWU's 2009 strike had demobilised casuals. Even if there had been the stomach to launch a strike for SAGWAWTU's recognition, the legal path was still not open; TAS responded to the CCMA's ruling by going to the Labour Court for an injunction against the strike on the grounds that the dispute, a matter of rights, should have been referred to the Labour Court, rather than been granted a strike certificate. The hypocrisy of this approach takes the biscuit; TAS was using the law to stop a strike on the grounds that SAGWAWTU was seeking a right that TAS was refusing to recognise. In the end, getting the CCMA to issue a strike certificate was a pyrrhic victory, a kick of the dying SAGWAWTU initiative.

MP Lepheane and the CWU's A-Team: Second to fold

The divisions within CWU over the union's response to the use of casuals has been described in Chapter 7. After Freddie Marutha's death, MP Lepheane (interview), CWU's Gauteng provincial secretary, took on responsibility for casuals within CWU's Gauteng provincial structure. He was a CWU office-bearer and part of the A-Team described in Chapter 7. Via its affiliation to the Congress of South African Trade Unions (COSATU), CWU was aligned to the ruling ANC and its ally, the South African Communist Party (SACP). The complicated politics around labour broking and the glacially slow legislative action on their regulation has been described in Chapter 3.

Lepheane unilaterally allocated 40 per cent of his time to organising casuals in SAPO. This was far from popular within CWU; permanent workers objected to him spending time on casuals' issues instead of their own. He also came under increasing pressure from the union's leadership – directly, when the union's national office instructed him that no money was to be used in organising casuals, and, indirectly, when he was assaulted in his office.

He had opened up a campaign for casuals to be recognised by TAS in April 2010 when he sent Daniel Tsotetsi, the company's human resources manager, a letter on CWU's Gauteng provincial office letterhead informing TAS that 'we have a substantial number of members that will qualify us to secure comprehensive rights' (Lepheane

2010). The letter went on to say that it would be a 'great honour to be afforded an opportunity to officially launch in your company' and proposed a meeting in May. TAS's response was less enthusiastic, and they ended up meeting in the CCMA. Here the number of bona fide TAS employees on the list that CWU presented was agreed at 217 or 45 per cent of TAS's workforce, clearly enough to constitute sufficient representation. The CCMA commissioner sent the parties away with 21 days to conclude an agreement. No agreement was reached, and the matter went to arbitration on 17 February 2011. TAS failed to attend the arbitration, which went in CWU's favour. TAS was given fourteen days to award CWU full organisational rights as laid out in Sections 11 to 16 of the LRA.

The arbitration ruling was, however, another pyrrhic victory for the casuals. CWU's organisational drive had already collapsed with Lepheane's marginalisation and then effective banishment from CWU. The CCMA award was never enforced. This time the damage to the organisational drive was not from outside, as when CWU's 2009 national strike had swept aside SAGWAWTU's legal mobilisation. Rather, Lepheane's attempt to get legal recognition from TAS was collapsed from within CWU.

The DSM's COSAWU: Third to fail

Activists from the Democratic Socialist Movement, the third organisation to seek recognition for the SAPO casuals from TAS, shared Bokaba's frustration with how organisations routinely condemned labour broking but did not engage with the problem. They were not referring, however, to their own structure, but rather to the Tripartite Alliance of the ANC-SACP-COSATU and, in particular, COSATU. Liv Shange of the DSM vented this frustration:

> By narrowly pouring pseudo-radical vitriol on the singled-out target of labour broking, they [the leaders of COSATU] hope to detract the focus from the increasingly burning need for an across-the-board class confrontation. As a result, the demand for a ban of labour broking is routinely added to wage increase campaigns, etc., as a sort of spiced-up afterthought (Shange 2011).

The quote also makes it clear that the DSM's politics is revolutionary and no friend of capitalism. Like the APC, the DSM's origins are in the ANC, but from the Marxist Workers Tendency, a Trotskyist grouping that operated within the ANC until 1996 (WASP n.d.). The DSM operated at that point within the Workers and Socialist Party (WASP), which it established in late 2012 when it held considerable influence among mineworkers' committees in the platinum belt post-Marikana (Sosibo 2012).[5] In the introduction to WASP's 2014 election manifesto, the party outlined the need for a mass working-class party, along with a revolutionary organisation that would direct the revolt against capitalism (WASP 2015).[6]

Despite the DSM's Trotskyist pedigree, its engagement with the SAPO casual workers was defeated by the same legal and bureaucratic constraints to which previous attempts to organise casuals had succumbed. Like the affair with SAGWAWTU, the casuals' involvement with COSAWU started by chance. Raymond Efela, a casual worker based on the Far West Rand, made contact with the DSM after it published an article on labour broking in its newspaper *Izwi labasebenzi* (*Workers Voice*). After meeting with Efela, the DSM saw an opportunity to organise workers in Gauteng (interview, Hamilton). Like SAGWAWTU, COSAWU was something of an 'off-the-shelf' union that could be used to organise SAPO casuals (interview, Sebei). COSAWU had been established in the Western Cape independently of the DSM, but had come into its sphere of influence when members of the executive had joined the party.

The DSM produced a series of leaflets for the SAPO casual workers. These were far more sophisticated than anything that had previously (or since) been produced, with professional layout, detailed text and a clear programme of action. What had been a fluid and fractious network of workers committees now became the Gauteng Labour Broker Workers Committee (LBWC). This consolidation was, as we will see, more textual than real. However, the LBWC was seen as a transitional step by the DSM. Several of the leaflets were headed, 'The Labour Broker Workers Committee Says: Organise or Starve! Join COSAWU!' It was explained in the text that 'the only way in which we can strike back at the invasion of the labour brokers in SAPO is by organising ourselves in a union. We have reached the limits of how far we can go led by a committee' (LBWC/COSAWU/DSM 2011a).

At a meeting held in October 2010, the LBWC was formally established. It consisted of five four-member working committees: Tshwane (Pretoria), Vaal, East Rand, Johannesburg Central and West Rand. The 'top' member of each committee was appointed as an office-bearer of the Gauteng committee.[7] A detailed document was drawn up outlining how the LBWC should establish itself as a branch of COSAWU and collect membership fees monthly. Forty per cent of these fees would be remitted to the union's head office and the remainder retained by the branch to fund its aims. These aims were laid out as:

- Recruit members to establish COSAWU in SAPO (Gauteng);
- build the union;
- pursue the legal challenge of enforcing the 2005 agreement between SAPO and CWU [to convert casuals to permanents];[8]
- seek recognition with the various labour brokers and eventually SAPO (LBWC/DSM/COSAWU n.d.).

However, what the DSM's initiative did not account for was the independence of existing workers committees, and their attempt to found a unified structure soon floundered. The two casuals who most enthusiastically worked with the DSM were Raymond Efela from the Far West Rand, who was appointed chairperson of the LBWC, and Desmond Moeketsi from the Far East Rand depot of Daveyton, who became secretary. The East Rand or Tembisa Workers Committee never came to the table and rebuffed requests to meet with a series of excuses. Meanwhile, the West Rand felt overlooked by the LBWC. East and West Rand committees had their differences as to who was leading casuals, but they shared common cause over the DSM's initiative that seemingly relegated both East and West to second-league teams.

The Vaal also had problems with the initiative. It was attempting to set up its own union of casuals, the National Communications and Allied Workers Union (NACAWU) (see Chapter 8). Members of the Vaal Workers Committee attended meetings of the LBWC, but the problem of two unions could not be resolved. Matters came to a head at a meeting in Johannesburg on 13 November 2010. In reserved language, the NACAWU minute book records the following:

> Comrades Bazil [Hlekiso] and Papiki [Mokoena] [of the Vaal Committee]: we [made it] clear to other comrades that we are not going to recruit for COSAWU union.
> Comrade Weizmann [Hamilton of the DSM] said that we must take decision to leave or stay. [He was] supported by Comrade Raymond [Efela] and Comrade Desmond [Moeketsi].
> Then we leave that premises, we [came] back home.[9]

The LBWC-DSM-COSAWU legal approach did not fare much better. Efela, with the support of the DSM, had opened a case at the CCMA's Pretoria office over interpretation and application of the 2005 collective agreement between SAPO and CWU, by which all casuals should have been converted long ago (CCMA 2010c). SAPO was cited as the respondent. SAPO sent a junior HR manager to the Pretoria CCMA hearing and the case proceeded to conciliation and then arbitration. Since Efela was not employed by SAPO but by a labour broker, and was not a member of CWU, it was luck that the matter proceeded without being challenged on the ground of *locus standi*. That luck ran out when the case came up for arbitration, under a different CCMA commissioner, in January 2011. Efela had no legal traction on either signatory to the 2005 agreement that he was asking the CCMA to enforce on behalf of all casuals in SAPO. Possibly under advice from the new commissioner, Efela formally withdrew the case from the CCMA.[10]

Looking back on their engagement with the DSM, leaders of the SAPO casuals made two criticisms over and above the feathers that were ruffled when the DSM organised without fully understanding the dynamics of the existing workers committees. First, the DSM was accused of being focused on building its own organisation – in other words, using the casuals' struggles to build the party. If this was the case, it was unsuccessful; it did not recruit a single member. A second criticism was that the time frame put forward for resolving the casuals' problems was too long. The DSM/WASP insisted that 'the living standards of the majority will only be improved by the working class leading a revolution to end capitalism and create a socialist society' (WASP 2015: 1). And the estimated time of arrival for that kept getting pushed back; a Marxist Workers Tendency publication entitled *South Africa's Impending Socialist Revolution* was, for example, published in 1982.

In contrast to the casual workers' frustration at the DSM's timelines for liberation, DSM leaders were struck by the impatience of the casuals; by late 2010 they wanted one thing: permanent positions. And they wanted it 'here and now!' (interview, Sebei). This demand for instant results, along with their internal divisions and double-footing, was frustrating for the DSM, but not surprising (interviews, Sebei; Hamilton). They saw the way in which casuals were trapped, ensnared by the confederation of labour brokers, SAPO Human Resources and CWU, which, in one configuration or another, blocked casuals' attempts to advance. The casuals saw themselves at war, explained Mametlwe Sebei, a DSM organiser who assisted the SAPO casuals.[11] It was 'a war psychology'. The rage of the casuals, identified by the DSM, was to feature in the coming strikes.

On the eve of rebellion

Just as Bokaba's use of SAGWAWTU to mobilise casuals in 2009 had been swept aside by CWU's strike, so too was the DSM's mobilisation overrun by wildcat strikes in late June 2011 that began in Tembisa and swept across Gauteng (see Chapter 11). The DSM's efforts, driven through the LBWC, were already beginning to falter, but the strike usurped the coordinating committee's remaining authority. What took over from the formally organised LBWC was a loose, dynamic command structure, whose membership credentials rested not on title or position, but on active involvement in the strike and their ability to persuade others. That structure included the DSM's most committed comrades: Efela and Moeketsi. Indeed, Moeketsi was to end up as one of the six named respondents to the Labour Court interdict brought by SAPO.

When the LBWC met on 11 June 2011, its main agenda item was a planned march to the Department of Labour, for which a date was still to be agreed. There was an item under 'Any Other Business' regarding rumours of a strike about to start in the Tembisa area. The information was vague; it was not clear who was behind the call for the 'whole of East Rand' to down tools the following Monday (13 June).[12] The rumours were wrong, but only in regard to timing. The strike started on Monday, 20 June. As described in the next chapter, the strike did indeed spread across the whole East Rand, and further.

The DSM/LBWC's vague sense that something was about to happen in Tembisa illustrates the siloed organisation of casuals across Gauteng. A snapshot taken at this moment captures five distinct groupings. There was the LBWC's campaign with key support from individuals from the Far East and Far West Rand. There was the Tembisa Workers Committee, which was about to initiate a break-out campaign from its six-depot power base. There was the West Rand, which remained close to, if sceptical of, CWU, and which would remain largely aloof from the Tembisa strike. There was the Vaal Committee, which had detached itself from the LBWC over the issue of NACAWU and whose members were to join the Tembisa strike. Finally, there was Pretoria. Its involvement with the LBWC had been minimal. Like the West Rand, Pretoria stood aside from the Tembisa strike until the final days, but then began its own strike as the Tembisa strike ended.

Despite the frustration of being left behind by the Tembisa strike, the DSM hung in for a few more months. They gave assistance when the strikers found themselves facing jail sentences at the Labour Court and with impressive tenacity initiated talks, hoping to achieve recognition with the labour brokers. They even made good on the long-planned march to the Department of Labour, which took place a few days after the Tembisa strike had crashed. The demonstration got considerable media coverage (Shange 2011), but with just 70 people marching, from a range of organisations, it was a last gasp.

At this point, the casuals had exhausted any constitutional option they had to end their bondage. This chapter has focused on the three, similar attempts by outsiders to assist them by getting casuals into the industrial relations system. All three attempts to secure recognition with the labour brokers involved distinct nexuses between political parties and trade unions. For different reasons, all three attempts failed.

However, the different reasons tell one story: that the institutional road pursued was not going to end labour broking. Victories had been limited and defeats repeated. The lesson that these defeats taught the casuals was that they would have to fight their own battles.

11

We Are the Union Ourselves!

Striking at the labour brokers
The six men who assembled on a piece of waste ground close to Tembisa's Tembi Mall on the morning of Monday, 20 June 2011 were about to kick off 'the first strike organised by casuals for casuals' (interview, Moeketsi). Strictly speaking, it was not the first strike by casuals; there had been stoppages or 'partial strikes',[1] a few one-day protests when casuals had marched to deliver a memorandum, and two strikes in the Vaal, one in 2005 and one early in 2009 (described in Chapter 8). But it was the first Gauteng-wide and sustained strike of casuals.

In addition to its scale and duration, this strike differed from previous stoppages, stayaways or strikes in another way: casuals were now seeking to end labour broking. Again, that was not entirely novel. Many casuals had pinned their hope on the promise that the 2009 strike called by the Communication Workers Union (CWU) would end labour broking, but that strike had been fought for the benefit of permanents. Until June 2011, the struggles of casuals had been over the terms and conditions of their employment, not who employed them. There were depot-level tussles over the fairness of work allocation and the issuing of uniforms; there were the ongoing 'time wars' described in Chapter 9, and there were the attempts, made with external assistance, to obtain legal recognition from labour brokers. These struggles were not, however, attacks on labour brokers' existence. Indeed, they acknowledged their existence and their legitimacy – at least objectively, even if that was not the intention. The aim of the six men was to end labour broking.

This chapter describes the strike, or more accurately strikes, of casual workers in the South African Post Office (SAPO) that took place between June and August 2011.[2] Strikes take different forms. Within post-1994 South African industrial relations, there is a distinction between strikes that are procedural and protected or wildcat and unprotected. This strike was the latter, but that is far from an adequate description of what took place. To understand events, we need to appreciate how this strike began, developed, spread, peaked and collapsed. The shape of the strike was moulded by structural constraints, organisational forms and happenstance. Ideas were put forward, tactics were developed, unforeseen consequences emerged and errors were made. All this taught the casuals how to forge strikes that had little resemblance to the procedural strikes promoted by labour law.

Between dismissal and danger: 25 June 2011
Sitting at Jerry's Place, a *spaza* shop and fast food outlet in Katlehong Township, Maja explained that he had a problem at work.[3] We had ordered *kota* and cokes and were sitting in the shade of the store's veranda, waiting for the shout that would tell us that our food was ready. The R14 *kotas* being prepared consisted of a quarter loaf of white bread filled with chips, a slice of processed cheese, polony and a fried Russian sausage. As usual, Maja had opted for tomato sauce with his *kota*. I had chosen atchar with the forlorn hope that it made the meal healthier.

Maja had been unemployed when I had first got to know him around 2005. Paying him for weekly conversation lessons in township Sesotho had worked well for both of us. On Saturday afternoons I would drive into the township and we would head to Jerry's Place for lunch. The veranda was equipped with plastic chairs and a battered metal table. I would fish my notebook out and scribble down new words and phrases that our conversation threw up. Along with vocabulary and *kasi* idiom, I was learning much about township life and, although I did not know it at the time, starting to write this book.

In 2009, Maja started working as a postman. In theory, labour brokers recruited the staff they placed with SAPO. But, by 2009, recruitment in the depots worked somewhat differently. When a vacancy arose, supervisors would find somebody who would then be placed on a labour broker's books. Maja's friend Tsu got him the job when there was a vacancy in his depot.

Stepping into the shoes of a dismissed worker had not involved a *tjotjo* (bribe) as is often the case. But there was the delicate matter of Maja handing over to the supervisor R600 from his first pay packet. It had been explained to him that the R600 was over and above what he would normally get at the end of the month.[4] Maja had agreed without hesitation. He was grateful for the opportunity to get his foot into the world of work. Initially, he thought that with a regular income he would be able to make headway. He started off that way, putting down a lay-by on a TV and paying the six monthly instalments. But it had stretched him to the limit. When he then tried to do the same on a fridge, he ended up defaulting.

After we had finished eating our *kotas*, we got onto the problem at work. There was a strike by casuals in Tembisa and it was set to spread; they would be coming to Maja'a depot and all the casuals would be expected to join. Maja was not entirely clear what the strike was about, though obviously it involved money. All strikes were about money. Despite this, the casuals in his depot were planning to work. They were worried about losing pay and losing their jobs.

For two years, Maja had been learning the ropes. He knew what had to be done and how to do it. He also knew what he could get away with. And the money he earned was the only thing keeping his debts afloat. What they got was not enough; over this they agreed with the strikers. But little as the money was, the prospect of going back to idleness in the township, asking for everything that they ate, drank or wore, meant that they were not going to risk losing their month-end salary.

So, collectively the casuals in Maja's depot had decided they would continue to work. They would go out to deliver looking as little like postmen as possible. The SAPO bibs and bicycles would be left in the depot. They would be indistinguishable, Maja hopefully suggested, from people delivering leaflets. Plus, they planned to work in groups of four and keep in contact with other groups who could come to help or at least call the police. Obviously, they were not going to deliver the same volumes as they usually did, but they would be working and staying safe. They had heard that the Tembisa strikers took no nonsense, but they were not going to put their jobs on the line. Maja was in agreement with the decision; he was not willing to lose what he had.

Sekoteng

The casual workers in the Tembisa area had made the piece of waste ground their own. Named Sekoteng (the hole) it served as their meeting place, debating chamber and assembly point. There were around 130 casuals in the area, spread across six depots: Birchleigh, Edenvale, Kempton Park, Midrand, Olifantsfontein and Tembisa Township itself (interview, Mabulane). Much as the Tembisa casuals eschewed formal positions and titles, a number of leaders had emerged. Prominent among them was Marcus Makhura in Birchleigh, Moraba Choshi in Tembisa and Mkwabe Mabulane in Edenvale.

The population of Tembisa and the adjacent Ivory Park Township is almost entirely African. There is considerable ethnic diversity, however, with Sepedi, isiZulu, Xitsonga and isiXhosa widely spoken or, more accurately put, widely used in crafting the township's argot or Sekasi. Sepedi, also known as Northern Sotho, is, at least in official statistics, marginally ahead of other languages in Tembisa. Many of the casuals were Sepedi speakers. Typically, they had come to Gauteng from Limpopo Province, in the north of the country, after finishing school. Sometimes they came having completed matric and sometimes not. Always they came looking for work.

A migrant has much to prove. The typical South African migrant to Gauteng, usually male but increasingly also women, comes for work and does not intend to stay. Their intent is to return *mahae* (original home). The primary purpose of employment is to remit money back, ideally to build a house.[5] They may live transiently in Gauteng, but they nurture roots back home and prepare for retirement. So, getting by is not enough; there is a hunger to make good and there is pressure to start saving from the word go.

Many migrants, such as Choshi, had relatives already living in Gauteng, which made things easier. Others, like Mabulane, had few contacts. He and a 'homeboy', Patrick, had arrived from Limpopo in 1999. They had rented a shack and waited outside factories for piecework. If they were hired to unload lorries, they could expect R50 for the day. Then they would buy mealie meal to cook pap, along with cooking oil, onions, tomatoes and chicken feet for *seshebo* (relish). A few months after arriving, Mabulane got a job as a security guard, something he had stuck with for four years. When he heard that T&L Appointments (later TAS) was recruiting, he had applied and been called three days later. He took the job even though the money was no better; he was leaving the security industry's twelve-hour shifts. Yet, while he could survive on R2 000 or so a month, he was not sending anything back home. He was living a temporary existence in Gauteng, but had nothing to show for it in Limpopo. As the years passed, he was ceasing to exist.

Mabulane had been in contact with Makhura after blowing off steam with a postman delivering mail in Tembisa. The postman had given him Makhura's number. Makhura had told him about Sekoteng and he had started attending meetings. By June 2011, the Tembisa leaders no longer expected concessions from the labour brokers. They had sent a list of demands to TAS but, as expected, there was no response and the 30 or so casuals who met at Sekoteng on Saturday, 18 July resolved that they would strike from Monday. But when Monday came, they were only six.

There was a seventh, though not at Sekoteng. Choshi was on leave in Limpopo. He kept in contact with the strikers by phone. The strike could have easily collapsed. Perhaps without Choshi's exhortations from afar it would have. They rang the *maqabane* (comrades) who had promised to strike with a mixture of appeals and pleading. Gradually, numbers at Sekoteng increased. The strikers included Themba Sibiya from Birchleigh, a 'strong' comrade who provided backbone to the still-fragile strike. Their number increased to twenty, but they still had to close a single depot. That, they resolved, would be done on the morrow.

Mutual mobilisation

When they met the next morning, numbers were down again, this time to a dozen. They had to bring out a depot or the strike would fizzle. The casuals needed to learn how to protect an unprotected strike. Under labour law, those engaging in a protected strike can return to their jobs when the strike is over.[6] That does not apply to unprotected strikes.

But there is more than one way to skin a cat, and the casuals learned to protect their strikes by intimidating each other.

On the second day of the strike, the twelve strikers moved from Sekoteng into the Tembi Mall, a double strip of shops on either side of an open walkway, where the Tembisa Depot was located. They stood opposite the depot entrance, next to a busy betting shop. The bookies' customers made the group look larger than it was. Two of the strikers went into the depot and asked the supervisor if they could talk to the casuals. The supervisor noted the crowd outside and acceded to the request. The casuals were not surprised by the visit; they were expecting to be asked to join the strike. Those who caught the supervisor's eye as they filed out shrugged their shoulders indicating that they really had no choice but to go along with the request. Now almost 40 strong, the strikers rode the Metrorail north to the Olifantsfontein Depot, where they repeated the procedure. Olifantsfontein being the largest depot of the six meant that their numbers doubled. They rode the Metrorail back south, past Tembisa to Kempton Park. Inside the Kempton Park Depot, the casuals had slowed down on their sorting; they knew that strikers were on their way to collect them. When the combined forces of Tembisa and Olifantsfontein arrived, the crowd was singing and *toyi-toying*. The supervisor was given the courtesy of being approached first, but they were going through the motions. Given their numbers, the supervisor could do nothing but stand aside.

Thus, the casuals established a process of mutual mobilisation, one group intimidating the other. Those joining the strike could claim they had no choice but to join, fearful of what refusing might mean. There is, however, a limit to the depots that can be pulled out in a day by one group. Outside commuting times, the Metrorail trains run an infrequent timetable and some depots are nowhere near a station. So, on the first day, Kempton Park was their last depot. And, on the second day, numbers were down again. It was over a week before all 130 casuals in the Tembisa area were reporting to Sekoteng each morning. Some depots had to be revisited, sometimes more than once. Once casuals went back to work, another visit, with sufficient numbers, was required to bring them out again. They could not, after all, go back to work and subsequently claim to be intimidated if there was nobody *toyi-toying* outside. The zeal of the casuals who returned to their depot with the strike still on might be in question, but as we will see there were very few, even among the most determined strikers, who did not waver on occasion. Almost every striker was conflicted; a day on strike meant a day's lost pay. You were striking because you wanted more money, but the strike meant you were not going to be paid at all. You could be for the strike but still sneak back to work. You were trying to balance two unattractive alternatives: work for a wage that you could not live on, or take home nothing in attempting to get a wage you could live on. To succeed, intimidation must be more than an idle threat; it has to be real. That reality may be little more than a game, in which you are waiting for comrades to arrive outside your depot, giving you the excuse you need; it may be persuasive in tipping the balance of your calculations from work to strike, or it may be the only thing that gets you out because however much you want to work you are afraid of what will happen if you do.

So, defining intimidation as a stand-alone category, as is frequently done, may shore up righteous indignation, but it provides only limited analytical power. What must be understood, rather, is the diverse role that intimidation plays within conflict. Clearly, the fact that some of the six Tembisa depots had to be revisited before the strike was solid indicates that not all the strikers were straining at the leash and willing to risk their job to end labour broking. But then, viewed from another perspective, it was clear that not one casual was happy with their lot. As in any conflict, combatants' resolve is unevenly distributed and the need for intimidation had to fit all sizes. But what the one-size-fits-all intimidation of mutual mobilisation was able to achieve was a measure of protection for those who joined the strike. All could plausibly claim, irrespective of their actual feelings, that they had no choice but to strike and should not be subject to disciplinary action for participating.

Spreading the strike

With their hinterland secured, efforts to expand the strike beyond Tembisa began in earnest. The subsequent escalation of the strike across Gauteng was influenced by two key determinants: the layout of the Metrorail network and relationships between the casual workers committees.

The strike followed the tracks, the cheapest way to travel. Metrorail had a longstanding practice of allowing strikers to travel for free. In theory, a strike certificate from the Commission for Conciliation, Mediation and Arbitration (CCMA) should be produced to verify the bona fides of the group, but, in practice, unions often wrote their own letters. Once these acquired an official stamp, they would pass muster in most situations. Given the number of trains torched by angry commuters left stranded for one reason or another, Metrorail would rather avoid frustrating groups of strikers who wanted to travel (interviews, Choshi; Lepheane). In any case, at smaller stations, one security guard at the turnstile, armed only with a baton, was hardly going to insist on the correct documents, or indeed any documents, when a group of 20, 30 or perhaps 200 singing strikers arrived. They would open the gate to let the men pass.

As the strike spread, its centre of gravity also shifted, from Sekoteng to Germiston, the Metrorail hub for the East Rand. The Tembisa strikers still assembled each morning at Sekoteng before travelling to Germiston. That was necessary to maintain discipline; meeting at Germiston Station would make it easy to *lofa* (take the day off) or even slip back to their depot. At Germiston, they would meet with other strikers and head for wherever was next to be mobilised.

The East Rand was swept into the strike, as was the Vaal some 30 kilometres south-west of Germiston. But the West Rand largely held back. Rivalry was at play. Without internal support, the mobilisation efforts of East Rand strikers in Soweto and elsewhere on the West Rand had little impact. When strikers made the journey from east to west, they found depots deserted. And when they did mobilise casuals, they often only joined for the day.

Three years later, when I interviewed West Rand leaders, they explained how protocol had not been followed by the Tembisa strikers, who had launched the strike without consulting them first. They talked about how there had been unfortunate breakdowns in communication. And they talked about how they had come to the East Rand's assistance, even if it had been late in the day. The division between East and West would later be put to one side, though never entirely forgotten, as new configurations of loyalty and division arose. At the time, however, there was intense anger over the West Rand's failure to join the Tembisa strike.

With the East Rand out and the West Rand largely ignoring them, strikers travelled north to Pretoria, but attempts to spread the strike there were initially also unsuccessful. This was not because the Pretoria casuals were against striking. When they did finally rally to the East Rand's last stand at the Labour Court in late July, they did not return to work but continued striking for a further three weeks. When the Tembisa strikers first journeyed to Pretoria, the plan was to disembark at Bosmanstraat Station close to the city centre, make their way to depots and mobilise casuals. But it did not work that way. When they got to the station, there were police everywhere. In the end, there was a negotiation. The strikers told the police that they had come to deliver a memorandum to the Post Office and the police agreed that they could leave the station with a police escort, but they would need valid tickets for the return journey.

The memorandum to the Post Office was hastily handwritten and delivered to SAPO's Pretoria retail hub under police escort. Marcus Makhura read it out before handing it over to a management representative (interview, Choshi). Back at the station, it was every man for himself. They had to find, or borrow, R3.50, the minimum single fare. That got them onto the platform and out of Pretoria. Next time they went north, they were wiser and alighted at smaller stations, though they had no more success in mobilising casuals in Pretoria than they had in Soweto.

Notwithstanding its northern and western limits, the strike was more powerful than anything the casuals had previously embarked upon. Like the winds ahead of a storm, the strike swept away debris. It swept away doubt. It swept up sceptics. It swept aside caution. During the first week, while Tembisa was still being consolidated, CWU's stalwart Charles Kwata came to warn them that the strike was unprotected and they would lose their jobs. As one of the A-Team who had gone out of their way to help casuals, he was heard out. But the response was defiant: they did not care; they were willing to lose their jobs. The claim that they were willing to lose their jobs was bravado fuelled by confidence. They had every intention of keeping their jobs.

The point of the strike was to convert their casual status to that of permanent SAPO employee. They understood they could be dismissed, but it was to avoid that danger that they mutually mobilised. Riding the storm gave a sense of invincibility and heightened hope. What they were telling Kwata was that they were through with the union's way of doing things. They would emancipate themselves.

Striking for permanent: 2 July 2011

A week later, and back at Jerry's Place with *kota*, Coke and notebook, Maja's approach to the strike had changed. He, along with the other casuals in the Germiston Depot, had continued delivering mail, in clandestine fashion, till Wednesday. But, on Thursday morning strikers - '*ba bangata*' (lots of people) was the best estimate Maja could provide - had descended on the depot. What struck me most was how enthusiastic he now was about the strike. From one Saturday to the next, he had turned from scab to striker.

What now occupied Maja's thoughts was not losing pay or his job but the opportunity to secure a permanent post. He was intoxicated with the possibly. He was enthusiastic as to what the strikers would be doing. As well as hunting scabs, he talked about closing down the Germiston Hub. If they could do that then nobody on the East Rand would be able to work, not even the permanents who had up until then been left out of the dispute. He talked about the protest going national, though his knowledge as to how far it had spread was sketchy. But he was not unsure about the power that he now felt. The strikers had adopted the slogan, 'We are the union ourselves!' They were now in control of events. They were going to seize what they had been denied: permanent status.

A roll call was taken each morning by the two elected leaders for the twenty or so striking casuals in his depot. Internal discipline was important; Maja pointed out that some people could simply stay in bed while others did the hard work of the strike. He knew that it would be difficult at the end of the month if this went on for long, but he was sure that it would be over soon. They were going to win. It was not they, but management, that was intimidated now.

Labour Court I: Defiance

While the strike spread confidence among casuals, it sounded alarm bells in SAPO. There was a flurry of correspondence and a hastily arranged meeting between SAPO managers and labour brokers (Labour Court 2011a, 2011b, 2011d). SAPO was trying to use the courts to end the strike, but it was not straightforward. That this was a strike by casuals could not be ignored or denied. It was also obvious that CWU had no part in the strike, and could do nothing to rein it in. Without a union to interdict, SAPO had little purchase on the strikers.

Over the first two weeks of the strike, SAPO pressurised the labour brokers to fulfil their contractual obligation to provide labour. The labour brokers' response to SAPO was that this was not possible; employees who wanted to work were being intimidated by strikers. They pointed out that SAPO was to blame for this since depot supervisors were permitting strikers to enter depots and identify which employees were still at work. SAPO arranged for security at the depots, but that made no difference. As outlined in SAPO's founding affidavit submitted to the Labour Court on 1 July:

> To avoid being identified the striking employees are making threats at depots at which they are not stationed by their respective labour broker employers. The modus operandi of the [strikers] . . . is to arrive at undetermined times on various occasions during the course of the day and then proceed to storm the depot in a grouping of approximately 20–30 individuals at a time. Upon gaining entry into the depots, they intimidate working staff and cause damage to property. [SAPO's] security is unable to preclude the unauthorised access to the depots by the [strikers] as there is literally a mob rushing onto the premises. Generally there is one security official on guard who is unarmed. The gaining of entry into the premises and intimidation is a blitz on the depot which lasts in the region of up to 10 minutes. The strikers thereafter disappear . . . . (Labour Court 2011a: Sections 60–3).

The triangular employment relationship between labour broker, SAPO and workers had delivered cheap labour; now this complex arrangement was causing complications. SAPO's requests for relief from the court were largely a continuation of what it had been trying unsuccessfully to do during the first two weeks of the strike: instruct the labour brokers to instruct their employees to end the strike, obey SAPO's instruction and deliver the mail.

The first three respondents cited in the interdict were the largest brokers in the strike-affected areas: TAS, N.T. Ngidi, and Marula; the other respondents were strikers, totalling several hundred, who were identified in a range of lists drawn up by depot management and collected together as Appendix A of SAPO's submission to the Labour Court. The number of strikers and the lack of any identifiable leaders meant that they were effectively anonymous; it was unclear how any court order was going to be imposed.

A hearing date was set for 5 July, two weeks into the strike. Before the hearing, the only casual leader who had broken cover was Marcus Makhura when he spoke to the weekly local paper, *The Tembisan*, which ran a story on the strike in its 1 July edition (Nemutudi 2011: 5). However, the court case was to flush out the strike leadership. A day before the court hearing, Makhura and Desmond Moeketsi faxed a handwritten letter from the Labour Brokers Employees Committee to SAPO.[7] The fax stated that they wanted to meet with the Post Office regarding the hearing. Makhura and Moeketsi saw the case as an opportunity to put their grievances to senior SAPO managers. A contingent of strikers arrived at the court in Braamfontein, close to the Johannesburg city centre, the following day.

It was, however, not SAPO management but SAPO's lawyers who spoke to a group of six strike leaders during an impromptu meeting in the lobby of the office block that houses the Labour Court. Later accounts from strikers were adamant that the Post Office lawyer, Imraan Mahomed, had promised that management was willing to talk to them about their demands, and had tricked them into giving him their names for the purpose of negotiations. Although the strikers did not know, among the lawyers that they talked to was SAPO's senior manager of labour law, Nyiko Magayisa. His affidavit, filed at a subsequent court hearing, outlined how the six had identified themselves as members of the Labour Brokers Employees Committee and that Makhura had 'described himself as a "shop steward" and the person nominated by the individual respondents [Fourth to Further of Appendix A] . . . as to whom the Applicant could liaise with' (Labour Court 2011a: Para. 31).

This engagement provided the Post Office lawyers a handle on the strike. The six who had met with the lawyers in the lobby were quickly elevated from the list of strikers in Appendix A in Case J1208/11 to First to Sixth Respondents in the subsequent Case J1355/11. The remaining strikers were included in a new Appendix A, now as Seventh to Further Respondents. The three labour broking companies no doubt vacated their place as first three respondents with relief and were, for the time being, able to disappear from the legal stage. The six strike leaders, in the order in which they appeared as respondents, were: Marcus Makhura, Mzwandile Mdlungu, Johannes Manamela, Desmond Moeketsi, Petrus Morenamela and Mkwabe Mabulane.[8]

According to Magayisa's affidavit, the six had talked defiantly in the foyer about the court process, and Makhura had even gone into the building and introduced himself to Judge Steenkamp, who would hear the case (Labour Court 2011b: Founding Affidavit, Para. 32). However, as the number of police outside the court building increased, the casual workers took fright. They scarpered before the matter was heard.

Judge Steenkamp ordered that the strikers must comply with their contractual obligations owed to the labour brokers – that is, work. The strikers were further interdicted from interfering with SAPO's business, intimidating non-striking employees, or damaging property. Unless coming to work, they were prohibited from approaching within 100 metres of any SAPO premises. The ruling was to have immediate effect (Labour Court 2011a: Order of the Court).

Golden Walk car park: Ke bo mang? (Who are they?)

The Golden Walk shopping mall is a vast, sprawling single-storey building in the centre of Germiston. On the north side, its entrances merge into the hustle and bustle of market stalls that line the streets between the mall and the busy railway station. When residents of Katlehong Township say they are going to shop in town they mean they are going to Golden Walk mall and the surrounding street markets.

Other than white or Indian shop owners, everybody in the mall and in the surrounding streets is African. Since most shoppers travel by Metrorail or taxi, the vast car parks on the south and east of the mall are only partially used. They are de facto public spaces. Taxi drivers park to wash their vehicles, lorry drivers use it as a rest area, and in between any space can be used for a meeting by those who need a free venue. Beyond the car park, across the road that runs along the south of the mall's unfenced parking area, is SAPO's Germiston Retail Centre or Hub.

Some of the strikers had handmade posters. Written on a piece of torn card was one particularly raw message: 'AIDS is better than Labour Broker.' This was my first time at a SAPO casuals' meeting. What I knew about the strike was what Maja had told me over *kota* and Coke on Saturday afternoons. This serialised narrative was far from complete. I did not know that the meeting I was joining was to give feedback from the Labour Court case that had taken place that morning. I did not even know there was a Labour Court case. Neither did Maja. He knew there was a meeting and, knowing I was interested, had let me know.

Working from below can approximate some of the uncertainty and imprecision within which social actors work. The sociologist Max Weber outlined the research method of *verstehen* (understanding), the need to understand the position of others and so to grasp why they act as they do. Seeking to know the rationality of others' actions is critical, not only in affording them dignity, but affording us a true understanding. However, there is a danger that in grasping the reasons for people's actions we forget that rarely are there moments when the line of march is clear, when the options are unambiguous, when the obstacles ahead are in plain sight, or when it is clear who stands where and with whom. *Verstehen* must also mean understanding what is not known. To see things darkly, partially obscured and changing; as they are often experienced by rank-and-file actors, such as the foot soldiers of a wildcat strike.

When feedback from the Labour Court was given to the circle of men standing four or five deep on an empty stretch of tarmac, we were told that the case that morning was following up on the unimplemented 2005 agreement between SAPO and CWU: the agreement that was supposed to have ended labour broking. But, it was explained, when they got to court they had found five Post Office lawyers lined up against them. Five! All of them had gowns. The point about the gowns was emphasised to the faces that craned forward in the circle of workers that was knitted tight in order to hear the speaker above the background chatter and shouts of other car park users. The line-up was: SAPO five gowns, strikers none. At the time, this made sense to me. Or at least I was able to make it make sense: the casuals had gone to court to enforce their rights, rights that had been agreed to back in 2005, but they had been out-lawyered by the Post Office. They were frustrated.

Then there was indignation. The labour brokers had not been there! It was asked, rhetorically, *Ke bo mang?* Who, the short question asked, were their employers? The labour brokers or the Post Office? They were always being told that it was the labour brokers and not the Post Office that employed them. But when they get to court, it was the Post Office gowns that they had to deal with. Again, at the time, it made sense to me, more or less. I did not know much about the Labour Court. I knew then almost nothing about the 2005 agreement. But I did know that the brokers and the Post Office were hiding behind each other.

Much later, and with access to the Labour Court papers, my notes on the meeting made less sense than they had at the time. Now, I saw that two of the strike leaders had requested to meet the Post Office at the Labour Court. The Post Office pitched (even if fronted by its lawyers), but the message given to the strikers at Golden Walk was an indignant one over the labour brokers not turning up.[9] Strike leaders had reported that they were in the wrong court, but they were not. What they were wrong about was who was taking who to the court. It was not their gig; it was the Post Office's. The casuals were on an unprotected strike and SAPO was taking legal action against them. The strike leaders knew that they were being exploited by the labour brokers who hid behind the Post Office, which would hide behind the labour brokers. But in the foyer of the court building, their anger and righteousness over the ducking and diving of those who employed them was blunted by fear. They could feel that they were losing ground to the gowns even before the case commenced. They had bottled out, but in reporting back to the meeting had hidden their humiliation.

By early afternoon, events of a few hours earlier had been reconfigured for consumption by a crowd of angry strikers. Yet, what was not said, or was mis-said, was merely detail. The larger narrative, of the casuals' exploitation, carried those reporting over any doubts there might have been about accuracy. An accurate report on the morning's embarrassing events would, in all likelihood, have been less comprehensible to the strikers than the version provided, which had the merit of meshing with an already well-understood narrative.

What the morning's events did make clear was that strikers were on their own. There was nothing for them at the courts. Even I, on my first encounter with the strikers as a group, could sense this was a turning point. Or, put another way, it was an event that shifted the balance of power towards hardliners within the strike leadership. They needed, it was explained, to use *matla* (strength) not *molao* (law).

After the report-back, there were questions for the three or four leaders who stood together as part of the tight circle of men. The chairperson of the meeting carefully explained procedure and when, at one point, there was a breakdown in protocol he berated his colleagues, telling them that a strike was about '*hlompo le* respect'.[10] Once there was a clear narrative, and we were at the point of *matla* not *molao*, the leadership conferred aside while the rank and file met depot by depot. There were small groups of men standing together, the leadership far enough away for their deliberations not to be overheard.

The reconvened meeting needed only to clarify the general direction for the following day's programme. It had already been settled that it was a matter of *matla*. What was emphasised by the leadership was that they had no other option. An SMS received by one of the strikers from their supervisor was read out. In bad English, it told the recipient not to bother coming back to work as he was already fired. They had nothing to lose now. The target the next day was the *magundwane* (scabs) who were still working, but details were kept to a minimum. Aside, I was told that it would be a matter of *thupa feela* (literally, 'stick only' – that is, violence). The strikers would assemble at Germiston Station at 8 a.m. There were to be no Post Office bibs or other items of SAPO uniform worn.

The shoes of desire

With the meeting finishing close to 3 p.m., Maja, Sibusiso, Tsu and myself walked through the mall to the KFC outlet for a late, finger-lickin lunch. Weaving through the shoppers, we passed a men's shoe shop. It was, by Golden Walk standards, smart and its brightly lit window display was filled with branded shoes: Arno, Lacoste, Kurt Geiger, Woodcutter and more. The stuff you wear in the *kasi* to show you are something. Shoes that would eat a casual worker's monthly pay twice over.

One of the three, maybe it was Tsu, started a joke by shielding his eyes from these unaffordable articles of desire. The others joined in, passing the shop with exaggerated ways of avoiding sight of the display. Once past the shop and the joke, we concurred that when the strike was won they would no longer have to walk past the display. No! They would be able to enter the shop to purchase the pair that had caught their eye!

Ho tsoma

It did not take long for the *ho tsoma* (hunting) tactic to become established. It meant transitioning from delivering letters to hunting strike-breakers. Typically, strikers left Germiston Station in groups of twenty. Alighting at selected stations, they would fan out in groups of three or four to comb the streets. If a police car passed, they would continue walking without hesitation, making a point of talking loudly to each other, just as friends always did, and the police would pass uninterested. As they honed new skills, strikers started to take pride in the hunt. Initially, they lacked coordination and scabs got away: fear and adrenalin assisting them to outrun their pursuers. The hunters adapted, learning to trap the *gundwane* before he knew he had been spotted.

The three men had seen the *gundwane* as they turned into the township street. He had just put his bike with its large, front-mounted, plastic basket up against a low front wall so that he could reach the mail box that was set slightly back in the front yard of the single-storey house. The three hurriedly backtracked, and when the postman returned to his bike and scanned the street there was nothing to concern him. But phone calls were being made. Standing off from the hunt, a striker who knew the walks of the township explained the direction the postman would be taking. Other groups hurried to cut off his path.

By the time he realised he was being hunted, it was too late. Both ends of the street were blocked and the hunters were closing in on him. He was pulled from his bike as he attempted to ride his way out of the encircling men. Once back on his feet and surrounded by strikers punching the air in triumph, he had to explain himself. Now that the strikers had him up close, they recognised him – a casual worker who they had seen at meetings, pretending to strike while working.

Cornered and fearful, he tried to convince them that he had not really been working. He had only left the depot because he had had no choice. His supervisor had told him that he had to either deliver or be dismissed. So, he would come out to deliver just 'one, two, three, four *feela*' (only). Desperate to convince his captors, he mimicked throwing four letters into imaginary letter boxes fanned out in front of him. But the strikers did not buy Four Feela's story. One group, hurrying to close the trap, had pulled switches from the branches of a tree. The question as to why he was still working was now reinforced. Four Feela jumped and twisted trying to avoid the strokes. Later, the strikers would joke that they had taught him to play guitar.

Much as they were now in control of Four Feela's fate, the group was unsure what should happen next. The hunt had been successful, but they had no plan as to what to do with their prey. Many suggestions had been made over the previous weeks as to what they would do when they had a scab in their hands, but it had been talk about what they would *like* to do. They had not actually decided what they would do. There were different opinions. What they did agree on was that they should not hang around in the street. The remaining letters were thrown across the road. They left the bike on a piece of wasteland, its plastic basket set alight and its tyres disembowelled of their inner tubes. That left them with the scab. They took him along to the Metrorail. He was too scared to shout out that he was not voluntarily with the group that walked unchallenged onto the platform.

On the train, heading back to Germiston, there was a discussion about throwing Four Feela out of the carriage. In the end they did not, but they took pleasure in debating the option in his presence. They let him go at Wadeville Station and laughed at how he sent stones flying up behind him as he bolted down the railway track to get away.

Labour Court II: The order to restore order

On 20 July, the strikers were back at the Labour Court. Two weeks earlier, they had done a runner and turned instead to hunting scabs. But the Post Office had also been hunting, tracking down the six names given to the SAPO lawyer on 5 July. A few days after the lobby talk, the sheriff served the six strikers with the legal papers for the second interdict application (Labour Court 2011b).

The bravado of the six strikers in the Labour Court lobby was now used against them. SAPO's senior manager of labour law, Nyiko Magayisa, outlined in the papers that one of the six had stated that the court's order was 'a piece of paper' and that they 'didn't care if the strike was lawful or not' (Labour Court 2011b: Sections 36 and 37). The striking workers were now to be nailed with their own gibes.

It was not hard for Magayisa to argue that Judge Steenkamp's order was being defied. Court papers listed evidence of further disruption to mail deliveries, stormed depots, assaulted postmen and two damaged vehicles in Tembisa. Magayisa noted that although the court had issued an order, that had not restored order. Any repeat would, he argued, simply perpetuate 'the present status quo of flagrant disregard of the orders of this Honourable Court' (Labour Court 2011b: Section 26). SAPO asked that the respondents be declared in contempt of court, sentenced to 30 days' imprisonment and required to pay costs.

SAPO wanted this applied to all strikers listed as respondents to the case, though clearly the six named respondents were first in line. On the second court date, 20 July, there were police everywhere. The six, now leadership in the eyes of the court whether they liked it or not, were arguing among themselves. Support wilted. Afterwards, there was recrimination because some strikers had refused to go back into the courtroom after a recess, afraid that they would be arrested there and then.

Indeed, Judge Basson, who was on the bench that day, made it clear that imprisonment was on the cards. When Makhura went into the witness box and attempted to outline the strikers' grievances he was given short shrift. Judge Basson told him that he was doing him a favour by letting him stand in front of him at all. He should already be in jail for failing to attend the first hearing (interviews, Mabulane; Makhura). The accused were dispatched to the court's pro bono office for legal advice. At the pro bono office, they were told 'what they didn't want to hear': that they needed to end the strike and return to work. The pro bono lawyer said he would take their case, but only on condition that they agreed to what the judge told them (interview, Makhura). Back in the courtroom, Judge Basson found them in contempt of Judge Steenkamp's order. They were told to appear a week later to explain why they should not be arrested or imprisoned for 30 days, and ordered to pay costs.

The six were now caught between the strikers on the streets and the judges on the bench. Their defiance melted in the face of a jail sentence, the threat of costs of a magnitude they could not even begin to think about paying, and the inevitable unemployment that would follow jail (interview, Moeketsi). Before their appearance on 27 July, all six made affidavits at local police stations stating, quite improbably, that they had not known that they were supposed to appear in court on 5 July. They also scrambled to get legal representation. They ended up with two representatives: Booysen Mashego, a CWU lawyer, and Mametlwe Sebei, from the Democratic Socialist Movement (DSM). Getting them on board involved eating humble pie.

Those who had been working with the DSM were going back for help after they had abruptly abandoned the DSM's attempts to build a Gauteng-wide structure for the wildcat strike that was initiated by the Tembisa Committee. Despite frustration over the strikers' failure to focus on the DSM's strategy for building working-class power, they were forgiven. Sebei was dispatched by Weizmann Hamilton to see what could be done now. He ended up doing much of the, ultimately unsuccessful, work that the final court-sanctioned agreement required, but it was the CWU lawyer who held the key to keeping the strikers out of jail. CWU was the only recognised union in the Post Office. In the eyes of the court, it was the only organisation that could guarantee to channel the dispute from the streets and into the company's industrial relations framework (interviews, Sebei; Mutavhatsindi). Tutu Mokoena, who was then working for the still unrecognised South African Postal and Allied Workers Union (SAPAWU), told the strikers as much when they had come knocking hopefully on his door. He said he would be willing to represent them, but if he did they would end up in jail (interviews, Choshi; Mabulane). They needed CWU to speak for them.

That was not straightforward. The core of the strikers were from the Tembisa Committee, which had long rejected CWU's legitimacy, a position restated only weeks earlier when Kwata's warning over embarking on an unprotected strike had been dismissed. The committee with the best relationship to CWU was the West Rand Committee, the Soweto 'clever boys' with whom the Tembisa Committee had, at best, a cool relationship. During the strike that relationship had cooled further. The failure of all but a few depots on the West Rand to join the strike had been put down to the influence of key West Rand leaders who were deliberately holding casuals back from striking. In particular, Russel Mutavhatsindi was identified by the strikers and there were plans to remove what they saw as the main stumbling block to spreading the strike westwards.[11] Now they needed Mutavhatsindi's help; he and other West Rand leaders were their best chance of getting CWU's assistance. Given events of recent weeks, it would be unlikely that CWU would even unlock their doors should the strikers arrive at their Johannesburg offices. However, Mutavhatsindi and Thabiso Bopape agreed to assist. The former brokered the deal using his connection with a CWU national office-bearer, and Mashego represented the strikers on 27 July for their third court appearance.

Labour Court III: Unity in defeat

When reporting to the rank-and-file strikers, the bleak legal prospects were played down by the leadership, who still hoped to save something from the strike as well as save themselves from jail. Indeed, many rank-and-file strikers were under the impression that the legal process was going their way.

Over *kota* and Coke three days after the strikers' 20 July court appearance, I was told that their return to the Labour Court the next week was a sign that they were close to victory. Maja put the strikers' progress down to two Post Office vans being *tubilwe ke majwe* (trashed with stones) in Tembisa. The escalation that such destruction represented had got the matter back into court. He was confident that there would be a settlement: he would soon be a permanent employee. But before they returned to court in four days' time, the instruction was that nobody was to touch the scabs. The hunting was being reined in. They wanted to make a good impression on the judge. Maja concurred with this order: their efforts on the streets, especially that of the Tembisa *maqabane*, had brought their plight into the open. It would now be resolved. He was more than willing to believe the argument: they had already as good as won.

Others were mobilised to demonstrate outside the court, similarly unaware what exactly the court case now revolved around. In addition to the mangled explanations and spinning of the situation, there was a conflation of SAPO's case with the Vaal Workers Committee's application to the Labour Court (see Chapter 8). In the end, there was a strong turnout with supporters arriving outside the Labour Court from all quarters of Gauteng. The West Rand Committee now joined the strike, if only for the day, while hundreds of Pretoria casuals rode the Metrorail to Johannesburg's Park Station, from where they marched into Braamfontein.

Much as the final Labour Court appearance brought all the Gauteng casuals together, it also illustrated just how divided they were. The momentum of the wildcat strike had temporarily obscured some, though not all, of the divisions between the Gauteng workers committees. Outside the court, their differences were again on display. The Tembisa Committee marched, as always, under its own, non-aligned colours. The Far East Rand was back, at least for the moment, under the banner of the Commercial, Services and Allied Workers Union (COSAWU). The Vaal Committee was flying its National Communications and Allied Workers Union flag; it still hoped that the union would be recognised by the Department of Labour. The West Rand was still double-footing between CWU and its own committee, but for the day, with the union's lawyer prominent in proceedings, stood with the standard of CWU. The Pretoria Committee's strike was out of sync with that of the other committees; the day they came to the Labour Court was the first day of their own strike, one that would continue for some three weeks.

Inside the courtroom, the humiliation that securing legal representation had entailed was intensified. The strategy of Mashego, the CWU lawyer, was to portray the strikers as uneducated, unable even to read. In getting them off the contempt of court charges, he argued that they did not understand the law. Now that it had been explained to them what they had done wrong, they were sorry and were asking for forgiveness. It was a nadir: the strikers were being presented as objects of pity – not for the precariousness of their employment, but because of their ignorance. Order was re-established. The strikers' representatives were speaking for them; they were no longer speaking for themselves.

Judge Francis was the third to deal with the casuals' strike. His order issued on 27 July sentenced the respondents to 30 days' imprisonment, suspended for six months. The strikers were ordered to return to work the following day. The six named strikers, CWU and COSAWU were charged with effecting the return to work of all strikers listed in the court papers and also the Pretoria strikers who had arrived that day. Any breach of the order was to be referred back to the court on an urgent basis (Labour Court 2011d). No cost order was made. Any such order would have been pointless given the strikers' limited means. As Levy Zwane (interview), a Vaal Committee member, explained, it was 'checkmate'. The strikers were out of options. Only the Pretoria casuals were to continue, though with no more success. The strike was over: crushed without concession.

A bitter postscript
SAPO had brought the strike to court, seeking first to compel the labour brokers to fulfil their contractual obligations, then to interdict the strikers and finally to have the strike leaders imprisoned for contempt of court. What was not brought before the court was SAPO's two-tier labour market. The Vaal Committee's legal bid, described in Chapter 8, had attempted that, but the casuals had lacked the resources to get their case taken seriously, justice being an expensive and difficult business.

Yet, alongside the order, there was an understanding, taken up to very different degrees by those in the court, that there needed to be a resolution to the problem, or at least that they should leave the court heading in the right direction. Although Judge Francis' order only instructed CWU and COSAWU to ensure the return to work, at least some in the court understood that they were being instructed to deal with the problems that underlay the strike (interviews, Moeketsi; Makhura; Sebei).

The CWU lawyer paid lip service to this. Outside the court, he told the assembled strikers that they had won a victory. The court order that they had been up against was not *pap 'n vleis* (that is, an easy thing; literally, porridge and meat); the police could have arrested everyone (interview, Mabulane). But things had been worked out. They were not going to jail; they could now go back to work! (interview, Montoedi). They should return to their depots and their grievances would be addressed. That was the last that the casuals saw of Mashego. COSAWU, on the other hand, took the injunction seriously. Sebei had argued in court that there could be a resolution to the dispute without the strikers being jailed. Once the strike was over, he attempted to open negotiations with SAPO on behalf of the Labour Broker Workers Committee (LBWC), which briefly spluttered back into life. SAPO, however, was not drawn into negotiations. It had got what it wanted from the Labour Court – an end to the strike.

Sebei made more headway with one of the labour brokers, Marula Staffing. Marula had made an open offer, addressed to all SAPO casuals, on 25 July. It was a bid by the company to increase its footprint in SAPO, and the company needed a negotiating partner (see Chapter 12). Meetings took place between Marula and COSAWU. What was being suggested was that Marula would give COSAWU organisational rights and a negotiated pay increase for casuals. The quid pro quo was that COSAWU would bring workers employed by other labour brokers onto Marula's books. In the end, these talks came to nothing. Sebei was wary, on the one hand, of being used by Marula and, on the other, of being seen to be working hand-in-glove with a labour broker, even if one of the more progressive when it came to labour relations. Whether deliberate or not, the response that COSAWU/LBWC gave to Marula's open offer made any agreement all but impossible. All casuals were to be made permanent employees of SAPO, which would have left Marula without business. And if that was not enough to put an end to the prospects of agreement, Marula's offer of a 5 per cent wage increase was countered with a demand of more than 300 per cent: from R14.55 to R45 an hour (COSAWU/LBWC 2011).[12] These demands were eventually to be realised, but not until COSAWU had long departed from the field of battle.

Finally, there was Marcus Makhura, a casual at the Birchleigh Depot in the Tembisa area who was employed by TAS. He had worked alongside Kodisang Bokaba in the 2009 attempt to unionise casuals under the South African Gaming, Waitron and Admin Workers Trade Union. He had been at the centre of the Tembisa strike, and he had seen the Labour Court as an organisation that could resolve their grievances, but had ended as the first respondent on SAPO's interdict. Makhura worked alongside Sebei in the aftermath of the strike. Frustrated by what he felt was SAPO's unwillingness to address the cause of the strike, he and two other strike leaders from the Birchleigh Depot, Johannes Manamela and Petrus Morenamela, had written to the company's regional manager, pointing out that nothing had been resolved. As described in Chapter 8, he was accused, inter alia, of requesting to meet Mpai without TAS's authorisation and failing to follow the proper grievance procedure. The three were found guilty and dismissed on 21 September 2011 (CCMA 2011).

When I interviewed Makhura in late 2015 he had a temporary job working nights at a factory in Clayville, north of Tembisa. He was proud of his role in the SAPO casual workers' struggle, but he felt cheated. He had worked as a casual for ten years and had shouldered the struggle, but he never reaped the benefits of permanent employment as others did.[13] As he bitterly described it, 'We won, but I lost.'

12

The Long Tactics of Labour Broking

Part I: Introduction
A giant slow to fall
This book narrates the agency of casual workers in the South African Post Office (SAPO). How David took on Goliath. How the underdog felled a far more powerful adversary. In the biblical story David slew the giant with a single slingshot; it was over almost before it began.[1] Not so the casuals' struggle. The labour broking system in SAPO lasted for over a decade. If mid-2005 is taken as the start of resistance, then the casuals' struggle lasted close to seven years before the giant buckled and fell.

Just as casuals struggled against their contractual bondage, so too were there struggles to maintain it.[2] This chapter explores how broking, as a labour regime,[3] was upheld using psychological, organisational and legal tactics to maintain the precarity of casuals' labour.[4] Labour brokers did not act alone in this endeavour but were allied, in different ways, and at different times, and for different reasons by confederates: Post Office management, supervisors and even at times office-bearers, officials and shop stewards of the Communication Workers Union (CWU). There were also the paid allies of this confederacy, attorneys and advocates hired to wage lawfare.

Just as there was never a conscious strategy to introduce labour broking into SAPO, so there was never a plan for maintaining it. Over time, a span of tactics emerged. Defences of the system emerged in response to the challenges of maintaining the labour broking regime. Some of the earlier defences were likely not considered tactics at all, but just the way the labour broking business was run. But as the tempo of struggle quickened so also did cognisance of what both sides were engaging in: a battle to end labour broking on the one side, a fight to maintain it on the other. Just as the casuals built a repertoire of tactics, so too did the confederacy.

Unemployment and precarious work

South Africa's staggeringly high unemployment levels have been an essential support for the system of labour broking. The country's Constitution and labour legislation blunted the power of employers with the guarantee of workers' individual and collective rights, creating a level working field. But labour broking created a new stratum of workers chained by class insecurity. Unemployment provides a power resource to employers who are able to say, 'Take what's on offer or someone else will!' And both sides know this is no idle threat.

Labour broking may have arisen in response to the levelling of the working field, but its success has depended on inadequate economic growth, increasing capitalisation of production, structural imbalances in the skill profile of the workforce, and limited investment, alongside other constraints on employment creation. Within this economic stagnation and permanent, generalised joblessness the labour broking system could flourish.

The confederacy

The casual employees in SAPO were employed by multiple brokers, who competed for business with SAPO. But since SAPO specified what labour brokers could bill for casuals and how much of that would be paid to casuals, as described in Chapter 4, competition boiled down to the management of labour. All of the labour brokers were on the front line when it came to keeping order among SAPO's casual workforce. There were, however, differences in how this was done.

The management of Marula Staffing, a front company for the Kelly Group, generally followed legal procedures when it came to disciplinary cases, and some of its area managers would stick up for their placements in the event of a dispute. At the company level, Marula entered into negotiations several times over union recognition. Little came of these talks and the union negotiators came away with the impression that the company's interest was based on an expected quid pro quo. As a union partner, they would be expected to promote Marula as a preferred employer among the SAPO casuals (interviews, Bokaba; Lepheane; Sebei).

Machiavellian as this might be, it was benign in comparison to the attitude of TAS Appointments and Management Services (TAS), run by the black entrepreneur Colleen Ramaphakela. Its approach was openly hostile to unions and it bent over backwards to please clients. TAS dealt swiftly and decisively with unprotected industrial action. In a 2012 letter to SAPO's lawyers regarding TAS's responses to the Mabarete strike (see Chapters 13 to 15), Ramaphakela explained: 'TAS Appointments & Management Services has [a] code of conduct which is binding to all its employees and has been consistently applied when dealing with discipline. Our disciplinary processes have on numerous instances led to the dismissal of casual employees found guilty of participating in unprotected strikes' (2012: 75).

The development of methods to control the casual workforce involved innovation, but not the beneficial innovation envisaged by the architects of South Africa's post-apartheid society. Rather than develop human potential in support of high-skilled, high-productivity growth, the growth of precarious employment, labour broking included, is about squeezing a segment of the working class beyond anything that the country's labour laws permit. Within this arena of competition, Marula's relatively progressive human resource (HR) approach was at a disadvantage to that of TAS in the Post Office.

The commercial contract to supply casuals is between two companies: client and broker. But in the system of labour broking, the executives who sign the contracts are not those who manage labour on the shop floor. The client's line managers do the supervision while the brokers' staff step in to deal with disputes, initiate disciplinary action and, if necessary, replace fired workers with fresh hands. This division of supervision and discipline, and the axis developed between the client's supervisors and the broker's representatives, is a critical factor in making labour broking work on the ground.

It was a confederacy of agents, with the supervisor-representatives dyad at is core, which implemented the rolling tactics that maintained labour broking for so long in SAPO. It did this within the workplace and, when this failed, in the courts.

Part II: Order in the workplace
Workplace order begins in the mind

Neither law nor fear provided the first lines of defence for the labour broking system. As Steve Biko ([1978] 1996: 68) understood, it is through psychological manipulation that domination is best maintained: 'The most potent weapon in the hands of the oppressor is the mind of the oppressed.' Initially, tactics to maintain order among casuals needed only the lightest touch. Newly employed casuals knew that countless others were desperate for the opportunity to work, and that a job, any job, was an opportunity to be grasped with both hands. Tovey Montoedi (interview), a postman at the Vereeniging Depot in the Vaal, whose experiences were outlined in Chapter 9, had grabbed his ID book and rushed out of the house when he had been rung with the offer of full-time work by the labour broker.

However, once employed, casual workers started to realise that, much as they might have secured a job, it was not what they needed. True, sometimes their expectations were naive. Themba Sibiya (interview), a postman in Tembisa, laughingly recalled how he had arrived for a job interview at the Bramley Depot in a shirt and tie. After completing matric, Sibiya had enrolled for a diploma course in Human Resource Management at Damelin College in 2007. But there was a crisis at home, his father could not pay the college fees and he never graduated. Instead, his father asked a cousin, employed in SAPO, to help his son get work. Called to an interview, Sibiya thought he was going to be working behind a counter, perhaps even at a desk. So, he was puzzled when he got to the depot and was asked if he knew how to ride a bicycle. But he soon learned the job and was completing his walk in record time.

But enthusiasm for the job rarely endured past the end of the first month. Employed casuals soon knew their walks as well as the permanents and could get around them just as fast. But they were not able to take pride in their work. The pay cheque they received at the end of the month stripped them of dignity.

Promoting hope

Promoting hope was a tactic that slowed the development of a collective understanding or consciousness of their situation among casuals. The prospect that casuals might be converted into permanents was one that was tantalisingly kept alive. Occasionally, casuals did land permanent positions, though this became increasingly rare as the labour broking system developed. The hope manipulated around these isolated instances was an important way of staving off dissatisfaction. Everybody wanted to be permanent; there would be no shame at the end of the month. By and large, recruited casuals knew they were being employed by a labour broker and not SAPO, but they still hoped that they would be made permanent. The possibility of a permanent position was a powerful incentive to stay put. It was also a powerful incentive not to complain too much.

The promises of permanence were augmented by smaller pledges, pledges that gave hope for something in the immediate future. TAS's representative for the Vaal talked to Montoedi (interview) and other casuals about computer training, but, like other promises, it came to nothing.

Montoedi's co-worker at Vanderbijlpark, Sam Khanye (interview), had been initially recruited by SAPO in 1998 as an S32 – SAPO's terminology for a temporary, but directly employed, worker. S32s were paid at the same rate as a permanent worker. In fact, when it came to cash in hand, they came out with more than a permanent doing the same work as there were no deductions. One afternoon, the S32s were informed by SAPO's area manager that they were being transferred to Interim, a labour broker. Payment would now be calculated by the volume of mail delivered. At the end of the month, they found out that they were taking home between R200 and R400 less than they had as S32s. The transfer did, however, have its upside; the transfer had come with the reassurance that 'one day' they would be converted to permanent status.[5] Hanging onto that hope, Khanye decided to stay in the job.

It was stressed that the old S32s, including Khanye, would be top of the list when conversion came. They were issued with SAPO bibs. This was not the uniform issued to permanent workers, but the SAPO-branded item made Sam feel that conversion was closer. In 2005, Interim got into difficulties, and Khanye and other casuals were not paid. Eventually, they were transferred to TAS. More promises were made, which also did not materialise.

Paternalism and patronage

Labour brokers believed they were doing casuals a favour by employing them. Colleen Ramaphakela, TAS's owner, started off with a paternalistic approach. There were gifts at Christmas. As described in Chapter 6, in 2002 she had personally driven around the depots to drop off hampers for each TAS employee. These gifts were supposed to affirm harmonious employee relations, but their paucity meant they backfired. Rather than cement bonds between employer and employee, they provided illustrations of the casuals' plight that were frequently dredged up in interviews.

Ramaphakela's annual nod to paternalism had limited impact in containing resistance and, given its parsimoniousness, fuelled resentment. More significant than this paternalism between labour broker and casuals were the networks of patronage within depots, established through recruitment and retention. Typically, depot supervisors and controllers were at the centre of these informal networks. Though area managers might determine which labour broker was to provide casual workers, it was depot-level management who recruited. Providing employment was doing somebody a favour, even if that favour turned out to be threadbare and needed buttressing with the hope of better to come. Providing work to a relative, friend or neighbour brought social ties into the workplace. A supervisor might have half a dozen casuals in the depot who owed him their jobs: *matsoho a hlatswana* (hands wash each other).

Once the labour broking system was entrenched, recruited casuals had minimal contact with their legal employer. It was their managers, SAPO supervisors, who called the shots on the ground. The labour brokers would be contacted only if things got out of hand. Most supervisors just wanted to keep things sweet in the workplaces that they managed. Depot supervisors rallied the flagging hopes of casuals over the prospects of conversion. They also played on casuals' fears of what would happen if they protested.

Other than those cases where supervisors proactively supported the casuals' cause, protests were led by those outside of the supervisor's immediate network of influence. In the optimism of the Tembisa wildcat strike, casuals in many depots were swept up wholesale, irrespective of whether they were in or out of supervisors' networks. When the strike collapsed, the supervisors' power was boosted, their previous advice over the folly of striking seemingly verified. When casuals in the depots split, as was the case in the later Mabarete strike, those who remained at work would always include the casuals in supervisors' nepotistic networks.

Pillar to post

Once casuals gave up on promises of conversion and began to organise, the problem was who they were to engage with. In legal terminology this later came to be known as the 'deeming' issue. Who is deemed to be a casual's employer is important since it determines responsibility for workers' terms and conditions of employment and, therefore, against whom demands must be made. Additionally, it becomes important in the event of dismissal. If the dismissal is unfair, who is to be taken to the Commission for Conciliation, Mediation and Arbitration (CCMA)? If you get this wrong, any legal process will fail on procedural points. Legal responsibility also depends on the piece of legislation cited. But that aside, the pillar-to-post tactic, in which labour brokers and SAPO bounced responsibility for employment between each other, was effective in dissipating casuals' attempts to challenge their situation.

On occasion, there were genuine disputes between SAPO and brokers when responding to casuals' demands – for example, who was responsible for providing them with uniforms? But a lack of clarity could also be usefully deployed to frustrate attempts by workers to organise. It started with pointing out that casuals were talking to the wrong person, something that often deflated challenges. The possibility of improvement was tossed from SAPO to labour broker, labour broker to SAPO. The casuals ran between the two, hoping to snatch the dream being tossed over their heads.

In the Vaal, Tovey Montoedi (interview) started attending meetings of the workers committee initiated by Papiki Mokoena and Bazil

Hlekiso. Many of the meetings were taken up with people complaining to each other, but eventually they had resolved to confront the SAPO area manager. The demand to be made permanent employees had still not emerged at the casuals' goal. Rather, their complaints were over the different terms and conditions of employment: pay, leave, uniform, work allocation and more. A delegation met with the manager, and Tovey was among them. They outlined their grievances. Tovey recalled that it must have taken them at least 45 minutes for them to say their piece. The manager had listened to what they had to say and had taken notes. Tovey started to think that something might come of the meeting. But when they had finished the manager told them that they were not employed by the Post Office. They were employed by TAS. They must talk to TAS. There was nothing he could do.

Telling not talking

While the less determined could be frustrated by the confusion generated over who was responsible for their situation, the pillar-to-post tactic could only work for so long. To the extent that negotiations could be stalled they were, but as casuals started to dig in their heels talks became hard to parry. But getting to talks did not mean resolving the casuals' problems; talks were another opportunity for delaying tactics.

With talks conceded, a new tactic was to steer away from engagement and rather make a take-it-or-leave-it offer. The Vaal casuals eventually secured a meeting with TAS management and repeated what they had told the SAPO manager. The TAS manager said he would get back to them. And he did. His arrival was preceded by a memo; TAS employees were to receive a pay increase. This was in early 2008. When the meeting started, everybody was expectant. The TAS manager built up to the moment, explaining to the assembled TAS employees that the Post Office was not increasing what it paid TAS, but TAS had heard the workers. The increase was being taken from their own pockets! 'Yes', the workers said, they were grateful that TAS was looking after them, 'But, please tell us, how much is the increase?' The punchline was a blow to the generated expectations: ten cents an hour. The meeting didn't end well (interview, Montoedi).

Fudging the contract

In 2009, talks again took place with TAS but amounted to a take-it-or leave-it offer of an increase of 50 cents an hour, nowhere near what the casuals were asking. In 2010, there were more talks, held in the Vaal's Sebokeng Depot. The Vaal Workers Committee negotiators were stiffened by the inclusion of leaders of the West Rand Committee. It was, effectively, negotiations for TAS's SAPO workers across Gauteng. However, they quickly floundered when it was explained by TAS management that salaries could not be increased because of the 'laws of labour broking'.[6] There are, of course, no laws of labour broking outside of what can be found in the Labour Relations Act. And there is no chapter, section, sub-section, clause, sentence or phrase in the LRA that says 'labour brokers shall not increase salaries'.

Rather, when TAS managers said an increase was not possible, they were referring to the pay rates set by SAPO for the casuals they provided. The rates that labour brokers would be able to pay to casuals were introduced to prevent casuals moving between labour brokers to exploit marginal differences in pay (interview, Petersen). Once these rates had been set, they remained unchanged for several years.[7] Citing the 'laws of labour broking' was effectively pointing to the outcome of the contractual move previously outlined: SAPO was the budget holder, and labour brokers were in effect a buffer between workers and any claim on that budget.

At the 2010 talks, the West Rand and Vaal workers were told that their committees were not recognised 'as per collective bargaining'.[8] In other words, they had no legal standing to negotiate. The workers committee in Tembisa, ahead of other committees in recognising the limits of a constitutional road to ending labour broking, was told much the same thing: as labour broker employees they did not have the right to join a trade union. When they took advice from the Department of Labour, they were correctly told that they could join a union; it was a constitutional right. When they told that to Ramaphakela, she told them that they would be dismissed should they join a union (interview, Mabulane).

Buying leadership

Should the casuals manage to organise, one way in which the potency of any collective action could be attenuated was by buying off leadership figures. How prevalent and how effective this was within the SAPO casuals is impossible to ascertain. In some cases, casual workers' leaders publicised offers made to them by labour brokers but, obviously, where bribes were accepted there was not going to be publicity (interview, Maja). Accusations would be made, as in the case of the failure of the Vaal's Labour Court case described in Chapter 8. That accusations are easy to spread is a problem in evaluating the extent that labour brokers bought off the casuals' leaders. Slandering other leaders played into the rivalry between workers committees and between individuals. The eventual hiding of leadership, as will be described in Chapter 13, would have limited, though not eliminated, the ability of labour brokers to bribe casual workers' leaders.

Doubts

In early 2009, the Vaal Workers Committee, assisted by Vaal University of Technology lecturer Toto Molaza, obtained a 'strike certificate' from the CCMA.[9] The subsequent action was the only protected strike of the casuals' struggle in SAPO. Yet, support for the stoppage was limited. Much as strikers were legally entitled to return to their posts once the strike was over, in practice casuals had to weigh up a range of possible outcomes.

Tovey Montoedi (interview) recalled how in the Vaal's Vereeniging Depot casuals had weighed up the pros and cons of joining the strike and decided to carry on working. He outlined what had influenced them not to support the stoppage. The strike had been framed for them by SAPO supervisors and TAS managers as being 'Toto Molaza's dispute'. The message was that the strike was organised by outsiders who did not have the casuals' interests at heart. Casuals were being used. CWU shop stewards had the same message and cast aspersions on 'your advisers who are not working in SAPO'. Toto Molaza and others who assisted the casuals would, it was argued, move on to wreck another company when the strike failed. This was despite Molaza having steered casuals' frustrations into legal channels. The argument,

Montoedi recalled, was unsettling; could they rely on Molaza if things went wrong? So ironically, the assistance provided to the Vaal Committee in helping them navigate labour law and obtain a strike certificate was used to undermine the strike.

In addition to attacking the strike on the basis of outsider involvement, the value of the strike certificate was challenged by SAPO supervisors in ways that undermined confidence. Casuals were asked, 'Who are you fighting? SAPO or the labour brokers?' The strike would stop mail delivery so they would be fighting SAPO, but was it not the labour brokers with whom they needed to bargain? They were the labour broker employees. This was the pillar-to-post strategy in a slightly different form. Montoedi conceded the argument had created confusion. The truth was that in 2009 the casuals were not clear about their strategy (interview, Montoedi).

The likely success of any strike was also questioned. It was pointed out that if casuals were to strike, the labour broker would provide replacement workers.

An alternative argument against the strike implicitly accepted that they would not lose their jobs, but was nevertheless demoralising. The strike, it was pronounced, would collapse and they would come back to a mountain of mail that needed to be delivered. They were reminded that if they went on strike, protected or not, it was 'no work, no pay'. They would come back defeated, facing the end of the month without pay, and a pile of work to clear (interview, Montoedi).

Bad books

Montoedi's supervisor discouraged them from joining the 2009 protected strike. She did not issue threats, but offered friendly advice – or, at least, indirect threats wrapped nicely in friendly advice. She knew that the casuals wanted to be permanent. Maybe, she conceded, the strike certificate would mean that they would keep their jobs. But, was it sensible to join the strike? They should, she counselled, think about their future. She did not have to spell it out: everybody knew she had the power to determine who would benefit should permanent positions became available. As Montoedi explained:

> If you strike or if you do anything wrong [your] supervisor always keeps the record, they can keep your record until such time that Post Office employs people. [The Post Office] will say, 'Supervisor please tell us how is Tovey [Montoedi] behaving? Is Tovey always on strike? What is happening with Tovey?' If I am on his or her bad books then I am not going to be employed permanently in Post Office (interview, Montoedi).

Supervisors also hinted at more immediate consequences for striking: when the dispute was over, those who had been on strike would be called in, one at a time, by the labour brokers to face disciplinary charges. The strike might be protected, but what did that mean when the strike was over?

The pressure applied on those contemplating joining the protected strike created the impression that there was pressure from SAPO's top management on local managers and supervisors (interview, Montoedi). Management was watching. That raised the stakes. If they joined the strike, what happened afterwards would not be in the supervisor's hands. It would not be up to him or her to call the shots. There could be no turning a blind eye. This upping of the ante served as a deterrent, one that was especially effective with a workforce that had never before mounted collective action, which was divided over strategy, and which was still unsure of its own strength.

A rainbow of fear

Fear is not the ideal way to manage workplace order. Control through fear means that earlier, more subtle ways of controlling the workforce, whether through paternalism, nurtured hopes or engendered fears, have failed. The intimidation of workers appears as a response to emerging discontent. But since people generally prefer to be respected without having to intimidate, fear is, at least initially, installed in disguised form. It relies as much on the shadow of consequences as in actual action. It works best when there is nothing that can be pinned down. When Kodisang Bokaba's drive to organise SAPO casuals through SAGWAWTU gained traction in 2009 and a hearing at the CCMA for their recognition bid was set down, one of the key activists was suspended on, as Bokaba (interview) put it, 'a funny charge'. The casual was sitting at home idle, but no steps were taken to proceed with a disciplinary case. As far as Bokaba was concerned, it was a warning. Others took heed and casuals stopped attending meetings. When the CCMA date came, it was only Bokaba and the fearless Marcus Makhura in attendance.

The power of unspecified consequences worked differently in the minds of each casual worker. Fear focused their minds onto the arguments against resistance that resonated most with their own insecurities: uncertainty of their own legal standing, certainty of their own vulnerability, doubts over the success of industrial action, and anxiety over consequences. As individuals, it was always possible for them to talk themselves out of taking action. Then anger over their situation would subside into offstage griping and grumbling.

Disciplinary hearings

Fear paralyses but courage is contagious and becomes easier in numbers. If fear has become necessary to maintain workplace order, then deterrents need to be imposed swiftly. Should the numbers of those willing to resist grow, the dynamics of order change. The power of authority is countervailed by the power of numbers. Dismissing individual workers is relatively easy, dismissing an entire workforce and starting afresh is not.

For those responsible for maintaining the system of labour broking, it was important that open defiance be nipped in the bud. Those who first openly challenged labour broking needed to be neutralised to prevent contagion. That required discipline that others could see and from which they would learn to keep their place. Discipline constitutes any action that maintains workplace order; pretty much everything described in this chapter is about discipline. But there is also a narrower definition of workplace discipline – formal charges of misconduct, hearings, judgment and sanction.

Much as a disciplinary hearing is a formal process of accusation, evidence and ruling, it is also a power struggle between individuals and their employer and between workers and management. Distinguishing between what is disciplinary action for infringement of workplace rules and what is about maintaining workplace order is not always easy. Sometimes there is no difference. In a society as unequal as South Africa, rules are broken as a matter of course. Sanctioning transgressors is less systematic and often a matter of selection influenced by contextual factors. Take, for example, the first case in which Gibson Ramotsi, a postman and casual workers' leader in Katlehong, defended a fellow casual worker.[10] He forced his way into the hearing after being told that he was not permitted to be present. Casual workers were not entitled, he was told, to represent casual workers. This was, of course, made up. The case, he realised, was really about the supervisor putting pressure on the worker. The supervisor had lent the casual money, at interest, and the casual was struggling to repay. It was easy for the supervisor to find a pretext and call in the labour broker to conduct a disciplinary hearing. Ramotsi won the case because he called the bluff about who could represent whom and threatened to take the matter further. The supervisor, realising he was himself vulnerable should Ramotsi make good on his threat, backed down (interview, Ramotsi).

As this case illustrates, a supervisor's individual interest can serve the general purpose of maintaining compliance in the workplace through setting an example as to what happens if you fall out of line. It was the labour broker's responsibility to run disciplinary hearings, but the hearing would be called for by the supervisor, and the labour broker was dependent on the supervisor for business.

Take the strange disciplinary case of Dennis Matsile, a mail handler at the Witspos Mail Centre, employed by TAS. A common, and understandable, cause for disciplinary hearings is *not* turning up to work. On 31 March 2011, Matsile was charged for *coming to work*. Seriously. The TAS charge sheet outlines how he was 'informed prior to reporting for duty that you should be off as per rotation but you still reported [to work]'. As we find out from the appeal submitted by the Vaal Labour Broker Committee, which represented Matsile, he was on his way to work when he was informed by the (SAPO) supervisor that he was not needed that day.[11] Already on his way, he pitched up anyway, which led to the charge of 'failing to take a lawful instruction'. When he arrived at work and confronted his supervisor, there was an exchange of words, resulting in two further charges: insubordination and bringing the company (that is, TAS) into disrepute (TAS 2011a). The incident reveals the power of supervisors to control the work of casuals, and the power of the supervisor-labour broker axis to snuff out individual acts of defiance.

Over time, that vulnerability was tempered, though only to a degree. As cases started to trickle into the CCMA and the lack of any process was exposed, Post Office management insisted that disciplinary hearings be held. That probably reduced the trigger-happiness of supervisors to call in a casual's labour broker to run a disciplinary hearing. But when such hearings were called, they usually ended up with the same result: dismissal (interview, Papiki Mokoena).

Disciplinary action served both to deter others and also to decapitate emerging organisations. Marcus Makhura's dismissal after the mid-2011 strike, told in the previous chapter, was exactly such a decapitation: the Tembisa Committee lost an important leader. But advancing through the span of tactics is risky; disciplinary action risks bringing matters to a head. This was to be the case less than six months after the collapse of the mid-2011 strike. Workers from the West Rand Workers Committee were charged with misconduct over a one-day stay-away; refusing to be cowed, those charged were defiant and were dismissed. Their response was to launch the strike that would end labour broking.

Representation denied

That Gibson Ramotsi had to force himself into the disciplinary hearing of a co-worker illustrates how the formal process of law need not hold sway in organisational praxis. As he pointed out, summaries of the Basic Conditions of Employment Act and other legislation might be displayed on workplace walls, but, in practice, they were not observed (interview, Ramotsi). TAS charge sheets always listed the employees' rights going into a hearing. Top of the list was the 'right to a representative'. But often it was casuals' representatives who were the first thing knocked out in hearings.

Other reasons to prevent representation were based on arguments with at least some legal rationale. In late November 2009, Jabulani

Mabena and ten other TAS casuals were fired from the Springs Depot for leaving work early to attend the Department of Labour hearings into labour broking in Germiston (see Chapters 3 and 7). Moeketsi 'MP' Lepheane, one of the CWU's A-Team, had agreed to represent them. Neal Lakey, HR manager for the Moloko Group, chaired the disciplinary hearing for TAS, and outlined how the official 'could not prove that he had *locus standi* [legal standing to represent the charged workers] . . . He could not produce any documentation to show that the union had any organisational rights and was excused from the proceedings' (CCMA 2009b).

Not surprisingly, the workers reacted angrily to this bouncing of their representative. They began *toyi-toying* and refused to participate in the hearing. Lakey then asserted: 'If the employees had conducted themselves in a manner which would be conducive to these proceedings, I would have given them fair opportunity to state any concerns they might have had . . .' (CCMA 2009b). He continued with a pro forma list of rights afforded to the charged employees at the hearing, top of which was the right to representation.

Lakey ruled that TAS's employment relationship with the eleven casuals be terminated with immediate effect. They still, however, needed to be served with letters of dismissal. This was attempted by TAS's Jaco Koto on 13 November. Koto reported waiting for the casuals to return from their walks. He waited a long time but none of the eleven returned to the depot. Finally, he gave up waiting, whereupon he found all four tyres of his car deflated (CCMA 2009b). The notices were successfully served on 3 December and replacement casuals brought in the following day.

Part III: Lawfare
If fired workers are reinstated, the problem is not only the return of emboldened workers, but the example it sets to others. Labour brokers therefore continued their fight in the courts when dismissed workers attempted to be reinstated. The courts become an extension of workplace struggles. However, since legal processes have to be more closely followed here, the struggle takes place in a largely legal framework. But it is still a struggle, war with law: lawfare.

To the Labour Court

The dismissal of the Springs Eleven in December 2009 was not, by a long shot, the end of the matter. As outlined in Chapter 7, the eleven won their case at the CCMA with the help of Lepheane. The commissioner who heard the case had found the charges against the eleven 'baseless' and the procedures followed by TAS unfair. The fired casuals were awarded compensation for the five months since their dismissal.[12] Given monthly salaries of between R1 900 and R2 670, this came in total to R108 571.50. The CCMA commissioner also ordered their reinstatement within seven days (CCMA 2009b). However, when they reported for duty, the supervisor at Springs told them that they worked for TAS, not for SAPO. If the CCMA had reinstated them, then they must go to TAS to be re-employed (interview, Mabena).

Mabena had worked at the Springs Depot for ten years, but he had never once been to TAS's office. He did not even know where it was. Knowing a runaround when they saw one, the workers ignored the supervisor's suggestion. Instead, they started sorting mail at 'their' presses. The replacement workers who had been recruited following the Springs Eleven's dismissal stood aside, knowing the reputation of the group. The police were called. First to arrive were black (African) cops. They had been told the group was rioting, but found the legally-reinstated-but-unwanted workers sorting mail and left. Next a pair of white cops pitched up. They came in aggressively with a no-nonsense approach, but also backed off when shown the CCMA reinstatement order. SAPO area management then resorted to closing the depot completely. Now nobody could work. This went on for close to a week before, fearing that they would be charged and re-dismissed for delaying mail, the unwanted casuals went to the Labour Court to have the CCMA award made an order of the court.[13]

Silence

The Labour Court granted the application, but TAS proceeded to ignore it. Silence is a weapon; one that can drag out a dispute. And in an unequal lawfare conflict enough obstacles placed in the legal path means that the richer side will prevail, irrespective of legal merits. Eventually, something or some combination of problems will bog down the weaker party: unaffordability, a lack of good advice, weariness, a lack of time, a lack of energy. Each and every hurdle that can litter the legal road saps the energy of those seeking justice. Silence helps cull legal challenges without having to actually do anything.

A legal pincer movement

Jabulani Mabena and the other ten Springs dismissed casuals refused to be deterred by TAS's stonewalling. On 9 July 2010, the Springs casuals obtained a writ of execution from the Labour Court for the R108 000 compensation order. They took it to the sheriff, who went to TAS's Sandton office in the north of Johannesburg and attached two of the company vehicles for auction should the debt remained unpaid (Labour Court 2010c). For a moment, TAS was no longer able to ignore the fired Springs workers. It could, of course, have accepted the CCMA ruling, now made an order of court, but instead it fought back. The legal war between the two sides escalated. Fortunes ebbed and flowed as three, arguably four, cases in the Labour Court ensued over the next four-and-a-half years.

First up was JR1295/10, in which TAS filed for a review of the CCMA arbitration (Labour Court 2010a). TAS's main argument was its original line of defence: that CWU should not have been representing the workers. The union did not have *locus standi* to do so because the casuals were not CWU members – or at least they were not members when dismissed. Joshua Jabangwe, TAS's HR consultant, outlined the labour broker's argument in his submitted affidavit: '[CCMA] Commissioner Stapelberg should not have accepted stop order forms signed after the dismissal of the Third Respondent [the Springs Eleven] as evidence of Communication Workers Union membership' (Labour Court 2010a).[14]

JR1295/10 was, however, only half of a more powerful tactic that TAS was mobilising. In parallel to the requested review of the CCMA's ruling, TAS also filed for a stay of execution on the sheriff's warrant while their challenge against the arbitration ruling proceeded. This was Labour Court Case J1398/10. A preliminary order was granted by the Labour Court on 20 July 2010 to stay the sheriff's warrant (Labour Court 2010c). CWU opposed the stay of execution on 21 July 2010. This was the last involvement of CWU in the case, as Lepheane withdrew first from actively assisting casuals and then from the union itself. The action failed and the stay of execution was confirmed by the court on 19 August 2010.

TAS had now regained control. In a legal pincer movement, the two cases supported each other to block the casuals' advance. The writ of execution was now stopped by J1398/10 and could only proceed once J1295/10 (the review of the CCMA award) was completed. Not surprisingly, TAS did nothing to advance the latter case. Having stymied the Springs Eleven legal assault with this manoeuvre, TAS could keep legal action against them in abeyance by doing absolutely nothing.

In the wider picture of tussles between employers and employees at the CCMA, TAS's strategy followed a well-trod path. In a report on judicial decisions and the operations of the CCMA, Paul Benjamin (2007), outlines how arbitrations, which most commonly deal with dismissal, could not be appealed but only reviewed by the Labour Court under Section 145 of the LRA.[15] Benjamin described reviews of CCMA arbitration awards as having become 'a predominant feature of labour litigation in South Africa'. Reviewing the data on 1 597 reviews of CCMA arbitration awards in KwaZulu-Natal between 1997 and 2004, Benjamin found that 18 per cent were dismissed (that is, the CCMA award was upheld), 16 per cent resulted in the award being set aside, 11 per cent were withdrawn and 52 per cent were neither processed nor withdrawn (2007: 26). In other words, the original arbitration ruling was, in more than half of cases, put into a legal coma. As Benjamin explained, 'This indicates the extent to which reviews are instituted for the purpose of frustrating or delaying the enforcement of awards in favour of employees' (2007: 26).

Without assistance, this might well have been the end of the Springs Eleven fight. However, with Lepheane off the scene, Mabena realised that they were going to lose unless they had help. He brought in Attorney Ndumiso Voyi of Ndumiso Voyi Incorporated: Attorneys (interview, Mabena). Voyi went into action, informing TAS on 13 May 2011 that he represented the Springs Eleven, noting their lack of action on the review application. He sent TAS four letters in succession, demanding that they progress the case. All were ignored (Labour Court 2010c: 168). On 16 September 2011, he requested the Labour Court dismiss TAS's review application on the grounds of excessive and unreasonable delay (Labour Court 2010c: 144). The court granted Voyi's application on 7 December 2011: J1295/10 was dead!

With one thrust of TAS's pincer movement now parried, Voyi went on the offensive and applied for a second writ of execution (Labour Court 2010b: 37). The sheriff attached one of TAS's bank accounts, the details of which Mabena had obtained from a contact within SAPO's HR office (interview, Mabena). TAS was again rudely awakened to the tenacity of the Springs Eleven when, on 4 January 2012, ABSA bank informed them that R108 571.50 from their account has been handed over to the sheriff.

TAS was in a corner, but not out of the fight. Two days after the call from ABSA, the company launched another case in the Labour Court: J11/12 (Labour Court 2012a). This was an application to stay this second writ of execution while they challenged the court's 7 December ruling against J1265 (Labour Court 2010b: 37). Could J1295 be revived from legal death? Perhaps not, but that was not the important point for TAS. What it sought was to re-establish its pincer movement: to stay the writ of execution on the basis of an appeal that could then be strung out indefinitely.

J11/12 was heard on 19 January 2012. In court Voyi pointed out that what 'the Applicant [TAS] is avoiding to state is that the review application [JR1295/10] has been dismissed' (Labour Court 2010b: 65). Voyi won hands down: J11/12 was dismissed with costs. Voyi then upped the ante with a compensation claim of R500 000 since the Springs Eleven had not yet been reinstated; back pay amounted to some R400 000 and there was interest (Labour Court 2010b: 67, 144).

Having failed to block the writ of execution, TAS was now running out of road. But on 23 January the company launched an urgent application in the Labour Court to interdict the writ of execution; they used J11/12 in their arguments. Yes, that is correct: J11/12 – the same case that had been dismissed just four days earlier. Yet, *this* application was to stay the writ of execution on TAS's bank account while seeking a dismissal of the dismissal of JR1295/10. TAS was trying, for the third time, to get a legal pincer movement in place. Voyi responded with what he must have hoped was a sliver bullet: *res judicata* (the matter has already been judged) (Labour Court 2010b: 142).

When J11/12 [mark II][16] came to court on 20 February 2012, the judge found in favour of the Springs Eleven; TAS had failed, without good reason, to prosecute its review application of the CCMA arbitration (that is, JR1295/10). They had only themselves to blame.

A long end game
Finally, TAS was down. The first blow was the R108 000 to be paid with interest, plus the sherriff's charges and the court costs awarded against them. Then came the R500 000, and the compensation claim that Voyi put in motion. In February 2013, Voyi got the Labour Court to (again) make the April 2010 CCMA settlement an order of court, including the original order to reinstate the Eleven. Further, the court also made TAS and its owner, Colleen Ramaphakela, jointly and severally liable for all due back pay. TAS was given seven days to comply.

But seven days did not bring matters to an end. Finality was reached only in 2015 with an out of court settlement. Each of the eleven were paid R40 000. In return, they acknowledged TAS had discharged all of its obligations, and waived any right to further claims.[17] Voyi told them it was the best they could expect and they accepted the offer by majority vote (interviews, Mabena; Vilakazi).

The Springs case was uncharacteristic of the lawfare waged on casuals. It was a rare victory for the underdog. The Springs Eleven won only because of the persistence, and balls, of Mabena, assisted by Lepheane and then, when he fell victim to CWU's internecine conflict, an enthusiastic and competent lawyer. Justice was a long time coming and partial. The final settlement did not see the Springs Eleven reinstated and the financial compensation was a compromise on the original order, which set compensation on the basis of lost earnings. But still, it was a victory, and an unusual one. More common were victories for those using the legal system to maintain labour broking.

Part IV: A triangular workplace relationship
The discourse on labour broking, and other forms of externalisation, is dominated by the model of the triangular employment relationship that links the broker, client company and casual worker. It is a powerful tool for illustrating the legal position and the relationships of these

three parties to each other. Yet, the model is one-dimensional in that it provides an outline of the legal positions and relationships of the parties, but little else.

In Chapter 1, this model was expanded beyond the three-point triangle to incorporate the usual multiplicity of labour brokers contracting with a single client and the corresponding plurality of casual workforces that exist alongside a client's permanent employees.

This chapter allows us to further develop the model in two ways. First, it identifies a triangular *workplace* relationship that links not client, broker and casual but rather supervisor, labour broker representative and casual. The relationships in this workplace triangle are only indirectly those of contractual obligations. Rather, their essence comprises day-to-day working relationships. Unlike for a permanent employee, the combined responsibility of supervision and discipline is now split. The supervisor directs, or supervises, while the representative disciplines. The representative supports the supervisor's control of the workplace: the supervisor-broker representative axis. This alerts us to actors that are unrecognised in the basic triangular employment relationship model. It also draws attention to the dynamics of workplace power, and the particular configuration under labour broking, which operates below the legalities of contractual relationships.

A second departure from the basic model explored in this chapter is how the law is used in practice. Law and practice should not diverge, but of course they do; it is an outcome of human agency. Conceived within a lawfare perspective, the law-in-practice can be regarded as another disciplining force on the casual workforce, one that originates outside the workplace but supports internal disciplining mechanisms. Lawfare is not, however, the only external disciplining force that bolsters the internal disciplinary structures. Mass unemployment powerfully strengthens the hand of supervisors over casuals. There is also the intra-class disciplinary pressure that permanent workers bring to bear on casuals, as described in Chapter 5. Figure 12.1 illustrates the triangular *workplace* relationship, its overlap with the triangular *employment* relationship, and the various sources of discipline bearing on casual workers.

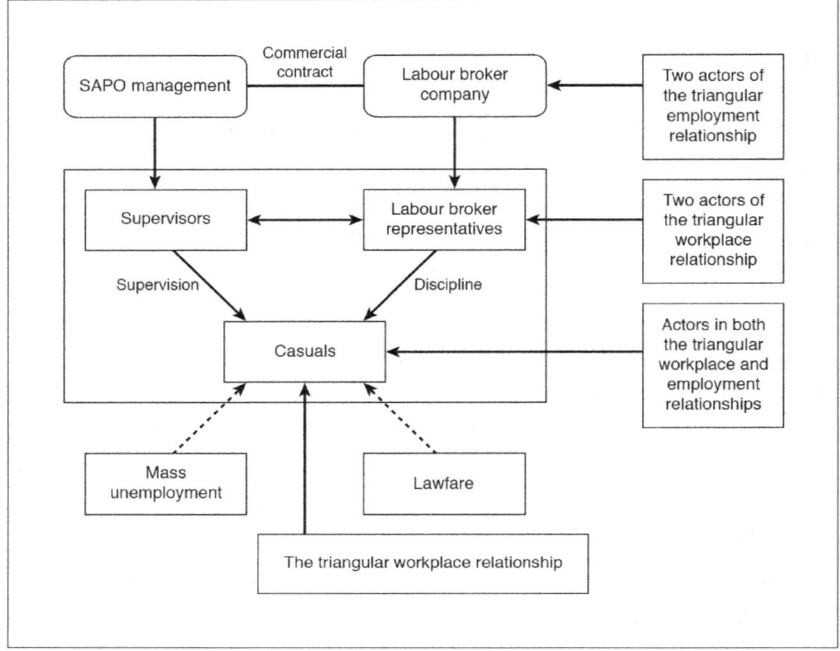

Figure 12.1 Triangular workplace and employment relationships.

Part V: The long tactics of labour broking

When I first planned this chapter, I was thinking about *labour brokers*. I was intending to single them out as the villains of the piece. But as I wrote, it became clear that the structural abuse of casual workers in SAPO did not rest on labour brokers alone. Casuals were victims of a system that had developed around a confederacy of agents. Labour brokers were critical, obviously, but they were not alone. And so, the chapter developed as one on *labour broking*. It is a difference of a few letters, but it makes an important point.

Michel de Certeau (1984), in his exploration of everyday agency, uses the terms *strategy* and *tactics*. His use of these two words is different to how they are commonly understood. Strategies, for De Certeau, are the visible projects of power in the social world: systems of authority that require conformation to prescribed behaviour. These are the behaviours set out, with different degrees of clarity, by the legal system, the educational system, the political system and so on. The power of these systems rests on acceptance of their rules and, if necessary, coercion through discipline, sanction, exclusion and punishment. In contrast to strategies, tactics are temporary advantages: creative moments, subversive actions, snatched advantages, jokes, improvisations and the like, often within the territory of a system. James Scott's (1985) anthropological analysis of struggle introduced the phrase *weapons of the weak*, which, as with De Certeau's tactics, are rarely employed openly or explicitly to challenge the dominant systems. Rather, they are practised opportunistically, in secret, in disguise, or at least unattributably: theft, fraud, sabotage, slander, tricks and lies. If confronted by the agents of a strategy, tactical practitioners will rarely stand their ground, even for a moment, but will disappear, deny, dissemble or otherwise melt away . . . for as long as authority remains present. Following the casuals' constitutional crusade and the open defiance of the wildcat Tembisa strike of mid-2011, the casuals' struggle in SAPO was increasingly clandestine. Much can be categorised as De Certeauan tactics and Scott's weapons of the weak. Yet, this chapter is not focused on what the casuals did, but on how labour broking was maintained for so long.

The work of both De Certeau and Scott speaks to binaries: the rulers and the ruled, the powerful and the weak. Applied to the casuals' situation, it works well enough. Applied to labour broking, there is a need for qualification. The combination of state-owned enterprise management, labour broking companies, hired lawyers and a dominant union can hardly be classified as weak, but they were using De Certeauan tactics. When it came to labour broking, they did not hold fast to a 'territory' by consistently applying a set of rules. Rather, they used shifting tactics to, collectively, maintain this system of exploitation.

Legally, lawyers had pushed open loopholes in the post-1994 legislation to create a grey zone within which labour broking could be practised. What was happening lacked social legitimacy, but the law was slow to catch up. However, on the ground, there was increasing conflict, and to maintain the system of labour broking there had to be shifting tactics, which this chapter has documented. As I slowly realised that the duration of labour broking needed explaining, I came to see these combined and compounded responses of the confederacy of agents, which operated over years, as *long tactics*.

The confederacy of labour broking actors allowed parties to benefit from the actions of others. Thus, labour broker representatives were in partnership with supervisors, throwing responsibility back and forth between each other, but collectively providing SAPO management with what it had requested: cheap labour to cut costs. In this regard, management were part of a largely invisible class war fought out not in dramatic public confrontations but in day-to-day conflicts that remained outside of the Post Office's managerial line of sight. Aloof from the fray, but ultimately responsible for this labour regime, the senior SAPO managers said what it wanted but then looked elsewhere as the dirty business of broking was implemented.

The implementation of such a system was assisted by mass unemployment, but it also sometimes had additional assistance from unlikely quarters, the casual workers themselves. This chapter has illustrated how they also contributed to their bondage. Shame slowed down the process of collective resistance as individuals initially sought to hide their precarious status, a problem compounded by the expectations of what a postman, as a government employee, should be earning. Even when this shame was converted to anger and they started sharing their common experiences of exploitation, much time and effort was taken up by complaining to each other, rather than working out how they could change the situation. And action was hampered by real and imagined mistrust and division. It was also hampered by the duplication of initiatives as described in previous chapters. Yet, despite their own divisions, and despite the confederacy's ability to keep shifting tactics to maintain the system, it was eventually the agency of casuals that ended labour broking in SAPO. The Mabarete strike, to which we now turn, smashed asunder the confederacy and ended the casuals' contractual bondage.

13

The Mabarete Strike I
Striking and Scabbing

Part I: A different strike
Drafting their own laws

The Mabarete strike began on 12 December 2011 and ended on 4 April 2012. With hindsight, the Tembisa strike of mid-2011 was a transition between the casuals' constitutional crusade and the Mabarete strike, which, at times, was closer to low-intensity warfare than industrial dispute. When the South African Post Office (SAPO) brought an interdict against the strike in January 2012, they sanctimoniously argued that the casuals could 'strike lawfully, they are entitled to exhaust the procedures set out in . . . the LRA [Labour Relations Act]' (Labour Court 2012b: Section 64).[1] But while such legal cant might work in the courtroom, it would no longer wash with the casuals. Alfred Mosito explains:

> We said, 'You know what? In South Africa the law is there and it's a nice law, but if ever you are poor it will never work and you will never get what you are supposed to get . . . your rights. Because you don't have money, because it's limited [compared to] the person who can violate your rights and [who can] use money against you and oppress you.' Then we end up saying that we are not going to use any law. We are going to draft our own law to fight this labour broker . . . we would rather fight like soldiers. And fight until we die! . . . We are not going to stop until we get what we want (interview, Mosito).

This is the first of three chapters that describe how, against the odds, 294 strikers made their own laws and ended labour broking in the Post Office. This chapter covers the first phase of the strike, and, in particular, the vacillation of casuals who were often unsure whether to join the strike or not.

A dark Christmas

The decision to launch the strike was taken at a Saturday morning meeting of West Rand casuals on 10 December 2011. The meeting was held in the committee's usual venue, Thokoza Park, a short distance from the Regina Mundi Church.[2] Several key leaders, including Thabiso Bopape and Alfred Mosito were absent. Russel Mutavhatsindi, who was present, later informed them of the decision. December is not seen as a good time to launch a strike in South Africa. Many companies close down. But since the Post Office only stops operations during public holidays, postmen's leave is staggered throughout the year. The festive season, which coincides with summer, is a time of expense; cultural expectations in South Africa require a spike in expenditure over Christmas (Dickinson 2015b). So striking in December is not something you would readily rush into; especially if you are a postman and there are Christmas boxes to be collected.

That the strike was not postponed was, in part, because disciplinary action against West Rand leaders was forcing their hand. At the meeting, Mutavhatsindi had also put forward another argument for an immediate strike (interview, Mutavhatsindi). He agreed that if they did strike, it would be a 'dark Christmas'. The December pay cheque would amount to the seven working days of the month already completed. But for casuals, it would be a dark Christmas, strike or no strike. As labour broker employees, Christmas was not a time of celebration. Seven days' pay or a month's pay, it still was not going to amount to enough. Mutavhatsindi's argument was about screwing up his and other's courage. It was clear what was needed: labour broking had to end. They had to become permanent employees. They had, he was saying, nothing to lose but their contractual chains.

To Tembisa

Apart from the 2009 dispute initiated by the Communication Workers Union (CWU), which casuals had joined, this was the West Rand casuals' first all-out dispute. They had held back from the East Rand's strike six months previously, but now they needed the East Rand. That was apparent when the strikers took stock of their situation after their dark Christmas. They had met on 3 January 2012, again in Thokoza Park. Since the strike had commenced on 12 December, they had been successful in bringing out West Rand casuals, but most had returned to work. The strike was fizzling out. There were just sixteen strikers at Thokoza Park. All of them had now been dismissed by their labour brokers (interviews, Bopape; Mutavhatsindi). If Mutavhatsindi had been talking up the misery of the casuals' condition in December, in January it was bleaker.

But the support of the East Rand could not be taken for granted. There was the long-standing rivalry between the two groups and the failure of the West to rally to the East's 2011 strike until the final day at the Labour Court. There was also the court's suspended jail term hanging over the East Rand leadership. The 30-day sentence had been suspended for six months. That order had been confirmed on 27 July and was therefore still applicable. If they had waited another six weeks, the suspended sentence would have expired and the East Rand leadership would not have to worry about this consequence of joining the strike. However, given the disciplinary action against the West Rand leadership, to wait six weeks would have seen the casuals' committee decapitated. Some East Rand leaders, particularly those in Tembisa, took this into account and buried the hatchet. For others, however, it was a good reason to hold back. The result was to be bitter division.

Two strikers went east on 4 January. Their brief was to bring out the East Rand. They met with Moraba Choshi, one of the mid-2011 strike leaders based at the Tembisa Depot. Choshi's reaction was that if the East Rand was to come on board, the West Rand needed to come back 'in numbers'. He was not going to persuade his depot to join if there were just two strikers outside the gate! Numbers were needed to convince casuals that it was safe to join an unprotected strike.[3]

Of course, the embarrassing fact was that the West Rand did not have numbers. Choshi assisted the following day by boosting the influence of the small group of West Rand strikers with a piece of theatre. Having talked up the strike to the casuals in his depot, he arranged to go on an errand and returned as the strikers arrived. They then attempted to capture him in full view of the depot, giving the impression that, if caught, he would be beaten. At one point, things threatened to get out of hand as some of the more enthusiastic West Rand strikers grabbed his bicycle. For a moment he feared that he really was about to be thrashed. Much as this was theatre, not all the actors at been briefed on their lines. However, he broke free and managed to reach the depot unscathed. The close shave only heightened the realism of the strikers' demonstrated anger. Those in the depot chose to join the strike. After that, matters became easier; numbers increased with each depot visited in the Tembisa area (interview, Choshi). The strike was back on its feet.

Rage against the machine

What propelled the strike was the casuals' rage. As the inventory of failed attempts to break from their contractual bondage had grown, so too had their anger. While casuals might be one corner of the triangular employment relationship, what the SAPO casuals came to see was another triangle – one that they were trapped within. They were hemmed in by the company, the labour brokers and the union. Together, these three organisations kept them in slavery.

As the casuals' struggles intensified, the list of those oppressing them grew longer. Many organisations were approached for assistance, but as promises faltered they ceased being sources of hope and became defenders of the status quo. The Commission for Conciliation, Mediation and Arbitration (CCMA) commissioners and court judges were bought by the company; the company's Human Resources Department and CWU were one and the same thing; CWU was aligned with the Congress of South African Trade Unions (COSATU); COSATU was aligned with the African National Congress (ANC);[4] the ANC was the government; SAPO was a state-owned company; SAPO's board and management were corrupt; the labour brokers paid off managers and the union to get business. The law only reinforced the walls of their prison. It promised justice, but gave them only referrals – referrals back to the very people who constructed the jail. Alfred Mosito again:

> To say that you must open a case: to go to the CCMA? [No,] we are not going there anymore. Because when you go to the CCMA they will say, 'You cannot come here, CWU is there [in SAPO], come [back] with the union.' [But if] you call CWU, they sabotage everything, everything is stopped . . . (interview, Mosito).

Weizmann Hamilton (interview), who as general secretary of the Democratic Socialist Movement had been involved in the attempt to organise SAPO casual workers in early 2011, had been acutely aware of the casuals' anger. He described it as a 'rage against the machine', a phrase that captures the frustration of casual workers and their seething wrath.

A *paper tiger*

The mid-2011 strike had been defeated by the Labour Court's interdict. The courts, the casuals had learned, had teeth. The strikers now saw the Labour Court as the Post Office's attack dog. It could be set on the strike's leadership. But if there was no leadership, there would not be anyone to bite. It would not matter if its leash was slipped. It would run around barking. All sound and fury, but not a postman in sight.

On cue, on 19 January, the Post Office made an urgent application to the Labour Court for an interdict against the strike (Labour Court 2012b). Section 39 of its founding affidavit outlined that the unprotected strike had started on the East Rand 'on or about 6 January 2012'. The strike had, in fact, started a month earlier on the West Rand. TAS Appointments and Management Services (TAS) had, a few days before the court hearing, responded to SAPO lawyers' demands that it fulfil its obligation to provide labour. TAS's four-page letter, penned by Colleen Ramaphakela, TAS's owner and CEO, was a sharp rebuttal of the accusations that it was failing to respond to the escalating strike. She pointed out that by mid-January 'almost 30 employees have so far been dismissed . . . The process is ongoing' (Ramaphakela 2012).

The problem was that the dismissals had not stopped the strike. Once again, the Post Office was having to deal with the labour that brokers were supposed to manage. SAPO's interdict followed the format of the mid-2011 Tembisa strike. The first listed respondents were the labour brokers: TAS, N.T. Ngidi and Marula Staffing. They were followed by the fourth to further respondents: a list of more than 200 striking casuals drawn up by depot supervisors and listed in Annexure A.[5] Six months earlier, once six strike leaders had been identified, they had been promoted to first to sixth respondents, allowing the labour brokers to step out of the legal firing line, but this time nobody was volunteering their names for the court papers.

Instead, the strikers gave the court a wide berth. Much as depot supervisors were able to compile a list of casuals who were not at work, nobody (except for the strikers themselves) knew for certain who was leading, who was following and who was simply afraid to pitch up for work. The court issued an order on the same day that the case was heard. The strike was unlawful and unprotected. The strikers were interdicted from interfering with mail delivery, intimidating non-strikers, damaging Post Office property, or coming within 500 metres of SAPO's premises 'save to render service to the Applicant [SAPO] in accordance with their contractual obligations . . .' (Labour Court 2012b). SAPO was instructed to serve the order to the striking casuals by displaying copies 'in a conspicuous manner' at all entrances to its premises. Quite how the strikers were to read the order from the prescribed 500 metres was not clear, but it did not really matter. Without having strike leaders by the scruff of the neck, the interdict was a paper tiger.

Strikes, intimidation and disruptive power

In popular South African parlance, a strike can encompasses any protest. Pretty much anybody can strike: students, residents, activists and others with a collective complaint. A strike in this wider sense does not even have to be disruptive; it is about drawing attention to grievances. A march to deliver a petition may, if boisterous enough, be described as a strike. Sometimes the term becomes interchanged with *toyi-toying*, the ubiquitous protest steps and songs that characterise street demonstrations in South Africa. Such strikes may escalate beyond noisy protest. This escalation mobilises 'disruptive power' (Piven and Cloward 1977); township-based 'service delivery' protests not infrequently escalate to barricading roads, stoning cars, burning buildings and battling police. These actions, the 'smoke that calls', bring attention to injustices, neglect, unfairness or simply desperation; they have become standard protocol when groups with limited influence feel that attempts to petition or lobby are being ignored (Von Holdt et al. 2011). They are so routine indeed that protesters may end up battling police to demand a stronger police presence in their community (Spies 2017).

In contrast to community, student or other protesters, workers can withdraw their labour. This is a power resource uniquely available to them. The Labour Relations Act defines a strike as 'a partial or complete concerted refusal to work . . . for the purpose of remedying a grievance or resolving a dispute in respect of any matter of mutual interest between employer and employee' (RSA 1995: Section 213). In other words, a *labour strike* has a key feature that strikes in the wider, South African sense of the word do not: the withdrawal of labour as a power resource within workplace conflict.

In theory, a labour strike can be won by staying at home. Withdrawing labour needs no other activity to catalyse its power: no labour, no production. But the withdrawal of labour must stop the employer's operation if concessions are to be achieved.[6] Production stops when hard-to-substitute workers with critical skills strike or when enough low- or semi-skilled workers down tools, making it impossible for production to continue. One categorisation of unions reflects these two forms of power: craft unions and industrial unions. Craft unions organise artisans or professionals. They may have few members, but much bargaining power. By contrast, the strength of industrial unions comes with numbers; if enough workers strike, operations come to standstill.

Despite the core of a labour strike being the withdrawal of labour, in practice no strike involves workers simply putting their feet up at home. All strikes are accompanied by some level of mobilisation. This is especially so in the case of strikes by industrial unions, which must ensure that low-paid workers with limited reserves heed the strike call.

Such mobilisation constitutes a visible, social dimension to a strike, alongside the economic trial of strength between labour and employer.

Recognising this, the Labour Relations Act, via the 'Code of Good Practice' drafted by the National Economic Development and Labour Council (NEDLAC 1998), regulates strike-related pickets. A picket line must be formally authorised by a union registered with the Department of Labour. It may be called only in support of a protected, CCMA-sanctioned, strike. In line with the Constitution, picketers have the right to protest peacefully and unarmed (RSA 1996: Section 17). Picketers may carry placards, chant slogans, sing and dance. They may not physically prevent anyone entering or leaving their employer's premises, or commit any unlawful act, 'including but not limited to any action which is, or may be perceived to be violent' (NEDLAC 1998: Section 6(7)).

This institutionalisation of conflict places violence and intimidation out of bounds. To the extent that it is effective, this prohibition strips strikers, especially those organised in industrial unions, of a means of enforcing strike solidarity. However, in practice, labour strikes in South Africa usually involve more than the withdrawal of labour and the mounting of picket lines. Physical violence is inherently intimidating, but intimidation can be generated through threats (Von Holdt 2012). Intimidation can be produced by a range of actions that fall short of physical assaults but generally go beyond carrying placards, chanting slogans, singing and dancing as envisaged in the NEDLAC Code.[7]

Thus, strikes by industrial unions may involve vivid demonstrations of anger against those still at work. Most of the time, this does not spill over into direct attacks or assaults, but involves threats supported by, inter alia, blocking entrances, shouting and stone-throwing at premises where a strike call is being ignored. Such 'sieges' are usually short-lived given the arrival of police, but can scare the pants off inexperienced managers. However, the real targets of this intimidation are those who are working. They should join the strike or know themselves to be *amagundwane* (rats; that is, scabs). In other words, the intimidation is intended to maximise the number of strikers, minimise the number working and strengthen resolve.[8]

The Mabarete

There are different accounts as to who coined the name 'Mabarete', or its isiZulu version the Amabarete (The Berets), but there is agreement that it was a reference to the then Minister of Police, Bheki Cele's paramilitary Tactical Response Teams. The units were created in 2009 as a high-profile initiative billed to fight housebreakings, bank robberies and cash-in-transit heists. In the end, the newly created units spent a lot of time patrolling townships. In the minister's words, 'They are the ones who put the berets on . . . They are the kind of (specially dressed) police who, as they walk around, you check yourself' (Rantao and Bailey 2011). Nicknamed the Mabarete (or Amabarete) on account of their black berets, the unit meted out corporal punishment for minor offences rather than having the hassle of opening criminal cases at the local South African Police Service stations. Punishments included press-ups at the side of the road, slapping, crawling through sewerage spills,[9] and beatings – all humiliating in one way or another (Chernick 2015).[10] Those at the receiving end of this treatment resented it, but there was also support for the Tactical Response Team's heavy hand from those tired of crime and lawlessness.[11]

The striking SAPO casuals did not wear berets, but they did administer corporal punishment. One account of how they appropriated the name Mabarete from the Tactical Response Team was when a township resident rang a local radio station to report seeing a postman pursued down the street by an angry mob. The station presenter, who must have known something about the situation, referred to the Post Office Mabarete.[12] Nobody had a problem in seeing a parallel between the two groups. The strikers adopted the title with relish.

Applying labour: Stopping the mail

The Mabarete's key weapon in their battle to become permanent employees was stopping mail delivery. They might be employed by labour brokers but it was the Post Office that was in their sights. This could only be achieved using disruptive power. Generally, disruptive power hits parties with no direct connection to the dispute, for example motorists forced to re-route when township protesters block a nearby highway. The disruptive power that the

Mabarete used was a substitute both for the lack of a protected strike and their limited numbers.

The strike's numerical zenith was, at most, 500. That included those who came out for a day or two before returning. For most of the strike, the Mabarete were far below that number. When the strike eventually ended there was an agreement for conversions of the strikers to permanent positions. A list of 294 strikers was drawn up, a number that became synonymous with the Mabarete.[13]

The disruptive action of the Mabarete did little to increase the number of strikers. Occasionally, a beating would bring about a change of heart. Several times I was told about how a strike-breaker had pitched at the Mabarete's morning meeting the day after being caught. His face was swollen and cut, but he made a short speech thanking them for helping him see where his interests truly lay. To applause, he announced that he was joining the strike. This was, however, the exception rather than the rule.

What stopped the mail across large parts of Gauteng was not their withdrawal of labour but the *application* of labour. Non-striking postmen turned up for work and sorted mail, but did not dare venture out to deliver. Despite there being fewer Mabarete strikers than in mid-2011, there was greater disruption.

> [There were] less people [than in the mid-2011 strike] but more effective people, because this was a hands-on strike. We didn't go on strike to just sit around. We were working very hard. When we came out early in the morning, we had a programme and just went to work on it. That was the strong point of the strike of 2012. We were working very hard on it . . . So the mail was piling up (interview, Zwane).

Part II: Casuals divided
Difficult choices
There were around 300 Mabarete, approximately 140 from the six Tembisa depots, another 40 from Far East Rand depots, some 80 to 100 from the West Rand, which included Soweto, and around 30 from the Vaal. In the six Tembisa or 'East Rand' depots the strike was total

among postmen. They were joined by a handful of casuals, including a few women from the Mail Collection Points. Outside of Tembisa there was not one depot in which every casual joined the strike, at least not for longer than a few days. In many depots, it was only one or two with the Mabarete, while the rest continued to clock in, if not deliver.

On the East Rand, a key leader of the 2011 strike, Desmond Moeketsi, held back. He was one of the six named in the SAPO interdict and was still under a suspended sentence. He was adamant that it had been agreed to wait out the six-month suspension, but the West Rand had pushed the strike onto them because of the dismissals of their leaders. He was also nervous because, when the mid-2011 strike had collapsed, workers had turned on him, blaming him for the failure (group interview, IICUSA members).

However, as it happened, he had been on sick leave when the West Rand spread the strike eastwards in early 2012. While mutual mobilisation provided protection to those wanting to join the strike, his absence provided an excuse not to join. Many Far East Rand workers responded to the strike call by saying that they first needed to consult leadership. When the strikers sought to mobilise depots in the Far East, they found locked gates and nobody in sight (interview, Dlamini). The theatre of industrial struggle does not work well without an audience. Other Far East Rand leaders joined the strikers for a day but went back to work unimpressed by what they had seen (group interview, IICUSA members). By the time Moeketsi came back from sick leave, the strike was in full swing and it was too late. Strikers and workers were now enemies.

Not surprisingly, strikers saw things differently. They accused Moeketsi and others of deliberately holding back the Far East Rand from the strike. Eighteen months after the strike had ended, I mentioned to a rank-and-file Mabarete member that I had interviewed Moeketsi. His response was spat out: 'That bastard!'[14]

But such clarity was easier with hindsight. At the time, it was often agonisingly difficult to decide whether to strike or to scab. Some casuals attempted to do both, hedging their bets but at the risk of being rumbled. The decision had to be made with incomplete information and without certainty. In early 2012, outside of the dismissed West

Rand strikers, those joining the strike risked their jobs. Against this was the prospect of the strike succeeding. To strike was to play with high stakes. SAPO raised the stakes when it offered, to CWU, the conversion of 205 labour broker employees to permanent positions (Petersen 2012).[15] The strike was being called to demand permanent positions, but here were permanent positions coming to you! If you stayed put and kept working. If you joined the strike you certainly would not get one of the promised positions. As Tovey Montoedi (interview) outlined, supervisors would be asked if you were always on strike and they would have to answer that you *were* on strike. You would come back to find the scabs were now permanents.

Dieho delays

There were other reasons for not striking. John Dieho did not join the strike immediately.[16] Rather, as a fervent church member, he put his trust in God and was reluctant to join the *zabalazo* or (earthly) struggle. At school he had hoped to become a teacher, but there was no money for him to continue his studies so he went to work as a security guard. A friend had told him that SAPO was recruiting. He was taken on and trained to sort mail, fill out Return to Senders and deliver. As a Post Office temporary worker (or S32), he was paid R500 in cash a week. Then he and other S32s were transferred to a labour broker. The pay dropped but he stayed on. He needed the money; he was a family man. More than ten years later, he was still a casual, still hoping that God would hear his prayers for a better life.

He wanted the strike to succeed, but he was afraid of joining. As with all those who had to make the choice whether to strike or to scab, it was a conflict between the need to earn and fighting for what you needed to earn. As a breadwinner, there are always demands. You can make choices for yourself, cut your cloth to suit your purse, but others are going to make demands: your wife; your wife for your children; your children, especially your children. It is not easy to keep saying 'no' to your children.

Dieho's faith also held him back from the strike. To join the strike was to show doubt in God's ability to answer prayer. He had been praying to be made a permanent worker since his very first day as a casual. To strike was to turn his back on God. He fought with himself over what to do. He talked to his wife. And he went to work.

He was afraid when working. He would get up early to catch the first train of the morning. He wore nothing that could identify him as a postman. He would check constantly, looking to see if anybody was watching him. He would sit hunched on a bench in the almost empty station and slip quickly onto the train as it pulled into the station. Once in a carriage, he would look for a seat where he could hide himself among the other commuters. Approaching the depot, he would again check around to see if anybody was watching. Inside it was safe; they kept the door locked; but only safe until they had sorted the mail and it was time to deliver.

He would tell Richard Tabane, his supervisor, that it was not safe to deliver. Tabane's response was that nobody was safe in a strike. Since everybody knew that, why had Dieho come to work? Now that he was here, being paid, he had to deliver. There had been the offer of police protection. That amounted to a phone number. Dieho had not even bothered to take it. What good was it going to be? Rather, he relied on God to protect him. Out delivering, he worked as fast as he could. Always watching. Looking ahead, looking behind, checking twice. When he got back to the depot, he felt a surge of relief. He had got away with it. Again. At least he had earned something! Then the relief would dissipate. He still had to get home. Checking, hiding, worrying.

After a week, Tabane called Dieho into the office. Mike Mashishini from TAS was there. Mashishini told Dieho that he was doing the right thing: by working he was looking after his family. The strike would crumble. He reminded Dieho about the permanent positions that SAPO was offering. He and Tabane were willing to put Dieho's name forward. Dieho waited. God might be answering his prayers, but he knew there would be T&Cs. Sure enough, they needed his help. Mashishini handed over airtime. He wanted Dieho to contact his striking workmates and get them to see that the strike was not the way to win. TAS was about to replace them. Once that happened, they could not come back to work, however hard Mashishini and Tabane pleaded for them. On the other hand, there was the sweetener: if they returned now, there would be no discipline and no grudges held against them. Tabane and Mashishini understood it was tough, but the strike was not going to get them anywhere. And Dieho, it was emphasised, would be first in line for a permanent position.

Dieho made the calls. He had to exaggerate to those striking how many casuals were back working, but pretty soon it was not an exaggeration. It was not long before there were more casuals working in the depot than striking. Each striker returning to work made Dieho feel safer. But Dieho did not trust Mashishini to keep to his word. Indeed, when he thought about it, he knew there was no guarantee that he would be made permanent. It could be another of those promises that would disappear from view.

One day, Dieho received an SMS while delivering mail. He did not know the number. 'Dieho', it started. The SMS was addressed to him. They knew he was working. They knew where he stayed. They would deal with him. Dieho cracked. He went back to the depot without finishing his walk, and then straight home. His wife, who had supported his decision to work, now told him to join the strike. God, they agreed, would make a plan for them.

That evening Dieho went to see Tobias Zondo, one of the casuals still on strike. Zondo was happy to see Dieho because he knew that he had heeded the warning and was joining the strike.

The next day, Dieho joined the other local strikers. Zondo vouched for him. Dieho, he explained, would not be going back to work. They would be out together until they were permanents. The process had to be repeated when they met with the other striking casuals in Germiston. This was a bit tougher; he had to stand in the middle of the crowd and explain why he had been working. Working out the best way to navigate this, he confessed immediately, omitting the bit about the airtime, telling the men around him that he had wronged them. He was sorry. He knew that sorry was not enough, but he was apologising and he promised that he would do his utmost to bring the rest of the depot out on strike. He was applauded. Accepted. Forgiven.

But joining the strike was not easy for Dieho. It compromised his standing as a man of faith. When working, he had been afraid of being seen by strikers; now he was striking, he was afraid of being seen singing struggle songs on the train. If church members saw him, they would be shocked. They thought he was a man who put his trust in God – which he was, except that his prayers were now for God to give the strikers victory.

Dieho was a *maqabane* (comrade), but as a turned *gundwane* he had to be careful. He made a point of turning up for the strike each and every day. If he skipped, he knew there would be suspicions that he was back at work. He was being watched as a possible *impimpi* (informer). He also had to make good on his promise to bring out the rest of his depot. He had to persuade the casuals he had helped get back to work to rejoin the strike – undoing what he had done, now with his own airtime.

The complexity of lived history

History, Madeleine Albright (2003) reminds us, is written backwards but lived forwards. This chapter has described how the Mabarete strike began, and provides an account of subaltern rebellion, in which a minority of SAPO's casual workers, realising that they could do no other, made their own rules and changed things: a history of how history was made.

But written history sharpens narratives that the complexity of lived history obscures. This chapter provides such a narrative. In telling it, I have striven to present an account that explains how the strike began and the form that it took. I believe the account to be accurate, even if interpretation rests on my own perspective. But accuracy does not mean a full or complete account. The chapter has also attempted to deepen this account in one important way: to underline the acute uncertainty of lived history in the opening weeks of the strike.

In telling the stories of individuals who vacillated over whether to join the strike or continue working, I have sought to highlight just how difficult the line of march, now clear with hindsight, was at the time. What separated those who joined the Mabarete strike and those who held back was often nothing but differing, contingent circumstances. It was not about ideology or political discipline; it was not about courage or endurance – though those were important qualities – and it was not about strategic and tactical ability, much as these were to be crucial to the eventual success of the strike. Much came down to the particularities of personal circumstances and how these were perceived by the actors themselves. And being human actors, these perceptions could change from one moment to the next, just as Dieho U-turned, yet again, after receiving an SMS.

The accounts of uncertainty reveal the complexity of struggle, whether for rank-and-file strikers or strike leaders as they navigate a way through the complexity and unpredictability of the present. Much as SAPO casual workers began to see an increasingly clear picture of the enemy – the confederates who maintained the system of labour broking – there was a much closer enemy. As the next chapter outlines, the Mabarete Strike was in large part waged by striking casuals on working casuals.

14

The Mabarete Strike II
Invisible Violence

A township battleground

By mid-January 2012, further mobilisation of casuals came to a halt. As the strike continued, the strikers' ranks were thinned: some returned to work out of desperation, others found work elsewhere. This attrition was only reversed when casuals in the Boksburg Depot on the East Rand, led by the indomitable Jerry Kgodu, joined the Mabarete en masse after the Commission for Conciliation, Mediation and Arbitration (CCMA) made it clear that it could not guarantee the safety of workers. The lines of battle were drawn. The Mabarete rode the trains and roamed the townships; working postmen took their chances should they venture out to deliver. As the Post Office explained in its appeal to the Labour Court for an interdict against the strike, 'staff remain within the depot to sort mail and do not deliver fearing for their safety' (Labour Court 2012b: Founding Affidavit, Section 81).

In fact, not all postmen remained in the depots. There was a geographical configuration of fear. Those truly afraid to deliver worked in townships, especially those with Metrorail stations. The geography of the Mabarete strike, like the mid-2011 strike, was shaped by the lines of the Metrorail.

Suburbs, by contrast, were all but off-limits to the strikers. Early in the mid-2011 strike, the Tembisa casuals had attempted to hunt replacement workers delivering in the 'white areas' that their depots serviced. The trip had been a disaster (interview, Choshi). The bakkie that they had hired to transport them had been stopped by traffic cops and the driver fined R200 for overloading. The fine went on top of the driver's hire charge and came out of the strikers' pockets. But never mind the transport, they quickly realised that they stood out like a sore thumb in the suburbs. Police or private security officers would soon be asking what their business was in the tree-lined streets. City centres were also off-limits even though they were often serviced by Metrorail: too many cameras, too many security guards, too many police.

The *ho tsoma* (hunting tactic of the Mabarete) operated on the last, and most dispersed step in mail delivery: door to door. Hunting required the Mabarete to disrupt the South African Post Office's (SAPO's) business walk by walk. Somewhat paradoxically, the strikers' desire to stop mail delivery led to a greater consciousness of how the daily delivery routes fitted into a national mail system. They realised that closing the hubs that processed mail before it reached the depots would be much more potent than tracking down postmen one by one. Bringing these to a halt would stop delivery in its tracks. Nothing would even get to the depots.

But the hubs were beyond the reach of the Mabarete. Despite the hubs using a large number of casuals, mainly women, the workers committees had never made inroads there. There was also more administrative and supervisory work in the hubs; they were permanent worker territory and the Communication Workers Union (CWU) was strong. When the Mabarete attempted to close down Witspos, the key national hub for the country, on 20 January 2012, they failed. They had nobody on the inside to work with and, when they attempted to block the main entrance, permanent workers, some brandishing guns, had chased them away (interviews, Bopape; Mulaudzi).

This and failed attempts to close regional hubs had seen the Mabarete fall back to hunting in the townships. The *ho tsoma* tactic was elevated from a piecemeal response to the deployment of replacement workers to their stock weapon, which they increasingly perfected.

An evolving structure

There is intense interest among labour scholars over what organisational forms are available to precarious workers given that traditional trade unions have, almost everywhere, struggled to advance their interests. This debate is sometimes constrained by the assumption that the purpose of organising casuals is to facilitate their participation in the industrial relations system. When it comes to the Mabarete, such an approach is putting the cart before the horse. The Mabarete organised to smash their way out of the system. It was only after this was achieved, once they had become permanents, that it made sense to think about re-entering the system. While the Mabarete sought to destroy labour broking, their aim was not to overturn the wider economic system but to participate in it on a different basis. If there is a key to understanding the Mabarete, it was their determination to prevail in a conflict waged outside the industrial relations system so that they could join it as full members.

The Mabarete, despite their worker membership, were closer in organisational form to an anarcho-syndicalist militia than to a trade union. There was a command structure, which came about through individuals taking up roles through the consent of others, and not through establishing formal ranks or positions. Loosely, an approximation to military organisation can be made. This is not one provided by the Mabarete themselves and I therefore use inverted commas throughout in this analogy.

The handful of leaders who were separated, deliberately, from day-to-day activities can be seen as the Mabarete's 'political leadership'. On the ground, there were a number of 'officers'. They would collectively make day-to-day operational decisions and then split up to lead different groups. When these groups arrived at their destination and split further in order to *ho tsoma*, to the extent that one striker led these smaller units they made an 'NCO' (corporals and sergeants) level of leadership. Alongside this fluid command structure, there was a culture of participatory democracy. At meetings, any striker could speak and votes by a show of hands would be taken, though often decisions were made by acclaim. They were never made by secret ballot. Yet, the need for secrecy curtailed how open such decision-making could be and operational decisions were delegated to the 'officers'. Although the 'officers' might be trusted, their positions lasted only as long as they retained the confidence of the Mabarete collectively. The morning meetings were a space where inadequacies or grievances could be raised. Throughout the Mabarete strike, no elections took place. Rather, leadership roles emerged from what responsibilities individuals shouldered and what respect they earned in the strike.

That was in line with the voluntary nature of strike participation. While the Mabarete's stock in trade was to deny scabs the right to work, they could not make people join them. The Mabarete had no real sanctions over each other. If a striker chose not to turn up at the morning meeting, there was little, other than moral suasion, that could be applied. There would be bursts of intense activity, riding the trains day after day in numbers when morale was high. But then people would take days off to rest, to attend to family matters and, increasingly as the strike lengthened, to attend court hearings. The strength of the Mabarete on any day amounted to who pitched up. Thus, although the Mabarete counted themselves at 294, this was never the total number of strikers active on any one day. They pitched because this was their last chance to become permanent. It was also because comradeship developed between them and because what they were doing was far more challenging, far more fulfilling and far more exciting 'work' than working.[1]

Other than what had been learned in the mid-2011 strike, there was no blueprint. Their transition from postmen to hunters of postmen came through experience. Given the organic nature of this process, nobody assigned titles, nobody wrote anything down, nobody conceptualised it as a structure. In part, this was because of the need for deniability, something that also saw leaders readily adopt *noms de guerre*. In part, it allowed the Mabarete to downplay the regional tensions that had divided the workers committees and, rather, focus on their mission. It also reflected the limited education of most Mabarete. Labour broker recruitment had lowered the educational requirements for recruitment into the Post Office. The previous SAPO requirement for completion of secondary schooling had fallen by the wayside. With few exceptions, writing beyond text messages, in any language, was a strain and rarely attempted. Those confident enough to write basic meeting minutes fell into a single-figure quantum. The Mabarete had no secretariat, no office, no bureaucracy. Nothing was formalised, especially in terms of leadership, until the strike was about to end.

In interviews, even when confidentially was guaranteed and it was understood that I did not want to know names, individuals who had played central roles during the strike were at a loss to describe their organisational form, though they could readily describe what they did. That contrasted with the ease with which the formal positions of earlier workers committees, particularly on the West Rand, were provided. Long-departed comrades were recalled alongside the positions they had held in structures that had been abandoned years previously. Here, I was given what amounted to a genealogy of the early workers committee structures. There was nothing comparable for the Mabarete despite it being the vehicle of the casuals' victory.

Cats, mice and mob squads

While the reach of the Mabarete's activity was prescribed by geographical opportunities and limitations, as described above, the *forms* of their activity was shaped by the resistance that they faced. Uncertainty was a key 'force multiplier' – if nobody knew where they were, they were in effect everywhere. The strategy was therefore to keep secret their planned activity; scabs and their supervisors must be kept guessing. The principle of hunting in areas where you were not known meant that the default activity involved multiple groups operating in different townships. To further uncertainty, tactics were varied. One day in February, all the Mabarete travelled south to the Vaal. Once in the area, groups disembarked at different stations on the line and the kasipolis[2] of the Orange Farm, Evaton and Sebokeng townships were swept clean of working postmen. The Mabarete were everywhere. And then they were gone. Subsequently, several similar 'spectaculars' were mounted, in which all Mabarete were mustered to saturate a large township or group of adjacent townships.

Generally, the odds were stacked against the scabs in any encounter on a township street. The Mabarete hunted in groups and generally postmen deliver alone. Beyond outnumbering a scab, the Mabarete held the moral high ground as well as the balance of fear. Only on one occasion did working postmen attempt to fight back. This was in Tembisa Township where replacement workers armed themselves and delivered in a large group. Unaware of this development, a regular

Mabarete hunting party had gone into the township but came back with their tails between their legs. This was a humiliating event given that it had taken place in Tembisa, the heartland of the strike. The next morning, after receiving the report-back, the meeting resolved to take revenge on the *amagundwane*.

Initially, the ten or so postmen that were delivering together thought they were dealing with a similarly sized group of strikers to the previous day and were preparing to again put them to flight. The bulk of the Mabarete were behind them, however, and on the cry of 'Move!' charged from side streets. The road was littered with abandoned bicycles and scattered letters as the scabs fled. Some made it back to the depot where they thought they were safe. But buoyed by success, the Mabarete 'mob squad', as these large groups became known, stormed the depot and beat those cornered inside. That was the end of the Tembisa strike-breaking and the birth of another operational tactic.

More sustained resistance to the Mabarete's efforts came from depot supervisors. Early in the strike, the owner of TAS Appointments and Management Services (TAS), Colleen Ramaphakela (2012), had berated SAPO supervisors in a letter to the Post Office's lawyers. She had been responding to demands that the labour brokers provide replacement labour, a necessary step before SAPO could approach the Labour Court. Supervisors, some of them trade union shop stewards, she alleged, were sympathising with the strike. They were not alerting the South African Police Service (SAPS) in a timely manner, they were allowing strikers to 'address and/or intimidate employees at depots unhindered', and they were 'not willing and/or reluctant to be witnesses or identify culprits'. What did SAPO think the labour brokers could do when their own line managers were sympathetic and/or running scared of the strikers?

Ramaphakela's observations were true, if uncharitable, of supervisors who had to think of their own safety. However, under pressure from senior managers, some supervisors attempted to continue delivery in what became a game of cat and mouse (group interview, SAPO supervisors). But the supervisors who played this game were neither cat nor mouse; rather, their part was to send the mice out while promising that the cat was elsewhere.

Saturday morning deliveries were organised, since the strikers were not active on weekends, with postmen sent out in groups for mutual protection, just in case something should happen. During the week, whenever supervisors got information of the whereabouts of the Mabarete, they would share it with each other. They knew that the Mabarete used the Metrorail and they knew they did not stay for long in one area. The theory was that it was safe to send out postmen once the Mabarete had passed through and were heading elsewhere. In response, the Mabarete kept changing tactics. Groups would criss-cross the region and sometimes deliberately double-back on themselves, or return to an area unexpectedly the following day, to deny the mouse-masters certainty over where the Mabarete would be next.

As the strike ground on, the levels of violence rose. The Mabarete were focused on stopping mail delivery. It was frustrating, as sometimes happened, to return after a long day's striking to find mail in your mail box. However, it was far more frustrating to believe that you were stopping the mail, but that it added up to nothing. After the Post Office's interdict fell flat, it tried to defeat the Mabarete by pretending there was no strike. It then attempted to portray those disrupting mail delivery as criminal elements, hooligans. As both sides sought to win this strike, the ferocity of the beatings increased. It was one thing that the Mabarete's foot soldiers controlled.

Move!

It was not until negotiations began in March 2012 that any publicly identifiable leadership group, the 'Top Nine', became visible. Fearful of organisational decapitation, the Tembisa eschewal of formal positions was adopted. Additionally, Chinese walls were put in place; the 'political leaders' of the Mabarete did not know, nor wanted to know, what happened after the morning meetings. When the Top Nine began negotiations with SAPO, they were able to plausibly argue that they did not know what was happening on the ground. Despite some close calls, this separation held. Of course, on the ground, the Mabarete knew who their leaders were. Indeed, one way to test an unfamiliar face was to ask who was leadership. If you had not been around you could not answer (interview, Kubheka).

An important channel of communication for the Mabarete, enabling them to coordinate activity, was the 'office phone', which allowed anonymous instructions to be issued. The phone had been purchased by the remaining hard core of West Rand strikers in January 2012 (interviews, Chauke; Mutavhatsindi).[3] It belonged to nobody. It was rotated among the Mabarete leadership and the number given only to trusted strikers. Those receiving a message from the number did not know who had sent it, but they knew it was an instruction (interviews, Chauke; Choshi; Kubheka).

It was essential that nobody be recognised as they hunted. If that happened, charges could be laid against them.[4] This was achieved by strikers avoiding areas where they were known, save one or two locals who would act as guides to the hunting parties while keeping a low profile. It was also essential that nobody knew where the Mabarete were headed. If their destination was known, the working postmen would quickly head back to the depots. The cat would be hunting with a bell on its tail. The bell was not full-blown *impimpi*, but 'indirect informants'. Early on, the Marbarete 'officers' realised that a hunting party would set off and find the streets empty of postmen. Someone in the group would have tipped off a relative or friend to save them a beating. But one person would tell another and it was not long before every postman in the area was peddling furiously back to their depot, making sure that their route did not take them close to a Metrorail station.

This problem was resolved with 'Move!' The word became the Mabarete's battle cry. Like much of the cultural repertoire established during the strike, it was borrowed. In this case, it originated with security guards at Park Station who had been dealing with crowds on the platforms as a Mabarete group was passing through.[5] They took it for themselves. 'Move!' meant to spring into action. It could be used offensively (Move! and catch him before he has a chance to escape) or defensively (Move! now that we are done here everyone must make their own way to the station where we will regroup). But when riding the Metrorail, 'Move!' was the command to alight at the approaching station. Once the problem of indirect informers was identified, it was the 'officers' who decided where each group would be hunting. The *batsomi* (hunters) were told only which train to board. They knew their exact destination only when 'Move!' was shouted as they approached a station (interview, Mabulane). Of course, it was still possible for indirect informers to warn others towards whom the train was heading, even if they did not know where on the line they would be disembarking. The Mabarete policed each other in this regard: no phone calls. If there were concerns that someone had leaked information, the suspect would be taken to one side and his phone checked.

The Mabarete and the *lex loci* of the *kasi*

In pursing their objective, the Mabarete focused on the bodies of those postmen attempting to deliver mail. The most graphic evidence provided to the Labour Court and served on the first six respondents in the mid-2011 strike had been photographs of vandalised Post Office vans at the Tembisa Depot. Page after page of the SAPO submission showed the smashed windscreens and damaged tyres. It was concluded that destroying Post Office property provided easy evidence for the courts to act upon. The result was a macabre focus on people rather than property.[6] It meant, in principle at least, that scabs could be dealt with while bicycles and letters should be left alone.[7]

Leaving letters untouched was also rationalised on the basis that they did not want to make enemies in the community. Destroying a letter could cause problems; perhaps it contained a cheque or a certificate.[8] Finally, there was their image to think about: the Post Office was portraying them as criminals or hooligans. They needed to show that they were not. Why safeguarding letters while beating the man delivering them demonstrated that the Mabarete were not criminals will require most readers to step into a different value framework – the *lex loci* (local law) (Thompson 1991) of the South African township or *kasi*.

Unlike the suburbs, in the township the Mabarete, as African men, were as 'good as anyone' (interview, Bopape). It was not only their black skins that were the same as others, but also their world view, their perspective on the struggle they were prosecuting. In the context of a strike against labour broking, it was strikers who held the moral high ground. Townships are not homogeneous and neither are their residents' beliefs, but if there is a dominant world view within them it includes two important facets: that people should not be selfish and that punishment, including physical, is necessary to teach right from wrong.

Of course, world views affirm most vigorously the very values with which communities are struggling in practice. People's perceived selfishness is understood to be central to the everyday strife that constantly courses through families and between neighbours in the *kasi*. And while in the *kasi* there is a lot of talk about beating children as part of their upbringing, it is usually only resorted to in desperation. Parents would like their children to be given a hiding when necessary, but would rather not do it themselves.[9] Nevertheless, none of this detracts from the validity of these widely held norms. Applied to a strike, especially one against the selfish exploitation of Africans by labour brokers, scabbing is a moral infringement and thrashing the guilty is understandable.

One of the Mabarete's struggle songs, *Thiba ka Mona!*, captures the moral justification for this punishment.[10]

> *Thiba ka mona!*
> *Thiba ka mona!*
> *Re boloya ntja tsena!*
> *Di ya re usa.*[11]

> Stop [them] on this side!
> Stop [them] on this side! [Singers indicate with their arms the alternative sides that they are blocking]
> We kill these dogs!
> Those which use us.

As the last line makes clear, the scabs, other casuals in particular, were using the strikers. The strikers were sacrificing to end labour broking while, by working, the *amagundwane* continued to earn. Yet, all casuals would benefit from a Mabarete victory. Under these circumstances, working during the Mabarete strike was clear-cut selfishness and needed to be corrected.

Captured scabs were not necessarily beaten; it depended on circumstances. It was seen as a greater infringement for a casual to be scabbing than a permanent worker. Then there was the question of whether warnings had been heeded; if a casual was caught delivering a second time, they were committing a far more egregious violation of the strike and clearly the severity of the first lesson had been insufficient to correct behaviour. If a scab 'gave lip', it indicated an unwillingness to accept they were in the wrong and necessitated strong medicine. There was thus a moral code, even if its application was not always consistent. Earlier in the strike, there were more warnings, threats, slapping, mocking and forced stripping – humiliations that stopped short of serious physical harm. Beatings became increasingly the norm, and were more severe and more prolonged as the strike continued.

What was constant was the belief that such beatings were justified. That did not mean everyone relished what happened. Some did, but many did their best to avoid taking part; there were always more than enough volunteers to act as lookouts while beatings took place. But nobody thought it was not necessary. The beatings might be justified reluctantly, with regret that they had to happen, but they were justified. This did not put the Mabarete apart from the wider township communities to which they, and the punished strike-breakers, belonged. Far from it: what they did conform to was widespread, culturally grounded beliefs. They were outside the law, but within the *lex*.

The police, the law and the *kasi's lex loci*

So, what of those responsible for upholding the constitutionally governed laws of the land? The dilatory response of the SAPS was bemoaned by SAPO. When it returned to the Labour Court on 9 February 2012 to have the January *rule nisi* confirmed, Janras Kotsi's affidavit had complained that the SAPS 'have been ineffective in enforcing the initial court order' (Labour Court 2012b: Supplementary Affidavit). SAPO was, Kotsi continued, drafting a court application to compel SAPS to enforce the court order. However, even if the application had been made an order of court, it is not clear what would have come of it.[12] It was not only the difficulty of dealing with hit-and-run tactics across scores of townships, nor the limited capacity of the SAPS, that was on the Mabarete's side. The approach of the police to the strike, on the ground, was equivocal; at least it was so in the townships where most action took place.

On one occasion, when strikers caught a working postman, they took him to a piece of waste ground where he was forced to strip. The opening stages of a thrashing were unfolding when a police car passed the scene. The officers hooted and waved but did not stop. It was assumed that the police had clocked the scene as community members dealing with a criminal; perhaps a nyaope smoker driving them to distraction with incessant burglaries, perhaps a rapist. The police's job was being done for them. Officially, the line is that communities should not 'take the law into their own hands'. But when that happens, officers frequently *sheba thoko* (look away) because they tacitly approve, and because once it has got to this point it is not wise to intervene on behalf of the criminals until the community anger has cooled.[13]

But it was not only over methods that many police officers would see eye to eye with the Mabarete. It was also the issue of labour broking. As members of a highly unionised organisation, police officers frequently took a dim view of strike-breakers, especially if it was a strike against labour brokers. In township police stations, where the vast majority of officers are Africans, the assumption that the dispute was one between African worker and white bosses reinforced this perspective (even if, as with TAS, this was not always the case). *Amagundwane* reporting assaults at township police stations could get short shrift.[14]

If, however, the Mabarete's *ho tsoma* activity was framed neither as community chastisement, nor dealing with strike-breakers, police would respond as they would when called to the scene of any street assault and attempt to arrest the perpetrators. The Mabarete increasingly took care not to beat scabs openly and rather escorted them to more secluded places.[15]

Sometimes, however, captured scabs would see an opportunity and shout for help or make a run for it. Sometimes arrests were made and charges laid. In this case, Mabarete leaders would go to the station to explain the situation. Sometimes this could turn things around:

> There was a case . . . and we went and explained our side of the story. The investigating officer said, 'Are you saying these guys who are opening the case, they don't want to participate in the strike?' We said, 'Yes.' He said, 'But when you win they

are all going to win also. Are they happy working for the labour brokering companies?' And we said, 'That's what we suspect; that they are happy working for these companies.' He said, 'No.' He even took the [case] docket and he tore it apart and threw it in the dustbin. He said, 'Deal with these people because they are sell-outs' (interview, Mutavhatsindi).

This was not always the case, however. Sometimes the charges stuck and Mabarete ended up in court. Usually the accused were released on bail. Typically, cases were repeatedly postponed. No cases ever got to trial, often because accusers would withdraw charges or because witnesses retracted statements or provided useless information (interview, Kubheka). As much as company managers might want prosecutions, those on the front lines of the strike had additional factors to consider.[16]

Kasi heroes

An incident during the strike in one East Rand township illustrates how *kasi* morality, the stigmatised status of labour brokers and police sympathy could synergise in favour of the Mabarete.[17] After a heavy night, two strikers had been making their way on foot to a funeral early one Saturday morning. Unexpectedly, they had encountered a group of replacement workers delivering mail. Initially, they had spotted two of the group on bicycles. It was their neighbourhood and they knew that nobody had delivered for weeks. But now it was happening in front of their eyes! Outraged as they were, they figured cunning was in order and continued talking to each other until the cyclists were in range of the stones they had picked up. Though neither rider was hit, both came off their bikes and fled on foot.

Breaking Mabarete protocol, the two then took the bicycles with them. But as they turned a corner, they came face to face with a much larger group of scabs. How many were in the group varied between ten and fifteen as the story was subsequently told and retold. They realised they had stumbled into a new SAPO strike-breaking tactic: group delivery in the township on Saturday morning. They recognised one person: Ronald, a permanent worker who lived only a few streets away. After the first encounter, the *amagundwane* must have gathered together, realising that there was trouble. By chance, the two sides now ended up face to face, two against many. The strike-breakers had likely been assured that the Mabarete did not operate on weekends. But since two of their number had just been attacked, for all they knew, there was an entire mob squad hunting in the township. The two Mabarete stood their ground with courage – part Dutch, part moral indignation. They pointed at the group, told them they were scabbing and that they would remember their faces. It was the strike-breakers who fled, two bicycles short, back to the depot.

The two strikers hid the bikes behind the *mokhukhu* (shack) where one of them lived and got back to the business of the night before. At some point, they dozed off. They were woken by knocking on the shack door. Outside were two police officers accompanied by an African woman, the supervisor of the local SAPO depot. She was on the warpath and wanted the police to lay charges of theft and assault. However, she did not get far. In the ensuing arguments, the two Mabarete made it clear to the police officers that they were not common thieves but striking workers. Striking against labour brokers! They were postmen, but still casuals after so many years! They were striking against exploitation! Yes, they had taken the bikes, taken them from scabs! They showed the police the bicycles, the bundles of letters still in the front baskets.

The police were annoyed that they had not been informed about the background to the incident and made the supervisor's attempts to lay charges an uphill task.[18] Since the bikes and the letters had been recovered, there was no case of theft. Since nobody had been hurt, there was no assault. One of the police officers started tapping his watch. The other wanted to know what the legalities of the Post Office working on a Saturday morning were. Both agreed that their police van could not be used to transport the bikes, even though the supervisor had travelled with them after first reporting the matter. She would have to get them to the police station herself. If she did manage to open a case, nothing further came of it.

The two Mabarete were now heroes. But there remained a question about Ronald's role. Had he informed on them? The matter was debated with friends, neighbours and Mabarete *maqabane* over the afternoon. If Ronald had informed on them, it was not a matter that could be ignored. In the end, consensus was that he would not have been so stupid. He would know there would be consequences. In support of this line was that the supervisor had not known their names when she came knocking with her police escort. It was concluded that she must have tracked them down some other way.

A few streets away, Ronald must have been having similar conversations, or at least thoughts. The next day, one of the Mabarete received a message, via an intermediary, from Ronald to say that he had not grassed on them. The township *lex loci* had prevailed.

Broken promises and imagined papers

The strike hardened Maja.[19] He seemed to gain years during the first few weeks of the strike. Before the strike he knew he was at the wrong end of a raw deal. He had joined the previous strike, but now he was much clearer about the problem. The government, he told me over our *kota* and coke, are *tsotsis* (criminals) and the unions have been bought by management. People get what they fight for, and he was fighting for what he wanted. Now when he rode the train in the morning he was no longer travelling alone; he rode with other strikers, people he hardly knew before but who were now *maqabane*. They rode unafraid of the ticket inspectors. If there was a problem they were not alone. They would deal with whoever opposed them.

One afternoon, Maja suggested we visit Mabarete friends: strikers who live in another section of the township. Ahead of us the sky was dark and the first gusts of a storm were starting to blow. Making the journey on foot had put us at the mercy of the elements. The darkening sky had taken both of us by surprise. But we were lucky; the first spots of rain started as we reached the *zozo* (prefabricated corrugated-iron shack) where Solly lived with his girlfriend. It was squeezed into the yard so tightly that one window looked directly onto the sidewall of the house some 20 centimetres away. We entered hurriedly as the rain began to fall. The single room had a double bed, two plastic chairs, an old kitchen cupboard with a two-ring stove on it, a TV and a huge fridge. A single light bulb was suspended above the stove. The bed was partly screened with a purple cloth hanging from a wire stretched across the room.

Maja and I took the two chairs while Solly found a paint tin to sit on. His girlfriend pulled back the dividing curtain so that she could see the TV from the bed. She and Solly were part way through a Nollywood movie full of flashy cars, gold jewellery and an implausible story line. Every now and again the screen froze and we would miss a few seconds of the film, a *fongkong* (pirated) DVD. The rain beat down so hard on the zinc roof that we could not hear each other, even if we shouted. We watched the bright colours on the TV screen until the rain slowed and the three of us headed off, leaving Solly's girlfriend behind to watch the end of the film.

Shitas Selota, another *maqabane*, lived only 100 metres away. We went around to the back of the four-room house. There were three rows of shacks filling the long, narrow backyard. It was the same for neighbouring properties, a mini shack city within the township. There were narrow passages between the shacks leading to the toilet at the back. After the rain, puddles of water filled the passages.

Shitas came from Limpopo to Gauteng after he completed his matric. He came to study at college, but things did not work out and he had worked as a permanent casual in the Post Office since 2000.

We headed for a tavern. Inside there were a dozen customers, most of them watching a huge flat-screen TV fixed to one wall. It was tuned to the SuperSport channel, and Liverpool was playing Manchester United. I sponsored the round: Maja had a Castle Light, Solly and Shitas drank Zamalek and it was Coke for me.

We chatted, or rather we shouted across the table. About the strike. Solly, a man of few words and much *matakwane* (cannabis), said little. Shitas was eager to talk. He was at one with Maja over unions: CWU was only interested in the permanents. Like the government, they were part of the racket. The ANC and Zwelinzima Vavi [then general secretary of the Congress of South African Trade Unions] talk about ending labour broking, but what do they do? He spat out the answer; they do nothing! Later, walking back with Maja I raised this point again. There is, I told him, legislation in the pipeline. Maja laughed at my suggestion and told me that if he waited for the ANC he would be permanent when he was walking this way, and he mimicked an old man doubled up, using a stick to painfully step forward. When we stopped laughing, he became angry again. What had the ANC done for him? What about [President] Zuma's *ditsepiso* (promises)? Nothing!

While uncertain as to what exactly becoming a permanent employer would mean, beyond the increase that they craved, the three were in no doubt that victory would be sweet. They promised each other that if they pulled this off, they would slaughter a cow at Germiston Lake. Maja, for one, had already imagined the moment when he signs his permanent contract. He could not wait to have it in front of him so that he could say, 'Give me your ballpoint!' He illustrated this triumph with repeated flourishes of his hand as he signed the imaginary papers that would set him free.

Stories of struggle
Participants in any social action conceptualise and justify what they are doing. Conceptualisation and justification are interwoven processes, each fashioned to support the other. The Mabarete conceptualised and justified the strike in a range of ways. The foundation for these efforts was a moral economy, or a just distribution of opportunity and wealth, which contrasted to their actual situation (Thompson 1991). At an individual level, each member of the Mabarete knew this intimately; it was rubbed like salt into a wound every working day by the difference between themselves and the permanent SAPO workers.

It was not hard to extend this workplace discrimination between casual and permanent to their position within the new South Africa – a new South Africa that was not so new and which was not, for them, living up to expectations. In a reflective piece written after the strike, Mashita 'Shitas' Selota stated:

> It is really hurting to see individuals benefiting and the rest of South Africa suffering. Rich people get richer and privileged, poor people get poorer. The gap between poor people and rich people becomes wider and wider every day. Democracy is for all South Africans, not only political leaders who own companies and have shares in big companies and mines. We all deserve a

better life and better living wages. Away with labour brokers, away! (Selota 2012).

The Mabarete's struggle, it can be seen, was fought at three levels. First, individually each member of the Mabarete was fighting to become a permanent employee; second, collectively they were battling to end labour broking in the Post Office; and third, some of the strike's leaders came to see their struggle as a step to end all labour broking in South Africa. The first two levels of struggle were bonded; the first could not happen without the second. To end labour broking had become a mission. It was not hard to see this as a noble endeavour, especially when projected onto the national landscape; the difficulty was that those who stood in the way of victory were largely also victims of what they were fighting against – labour broker employees just like themselves, African men close to the bottom of the occupational pile. But by delivering mail, they took the side of the oppressor. Russel Mutavhatsindi explained it this way:

> If you go to work . . . you take the company's job, you go out for delivery, definitely you have a demon [possession] because how could you do that while others are fighting for what's right? . . . If you are delivering then you are saying, 'I don't care about decent salary, I don't care about decent job, I don't care about job security', and we could not allow that and we could not allow anyone who will help the company to defeat our, our *mission* . . . (interview, Mutavhatsindi).

I have outlined how the township *lex loci* justified corporal punishment. Yet, it did not provide an unequivocal licence for violence. There were limits and boundaries, even if these could be shifted and flexed. Just as the extremities of wealth raise moral ire, so too do extremities of behaviour. Justification requires some proportionality between means and ends. The recognition that corporal punishment is necessary to correct transgressions has to compete with other values and considerations. Beating scabs could be justified, but it did not mean it was something to be unequivocally proud about. This ambiguity and uncertainty over the tension between mission and means came out when I asked Siphiwe Kubheka (interview), who was on labour brokers' books in SAPO for over a decade, if he thought that God had been on the side of the Mabarete.

> SK: I think God helped. Why I say that [is] because . . . the way this strike happened I think maybe God said, 'Now it's time [to end labour broking in SAPO]', because we have been suffering for a long time in this company. And then for each and every thing that we did, we were successful. We did what we did, [yet] we were never arrested [convicted]. You see everything like it was guided by him . . . [But] I wouldn't say that, er, when it comes to the beating, that wasn't God. No, that was not God. God did not want us to do that. Yes, we did wrong by doing that . . .
>
> DD: Do you see it as wrong?
>
> SK: Yes, I know, yes, we knew it was wrong, it was not okay, but it was the only way to stop these people from doing this work for this company which is playing with people. Paying them this money, this R2 000 every month. You can't even do anything, you can't even buy yourself underwear with this money of R2 000. Because when it comes to you, you already have debt owing to the *mashonisas* [moneylenders].

Not surprisingly then, the narrating of the strike by the Mabarete was complex and took different forms. Perhaps the least complicated was the image of themselves as brave soldiers fighting for a cause. It was an image that matched their, previously discussed, militarisation and their name. In the words of one of the songs with which they maintained morale, *Pelo tse Thata*:

> *Makwala a tjhetjhe!*
> *A tjhetjhe ke marao.*
> *Ho ya rona!*

Ho ya rona!
Ho ya rona!
Ba pelo tse thata ko pele.

The cowards retreat!
They retreat back.
It is us!
It is us!
It is us!
Those with strong hearts who go forward.[20]

Not only were they courageous, but they were fighting for others. Selota (2012) again: 'It was the brave workers who put their careers and livelihoods at risk by taking part in an illegal strike, who fought like soldiers protecting their country, that won the struggle. With the help of Almighty God nothing is impossible.'

Religious beliefs played a varied role in the strike. Zion Christian Church members would leave their badges at home when they were with the Mabarete. The strike was not a thing of the church. But that did not mean that the lay preachers among the Mabarete would not be asked to pray for the success of their endeavours when they gathered together each morning, a ubiquitous practice at South African gatherings.[21] Those endeavours were frequently placed within a three-part account that, loosely, paralleled the Old Testament account of the Jew's enslavement and escape from Pharaoh's Egypt to the Promised Land. There was a time of suffering (the 'slavery' of labour broking), a time of struggle in the wilderness (as the Mabarete), and an (imminent but not yet achieved) time of reward (as permanent employees in the 'House of the Post Office') when they reached the Promised Land.

This narrative did not, of course, strictly conform to the biblical text. Religion was one resource among others that could be used to explain and justify their actions. They told each other that nothing was achieved without effort. *Mamello a tswala katleho* (Patience brings success)[22] is a Sesotho saying, while *O tla ja bohobe mofufutso wa phatla ya hao* (You will eat bread by the sweat of your brow) is a verse from Genesis (3: 19).[23] Both were used for the same purpose: to reassure themselves and each other that they would prevail and that their efforts would be rewarded.

The Bible, being a vast resource, can be used in multiple ways. George Ramagaga likened the Mabarete strike to the Children of Israel's conquest of Jericho under Joshua.[24] On another occasion, Ramagaga (interview) used a different metaphor to explain what they had done, one that mixed the Old Testament with a distinctly modern substance. In seeking the Promised Land, he explained, you could not simply wait for deliverance. You had to march. And if you march, there will be obstacles. If you came across a rock that blocked your way, you had to dynamite it.

As we discussed this metaphor, Ramagaga conceded, jokingly, that one should use only small sticks of dynamite: just enough to clear the way, not more. All groups working together develop jargon, codes and jokes. Euphemisms and jokes ease the discussion of embarrassing, difficult or sensitive matters. Karl von Holdt (2012), in his research on strike violence in South Africa, outlines how a striking nurse talked about the effectiveness of the medicine (that is, beating) that had been administered to scabs, while others joked about rat poison for *amagundwane*. Early on in the strike, the Mabarete played with the idea that those they were hunting were one or another type of food.[25] They were hungry and needed to 'eat'. This played on their actual hunger over long days travelling across the province, but also the enjoyment, or at least professed enjoyment, of punishing a scab.[26] These euphemisms were sometimes used when they were taking a captured strike-breaker to a place where punishment could be administered undisturbed. Strikers would banter with each other in a way that a terrified victim would half understand, or would hope he had not understood.

However, what became the dominant code of the strike was a religious metaphor in which the Mabarete 'prayed' for the strike-breakers. This idea was elaborated in multiple ways. Among the Mabarete there were archbishops, bishops, priests, preachers, deacons, elders and so on, who would remove the demons that caused them to sin against their fellow brothers by breaking the strike. Those whom they prayed for were to be born again and needed to be as naked as a newborn baby, stripped of their clothes. The Mabarete's prayers would immunise the person from contracting the sickness again. Should it not, as on the odd occasion when a warning *klap* (slap) or two had not been heeded, stronger prayers were necessary: a full-on exorcism of a particularly persistent demon. When those escorting a captured postman felt they had reached a suitable place for punishment to be administered undisturbed, members of the hunting party would call out, '*Ntate Moruti aku o qale sefala*' (Mr Preacher, please will you start the hymn).

In contrast to the religious narrative of their journey from slavery to the Promised Land, praying to remove demons was never taken for anything more than a metaphor. Although the belief that it put them on the right side of a moral equation helped to explain why it was so enthusiastically embraced. It also served as code; everybody knew what 'we have prayed' meant. And it provided a way to gloss the reality of blooded bodies. The metaphor became a leitmotif of the strike and endured long afterward as a threat and as coded communication in the turbulent strikes and confrontations that were to follow the Mabarete victory.

An invisible strike

As much as praying, Mabarete style, became a symbol of power, it also indicated that they were not full industrial citizens who could claim their rights. Rather, they must speak in code. For all their prowess, they remained a liminal entity. Their tactics were hit and run. Attempts to close the SAPO mail hubs failed. At Witspos they had been chased away by CWU militants. When they tried to close the regional mail hub in Germiston, police came and wanted to know where their strike certificate was. When they could not produce one, they were threatened with arrest and told to move on (interview, Choshi).

Early on in the strike, they had used a park in the Johannesburg city centre for meetings. This was equally convenient for strikers coming from the Vaal and from the East and West Rand. But meetings there had been harassed by mounted police telling them that they needed a permit (interview, Mabulane). They had retreated from the metropole to the periphery, back to the Germiston Golden Walk mall car park, which, although only 50 metres from SAPO's mail hub, was de facto asphalt commonage. This became the Mabarete's head office. Their pressure point, the township where they could disrupt delivery, was even further from the metropole. The disruption the Mabarete caused was confined to the townships.

Operating in socially marginal spaces, they acted against marginalised citizens. Their primary target was the casuals who were delivering – people like themselves, working and living in the precarious margins of South African society. The Mabarete's primary objective was to stop mail delivery, but it was achieved only in townships. The disruption burdened township residents, who, despite the rhetoric of the new South Africa, do not count in the way that suburban residents count. The Mabarete's message, delivered through the punishment they meted out to *amagundwane*, was not getting through. The reality was that the Post Office put little value on its labour broker staff, whether working, striking or in intensive-care wards.

For all its fury, the strike was invisible.

15

The Mabarete Strike III
Manifest Fear

Talking with hooligans

Although the Mabarete strike was all but invisible beyond Gauteng townships, their *ho tsoma* (hunting tactic) activity laid the platform for their next move: home visits. These created fear beyond the socially marginal, but it was the township beatings that made home visits effective. From the perspective of the Mabarete, the visits 'changed everything', although it can perhaps be better understood as tipping the scales for South African Post Office (SAPO) management over labour broking.

This chapter looks at the Mabarete's home visits and the negotiations that followed. However, it starts by exploring the failure of a popular, alternative resource available to precarious workers – symbolic power. Activity in the Mabarete strike did not focus solely on disruptive techniques. Despite their experiences of how constitutionally framed efforts had failed, these continued, albeit with less vigour, alongside the Mabarete's use of disruptive power.[1]

Striking over a long period, in any form, requires that participants sustain themselves, since once on strike they receive no wages. Nor could they claim Unemployment Insurance Fund (UIF) benefits since striking Mabarete were dismissed for being absent without leave. Some were on strike for four months. With savings and accumulated assets, it would have been hard. Starting, as most of them did, with nothing in reserve, these were long, grim months.

By surviving over months, in ways explored in this chapter, the Mabarete held out until SAPO was forced to negotiate peace. As long as their messages came through the bloodied bodies of workers, SAPO continued to see them as hooligans with whom they refused to talk (interview, Tutu Mokoena). That changed when the strike came knocking on their front doors. The subsequent talks were not straightforward, however. The Mabarete were entering into unfamiliar terrain, for which they were not prepared. SAPO had to end what had been a lucrative arrangement, with many beneficiaries, which had kept the organisation in the black, and there was the problem of the Communication Workers Union (CWU) being the only recognised labour representative. Despite the difficulties, though, an agreement was reached and labour broking ended.

The limits of symbolic power

Jennifer Chun (2009) outlines how precarious workers employed by agencies in a triangular contractual arrangement have mobilised 'symbolic power' in their struggles for better pay and conditions. Key to leveraging symbolic power were protests covered by the media that publicly shamed the client company by making employment conditions visible. This enabled organisers to bypass the legal contractual arrangements and appeal directly to public sentiment. What makes an organisation vulnerable to symbolic power depends on a range of factors, but since symbolic power requires an audience to form an opinion on what is presented, publicity is essential.

Over the years, SAPO casuals had attempted to mobilise symbolic power by contacting the media. These efforts had produced minimal results. It was not as though there was no potential for symbolic power in the casual workers' struggle; the mixed approaches of the police to the Mabarete, as outlined in the previous chapter, indicate the degree to which labour broking had become stigmatised in South Africa. The challenge for SAPO casuals was to bring this symbolic power to bear directly onto the Post Office. Even though the Mabarete strike increasingly focused on using disruptive power, there were sporadic attempts to mobilise symbolic power.

In late January 2012, Thabiso Bopape and Russel Mutavhatsindi put together a leaflet addressed 'To the Communities of Gauteng' in an attempt to build public support for the strike.[2] The leaflet apologised for mail not being delivered, but blamed 'the Post Office and their labour broker friends'. The leaflet outlined the casuals' exploitation and asked for the public's support. 'Do not,' it requested, 'accept mail from the *Amagundwane* (non-strikers) during the strike and ask them why they are not part of our struggle.' The leaflet then called for people to 'Join us in our march for justice' to the Public Protector's provincial office in Johannesburg on 7 February (Bopape and Mutavhatsindi 2012).

The march to the Public Protector's office went ahead. The petition was delivered, but disappeared without trace.[3] As far as anybody can recall, the strikers were not joined by members of the public. If anything, it was a day when strike-breakers could deliver without having to worry: the Mabarete were in Johannesburg and not in the townships. Nor was there any evidence of residents refusing mail. Possibly it happened. Probably it did not. Residents standing guard over their post boxes each morning in solidarity with the casuals seems unlikely. The march to the Public Protector's office was something of a nod to the Mabarete's past, to the constitutional road and the politics of petitions.

Nevertheless, the demonstration was one of the few times the Mabarete got media coverage. Soweto TV, a widely watched, free-to-air community TV station, sent a film crew. There were other protests organised by the Mabarete, but these attempts at mobilising symbolic power did not get far; media attention was slim. Soweto TV and Jozi FM, a local radio station that also had its roots in the township, provided some coverage. Despite efforts, there was no coverage on the most widely watched TV stations run by the South African Broadcasting Corporation (SABC). At one point, there was even a march to the SABC to complain about the lack of coverage, but nothing changed, something that was put down to CWU's influence in the organisation (interviews, Bopape; Chauke).

The one event that did bring extensive media coverage was, ironically, the national march organised by the Congress of South African Trade Unions (COSATU), including CWU, against labour broking and e-tolling on 7 March 2012. This was part of COSATU's long-running national campaign against labour broking. The issue was hitched to the unpopular introduction of electronic road tolls in Gauteng, and a national one-day strike was declared. An estimated

200 000 people joined protests nationwide, with the largest march in Johannesburg.[4] A group of Mabarete joined the march. What made them stand out was their SAPO bibs, while other protesters wore the standard march wear of union-issued T-shirts. They also had handwritten placards that fingered the Post Office for using labour brokers. Nobody else on the 50 000-strong march identified client companies using labour brokers. This was not surprising, given casual workers' vulnerability. The Mabarete did not have to worry about dismissal for bringing the client company into disrepute since they had already been dismissed. The SAPO bibs were a magnet for the media, who circled, snapped and interviewed the group. It was a tangible story that spiced up journalists' reports, which otherwise had to rely on the well-worn official slogans of the march. Pictures of the *toyi-toying* Mabarete-in-SAPO-bibs were widely used in reports. Yet, much as the publicity gave a boost to the morale of the Mabarete, and was noted with embarrassment by SAPO managers, it did not bring about any dramatic shift in attitudes (interview, Petersen).

The limited publicity given to the Mabarete strike was frustrating. Management appeared to care no more about the mail being delivered (in the townships) than they cared about what happened to postmen caught delivering. One attempt to dispel the invisibility of the Mabarete strike was to make major SAPO clients aware that they were paying for a service that was not delivering. It was hoped that they would then complain and SAPO would have to deal with the problem.

Their approach to the University of South Africa (UNISA), South Africa's distance learning university, was the most creative of these efforts. Some of the Mabarete were studying with UNISA. So, swapping hats for the day, they went to UNISA's head office in Pretoria to complain, as students, that they had not received their study material. They backed up this protest by showing date-stamped pictures of UNISA study material sitting in Post Office depots long after students should have received them (interview, Bopape). But even the chutzpah of the UNISA ploy did not appear to have any impact on the Post Office's steadfast refusal to acknowledge the strike for what it was.

In juggling disruptive and symbolic power, the Mabarete were hedging their bets, seeing which would work best for them. There was an obvious contradiction between the two strategies. Much as the Mabarete wanted publicity to leverage symbolic power over SAPO on labour broking, publicity about their disruptive activities could only have damaged, perhaps destroyed, their standing in any national public debate.[5] But unlike the use of disruptive power and the withdrawal of labour, which can be tacitly combined, this was not possible with symbolic power. The two power forms were alternatives. One was to force the Post Office to concede because otherwise it could not operate; the other was to force the Post Office to concede because reputational damage was exceeding financial savings. As the latter failed to gain any significant traction, the former was stubbornly maintained by the Mabarete.

Surviving the strike

As the strike dragged on, things got harder. For those who know exactly how many days there are to go until pay day, skipping a month's salary is hard and even harder the following month. Soon it is not just about money, but about relationships, which either hold despite the strain or disintegrate.

Recalling their time of struggle, Mabarete often inflated the strike's duration to six months. It must have felt like that, but in fact it was just shy of four months: seventeen and a half weeks. This was long enough, even if joining the strike in January cut three weeks from the total for many. So, how did the strikers survive without pay for that long?

The easy answer to that is that they survived just as they would have survived if unemployed. Unemployment in South Africa, depending on which measure you use, has for long remained around the mid-20 or mid-30 per cent level. It is higher for Africans than for those of other race groups and higher still for those with lower educational qualification and skill levels. Few African residents of the townships have not experienced periods of unemployment and the hardship this brings. Social security for those of working age is limited to the UIF, which provides limited relief.

The most important factor in surviving is family – specifically, relatives who are able to provide or pay for accommodation, groceries, transport or whatever else is needed. Viewed from the other end of the dependency relationship, this is 'black tax': too many dependants hanging onto too few breadwinners. When a SAPO casual postman went out on strike, another set of appeals was being made to those likely already overburdened by a carousel of requests. Nevertheless, by and large relatives were sympathetic to the casuals' strikes. They knew how the strikers had struggled to make ends meet when working. That they were striking for something better made sense, both for the casual and for the relative. In a best-case scenario, should the strike be successful, there would be one less set of demands to juggle in the future and another person to share the family's black tax.

Those still living at home fell back on parental or sibling support now that they could no longer contribute to household expenses. Mabarete living with partners who had stood by them expressed deep gratitude (interviews, Chauke; Mutavhatsindi). Others were not so lucky and lost girlfriends and wives, sometimes for good.

A key problem for all strikers is existing financial commitments that can now no longer be serviced. Furniture on hire purchase is repossessed, loans from banks have to be rescheduled leading to higher deferred repayment schedules, DSTV subscriptions lapse. Even worse is when there are children. They still have to have transport money to get to school; they still need something in their *skaftin* (lunchbox) or *mokeri* to eat at break. You can go to the *mashonisa* (informal moneylender) but that only defers the problem. However strong the mother of your children, she must eventually leave for her parents or another relative who can provide what the children need.

As much as public opinion, especially in the townships, might have been against labour broking, this did not translate into public support. The Mabarete had no channels through which to make appeals. Their strike had been almost invisible; they had no press officer and few links to organisations that might take up their cause. Any assistance they received came informally. Perhaps the greatest help came from Justice Mokoena, a hawker at the Germiston Railway Station. Mokoena has run a platform stall for some twenty years selling crisps, bananas and other items to commuters. He was as much a part of the place as the trains. Over the years, he had seen many strikers pass through the station, singing struggle songs. The Mabarete stood out because of the length of their strike. And with the length of the strike came evident hunger. So, morning and evening, he called the Mabarete over and handed out his over-ripe bananas. And, when they were finished, he went into his fresh stock. Mokoena's response was humanitarian, *ubuntu*: '*tlala ke tlala*' (hunger is hunger) (interview, Justice Mokoena).

Beyond Mokoena's bananas, the Mabarete had to find their own way through the strike.

Home visits

The breakthrough for the Mabarete was visiting the home of E.T. Mpai, SAPO's Wits Region general manager for mail delivery, on 12 March 2012. The idea to take their message directly to SAPO management had been raised at the Mabarete's morning meeting. A postman knew Mpai's home address, having delivered mail there in the past. Why not go and deliver their message directly? The idea was taken up with enthusiasm. After months without any tangible sign of success, they were willing to give anything a try.

In fact, this was the third home visit made by the Mabarete. The three home visits happened for different reasons. Yet, they represented the three sides of the casuals' confinement: labour broker, union and company. The purpose of home visits was to deliver messages, but on the third visit they quickly realised that they had stumbled on a power resource. The last visit, it was unanimously agreed, 'changed everything'. There was no need for a fourth.

The first home visit was spontaneous and happened early in the strike. A group was passing the Tembisa house of the mother of the owner of TAS Appointments and Management Services, Colleen Ramaphakela. In an act of bravado, they made an anonymous phone call to Ramaphakela telling her where they were and that they would be back.

The second home visit was to Clyde Mervin, then the chairperson of CWU's Gauteng Region. It took place on 21 February. This visit was planned and provided a template for the later visit to Mpai. It was two months into the strike and, with absolutely no sign of progress, CWU was seen as part of the problem. It was meddling. Working, the casuals suspected, hand in glove with management. What the

Mabarete wanted was for CWU to 'leave the issues of casual workers alone' (interview, Bopape).

The Mabarete went to Eldorado Park, a historically Coloured township south of Soweto, where Mervin lived. Before going to the house, a smaller group went to the local police station. They told the duty officer there were workers with a petition for their manager.[6] The police told them to go ahead. Any group that came to report to them first was clearly going to behave itself. The small group left the police station; the full group arrived at Mervin's house. Mervin was not in, but members of his family were, including a teenage child who was surrounded and pinched by the crowd. The family was traumatised by the experience (Mervin, personal communication). There were angry phone calls after the visit between Mervin and Mabarete leaders. Mervin threatened to lay charges but in the end he did not (interview, Mutavhatsindi). The message he was left with was that he should stay out of their strike; casual workers were now fighting their own battles.

Mpai, the SAPO manager, lived in a gated housing complex on the East Rand. The Mabarete took the Metrorail to Elsburg Station and then trekked on foot. When the long line of strikers finally reached the complex gates, they posed as workers come for unpaid wages from their employer. The police were called by security, but eventually the group was allowed to enter. Mpai was not there. A domestic worker was and so was one of Mpai's children. Their message was that Mpai needed to make their demands his business. If he did not, they would be back. They were hungry. If they had to come back, they would be coming 'to eat' with Mpai. The seriousness of this threat was dramatically underlined when, by chance, a postman who was delivering in the complex was captured. His bike was left at Mpai's gate, while the scab went with the Mabarete. He was found later that evening on a piece of open ground and admitted to intensive care.

The strikers had not even reached the Metrorail station when a call came to the office phone. Brokered through an intermediary, the message was that Mpai wanted to meet.

Negotiations

The home visit to Mpai was a lucky break for the Mabarete. There had not been the slightest sign that they were any closer to their goal after months of hard slog and intensifying difficulties. Individually, their financial and domestic situations were increasingly stressed, and some had already snapped. The arrests and court appearances sapped their collective strength and threatened to neutralise key activists. The strike was close to collapse.

So why did they not go to Mpai's house from the start? The answer is straightforward: it had not occurred to them. It was not in their repertoire of action. But in any event, if they had gone earlier it would not have had the same effect. For the visits to be effective, they had to scare the target of the visit. Really scare. There had to be manifest fear. Any group of workers pitching at a manager's house with a grievance would be scary, likely menacing, embarrassing and humiliating. But the previous down payment of violence that the Mabarete had invested meant that this visit was terrifying.

Preventing mail delivery across much of Gauteng had dramatically increased the real cost of using casuals. Using labour brokers was becoming more liability than asset. The fear of the visit tipped the scales. Mpai could no longer go along with the organisation's denial over labour broking; his family was now on the front line of an industrial war. He confronted his superior, Pieter Swart, SAPO's general manager for mail delivery, and told him he did not care about the technicalities of the strikers being fired labour broker employees; the strategy of riding the strike out was not working (interview, Tutu Mokoena). He was not going to sacrifice his family. He was going to talk to the strikers. Faced with dissent in their own ranks, senior management agreed to talks.

These were not easy. The Mabarete hiding their leadership meant that the Post Office did not know who to negotiate with. Nor were the Mabarete clear who they should be talking to in the Post Office; their understanding of the managerial structure at higher levels of the organisation was hazy. Mpai wanted to meet there and then, but the Mabarete stalled the request. Thabiso Bopape and Russel Mutavhatsindi, who would be central to any talks, were out of town. The pair got back that night and the entire leadership met the following day. Initially, there had been fifteen in the Mabarete delegation, but the eventual decision was that they should be nine (interview, Choshi).

This established the 'Top 9' leadership that became, in effect, the executive committee of the Mabarete.[7] It was these nine who went into the negotiations. This surfacing of leadership was a first, tentative step in moving into the formal industrial relations system and it was taken cautiously.

Their emergence quickly revealed a problem; the Mabarete, despite their long campaign, were unprepared for talks. Negotiations were not the skills they had been developing. The first meeting did not go well. For all the exhilaration of reaching this point, the Top 9 were also fearful of what might happen, that they might in some way be ambushed. They were now talking to SAPO, but that was exactly what Marcus Makhura, Johannes Manamela and Petrus Morenamele had requested in their letter to Mpai after the mid-2011 strike and for which they had been dismissed. In the initial meeting, not all of the nine gave their true names (interview, Choshi).

With the help of a group within the South African Postal and Allied Workers Union (SAPAWU, then called SAPWU), particularly Tutu Mokoena, a SAPAWU official, supported by Malandela Radebe, a working relationship between the two sides was established. Both were desperate to settle. The problem of establishing credentials was resolved with the Mabarete marshalled in their head office, the Golden Walk car park, just across the road from the Germiston Hub where the negotiations took place. There was what amounted to a three-line whip; everybody was to report to head office each day and no one was to touch working postmen (interview, Kubheka). When no incidents were reported, SAPO management knew it was talking to the right people.

The Mabarete realised that they needed assistance. An important reason for turning to SAPAWU, still not yet recognised by SAPO, was because it was not CWU. There was also a personal link; Caphus Chauke, one of the Top 9, knew Tutu Mokoena from Witspos where he had worked for a while (interviews, Chauke; Radebe). Members of the Mabarete's Top 9 met with SAPAWU's Mokoena and Siphiwe Nenjelele in Joubert Park (interviews, Tutu Mokoena; Radebe).

Mokoena had been manager in SAPO and had held various positions within CWU. After being ousted from CWU in 2007,[8] he had assisted in setting up SAPAWU, the rival union to CWU in the Post Office, and was employed as an official by the union. Now, he was in a factional fight within SAPAWU over the direction of the union. Given his involvement in CWU and SAPAWU, his recognition of the casuals' plight within SAPO came late. When they met in Joubert Park, he was moved by the strikers' gaunt faces and sheer determination. He recognised their desperation to end labour broking, which he described as approaching zeal, alongside a fear that the talks would see them outmanoeuvred by SAPO. What he also saw was a power resource that could be used within his union and within the company, although it would need careful handling. He said he would help them with the negotiations (interview, Tutu Mokoena).

Because SAPAWU was still not recognised by SAPO, the union could not negotiate with management, nor could it represent the casuals. Casuals were not employees of SAPO; they never had been. They had been the employees of the labour brokers. But now there was even less connection to the company, because they were fired casuals, ex-non-employees. This difficulty was fudged with the SAPAWU team sitting in as observers. Their presence meant that the SAPO team could not pull anything over the inexperienced Mabarete negotiators (interview, Petersen). This gave them confidence to engage without distrusting every suggestion from management.

Two unwritten clauses

The industrial relations terrain that the Mabarete were now entering was one they knew little about. It was one structured by laws, regulations and procedures but also one of personal relationships and careful manoeuvring between players to reach agreement, sometimes despite the laws, regulations and procedures. Tutu Mokoena was critical in assisting the Mabarete. Nothing was straightforward; the SAPO negotiating team was not as one. Mpai wanted to settle quickly and was willing to concede the key issue of converting casuals to permanents but, given the financial implications, that required senior management's agreement. Senior management initially came in with a different approach. As Mokoena outlined, 'They came in with an attitude of "These are the guys who are beating people up, who are causing one, two, three. In fact, we want to identify them . . ." They even brought the general manager of [SAPO's] Security & Investigations' (interview, Tutu Mokoena).

Tutu Mokoena and Mpai knew each other well. Mpai had been Mokoena's manager in SAPO. Working behind the scenes, they reached an agreement. Mpai was desperate to settle; the Mabarete were desperate to become permanents. That gave Mokoena a lot to work with and the two sides were brought together (interviews, Radebe; Tutu Mokoena). The agreement was a stepped approach. The Mabarete were to be recruited by SAPO. The old S32 category was recycled for the position they would have before they became fully permanent. The salary would be equal to what the Post Office currently paid to labour brokers. Roughly twice what casuals were paid by labour brokers, but still half of what a SAPO permanent was paid. The rest of the SAPO casuals were to follow within three months. Radebe provided the financial knowledge to support the cost neutrality argument for SAPO of this first step (interview, Tshabalala). The back channel between Mpai and Mokoena was critical for the negotiations to reach an agreement. Except it was not an agreement. Or at least it was not a written agreement, and it is axiomatic in industrial relations that if it is agreed then it must be in writing. As everybody knows, unless it is in writing there is only going to be disagreement about what was agreed.

A key reason for the lack of anything on paper was CWU. It was still the only union recognised by the company and therefore the only one with the right to negotiate. While the SAPAWU representatives were classified as observers, there was a de facto negotiation taking place without CWU. They would object to the talks happening at all, as indeed they did.[9] The unwritten agreement between SAPO and the Mabarete also broke SAPO's agreements, dating from 2005, with CWU on casuals; that agreement had set out a hierarchy of priorities as to who within the company was to be converted into permanent positions, one that would see, should it ever be implanted in earnest, their members benefit before casuals (see Chapter 7). Now this was to be upended; given that the Mabarete were no longer employed, for SAPO to employ them it was, effectively, recruiting them from outside directly into permanent positions, over the heads of others in the agreed pecking order. And, lastly, many of those who would be appointed as permanents were, to put it plainly, embittered with CWU.

The first unwritten clause concerned the Mabarete's entry into the Post Office by transferring the payments previously made to the labour broker to the newly created casual-in-transition-to-permanent-employees. That was a transitional arrangement and it was also agreed that they would become permanents within three months. How that was to be funded was not clear, but it was three months away, and bridges would be crossed at that point. There was much that was uncertain. SAPO did not even know who it was agreeing to employ. The Mabarete counted themselves at 294 but remembered comrades who had been victimised or who had dropped out of the struggle before they had triumphed. The final list submitted was of 411 names. These individuals were given until 26 March to submit a CV, along with copies of their ID documents. Not quite the ballpoint flourish of Maja's daydreams, but good enough. There was a rush to get CVs typed up. The Mabarete returned victorious to their depots.

The second unwritten clause was that *all* labour broker employees in SAPO would follow a similar process to that outlined for the Mabarete.

That would be a good place to end this book; an uncomplicated finale to a complex, morally taut saga. An industrial fairy tale. So, readers may wish to put this book down and finish on a high note; the Mabarete triumphed and ended labour broking in SAPO.

But real stories never end. The unwritten agreement reached in late March 2012 was a decisive moment and an important step. Yet it was to be four years and three months before the second clause was to be fully honoured with all casuals employed as permanents.[10] The following chapter looks at those years of struggle, the messy aftermath to the end of labour broking.

16

Above and Below the *Lex*
Insurgent Unionism and Technologies of Struggle, 2011–2014

A beast disembowelled
The Mabarete strike between December 2011 and April 2012 was the tipping point in the struggle against labour broking in the South Africa Post Office (SAPO). The Mabarete had hunted for long months in the township. They had hunted scab workers, but their ultimate target was the Post Office, which used their labour but refused to employ them. Against the odds, they had brought their opponent to its knees and forced concessions.

But for SAPO, the crisis was far from over. SAPO is a big beast, but the Mabarete had brought it to bay. Now it was to be eviscerated. The low-intensity war waged by the Mabarete over four months was to rage hot and run for years as SAPO's industrial relations system imploded. There was the barest of respites between the Mabarete strike ending and what was to become known as the 'second strike' commencing. Only in late 2014 was the conflict contained after the entire SAPO board was fired and the organisation put into administration.

Entering the House of the Post Office
April 2012: the Mabarete were back at work and jubilant. They had made it to the Promised Land! They had achieved what nobody else had been able to do, although they were only 294. The Bible again served as a cultural resource to capture the scale of their achievement: *Ho thata ho kenya lesobeng la naleti* (It's hard to enter through the eye of a needle).[1]

251

The 25th of the month: pay day for the Post Office and now pay day for the Mabarete. The excitement before pay day was palpable. Their delight overwhelmed the reality of the debts they had to clear. The Mabarete held a celebration in June, each contributing R200. By then they were starting to get back onto their feet financially.

In lucid moments they knew that for all the difference their salary increase would make, it would not be enough and in a year's time; like everybody else, they would be complaining that they could not manage. But at that moment, they wallowed in the bliss of being able to afford what they had long desired. Each one had a list. Take Sello Ramokgopa who had scraped through to the end of the strike eating *pap* with NikNaks (corn puffs) as *seshebo*. In just two-and-a-half years since becoming a permanent employee he had bought a second-hand Ford Laser and got his driving licence. The car had cost just R7 500, the licence R4 000 for lessons and the test organised by a driving school. To finance this, he had taken out a loan with First National Bank. He had repaid the loan through monthly deductions from his salary. He did not want to be delivering mail all his working life. He was eyeing promotion within SAPO and for that he needed a driving licence. Now he had it. He was also a breadwinner, providing for younger siblings and his children. That included maintenance payments for his first child. He had taken out education polices for both his children with Old Mutual. He wanted them to be able to complete their studies.[2]

Of course, it was not all plain sailing. An immediate problem was that of going back to the depots. Outside of the six Tembisa depots, casuals across Gauteng had been divided between strikers and scabs, hunter and hunted. The Mabarete were returning to work alongside those they had stalked in the township. In many depots, they were outnumbered. Before reporting for work on 4 April, they put out the word; an attack on one would be an attack on all 294. If one of them was touched it would be the Mabarete that would retaliate.[3] The threat worked, holding back vengeance as they resumed their walks. But not for long; once the second strike began, the tables were turned.

Second strike

The agreement between SAPO and the Mabarete had consisted of two unwritten clauses, as explained in the previous chapter. The first clause was that the strikers would be employed directly by SAPO. This broke SAPO's own recruitment rules, but since it concerned only 294 strikers the bending was *smallanyana* stuff for an organisation the size of the Post Office.[4] However, the second clause, that all casuals in SAPO be made permanent within three months, presented a greater challenge. It involved thousands – according to employment equity data around 8 000 individuals (see Chapter 4). Eventually, this did happen, but was there actually a second clause? Over this there is disagreement. The second strike was based on the premise that there was no second clause. Why would casuals strike if the Mabarete had won an agreement that they would all be made permanent within three months?

Whether a second clause existed or not is important for the reputation of the Mabarete. Had they fought for themselves alone, or had they fought for all casuals? Within the rank-and-file Mabarete returning to the depots, there was a view that 'the train had left the station'. Entering into the House of the Post Office was their reward for the struggle and hardships they had endured.[5] Such a perspective contradicts, of course, one of the justifications for beating strike-breakers – that all casuals would benefit from what the Mabarete were doing.

By contrast, in interviews held with the leadership of the Mabarete from early 2014 onwards, the presence of the second clause was underlined. It had, respondents stressed, been a principled stand, a fight against labour broking and not a fight for the Mabarete alone. It was a view passionately expressed. Thabiso Bopape (interview) outlined how they had attempted to approach the leaders of the casual workers who had held back from their strike with the good news that labour broking was to be ended, but had been rebuffed.

What is clear is that the situation rapidly unravelled. Within days of the Mabarete returning to work, the second strike commenced. Following the struggles of the casual workers in SAPO that would make this the third, not the second major strike by casuals; it followed the mid-2011 and Mabarete strikes. However, the idea of it being the second strike resonated in different ways for different groups of casuals. For the Mabarete, it was the strike that followed their own, the one that started it all, the first to be successful. This was all the more so for Mabarete from the West Rand who had held back from the mid-2011 strike. For those who had skipped the Mabarete strike, it was their second strike following that of mid-2011. That it was the third strike is probably the most accurate historically speaking, but nobody who was involved thought about it as the third strike. It was the second strike to all.

The Post Office negotiators had hoped that the process of conversion agreed with the Mabarete could be smoothly managed and did not want the agreement publicised. They had to deal with the existing contracts with labour brokers (interviews, Bopape; Tutu Mokoena; Petersen; Radebe). It was going to be a messy disengagement and publicity was not going to help.[6]

Perhaps clear communication would have averted what happened next, though probably not. In understated terms, Jaqueline Maja (interview), a leader of the Pretoria casuals, described how they had 'raised their eyebrows' when the Mabarete marched back into the company. Those who had held back from the Mabarete strike were fearful that they were going to be left behind. Those who had hunted them would be received into permanency while they would remain casuals. Like previous casuals' strikes, the second strike was unprotected (although not illegal since SAPO did not seek an interdict against it). Closer to the mid-2011 strike than the Mabarete strike in scale, there were thousands of Second Strikers. According to a 2014 attempt by SAPO to summarise labour agreements and disputes between 2004 and late 2014,[7] 6 220 casuals joined this strike. This is undoubtedly an inflated figure since the second strike was largely restricted to Gauteng. Desmond Moeketsi (interview), a central leader of the second strike, put the number at 2 500.But it was certainly far bigger than the Mabarete strike.

The Mabarete had catalysed the end of labour broking in SAPO and this was acknowledged by leaders of the second strike, even if they did not believe that the Mabarete had negotiated a second clause (interview, Moeketsi). In this regard, Sean Tshabalala's (interview) analysis is helpful: the second strike ensured that the second clause was implemented. This formulation works irrespective of whether there was a second clause, there was no second clause, or whether only some people in the negotiations thought there was a second clause.

Because of their numbers, the Second Strikers' withdrawal of labour had an impact on mail delivery. The strike, which was to last for two months, saw delivery disrupted or stopped not only in townships but also in suburbs and to business premises. Whereas the Mabarete strike had been almost entirely neglected by the media because its impact was restricted to townships, this strike was widely reported. The concerns of casual workers in SAPO became visible to a wider public only when the tide had started to turn against labour broking.

The strike did not, however, rely only on the withdrawal of labour. The Second Strikers had learned from the Mabarete and adopted their tactics to enforce the strike. The erstwhile rats now hunted the cats. The Second Strikers not only hunted in the townships but also mounted all-out assaults on depots, a tactic that earned them the name 'Stormers' (interview, Moeketsi).[8]

The second strike ended on 5 June 2012. This time the agreement was written (SAPO and Striking Casual Workers Delegates 2012). There were eight clauses. The first noted that SAPO had served the labour brokers with three months' notice to terminate their contracts. The rest of the agreement largely followed a similar process agreed with the Mabarete. SAPO would advertise the posts created by the departure of the labour brokers and current casuals were to apply for these positions, which they would fill as S32s (that is, directly employed, short-term contracts). However, the three months of the Mabarete's second clause was now a 'long-term plan to accommodate these employees [the S32 workers] in vacant permanent positions'. It was this decision to draw out the end of labour broking, particularly converting past casuals to full parity with permanent employees, that was to shred the Post Office's ability to deliver as strike followed strike.

Strikes three to further

An account of the strikes that were to follow the second strike in anything like the detail provided hereto would require another book. Most of the industrial chaos that convulsed SAPO over the next two or so years resulted from the slow, erratic and often inconsistent process of converting the 8 000 casual workers to permanent employees on equal pay. The process was not finalised until July 2016, and then not fully.[9] Adding fuel to the fire was intense inter-union rivalry. Two new unions emerged from the casuals' strikes. The first was the Democratic Postal and Communications Union (DEPACU), made up of the Mabarete and a significant number of the Second Strikers who, despite a history of conflict, joined what they saw as the union best able to complete the conversion of casuals in SAPO. The emergence of DEPACU was not straightforward, however. The Mabarete first joined the South African Postal Workers Union (SAPWU, later to become SAPAWU), the 2009 split from the Communication Workers Union (CWU). Later, they broke away with the SAPAWU officials/office-bearers/members (hereafter, simply 'officials' for simplicity) who had assisted them in the negotiations to end the Mabarete strike, to establish DEPACU. The second new union was the Intelligent Information and Communications Union of South Africa (IICUSA), which was drawn from the Second Strikers. There were two unions already operating in SAPO: CWU, which a small group of Second Strikers joined,[10] and SAPAWU. In total, there were now four unions in SAPO, arguably five since SAPAWU was deeply divided from late 2012 (interview, Radebe). All these unions claimed to champion the cause of conversion as they competed for members, the previous labour broker employees having now become part of the Post Office bargaining unit (interview, Tshabalala).

The result of this competition was a series of rotating strikes. One union would strike and gain a concession in the form of a specific agreement over conversions, or partial conversions, for a particular group or a particular number of ex-casuals. They would declare a victory, which would trigger one of the other three unions to launch its own strike to better the concession, as well as taking the opportunity to make other demands. Chaotic company human resources (HR) practices provided fertile ground for disputes; there were, for example, still five different rates of pay operating for postmen doing the same job (Dickinson 2015c). The slow pace of convergence stoked anger and was fuel for the strikes, while the heat of union rivalry set the tinder ablaze (interview, Bopape). The period of industrial anarchy during 2013 and 2014 also saw other groups (notably some 600 permanent employees known as the *Umnyango* [Door], who resigned to access their provident funds and then campaigned to be reinstated)[11] try their luck over matters unrelated to the conversion of casuals.

In November 2014, the entire SAPO board was forced to resign by the Minister of Telecommunications and Postal Services, who put the organisation into administration (Post & Parcel 2014; Zwane 2014; Nkosi 2015). In November 2015, a new CEO, Mark Barnes, a former investment banker, was appointed. He succeeded in raising significant capital guarantees, allowing the payment of creditors, many of whom were refusing to extend further credit to SAPO. In July 2016, he all but finalised the conversion process, bringing SAPO to something vaguely resembling normal industrial relations (Dickinson 2016; Goba 2016).

Technologies of struggle

Due to the labour broking system, SAPO casuals had been placed outside of the industrial relations system, as discussed in earlier chapters. Once they acknowledged this, the course of their struggles saw them develop 'technologies of struggle' – technologies that were prohibited within the legal system of industrial relations. Such technologies, while legally liminal, were nevertheless embedded within the Mabarete's social norms and values, the *lex loci* of the township. They were also the outcomes-focused products of a collective endeavour: stopping SAPO from delivering mail in order to end labour broking.

Technology of struggle describes innovations broader than the 'hard' technology produced by engineers and scientists. Rather, in this situation they were socio-technical processes, in which organisation and action are central to the technology itself. Despite the enormous influence that hard technology has on human society, and the advantage that advanced technology provides, forms of social organisation matter. Put another way, two groups may operate in the same environment, with the same resources and with the same goals, but one can organise itself to act in ways that makes it more effective than the other. This applies to groups in conflict. However, most conflicts are asymmetric; the opponents are not only organised differently, but also have access to different resources, and likely have different objectives. The will to prevail in asymmetric conflicts stimulates the development of new technologies of struggle suited to one group's organisational capacities. This was true of the Mabarete strike.

Denied the supposedly level playing field of the post-apartheid industrial relations system, SAPO's casual workers had to figure out how to beat a Goliath whose knees they could not even reach. Hiding their leadership did not advance their position, but it did deny their opponent of a key resource, the law and the courts. Operating outside the law, they developed and used two key technologies that have been extensively covered in previous chapters: the hunting of working postmen in the townships; and home visits. This section focuses on how these technologies of struggle can be transmitted once developed by looking at how this transmission took place in the second, third and further strikes that followed the Mabarete strike, which itself had drawn lessons from the mid-2011 strike.

I deliberately use the term technology. Technologies are, in themselves, neutral. It is how we harness them and how we control them that determines outcomes. I use the term in attempting to see past moral judgements that can prevent understanding of why struggles take place. Moral evaluations over the way struggles are prosecuted that are reached without understanding history or context are moral judgements of a special kind: ones that defend the status quo of privilege and exploitation.

One way of seeing the neutrality of the technologies developed by the Mabarete is to acknowledge how they could be used for different purposes. This was illustrated by an incident that took place in Thokoza Park, Soweto, a few weeks after the Mabarete strike had ended.[12] It was their first mass meeting since returning to their depots. Travelling from the East Rand, the carriages had been abuzz, dozens of reunions on the go simultaneously. Still to receive their first pay, they rode the Metro *mangober* (without tickets) as they had in the strike. It was a long journey in the slow Saturday trains, the final leg from Kliptown Station on foot. There were more reunions in the park with comrades from the West Rand and the Vaal. Then it was time for business; a report-back on the conversion process, the second strike situation and what would be their next move.

But as some 200 men and two or three women were seated on a patch of grass and about to start, there was a commotion. A thief had snatched the bag of a woman somewhere in the park. It took a moment to realise what was happening. Then there was the shout of 'Move!' Twenty or so Mabarete were up and running. Those remaining watched the chase; the thief, in a blue shirt, was sprinting up the slope towards the Regina Mundi Church, the Mabarete in pursuit. The man had a head start and the advantage that fear provides, adrenalin flooding his body. He disappeared from view, into the streets around the church.

Those around me confidently predicted that their comrades would bring him back. The Mabarete knew how to track a man down. But as the time dragged on, I assumed that he had got away. I changed the conversation to soften lost pride for when the posse returned empty-handed. Then, perhaps fifteen minutes later, a group came striding down the hill, a figure frogmarched between them.

As the phalanx of men came closer, we could see the thief. He was young, probably still a teenager. The smart blue golf shirt was now ripped open. His mouth was bleeding. Men and women were running up to *klap* (slap) him before scuttling out of the way of the fast-marching troop. Children were dashing around the periphery of the crowd. One man put in a punch and there were shouts that he was going too far. But then another man, from the ranks of the Mabarete, walked up to the advancing group and at the last moment spun around and kicked backwards, like a horse, a direct hit to the balls.

The thief's mouth opened in a silent scream, a bright red oval. The phalanx did not pause, not even the thief, keenest of all to get to the safety of the park office, to which they were headed. It was touch and go; there was a call for *thupa!* (sticks/a beating). Mabarete ran to trees to rip off switches. The phalanx stalled. In the melee there was an attempt to strip the thief, who lost what was left of his shirt and one of his takkies. It was an uneven application of the Mabarete's technologies. The hunting had been successfully implemented and the leadership now wanted the thief out the way and the meeting restarted, but other Mabarete had been triggered into another routine, that of punishing transgressors. Eventually, the former prevailed. The thief was pushed through the gate of the palisade fence that surrounded the park office to be taken away later by police and the bag restored to its owner.

When we re-assembled, the Top 9 leader chairing the meeting congratulated us for the excellent work. We had, he explained, demonstrated that the Mabarete were good South African citizens, contributing to the fight against crime. Just as the Mabarete's technologies of struggle could be applied in other situations, such as running a thief to ground, they could also be used by others for their original purpose, to prosecute an industrial dispute. Indeed, in the tempest of strikes that followed the Mabarete's victory that is what happened. The Mabarete might have developed the techniques, but anyone could use them. Once developed, all that was needed was for them to be picked up and used. The Mabarete's hunting and home visits had proved to be a 'magic wand' in their struggle (interview, Radebe). Who would not be tempted to pick up a magic wand? All you needed was 300 people and you could close down much of a 25 000-odd workforce operation.

The administrator appointed to run the Post Office after its board was forced to resign was Dr Simo Lushaba. He arrived during the rotating strikes of 2014. When Lushaba was interviewed for the *Power Lunch* programme on CNBC Africa on 24 November 2014, his message was that the strike was coming to an end. He illustrated this with the numbers reporting to work. Two weeks previously, he said, out of a unionised workforce of 17 000, there had been 1 100 failing to report for work, last week it had been down to 675, and that morning just 284.[13] However, given that much of mail delivery across Gauteng was at a standstill and many Post Offices were closed, telling how few strikers there were provided little solace. There were to be three more days before the strike ended, during which hardly a letter moved across Gauteng. Interestingly, 284 strikers is remarkably close to the 294 Mabarete, though the Mabarete never operated at full strength and it was unlikely that Lushaba's figure of 284 were all on the streets. When I interviewed Desmond Moeketsi, a leader of the mid-2011 strike, second strike and IICUSA, in November 2014 the strike that Lushaba was talking down was underway. Moeketsi disagreed with my suggestion that you only needed 300 men to close down SAPO using the Mabarete's techniques. Rather, he thought, 100 was enough (group interview, IICUSA).

And if the various groups of the fragmented SAPO workforce readily adopted the hunting tactics of the Mabarete, so, too, the home visit could be incorporated into their repertoires of action. Specifically, visits to managers were of interest, since the Mabarete had demonstrated, beyond any possible doubt, what such visits could achieve. During an IICUSA-led strike in September 2014, a SAPO manager was hospitalised after been attacked by strikers in his home.[14] The *Umnyango* adapted the home visit to office visits, with one female manger dragged out from a cupboard where she had been hiding during a rampage through Witspos Mail Centre (interview, Tutu Mokoena).

The Mabarete also had no monopoly on *developing* technologies of struggle. The Second Strikers, with greater numbers, took to storming depots (group interview, IICUSA). However, while demonstrating prowess, this only temporarily stopped the mail. If, as was often the case, those in the depots got wind of the raid and scarpered or hid, then there was not that much that the raiders could achieve. They could tip over the presses used for sorting mail and fling any letters they found to the floor. But the presses could be quickly righted and scattered letters resorted. Once the storm had passed, work could resume. However, if the strips on the presses, which label addresses in the order that the postman will deliver, are removed, then the press is all but useless. New strips must be printed, delivered and installed.[15] Thus, storming became far more effective when the strips on the presses were taken away with the storm, something that became standard practice.[16]

Some technologies of struggle, such as removing press strips, are specific to the business of SAPO. Hunting in the streets can be extended to other occupations that involve work on the streets, such as maintenance, delivery and transport workers. This was the case in the strike of labour broker employees of the Johannesburg Pikitup refuse company in March 2016 (Makhafola 2016). Technologies of struggle are not ring-fenced to a particular dispute. Home visits could, for example, be practised by any group, although postmen have the edge in knowing people's addresses.[17]

The flow of struggle technologies can go in any direction. There was an overlap between some of the SAPO 2014 strikes and the month-long, July strike in the metal and engineering sector, led by the National Union of Metalworkers of South Africa (NUMSA). SAPO strikers looked at NUMSA activists' tactics, such as checking who was wearing work boots at train stations to spot strike-breakers, and compared them to their own.[18] As has been previously outlined, some of these technologies overlapped with and borrowed from long-standing township practices of rough justice that replace inadequate policing. Technologies of struggle, once conceived and used to effect, are replicable. But if credit is to be given to the originators, excepting the Second Strikers' stripping of the sorting presses, it was the Mabarete who pioneered the key technologies of struggle and others that followed their lead.

Neither one nor the other
I began to interview the Mabarete's leadership in 2014.[19] This was a period of intense industrial action. The Mabarete had remained a coherent group, first within SAPAWU and then from March 2014 as the core of the newly established DEPACU. They had launched strikes, all unprotected, to pressurise management over the slow and erratic pace of conversion to permanency on equal terms and conditions during late 2012 and 2013. These were typically one-day events that targeted either the Witspos Mail Centre or SAPO's head office in Centurion, south of Pretoria. In 2014, the strikes continued with two longer DEPACU-driven periods of industrial action in July and September/October. These strikes were part of the previously described pattern of rotating, sometimes overlapping, strikes mounted by the different unions and collectives within the fragmented and fractious SAPO workforce.

I was, therefore, interviewing individuals about past events while they were engaged in current ones: the formation of their own union, DEPACU; industrial action over the still ongoing conversion process; rivalry with other unions and worker organisations; and, by the end of the year, internal conflict. This led to my own increasing involvement in contemporary events, something that resulted in unplanned informal interaction, discussions and a privileged observational position within what was now DEPACU.

Just as there were different perspectives and accounts of past events that my formal interviews probed, there were also different positions over contemporary events. However, one thing that struck me was a consensus among those who had led the Mabarete regarding the superiority of wildcat action over procedural disputes, of unprotected over protected strikes. On this they were as one and unequivocal. It was not surprising; they were still in the glow of their 2012 victory. As we drove from Tembisa to a meeting at SAPO's head office, Mkwabe Mabulane, one of the Mabarete's Top 9, outlined how unprotected strikes in South Africa produce results, but most protected or procedural strikes do not.[20] He even put a figure to it, suggesting that only five in a hundred protected strikes achieved anything. There were, of course, downsides to unprotected strikes; you ran the risk of losing your job, despite the informal forms of protection that could be used,[21] and there were the unpleasant things that happened to people. Nevertheless, despite the downside, it was obvious which was best. You needed to look no further than their experience. 'What had the country's registered unions achieved when it came to labour brokers?' he asked.[22] 'What had the Mabarete's unprotected strike achieved?' He did not need an answer to that question; he was on his way to negotiate with SAPO management, who had previously refused to talk with casuals.

Yet, despite this view, the strikes that I observed during 2014 were not either wildcat or procedural. They were neither one thing nor the other. Actual practice did not correspond to the dominant perspective. The strikes were unprotected in that the required process for legal protection had not been complied with. The Commission for Conciliation, Mediation and Arbitration was at this point all but ignored. They were wildcat strikes in that they were called without notice and all involved damage to property, intimidation and violence. Yet, at the same time, workers' leaders were engaging with management. This was, typically, on an oscillating basis. On the ground, there would be a rampage; this would be followed by talks. If the talks did not get anywhere, the cycle would be repeated. Sometimes this cycle turned at speed: *kak* (shit/problems) in the morning, unsuccessful or stalled talks in the afternoon, *kak* the next morning and so on.

Days of strategic anger

To be inside a strike is to be within a maelstrom. There is never a typical day. Rather, there are constantly changing circumstances, constant re-evaluations and constant speculation over what is going to happen next. Here, the account of a 'typical' day during the SAPO strikes of 2014 blends accounts from different, actual days that took place on different dates and at different locations during 2014.[23]

Our typical day starts with a morning of havoc. Rank-and-file activists, several hundred strong, have been active on the ground. When DEPACU is striking, the Mabarete assembly points are back in use. Familiar routines are resurrected. Depots have been mobilised to swell the strikers. Other depots have been stormed. Anybody working is a scab. It has been a quick sweep; the main rendezvous for the day is noon at Witspos, the regional sorting hub. By 1 p.m. there are enough strikers to close the street outside the huge warehouse and office building. One group of strikers arrives with old tyres picked up along the way. There are only two police cars and an attempt to confiscate the tyres is only partially successful; one is handed over but others make it to the main entrance. The shift working inside the buildings, due to knock off at 2 p.m., is wondering when it will be able to leave. Clearly, the afternoon shift is not going to make it in. The tyres are now alight; orange flames and black smoke. The police get their cars out of the way and call for back-up.

The active strikers are primarily those left behind in the erratic and staggered conversion process, those still not fully in the House of the Post Office. Those who have pitched to protest *toyi-toyi* up and down the road, closing it to traffic. They are *kwatile* (angry). They show their anger; every now and again someone runs alongside the palisade fence of Witspos with a stick, creating an improvised rattle. The noise adds to the chanting, singing and the stones thrown onto the roof of the warehouse. A knot of men are smashing a paving slab onto a concrete storm drain. Stone on stone makes stones. A window is smashed. A man kneels momentarily and fires off a shot from his catapult.

Behind the yard entrance, some distance from the offices, four Fidelity Strike Unit guards in black uniforms are lined up. They hold pump-action shotguns. The crowd edges closer as they *toyi-toyi* past the gate. Stones start to fly. The guards duck and edge back. Suddenly, a group of strikers peel off and grab hold of the long sliding gate. They shake it, and then heave with synchronised effort. The long sliding gate is rocked out of its runner and pulled open. Other strikers rush into the gap; one has a large slab of broken concrete held in both hands. The guards turn and run. The concrete is lobbed after them, but they are not pursued into the yard. There are limits understood by both sides.

The police are now forming up at the end of the road, twenty or thirty of them with bulletproof jackets and shotguns loaded with rubber bullets. A dozen public order police encased in body armour and helmets have arrived. The RoboCops have pistols strapped to their thighs and assault rifles in their hands. The last thing the police want is another Marikana, but nobody expects them to run like Fidelity. The situation needs to be cooled down quickly.

Then, right on cue, the union leadership arrives. They approach the police and there are hurried discussions. The workers are angry, they have been exploited for too long, they still have not received what they were promised, SAPO is dragging its feet. This is why people are angry. Some have lost their tempers, the union understands that it is a problem, but if they could just talk with management, perhaps they can find a solution, something to satisfy the workers. And before long the union leaders are calming down the strikers and a delegation is trooping into the building to parley. After delays in a sweltering, windowless conference room, we meet a scratch negotiating team that has been hurriedly put together. The *madala* (senior man) who leads the SAPO delegation talks nicely about it being better to talk than to fight, but we can all see that he cannot make the decisions that are needed. No matter, the union now has a foot in the door. It will push it open further.

The strikers are now waiting in the street; they are on standby while their leaders are in talks. Inside, the depth of their anger is periodically raised. How long the leaders can control what is happening is in doubt. SAPO must help the union; otherwise the rage is going to boil over. Of course, the *madala* agrees, but . . . After this has been repeated a few times, the union negotiator puts his foot down; they need, he says with respect, to speak to somebody who can help. If the *madala* is saying it is a problem that only government can solve then the union needs to talk to the minister! It is a bold gambit, but what is really sought is a step closer to whoever can authorise a concession to the union, something that means some workers will move further along the path of permanency. If *madala* pulls off a meeting with somebody with more authority than he has, a compromise to the demand to meet with the minister, then the union has won the day. The strike will be cooled, although the rank and file will need to be remobilised for the agreed talks with whomever has been nominated as substitute for the minister-demand.

If *madala* cannot assist, then we troop out to address those outside. They are told that SAPO continues to ignore their suffering and that they must now show these managers just how angry people are. The strike must be moved to third gear or to another level. 'Guys! Do your job!' An instruction easy to understand; they need to create enough *kak* to make people listen.

Nevertheless, the message was frequently laid thick with additional innuendo; SAPO's buildings, for example, did not meet health and safety standards and should be prepared for renovation. When DEPACU was on strike, the dominant trope of the Mabarete strike came into play; the bishops, ministers, prophets and preachers needed to assist those who still could not see how their brothers and sisters were suffering and should be prayed for.

Above and below the *lex*

The strikes of 2014 clearly operated both above and below the *lex*. I use the Latin *lex*, rather than English law, in part because I am drawing on E.P. Thompson's (1991) work regarding *lex loci* (local rules and practices), but it also helps us move away from the legal-illegal binary of a legal system that, in reality, is not applied equally nor practised uniformly. Though the strikes were unprocedural, in reality they blended the covert application of disruptive power with open negotiations. They did not fit the dichotomy of protected and unprotected strikes, wildcat and procedural disputes.

For the Mabarete, moving above and below the *lex*, between legality and disruptive power, started almost as soon as they had teamed up with the SAPAWU officials. Before then, the door into the industrial relations system had remained closed, however hard they had petitioned. But the magic wand that the technologies of struggle provided had seen the door swinging open when SAPO agreed to negotiations in March 2012. The problem they then faced was that they had no idea what to do once they crossed over the threshold into the world of negotiations. For the SAPAWU officials, negotiating with management was their bread and butter. Their services were therefore critical to the Mabarete. But the Mabarete's magic wand could still come in handy.

There was a moment in the 2012 talks when it looked as though a settlement was going to slip away. The outcome that the lead negotiators, Tutu Mokoena and E.T. Mpai, wanted was being resisted.[24] The negotiations became bogged down by procedural problems, of which there were plenty. A reminder was needed about the anger of those whose future they held in the balance. There were phone calls. The partnership between the Mabarete and SAPAWU was still new, but it did not take long to work out who to talk to about what.

The Mabarete's stock-in-trade tactics were hit and run, but they rose to the occasion and put the Germiston Hub, and the negotiators inside, under siege. Rocks were rolled from a piece of waste ground and the gates blocked; those inside would have to stay the night if they were not able to reach an agreement. But it was noise that was their strongest weapon. They knew which side of the building the conference room was and focused their efforts there. Inside the room it became impossible to hear what those across the table were saying (interview, Petersen). From the Mabarete-SAPAWU side there was no need to say anything; their point was being made for them from outside.

The effective mobilisation of anger is a skill. It requires balancing engagement with hovering threats, which are obvious enough to see, but not too obvious to be attributed directly. It also requires being able to adjust the heat of anger. Cool the anger too soon and your position collapses. Cool it too late and the flames may be beyond control. But for all the difficulties, the mobilisation of anger is a weapon that underdogs forego to their disadvantage.

A hard thing to balance

Over the course of 2014, DEPACU gained increased legal status. While this brought the union the benefits of recognition inside the system, it also decreased the organisation's room for manoeuvre outside the system. DEPACU was registered as a trade union with the Department of Labour in May 2014 and by June it had a provisional recognition agreement with SAPO. That agreement had still not been finalised during DEPACU's July 2014 strike. The union's leadership were aware that their room for manoeuvre below the *lex* would be constrained when recognition was finalised. Consequently, they pushed hard for the rank and file to give them negotiating advantage before this happened.

DEPACU's September/October 2014 strike still oscillated between disruptive power and negotiations, but there was a partial taming of the tactics employed below the *lex*. The high point of this strike was the occupation of SAPO's head office in Centurion, or at least the car park, which brought the organisation's centre to a standstill. Having rushed the gates, there was a long standoff as the guards of the Fidelity Strike Unit held the line and prevented strikers from occupying the offices themselves. Despite the tension, there were no shots and no stones. The occupiers even cleaned up the litter in the car park where they had slept when they departed the following morning, after assurances of progress in the conversions.

In comparison to what other groups were doing, such as putting a manager into intensive care, DEPACU were, in their September/October 2014 strike, model industrial citizens, the kind of strikers you could talk with. Obviously, bringing the Post Office's headquarters to a standstill for two days was a problem, but it was a problem and not raw conflict. The leadership would file into the office and sit down in a conference room on one side of the table, managers on the other.

Using *sub rosa* threats while talking was becoming more difficult as the Mabarete-now-DEPACU gained increased legal recognition; their magic wand was becoming harder to wave. The agreement reached during the head office occupation went rapidly pear-shaped. The anger of the rank and file was turned against DEPACU's leadership. A couple of weeks after the occupation, the leaders were taking heat from their own members in the Germiston car park. They undertook to resolve the shortcomings and set off for SAPO's head office. They would, they promised the restless crowd, collect the promised contracts themselves! But when they got to SAPO's headquarters, it was not that easy.

When Tutu Mokoena, leading the negotiations, explained the anger of the members back in Germiston in order to underline the urgency of the contracts being signed, the implicit threat he was making fell flat. In part, that was because the anger he was referring to was in Germiston and we were in Centurion. As the crow flies, it is close to 50 kilometres. But it was also because those sitting on the other side of the table knew that the anger was directed at both sides of the table.

As the afternoon wore on, it became increasingly apparent that none of the union leadership were willing to go back to explain that the promised contracts were not coming. A return to Germiston was seen as increasing risky. The crowd had been angry in the morning; there would be little sympathy for anyone who came back empty-handed in the afternoon. Some of those waiting impatiently for news would now be drunk and things could easily get out of hand. The default option was exercised: we sat the afternoon out at the SAPO offices waiting for the assembled strikers to disperse without a focus for their anger. It was not DEPACU's finest hour.

The position of the DEPACU leadership, trapped between company negotiators calling their bluff and the anger of their own members, was rubbed in with a lecture from a senior HR manager. That she was a white woman made it all the more humiliating: DEPACU was a recognised union; they could not throw around threats of violence; they had to control their members. If they could not do that, what was the point of SAPO recognising them?

Strike violence

Despite the difficulties of balancing *sub rosa* disruption with above-board negotiations, operating above and below the *lex* has distinct advantages for a union. You have access to a spectrum of tactics that transcend legality and illegality; you can fight a hot and a cold war at one and the same time. Striking above and below the *lex* is part of South Africa's real, rather than legislated, industrial relations. It is part of the relentless, but hushed, class war that takes place in the context of the country's obscene inequality. Yet, the violent projection of power in this class war takes place primarily as worker against worker.

In 2013, the South African Institute of Race Relations (SAIRR 2017: 434) estimated, on the basis of media reports, that 196 people had been killed during strike violence between 1999 and 2013. This included the shooting of 34 striking miners by police at Marikana on 16 August 2012, which followed the killing of ten people, including two police officers and two security guards. However, most fatalities during strikes are workers killed by strikers.

The Marikana massacre brought SAIRR's (2017: 434) tally of strike fatalities for 2012 to 62, along with 153 injuries and 644 arrests. Yet, 2012 is the second bloodiest year in the SAIRR's record: in 2006, 69 people died. All of these fatalities, murders in plain language, occurred during the security guards' strike that began in late March of 2006 (SAIRR 2010: 640).[25] The security guards' strike was initially focused on wages, but became a struggle over union recognition when fourteen of the sixteen unions in the industry settled. One of the two holdouts was the COSATU-aligned South African Transport and Allied Workers Union (SATAWU), the largest union in the industry. The Labour Appeal Court ruled that the signing by the fourteen smaller unions did not bind SATAWU, as the employer federations had argued (Labour Appeal Court 2006). The protected strike continued for almost three months with security guards divided. In the first week of the strike, marches had degenerated into rioting, but more deadly violence occurred after the division between strikers and workers. Much of this occurred on Gauteng's Metrorail network with strike-breakers killed as they travelled to or from work, often by being thrown from moving trains (Makgetla 2006).

Both the security guard and Mabarete strikes were violent, with workers attacking strike-breakers. That no strikers were killed by the Mabarete may have been in part luck, given the severity of some beatings. But there had also been some restraint; the lethal practice of throwing scabs from moving trains did not, despite opportunity, enter into the Mabarete's practice. The Mabarete made extensive use of the Metrorail, but in contrast to the security guard strike this was not to intercept strike-breakers going to or from work, but to travel to where they would hunt down postmen delivering mail in township streets and thereafter to escape.[26]

Crispen Chinguno's (2015) ethnographic work outlines the 'violent solidarity' used to enforce the 2012 platinum miners' strike. In contrast to the Mabarete strike, Chinguno describes how this intimidation was primarily directed at forcing labour broker and subcontractor employees to support the strike. The Mabarete, given their numbers, were in no position to enforce an effective withdrawal of labour, in which workers refrained from clocking in en masse, as the striking permanents were able to do in Chinguno's account of the 2012 platinum strikes. Rather, the Mabarete focused on preventing work from taking place by keeping working postmen, both fellow casuals and permanents, from delivering.

Insurgent unions

Labour conflicts, in practice, frequently straddle the covert and the open. In the 2006 security guard strike, strikers threw scabs from moving trains, but the majority union in the industry was also able to operate successfully in the courts. On the ground there was violence, but the union leadership remained in full view and lines of communication with employers remained open.[27] The strike on the platinum belt in 2014, which followed the 2012 strike broken by the Marikana massacre, provides another example. These were two different, but connected, strikes – the 2012 strike was wildcat ending in a paroxysm of state violence, the 2014 strike was protected and ended in a settlement. The 2014 strike was led by the Association of Mineworkers and Construction Union (AMCU), the major rival to the COSATU-aligned National Union of Mineworkers (NUM) in the mining sector. AMCU had shot to prominence and dramatically expanded its membership as a result of the 2012 strike.[28]

Although the 2012 strike was broken by Marikana, Luke Sinwell (2015) has documented how the network of workers committees that had emerged combined with AMCU, a registered union. As suggested by Sinwell's title, 'AMCU by Day, Workers' Committee by Night', the combination of registered union and workers committees meant that in 2014 strikers were able to operate above and below the *lex*. A key reason for the loss of faith with NUM by platinum mineworkers had been its opposition to unprocedural strikes and its subsequent failure to defend members dismissed for participating in these (Sinwell 2015: 594). Sinwell sees little difference between NUM and AMCU. However, he argues that AMCU was pushed by the militant culture of the workers committees, established around the 2012 strike, resulting in the protected but militant five-month strike in 2014. This, Sinwell explains, 'reveals the ways in which trade unions may be driven from below by the rank and file's collective, and in this case insurgent, agency' (2015: 603).

It would be simplistic to reduce the militant culture emerging from the 2012 platinum mineworkers' committees to the ability to use disruptive power during the later dispute. Any struggle, open or *sub rosa*, produces and tests leadership, establishes connections and networks, creates shared histories and intimate knowledge, establishes mobilisation repertoires, defines common values, teaches lessons and sharpens attitudes. All these are assets for an organisation in conflict. But they come fashioned around the activities from which they emerged. They can be refashioned but only over time and only if the individuals within the networks have the skills required for different forms of engagement. Among the Mabarete leadership within DEPACU, there was often a sense of relief when negotiations, inevitably led by the ex-SAPAWU officials, stalled and it was time for action. In negotiations, they had little role to play, but when it came to applying pressure on SAPO, they were professionals. I was told on several occasions during 2014, 'What we do best is strike!' And by strike, they meant creating the *kak* previously described.

In comparison to the 2012 platinum strike, the strike of 2014 was peaceful. Joseph Mathunjwa, president of AMCU, consistently called for discipline and warned against violence, but on the ground intimidation and violence was used to maintain the strength of the strike (Nicolson and Lekgowa 2014; Whittles 2014). This took place in a situation complicated by intense rivalry between the two unions and a provocative attempt by Lonmin, one of the major platinum producers, to organise a return to work on the basis of an SMS poll it conducted with employees (Nicolson and Lekgowa 2014).

The strike ended in a victory for the mineworkers; AMCU has become the largest union in the platinum mining industry and made significant advances in other mining sectors (City Press 2015). Given this, Sinwell's use of the term insurgent union suggests a symbiotic relationship between workers committees, formed, tested and hardened outside the industrial relations system, and the negotiators of a registered union. Further, such a symbiotic relationship creates a union on the offensive, a union gaining prominence, and a union able to rely on some of its members using disruptive power in parallel to negotiations.

Skidding below the *lex*
In SAPO, DEPACU operations above and below the *lex*, notwithstanding the limitations encountered, fit well to Sinwell's insurgent unionism. The organisation could field the Mabarete leadership to strike while the SAPAWU officials negotiated. Both knew what was happening, but what was below the *lex* was unattributable above. The result was capacity for direct and disruptive action combined with above-board negotiations. The primary recruitment ground for DEPACU was the 8 000 or so casuals who had previously been employed by labour brokers. Despite the complex history, the new union increased from the Mabarete core to a membership of around 4 000 SAPO employees.

But much as we can draw parallels between DEPACU and 'AMCU by Day, Worker's Committee by Night' of the second platinum strike, the SAPO strikes of 2014 present challenges to the idea of the insurgent union as a symbiotic relationship that supercharges the underdog organisation to best the efforts of bureaucratised and compromised established unions.

The industrial chaos in SAPO during 2014 was as much an internecine fight among worker organisations in the company as it was a fight against management. With such a crowded field of battle, it was a fight for survival and nobody was safe, not even CWU, which had dominated SAPO's industrial relations since 1996. The first serious threat to the CWU's dominance came in 2009 when SAPAWU (then SAPWU) was established by dissatisfied CWU officials and members. CWU fought the recognition of SAPAWU by the Post Office tooth and nail, both inside the company and in the courts. CWU's primary weapons in this struggle were its existing agency shop agreement and the close relationship it had with SAPO's HR department. The agency shop agreement meant that members of SAPAWU had CWU's membership subscription deducted from their salaries as well as voluntarily paying their subscription to SAPAWU, either by stop order from their bank accounts or by hand. Despite this, SAPAWU's membership grew among permanent workers (but not among casuals, who were effectively barred from union membership). CWU responded by reaching agreements with SAPO to raise the threshold for union recognition in the company. This delayed SAPAWU from getting a recognition foothold. It was only in February 2013 that these defences of CWU's monopoly in SAPO finally broke and SAPAWU won recognition within SAPO with 40 per cent of the bargaining unit (that is, of permanent employees). Yet, dogged and cynical as CWU's rearguard fight against SAPAWU had been, it had been fought within the rules of the industrial relations system.

By 2014, the threats to CWU had multiplied; not only had SAPAWU sapped the union's strength, but the former casual workers were now players in SAPO's industrial relations. DEPACU and, to a lesser extent, the unrecognised IICUSA both opposed CWU (group interview, IICUSA). Badly wounded and facing marginalisation, CWU had reached for the magic wand that the Mabarete had introduced into SAPO.

When SAPO's newly appointed administrator, Dr Lushaba, had been on CNBC's *Power Lunch*, he had talked about how few workers remained out on strike. The point previously drawn from this was how few strikers it took, using below-the-*lex* technologies, to bring postal deliveries to a halt across Gauteng. A second point that we now note is that when Lushaba talked about 284 strikers, he was talking about CWU members.

For part of late September and early October 2014, the strikes of DEPACU and CWU overlapped. On the ground, there was considerable scepticism among DEPACU leaders that CWU could manage the disruptive tactics that DEPACU members were then spearheading. The accusation was that CWU was piggybacking on

DEPACU's strike and that without DEPACU CWU's strike would collapse.[29] They were wrong; DEPACU reached an agreement with SAPO management on 8 October and called off their strike. CWU, however, were able to continue sustained disruption for several weeks. This was not simply the withdrawal of labour, as the still significant impact of 284 strikers on 24 November illustrates. They were using the technologies of struggle; on 21 October 2014 a large group of strikers arrived at the Kwenzekile Depot in Katlehong Township. Most workers there, including the attached retail section, managed to escape, but two were caught and hospitalised as a result of the beating they received.[30] While the ability of CWU to mount this disruptive action rested on a splinter group of the Second Strikers who had realigned with CWU, it was not doubted by those close to events that CWU's leadership was aware of what was happening (group interview, IICUSA). The willingness of CWU to tacitly permit such activities is noteworthy, though perhaps not surprising; if the technologies of struggle below the *lex* are useful for a union on the up, they can also assist a union on the skids.

When, in mid-October 2014, SAPO went to the Labour Court seeking an interdict against the strikes and accompanying violence that was roiling the organisation, CWU was listed alongside DEPACU as a respondent.[31] SAPO's approach to the Labour Court recalled similar actions in 2011 and 2012. Now, however, SAPO was seeking to interdict recognised unions, including CWU, and not shadowy workers committees. Susan Myburg, SAPO's acting group executive of Human Capital Management, outlined in an affidavit how, 'The level of violence and intimidation is unprecedented and is causing a tremendous amount of damage to the Applicant's property and reputation' (Labour Court 2014: Sections 47 and 48). Myburg framed the violence as the unions having 'lost complete control of their members' (Labour Court 2014: Section 47). However, she was missing the point. As much as unions do struggle at times to control their members, particularly when expectations are not fulfilled, the industrial chaos in SAPO, that reached a crescendo in late 2014, was the harvest of seeds sown when the organisation had introduced labour brokers more than a decade earlier to cut costs.

Conclusion: Reaping the whirlwind

It would have been nice not to write this chapter. Without it, the book would have been a much more straightforward account of how casual workers succeeded in becoming permanent employees. But in society's constant conflicts, nothing returns to where it started. The casuals in SAPO ended labour broking and achieved their goal of becoming permanents. But just as their struggle was far from straightforward, neither was the Promised Land, for which they had striven. Never mind the march of technology, which was seeing the letter become increasingly archaic; what the Mabarete returned to was not only permanency but a withered industrial relations landscape. At a time when SAPO needed to be repositioning itself in a changing world, it found itself engulfed by the long-term outcomes of short-term decisions. The Mabarete had added considerably, though not consciously, to this predicament by developing technologies of struggle that dramatically lowered the numerical threshold required for creating labour chaos.

The Labour Relations Act of 1995 opened the door for labour broking. Casual workers found themselves outside of the industrial relations system. To press demands they had to overcome the vast and varied tactics employed by the confederacy of labour broking. SAPO's casual workers finally overcame this with the Mabarete strike. But this was not achieved in a united fashion. Far from it: not only were casuals divided from permanent workers, but casuals were themselves divided. The Mabarete had to compensate for their limited numbers, which they did using the below-the-*lex* technologies of struggle. In a David and Goliath contest, they won their struggle, but in doing so gifted their technologies to all who saw fit to use them.

In what was now a chaotic and fragmented workforce, these technologies were picked up and augmented by practically every labour organisation in SAPO, including CWU, the union which for so long had ruled the labour roost. Using the technologies of struggle alongside open negotiations resulted in a hybrid form of union action, though one that is far from unique in South Africa. This symbiotic relationship between two wings of a union, one above and one below the *lex*, while necessitating a constant juggling act, brings benefits. It projects power in ways that a single strategy lacks, whether it be above or below the *lex*. Of course, a secure union, one that is confident of its position, need not take up this advantage. But in 2014, no labour organisation in SAPO was secure. They all picked up the magic wand.

Given the intense inter-union competition, the battles of 2014 in SAPO were as much union against union as about pushing for the completion of the promised conversion of casuals to permanency. And if everybody in a conflict has much the same weapons, the war can rage indefinitely without a clear winner. And there will be plenty of losers. In this case, this included SAPO, which was eviscerated in full public view. SAPO was both victim and perpetrator, however, reaping what it had sown when it introduced labour brokers.

17

Conclusion
Permanent Battle

The consequences of meeting targets
Despite the tenacity with which the parallel system of employment was maintained by a confederacy of agents, the casual workers in the South African Post Office (SAPO) prevailed. Their goal of entering the House of the Post Office as permanent workers was, however, only achieved by kicking down the organisation's door. When casuals finally crossed the threshold, it was not with any sense of gratitude but with resentment. The industrial chaos that convulsed SAPO from mid-2011 to late 2014 pulped what little credibility it had regarding its ability to deliver. In a world of rapidly changing communication technologies, to which the Post Office must adapt, the organisation was consumed by conflict and plagued by an indifference to service, which still endures. To the extent that this dysfunctionality goes beyond the South African norm, it is collateral damage resulting from the use of labour brokers that brought short-term financial gain but a long-term organisational meltdown. There is a lesson for management here. Perhaps someone will write an MBA case study based on SAPO's use of labour brokers that highlights the perils of meeting targets without assessing consequences.

Any such analysis would need to investigate why it was in SAPO that casuals defeated labour broking whereas the system remained (and remains) robust and intact in myriad forms elsewhere. One feature that would be prominent in any such assessment would be how unfairness was on open display. The concept of equal pay for equal work provides a powerful rallying point. Providing a reason, however contrived, helps neutralise resentment and maintains inequality by denying precarious workers a point of leverage. A distinction between core and non-core activity is one way in which this is done. In SAPO, there was not the slightest attempt to differentiate between the work of permanent and casual postmen.

A second factor explaining how SAPO imploded itself is that some managers were receiving kickbacks from contracts. When your objective is scoring for yourself, your decisions will not be in the interests of the organisation. Nobody in SAPO was able or willing to work out what was happening within the organisation over labour broking. Only a decade after the system began, in September 2010, did the board get around to instructing management to end the system, but it was a throwaway resolution that was ignored.[1] Eighteen months later, when the organisation's door was splintering under the Mabarete's assault, nothing had been done to mitigate the situation.

Developing struggles

Important as management's failures may have been, this book has focused on how casual workers mobilised to end labour broking. The struggle of SAPO casuals stands out as a rare example of labour broking being defeated by workers. It is certainly the only one in which a tiny band of men took down a Goliath the size of SAPO, and to the 294 this book pays homage.

The SAPO casuals were up against a labour broking system maintained by a range of confederates who fought tenaciously to keep themselves, and therefore the system, in place. Initially, resistance to labour broking was confined to clashes between casuals and the supervisor-broker representative axis, two points of the triangular workplace relationship described in Chapter 12. The Communication Workers Union (CWU), despite its avowed championship of the working class, was part of the problem, while attempts by smaller unions to assist were soon bogged down in the defensive lines that brokers constructed using provisions of the industrial relations system.

As casual workers developed a shared understanding of their position, conflict shifted from workplace concerns to collective action. Their predominant organisational form became geographically based workers committees. Initially, these committees engaged in constitutionally framed struggles that attempted to draw attention to their situation; the politics of petition. As these failed, there was a metamorphosis in the casual workers' objectives. Initially, they had sought to improve the terms of their employment, not to challenge their contractual status. In constitutional defeat, they came to understand how labour broking chained them as second-class workers.

Legally defined, a workplace strike is the withdrawal of labour. However, a strike often entails more than the withdrawal of labour and the picketing permitted by the Labour Relations Act (LRA). Nevertheless, the distinction is worth keeping: a strike as legally defined demonstrates the strength of the respective parties when work stops. Both sides' resolve and resources are tested: no work, no pay; no production, no profits. Only twice did SAPO casuals get to such industrial arm-wrestling. The first was the protected strike in the Vaal in early 2009, the second the CWU national strike later that year when casuals provided street muscle on behalf of the permanents, only to be shafted by the union that had called them onto the streets. Otherwise, it was all but impossible for the casuals to organise within the industrial relations system; when they attempted to negotiate, they would be bounced between their labour broker employers and SAPO, for whom they worked – the pillar-to-post treatment.

One common weakness of social analysis is to focus on how things *should* work and not *how* they work. One result of such over-reliance on the formal is that the informal, organic ways in which people organise are overlooked. That is not surprising; it takes time, effort and observational skills to work out what is really happening, all the more so when formal order is regarded as legitimate as with, for example, South Africa's post-apartheid, constitutional democracy.

This book has belaboured how the struggle of SAPO's casual workers was waged outside of South Africa's industrial relations framework. After backing out of the constitutional cul-de-sac, they groped their way forward, without explicit plan or strategy, to mobilise power against opponents that came into sharper focus as conflict escalated. Although the learning process of the SAPO casuals was uneven, always fragmented and subject to doubt, it is worth reflecting on the road that led to victory.

Struggles and the *lex*

To describe the critical turning point in the SAPO casuals' struggle – the Mabarete strike – as open conflict would be a misnomer given the asymmetric nature of the struggle with the Post Office, which continued to use the institutional system against them. Indeed, the use of the courts saw the Mabarete consciously hide their leaders and, though not their intention, the conflict itself.

To categorise the Mabarete strike as wildcat would also be incorrect. It was wildcat, but only in the sense that no agreed procedure was followed. A wildcat strike entails workers withdrawing their labour, even if this is intensified by a lack of warning and the raw energy that such stoppages display. The mid-2011 strike was wildcat, but the Mabarete strike was conducted by men who were no longer anybody's employees, having been dismissed by their labour brokers for absenteeism. Moreover, given their limited numbers, the power of the Mabarete was not the withdrawal of labour but the application of violence. This violence was not an 'add-on' to the withdrawal of labour but their core power resource.

The use of violence required not only that the leadership be hidden but also that the key activity of the rank and file – the hunting of working postmen – be conducted guerrilla-fashion. This was achieved using hit-and-run tactics in the spaces where they had greatest freedom and their opponent least traction: township streets. One factor demarcating the terrain on which the Mabarete could operate was that the *lex* depends on context: there is one *lex* in South Africa's townships, and another *lex* in the courts.

In later strikes, casuals-in-transition-to-permanent-workers combined institutional and disruptive modes of action, and this cautions us against there being rigid boundaries between struggle forms. It is possible, depending on circumstances, to operate above and below the *lex*. Indeed, the Mabarete strike ended with negotiations and entry into the industrial relations system. SAPO management's talks with what they had up until then regarded as hooligans were not smooth and did not entirely go by the industrial relations rule book, but it signalled a significant move from one form of struggle towards another.

Pluralistic systems of industrial relations entail an ongoing, never-final process. A settlement is the starting point for the following conflict. The typical result is incremental advances and reversals for both sides. With the SAPO casuals, the suppression of their demands for years meant that the conflict, when it came, was explosive. By the time the mid-2011 strike erupted, the casuals were demanding the end of labour broking and on this there could be no compromise. What became inevitable was a concealed yet unlimited conflict. For the confederacy of actors maintaining the labour broking system, it was a matter of maintaining the status quo. For the underdog, the casual workers, it was to press their struggle on to victory or face total defeat. Small wonder the Mabarete's millennial stance: they were fighting to end their slavery and to reach the Promised Land.

But it's fixed, right?
The battles of the SAPO casual workers provides a heroic, sometimes disturbing, account of struggle that overtook the grindingly slow process of legal reform. But since statutory reform finally came with the passing of the LRA Amendment Act in 2015, is their story only for the history books?

The ANC's 2009 election manifesto's promise on decent work included:

> In order to avoid exploitation of workers and ensure decent work for all workers, as well as to protect the employment relationship, [the ANC government will] introduce laws to regulate contract work, subcontracting and outsourcing, address the problem of labour brokering, and prohibit certain abusive practices; provisions will be introduced . . . to cover vulnerable workers in these different legal relationships and ensure the right to permanent employment for affected workers (ANC 2009).

At the LRA Amendment Bill's second reading in parliament on 20 June 2013, the then Minister of Labour, Mildred Oliphant, outlined: 'The Bill seeks not only to strengthen the legal basis for ensuring decent work in the South African labour market, but also regulates contract work, subcontracting and outsourcing, addresses problems of labour broking and prohibits certain abusive practices associated with it . . .' (RSA 2013). She was paraphrasing the ANC manifesto just quoted. Yet, while the new law regulated labour broking, fixed-term and part-time contracts, it said nothing about subcontracting or outsourcing, both alternative ways in which labour is externalised.

In theory, labour broking companies had three months to end the abusive practices of placing casuals in companies on an ongoing rather than a temporary basis; the amended law stated that a worker placed for three months would, with permitted exceptions, be deemed to be a permanent employee of the client company.[2] In practice, a protracted set of court cases culminating in a Constitutional Court ruling in July 2018 over the meaning of the word 'deemed' took the wind out of the sails of attempts to enforce the new legislation, and gave labour brokers over three years to reconfigure their business models. These business models include outsourcing and subcontracting forms of precarious labour, albeit often under different names. This should not surprise; the quest for cheap labour has a long history in South African (Benjamin 2014).

Sweating, separation and struggle

There is nothing new in the production of exploitation, nor is there anything restricting it to particular countries, even if South Africa has one of the highest levels of inequality globally. While the externalisation of work, in which contracts of employment are separated from work, has legitimate applications, it provides a powerful mechanism with which to exploit others. Contractual separation in the workplace is a key means of maintaining unequal relationships.

In 1891, David Schloss wrote an account of the different wage systems operating in Victorian Britain: *Methods of Industrial Remuneration*. In this and subsequent editions, he provided a detailed account of the 'sweating system', the centre of controversy for contemporary reformers. In his book, he cautioned that the sweating of workers, 'the exaction of an unreasonable degree of exertion' or in other words their exploitation, was not restricted to the widespread system of 'sub-contracting' operating in Victorian industry (Schloss

1898: 215). This practice was, however, in Schloss' view where sweating was prevalent. The essence of the subcontracting system was 'the supervision of labour by a person remunerated by . . . profit' (Schloss 1898: 220). The subcontractor of the Victorian era would take on a job for a larger company at an agreed price. Schloss (1898: 222-3) asserted that this system resulted in sweating not because of the size of the subcontractors' profit, which might well be tight, but because the subcontractor was 'remunerated by profit instead of a foreman remunerated by time-wage'. What profit he made depended largely on how little he could pay those who worked under him on behalf of his client.

There are differences between the Victorian subcontracting system and labour broking in South Africa. But Schloss identified the critical component in these systems where the employment relationship is in the hands of intermediaries whose own income rests on how cheaply they can provide labour to another. This externalisation, the insertion of intermediaries, is a critical way in which exploitation is incentivised, manufactured and maintained.

Contractual discrimination supplements the all-too resilient racial and spatial separation of South Africans. We should recognise racism, spatial division and contractual discrimination, often combined, for what they are: ways to deny the humanity of others without troubling our own. Such an understanding gives direction for a better world, but we should recognise that this story of precarious battle illustrates that the Promised Land is never reached, yet must always be our destination. Move!

Notes

Notes to Chapter 1
1. The African philosophy that people are fulfilled as people through their relationships with others.
2. Subject to certain exemptions.

Notes to Chapter 2
1. The province of Gauteng was created as part of the post-1994 re-demarcation of political and administrative boundaries. As an entity it had not previously existed, but was part of the much larger Transvaal Province. Johannesburg is situated on 'the Rand', short for Witwatersrand (an Afrikaans word meaning Ridge of White Waters). On either side of Johannesburg is the East Rand and the West Rand. The East Rand now forms the new Ekurhuleni Metropolitan Municipality and the names East Rand and Ekurhuleni are sometimes used interchangeably. The East Rand consists of nine formerly white towns and their respective townships. While historically the towns developed around mining, the area is now South Africa's industrial heartland. The West Rand also has some remaining mining activity and, to a lesser degree, industrial areas; the township of Soweto falls within the West Rand. Gauteng also embraces the city of Pretoria, South Africa's administrative capital, to the north and the Vaal Triangle in the south – hence the transitional name PWV region (Pretoria, Witwatersrand, Vaal) before Gauteng (a Sesotho word meaning Place of Gold) was agreed upon.
2. Throughout this book, 2011 rand prices are used. During 2011, the United States dollar was worth between R6.60 and R8.60.
3. Polony, a sausage made from finely ground meat and cereal, is typically a food of the poor in South Africa. The protein content for the most common brands is under 15 per cent (http://www.eskort.co.za/index.cfm?Aid=1885887822 [accessed 4 April 2016]). Fat cakes are often stuffed with some sort of savoury or sweet filler.
4. The racial categories used for equity purposes in South Africa post-1994 are African, Coloured, Indian (or Asian) and white. Collectively Africans,

Coloured and Indians are grouped together as blacks; however, black is often used interchangeably with African. Under apartheid, the legal racial hierarchy ran in the order: white, Indian, Coloured, African. The 2011 census identified the percentage of these racial categories in the population as: African, 79 per cent; Coloured, 9 per cent; Indian, 3 per cent; and white, 9 per cent.
5. Township women also travel to serve the new emerging black middle class, though these tend to be concentrated in newer townhouse developments, which are usually not serviced by the ageing Metrorail network.
6. The Unemployment Insurance Fund was extended in 2017 to twelve months, but with the additional four months at a lower rate.
7. *Lehaepharama* (plural *mahaepharama*) is a Sekasi term that draws on Sesotho to indicate, literally, somebody who lies down or rests (*pharama*) at home (*hae*).
8. The term bakkie brigade refers to a business based on the owner's vehicle (the bakkie), picking up day labourers waiting at various informal day-labour hire locations in South African cities.
9. This meme was in circulation in 2015 and the amounts (for monthly income) therefore refer to monetary values current at that time.
10. Literally, 'Person of God', but meaning somebody to be pitied.

Notes to Chapter 3
1. The levy was set at 1 per cent. The intention was to gradually increase it up to 5 per cent, but it has remained at the initial level as the ambitious training architecture has proved cumbersome, often inappropriate and more of a mechanism for middle-class enrichment than creating a skilled working class.
2. I participated in this research project as part of a four-member reference group that reviewed the commissioned research for the Department of Labour.
3. The structure is quad-partite in the case of the community chamber of the organisation, which, in addition to government, labour and business, has community representation.
4. Though there is a belief that the conference, in fact, passed a resolution to ban labour brokers. See, for example, Shange (2011).
5. Of course, labour broking (by whatever name) is not the only way to create cheap labour, a point will return to in Chapter 17.
6. *Government Gazette*, 17 December 2010, No. 33873, Notice 1112 of 2010.
7. The more relaxed approach of the 1995 LRA to the regulation of labour brokers made this statutory conjuring trick easier. The 1983 LRA had required labour brokers to be registered. The 1995 LRA did not require the registration of TES. This meant that the repeal of Section 198 of the LRA (1995) would not have resulted in the bureaucratic embarrassment of deciding what should be done with this tangible evidence of their existence.

8. This would then affect labour brokers but not outsourcing (see the distinction between the two in Chapter 2).
9. 'The proposals dealing with labour broking that are analysed are: the proposed repeal of section 198 of the LRA which has regulated labour brokers (Temporary Employment Services) since 1983; changes to the definition of an "employee" and a new definition of an employer; and provisions in the Employment Services bill dealing with Private Employment Agencies. These proposals would effectively prohibit labour broking. A prominent risk is that this would violate the Constitution on two primary grounds. The first is that it would violate the protected right to choose a trade, occupation or profession freely. It is noted that a similar prohibition in Namibia was struck down on this basis. The second such risk is that the definitional changes would significantly narrow the scope of who qualifies to be an employee under labour law. This would not only violate the right to fair labour practices and place South Africa in breach of international obligations but also have serious destabilising effects in the labour market' (Benjamin, Bhorat and Van der Westhuizen 2010: 4–5).
10. Though this argument depends on the increased cost of labour should labour broking be ended. It is implausible to argue that the work the casuals had been doing would disappear with labour brokers.
11. Though not until the house next sat two months later as there was no quorum when the vote was called at the June sitting. The National Assembly requires a quorum of 201 members (out of a total of 400). On 20 June 2013, 172 MPs had voted for the bill and seven against (suggesting a deliberate departure from the chamber of DA members, who had also vigorously opposed an attempt to conduct a vote on procedural grounds). When a vote was taken on 20 August, there was no point in avoiding a vote as there were 246 MPs who voted in favour of the motion; 81 voted against (RSA 2013).

Notes to Chapter 4
1. PNL was later absorbed, within Telkom, into the Solidarity union.
2. Excepting two unions operating in discrete areas of the organisation: the Banking, Insurance, Finance and Assurance Workers' Union in SAPO's Docex division and the South African Transport and Allied Workers' Union in the Courier and Freight Group division (SAPO 2012: 78).
3. Later renamed the South African Postal and Allied Workers Union (SAPAWU). In this book, the union will henceforth be referred to as SAPAWU.
4. The long period between SAPAWU's establishment in 2009 and its eventual recognition by SAPO in 2012 was largely the result of a protracted rearguard campaign by CWU (see Chapter 7).

5. Unlike Telkom, which was listed on the Johannesburg Stock Exchange in 2003 (with government holding 39.8 per cent and the Public Investment Corporation holding a further 10.9 per cent).
6. Transkei, Bophuthatswana, Venda and Ciskei: the four nominally independent homelands or Bantustans created under apartheid.
7. A percentage that continues, standing at 70 per cent in 2018 (SAPO 2018).
8. Given the preponderance of males employed to deliver mail, I use the male pronoun to cover postmen and specify that it was a woman in the few instances that this is the case.
9. In 2011/2012, there were 5 254 walks serviced by bicycle, 1 095 were foot deliveries, and 219 by motorbike (SAPO 2012: 32).
10. Sometimes in purpose-built boxes that can be locked, sometimes at *spaza* shops, sometimes with security guards of residential complexes or other secure locations. Sometimes, of course, they go missing.
11. Address boxes are effectively a form of mail collection point, but with containers of post office boxes placed within communities rather than forming part of post office premises.
12. This is based on approximately 8 000 full-time postal workers employed via labour brokers at an approximate cost of R4 000 per month, compared to the average entry level wage for permanent employees of some R8 000 a month.
13. By contrast, depots tend to absorb these fluctuations in volumes. Higher volumes mean more time spent on sorting by postmen before they can go out to deliver. However, increased volumes are integrated into the normal work of the walks: delivering one or a dozen letters to an address takes pretty much the same time. What does increase the workload is the number of houses that the postman has to visit. In this regard, the monthly municipal bills are particularly onerous since bills are sent to every single house, even to those of indigents who are being informed that they need not pay.
14. The agreement was named after the Magaliesberg hotel where it was negotiated. According to one interviewee, the agreement was finalised on the way to the Sparking Waters Hotel, but the two negotiating teams nevertheless enjoyed a three-day stay at the venue before signing the agreement.
15. Transman ceased providing labour to SAPO in 2006. Quest was the largest single provider of labour (by cost) to SAPO (Madonsela 2016).
16. T&L does not appear in the table of labour brokers and the amounts paid to them provided by SAPO to the Public Protector (Madonsela 2016).
17. SAPO's Wits Region consists of Gauteng, excepting Pretoria, which falls into its Northern Region.
18. Letter from Executive Supply Chain Management to Marula Staffing, 31 May 2005, pp. 56/7 of Labour Court Case J112/12. See also p. 55 for a similar

letter to N.T. Ngidi Consulting (from the Acting Group Senior General Manager: Human Resources) of 9 April 2003.

Notes to Chapter 5
1. The names of the three postmen and the SAPO manager are pseudonyms.
2. The Private Securities Industry Regulatory Authority, established by the Private Security Industry Regulatory Act 56 of 2001, certifies four levels of guards, A through to D, with A being the most skilled.

Notes to Chapter 6
1. Typically, African men were in the depots and African women in the hubs. Reflecting national demographics, there were significant numbers of Coloured workers in these operations in the Western Cape.
2. T&L later split to form TAS and T&T labour broking companies.
3. This was approximate because casuals' salaries varied month by month depending on the hours worked. There was also initially some variation in the hourly rate paid by labour brokers until a uniform rate for casuals was set by SAPO (interview, Petersen).
4. Public school education is free in South Africa. However, schools levy a range of charges or require parents/guardians to make certain purchases that are virtually compulsory.
5. By 2011, the term 'gain sharing/bonus' was being used in the CWU-management collective bargaining agreement, effectively conflating what had in 2005 been two separate issues.
6. This was split between 'small' and 'large' envelopes. The number of letters was the key measure for mail handlers sorting mail in the hubs.
7. Sacks of mail left at strategic points for postmen to pick up on their walks.
8. Clearflow is the practice of efficient mail delivery by not allowing mail to be delayed or to accumulate at any point prior to delivery.

Notes to Chapter 7
1. A bargaining unit demarcates the workers that the union negotiates for; this is usually defined by job grades. Any agreement reached between union and management is applied to all workers in the bargaining unit, irrespective of whether or not they are union members.
2. This section is based on documents in two CCMA (2008a, 2008b) cases GAJB25271-08 and GAJB25272-08; a Labour Court (2009a) case JR370/09; and information provided through interviews with Mkwabe Mabulane, Lerato Seema and Themba Sibiya.
3. This dimension of the strike never appeared in any document and is drawn from interviews.

4. The Moloko Group was run by Fulton Ramaphakela, husband of TAS's owner. The group included Vimba Security, a large township-focused security company, along with Moloko Information Systems, iSource and AssetCARE (https://www.entrepreneurmag.co.za/advice/success-stories/snapshots/moloko-group-holdings-fulton-ramaphakela/ [accessed 18 October 2014]).
5. Section 70 of the Postal Act of 1998 states: 'Any person who wilfully interferes with the conveyance of any mail . . . is guilty of an offence and liable on conviction to a fine or to imprisonment for a period not exceeding one month for each hour or part of an hour during which the delivery of the mail is delayed . . . or to both a fine and such imprisonment.' However, a labour broker disciplinary hearing clearly has no authority to try criminal allegations. The citation of the Postal Act illustrates just how much labour broking was a legal Wild West.
6. Marutha lodged cases with the CCMA on 28 August, demanding reinstatement and compensation for lost earnings. Conciliation hearings were held on 18 September and, not surprisingly, there was no meeting of minds. Florida's case went to CCMA arbitration on 18 November. The CCMA commissioner expressed incredulity at the process run by Lakey. 'One wonders,' the commissioner wrote in his arbitration award, 'how the chairperson of the hearing arrived at a guilty finding' (CCMA 2008b). He ordered Florida to be reinstated with immediate effect with three months' back pay, although this order was never honoured by TAS. For the Edenvale 18 it was otherwise: different CCMA commissioner, different situation, different outcome. Their commissioner stressed that the employees should have addressed their concern over Florida's transfer to their employer, TAS, but they had not done that and TAS was within its rights to dismiss them. Their dismissal was upheld as substantially and procedurally fair. CWU appealed the decision at the Labour Court but dragged its feet over finalising the matter. It took them over a year and a half to file a full set of papers with the court and when a hearing was finally set for July 2011 they did not pitch; the case was struck off the court roll.
7. This was despite the fact that they were not members of the union. A point the respondent, TAS, kept bringing up.
8. This section draws on the following interviews: Mkwabe Mabulane; Tutu Mokoena; Charles Peterson; Mathapelo Mphuti.
9. Employers required to submit an Employment Equity report are those with over 50 employees, or with an annual turnover greater than a specified figure, which varies by economic sector (RSA 1998a). These Form EEA2 reports are submitted annually to the Department of Labour. The ones referred to in this book cover the period 2007/2008 to 2011/2012, and can be sourced through the Department of Labour's website or from the author.

10. The data provided is for the number of disciplinary cases, not the number of people disciplined. In the event of somebody being disciplined twice in one year, two disciplinary cases should be recorded. Disciplinary action can be affected by a range of factors, including industrial action and periods of economic downturn when companies may be keen to downsize on the cheap.
11. What I am not doing here is asking the reasons for these quite astronomical percentages. While it is not hard to hazard some ideas, there has been little research; it is question that deserves more attention that it has so far been given.
12. There is a relationship between union activists and represented members; the latter frequently become the former. The development of a strong network of union activists, supported by indebted members, builds the strength of a union and enables it to organise effectively during periods of collective mobilisation.
13. That is, using their positions in the union to get ahead (interview, Mphuti).
14. A common union rule stipulates only members in good standing for a specified period should be represented. This is to prevent an employee free-riding on the union and only joining when they have a problem to benefit from the union representation.
15. Charles John (see Chapter 6) was also involved with the group, though less centrally than other members.
16. Not all cases are fully recorded by the CCMA. For example, Case GA41660/09 does not include CWU in the Applicant/Union column of the CCMA spreadsheet, though CWU acted, eventually, as the representative of the eleven dismissed TAS employees. Ten cases would represent 18 per cent of the 55 cases brought to the CCMA against TAS during this period (excluding four cases brought by other unions; see Chapter 8). The majority of the remaining cases were brought against TAS by individuals for dismissal-related disputes.
17. The other two had failed to appear at the CCMA hearing and their cases were dismissed by the commissioner.
18. See CCMA (2009b); Labour Court (2010a, 2010c, 2012b); interview, Mabena. What happened next is taken up in Chapter 12.
19. CWU insisted that it be provided with the resignation letters of members given to SAPO human resources for it to vet before their stop order could be transferred to SAPAWU (Labour Court 2012c).
20. Minutes of West Rand Workers Committee, 7 July 2009. Handwritten on pages 18–19 of diary provided by Russel Mutavhatsindi.
21. These views often included reference to racial solidarity; both Mervin and Roberts were Coloured.

22. Despite the obvious parallels, accounts of his illness given to me were never linked to HIV/AIDS.
23. The initial list presented had 279 names. However, through a verification process this was reduced to 217 (CCMA 2010a).
24. There was more progress with Marula and Quest labour brokers, but recognition agreements were never finalised (interview, Lepheane).
25. In the aftermath of the 2011 CWU congress, during which Lepheane was suspended from the union, there was an agreement with Telkom to transfer him to Durban where he would be out of the increasingly bitter CWU politics in Gauteng (interview, Lepheane). When he did return to Gauteng, it was as president of a rival union – the Information Communication Technology Union.

Notes to Chapter 8
1. The Far East Rand is something of a misnomer. A much clearer terminology would have been the Tembisa Committee and the East Rand Committee. Some of the depots in the 'Far East Rand' casual worker structure were geographically west of the six Tembisa depots. However, the Tembisa Committee was often referred to as the East Rand Committee, and the term 'Far East Rand' distinguished the far less organised depots on the East Rand that did not form part of the Tembisa/East Rand Committee.
2. 'Workers committees' is usually spelled, on the few occasions leaflets or letters were produced, without apostrophes. I use that form in this book when referring to the committees.
3. NACAWU Minutes Book, 9 July 2011.
4. In 2016, the CWAO successfully obtained a ruling from the Labour Court that CCMA commissioners had discretion to allow non-union representation in the CCMA (Labour Court 2016).
5. I have not been able to find a record of this dispute in the CCMA database. However, the protected nature of this strike was confirmed by several interviewees, including Toto Molaza. Their accounts describe going to the Johannesburg CCMA office where they were issued with the certificate of dispute, despite there being local CCMA offices that should have dealt with the matter.
6. The remaining two charges were: 'Refused to carry out lawful and reasonable instructions by not following proper grievance procedures' and '. . . that in your confessed capacity as the chairperson of the "Labour Broker Working Committee" you were responsible for organising the illegal strike in the East Rand . . .' (TAS 2011b).
7. A report that later emerged from the Public Protector's office on allegations of corruption in awarding labour broking contracts was a response to a complaint lodged by CWU, not to the casuals' petition.

8. This means that there have to be onlookers interested enough to be swayed by what they see. It is an informal public trial that is being held. Media coverage reaches, potentially at least, an extensive, if diffuse, jury.
9. This division helps explain why the Vaal Workers Committee did not organise south of the river despite the fact that the sprawling township of Zamdela, linked to the industrial town of Sasolburg, is only 5 or 6 kilometres south of the Vaal River.
10. There was some truth to this. In theory, labour brokers, as independent companies, negotiate the fee for the workers they place; in reality SAPO set the rate for labour brokers.
11. How the situation of SAPO casual workers in the Vaal came to the Minister of Labour's attention is not clear. There were no claims during the interviews of having either sent letters or organised a march that set this process in motion.
12. Bazil Hlekiso, Papiki Mokoena, Ernest 'Tovey' Montoedi and George Ramagaga. They were joined by three casuals from the West Rand Workers Committee, including, Russel Mutavhatsindi and Thabiso Bopape who were to play prominent leaderships roles in the Mabarete strike (see Chapters 13 to 15).
13. The South African Society for Labour Law runs pro bono (free) clinics in four Labour Courts around the country, including Johannesburg. The project 'assists the Labour Court with giving South Africans who cannot afford legal assistance, the right to have access to justice, and to receive advice on their labour matters from professional and qualified attorneys in a dignified and respectful manner' (http://www.saslawprobono.co.za/ [accessed 16 August 2018]).
14. This is no less than in the everyday conflict of the workplace where informing is ever-present. Indeed, at times it is impossible to distinguish between gossip, back channels and spying. Sometimes, it is all one and the same thing: both sides of industrial conflict are joined at the hip. Even if there are no back channels between worker leaders and managers, then workers and supervisors are in daily contact and both can report back what they have heard. To go beyond providing information to the other side, and sabotage your own side's efforts, you must have some position of leadership. Foot soldiers have little to trade beyond what they have been told. So, it is leaders who betray.
15. NACAWU Minute Book, 4 June 2011.

Notes to Chapter 9

1. Following Hirschman (1970), Freeman and Medoff assume that the option of remaining indicates loyalty to the organisation. What they do not explore is the option to remain, but without loyalty. In such a case and where problems

are not resolved, unofficial compensation can be extracted by, among other things, slacking, stealing, sabotaging and slander.
2. The demeaning term used for African males employed to look after family gardens.
3. In suburbs, numbers are allocated and sequenced by street. In the township, they are generally allocated by section, which will likely have many streets.
4. The approach in Pretoria with greater mobilisation of women casuals differed from this, but only to an extent. When mobilising working depots or retail offices to strike, female strikers would go in first and attempt to persuade workers to join them. If that failed, the women would withdraw and male strikers would then use tactics similar to those developed by the other casual workers committees in Gauteng (see Chapters 11 and 14; interview, Maja).
5. This section is based on interviews with Lerato Seema in September 2014.
6. Checkers is a South African supermarket chain. Lerato was not the only casual who told me about the Checkers voucher. Over the course of my research a dozen casuals must have brought it up when describing what it had been like to work for a labour broker; it was an insult still remembered.
7. Literally, 'what will you get sitting in the corner?' The line is used in the Kwaito artist Mandoza's *Uzoyithola Kanjani?*
8. I interviewed Seema during one of the 2014 strikes. At one point, the interview was interrupted when a male colleague came to collect his catapult. She had been carrying it for him in her handbag, a precaution against possible police searches.
9. It was also argued that it was demotivating for those not elected into leadership positions. A further reason put forward was the vulnerability that formal leadership positions created (see Chapter 11).
10. They would most likely have been the next generation of CWU leadership in SAPO had not the introduction of labour broking blocked that outlet for their talents (interview, Mphuti). Perhaps because of this they took far longer to abandon hope in CWU completely, double-footing far longer than the East Rand.
11. Tension between East and West Rand during industrial conflicts is not unique to this situation. In research I conducted on an East Rand plastic factory 'Flowco', following the merger of two of its plants, with workers from the West Rand transferred to an East Rand factory, the workforce was split into two unions along these lines. When the East Rand workers joined a 2001 national COSATU strike, the workers originally from the West Rand declined to join, despite their union also being a COSATU affiliate. During tense scenes, the striking workers chanted, 'This is the East Rand, not the West Rand!' (Dickinson 2004).

Notes to Chapter 10
1. A bargaining unit comprises the agreed categories of workers against which union representation is determined (as the percentage of signed-up union members in comparison to the total number of workers). Bargaining units start at the lowest skill level of employees in a company and extend up to supervisory level and sometimes higher. Sometimes there are different bargaining units within one organisation, representing different skill strata. Where exactly the parameters of a bargaining unit, or units, are drawn has, of course, an effect on any union's density (percentage representation).
2. The union's name was usually pronounced by casuals as 'Sagoti'. In fact, the name and acronym of the union was fluid. The union was registered with the Department of Labour in 2005 as the South African Gaming, Waitron and Admin Workers Trade Union, along with the acronym SAGWAWTU. However, it was as SAGWATU that the Department of Labour issued a notice of deregistration in October 2009. It appeared in the CCMA's case list as SOGWAWTU and SAGWATU on different occasions. The pronunciation 'Sagoti' may have originated with the APC's Moloko Mpolobosho, who introduced the Tembisa casuals to the organisation and who, in a 2014 email to myself, referred to the union as the South African General Workers Union and Textile Industries (SAGWUTI).
3. What the APC did do later was to provide support for a march of casual workers to the Ministry of Communications in Pretoria in early 2012 during the Mabarete strike (Moloko Mpolobosho, email communication, 30 December 2014).
4. Marula recognised that the LRA entitled the casuals to rights based on threshold representation in the bargaining unit. The problem was that SAGWAWTU had only recruited 51 Marula employees and it claimed to have a total of 1 500 employees (interview, Bokaba).
5. This influence subsequently waned with the rise of the Association of Mineworkers and Construction Union and the electoral success of the Economic Freedom Fighters, which emerged as the largest opposition party to the ANC in the area.
6. WASP received 0.05 per cent of the valid votes cast nationally in the 2014 election.
7. NACAWU minute book, no date (but between 23 October and 2 November 2010), p. 21.
8. It is not clear why the 2005 agreement was referred to given subsequent agreements and SAGWAWTU's experience at the CCMA when it was derailed by referring to a now superseded agreement. It does, however, indicate the siloed nature of much of the workers committees' initiatives.
9. NACAWU minute book, 13 November 2010, p. 28.

10. However, a LBWC/COSAWU/DSM (2011b) leaflet indicated that the fight to enforce the 2005 agreement was 'now proceeding to the Labour Court'. While that may have been the intention, the matter was never enrolled with the court and this line of action petered out.
11. Sebei subsequently assisted the workers committees on the platinum belt and outsourced workers in the tertiary education institutions in Gauteng, where he applied lessons drawn from his experiences with the SAPO casuals (interview, Sebei).
12. LBWC meeting, Minutes of 11 June 2011.

Notes to Chapter 11
1. A term coined by Neal Lakey when chairing a disciplinary hearing of SAPO casuals.
2. This includes the duration of the Pretoria strike, which started as the East Rand strike was collapsing.
3. Maja Mokhutsoane is a township friend, one of my language tutors and a rich source of information on township life. He was employed by a labour broker to work in SAPO in 2009. Note that this Maja is not to be confused with Jacqueline Maja, a worker leader at the Tshwane Mail Hub.
4. He was never sure where the additional R600 in his first month's pay packet came from. The most likely explanation is that Maja's start date had been falsified.
5. Historically, the purchasing of cattle was central to this strategy of asset accumulation; see, for example, Hunter (2010) and Steinberg (2008).
6. Though they can be disciplined on their return should they breach any workplace rule while on strike. Additionally, management may find alternative ways in which strikers, particularly strike leaders, are informally punished after returning to work, though care must be taken that these alternatives are conducted in ways that shield their true motive.
7. The slight name change from the COSAWU/DSM-backed Labour Broker Workers Committee (see Chapter 10) indicated that there was a new configuration of casual workers. However, not too much should be made of the name itself; it was something to put on the fax. If the term was ever used outside of judicial processes it was only ephemerally.
8. Four were from the Tembisa depots of Birchleigh and Edenvale, while Moeketsi and Morenamela worked at the Daveyton Depot on the Far East Rand. All apart from Morenamela, who was employed by Marula, were TAS employees. Interviewees had different views on the leadership role of the six. Some said that although the six included leaders, others were simply individual strikers who had made the foyer meeting their business. Others said that all six were leaders, although the six did not represent the entire

leadership of the strike. I am inclined to agree with the latter evaluation given the fluidity of the casuals' leadership, especially in situations of dispute, and that conflicting accounts need to be understood in the light of subsequent splits and realignments of the casuals' leadership.

9. Since three labour broking companies were the first three respondents to a case brought by their main (sometimes only) client, it is hard to imagine that they did not pitch. More than likely, they were present, but kept out of sight.
10. *Hlompo* translates directly as 'respect'; he was using the same word in two languages for emphasis.
11. Several accounts made it clear that the plan had been to kill him. Whether this was reporting the depth of anger at the time, or a concrete intention, was impossible to establish. Mutavhatsindi was aware of the plans to assault and, possibly, kill him, as result of the various back-channel communications between committees. Both he and Thabiso Bopape took a risk in meeting with the Tembisa strikers. By all accounts, the meeting was far from easy, but did result in the successful visit to the CWU offices (interview, Choshi).
12. The title of the response – *Response to Offer by Marula Staffing obo SAPO and TES Companies* – was a deliberate, but unsuccessful, attempt to tie in SAPO to the negotiations by the DSM. As Weizmann Hamilton explained in a communication to other DSM executive members, 'our position aim[s] at drawing in not only the labour broker monkey but the post office organ grinder into one process. We would thus effectively convert what is at the moment a de facto recognition into a de jure one' (email correspondence, Weizmann Hamilton to Mametlwe Sebei and others, 23 August 2011, subject line 'Fwd: Labour Brokers Demands').
13. Makhura appealed against the dismissal, assisted by Sebei. However, a signature was missing from one document and Makhura did not receive notification of this; he continued to wait for a hearing date. Realising that something was wrong, he finally went to the CCMA offices in August 2012. His application for condonation of the delay was approved and the case was heard on 7 September 2012. With Sebei now off the scene, Makhura turned to SAPAWU, then a registered SAPO union, and Tutu Mokoena took the case (interview, Makhura). At the CCMA (2011), it was agreed that the three would be reinstated by TAS, with effect from 1 September 2012. TAS, however, was no longer providing labour to SAPO, but the agreement specified, 'The purpose of this settlement will be to assist the union [SAPAWU] in getting the applicants absorbed into a contract with the Post Office.' When the three turned up for work nobody knew anything about their re-absorption. They went back to Mokoena, who said he would make sure the agreement was honoured (by SAPO), but it never was. Their names were also added to a list of casuals to be appointed as permanents following the Mabarete strike (see

Chapter 15), but were then removed. According to Levy Zwane (interview), management removed their names, arguing that since the three workers were fired by TAS before the Mabarete strike they needed to be reinstated though a separate process. The CCMA ruling provided this, but was never enforced.

Notes to Chapter 12

1. The Bible, I Samuel 17.
2. Rick Fantasia (1989: 27) points out how the building and breaking of worker solidarity are processes: 'Overall, the effort to break solidarity has as rich a history as the attempts to forge it.'
3. A labour regime encompasses all facets of the use of labour – how and where it is located, supplied, contracted, trained, deployed, managed, organised and remunerated.
4. This chapter draws heavily on interviews with SAPO casual workers. This account from below is supported by a range of documents, particularly those used in the various Labour Court cases. Additionally, I was able to speak to a number of SAPO supervisors, although my attempts to speak to labour brokers were unsuccessful. I did try. By the time my formal research project was underway, they had already exited the company. I have reconstructed the labour brokers' actions through the telling by casuals, court papers and the occasional newspaper report. One resulting limitation is that I cannot, and do not, attempt to describe how those in this broker-supervisor-permanent worker-management confederacy understood the situation: what it was that motivated them, how they justified what they were doing, what they feared and what they hoped for (things that I have attempted to describe for the casual workers throughout this book).
5. The transfer also meant they now had pay slips, which enabled them to open up store accounts and access formal loans. They were also now paying Unemployment Insurance Fund contributions. This small deduction from their salary was welcomed given the insecurity of employment (interview, Khanye).
6. Russel Mutavhatsindi, West Rand Committee Minute Book, 9 September 2010, p. 34.
7. The amount paid to the labour brokers was held constant at R22.72 per hour for postmen between 2006 and 2009. It was raised in 2010 to R23.67, with the stipulation that the labour brokers' employees at postman level should receive R14.59 per hour (TAS invoices to SAPO; SAPO 2010).
8. Russel Mutavhatsindi, West Rand Committee Minute Book, 9 September 2010, p. 33.
9. Officially, this is a certificate of outcome that the CCMA issues when it

concludes that the parties are unable to reach agreement and that the dispute may now proceed to protected industrial action provided that 48 hours' notice is given.
10. Ramotsi was a key leader in the mid-2011 strike (see Chapter 11). However, he did not join the Mabarete strike and later formed part of the leadership of the 'Second Strikers' and was a co-founder of the Intelligent Information and Communications Union of South Africa (see Chapter 16).
11. Workers Committee obo Dennis Matsile, 'Notice of Appeal: Disciplinary Action Imposed [on Dennis Matsile]', TAS internal disciplinary hearing, 31 March 2011.
12. In fact, two of the eleven failed to pitch and the award was specified only for the nine who were present. Typically, if applicants do not attend their hearings at the CCMA, their cases are dismissed. Nevertheless, subsequent Labour Court Actions included all of the original eleven.
13. A necessary requirement at the time for both reinstatement and compensation. The amendments to the LRA that took effect on 1 January 2015 made any financial awards given in a CCMA arbitration the status of a court order, though for other aspects of awards, such as reinstatement, the situation remained the same in that the Labour Court would need to be approached for enforcement. Although the law changed at the beginning of 2015, this interpretation was only confirmed by the Labour Appeal Court on 28 June 2016 (Labour Appeal Court 2016). This development has removed one step in the long and often difficult attempts by dismissed workers to challenge unfair dismissal.
14. Another factor TAS raised was that their key witnesses were not present at the arbitration. Neal Leaky, who had chaired the disciplinary hearing was permanently unavailable, having recently passed away (Labour Court 2010c).
15. The review application must be tabled within six weeks, half the norm for legal review applications. The average time for an arbitration to be awarded (from lodging of case) is 210 days. The majority of arbitrations are in favour of employers. Where the employee is granted an award, this is most commonly financial compensation (Benjamin 2007).
16. Hence there being, arguably, four Labour Court cases even if there are only three case numbers.
17. 'Agreement (Written Authorisation) for payments from TAS via Ndumiso Voyi Inc. Attorneys', October 2014.

Notes to Chapter 13

1. The document referred specifically to Section 64 of the Labour Relations Act which outlines the right to strike and the steps necessary for the strike

to be protected (Labour Court 2012b: Founding Affidavit, Section 94).
2. This church is well known for its prominent role in the anti-apartheid struggle (http://reginamundichurch.co.za/ [accessed 16 January 2018]).
3. As well as to parry any attempt to apply the suspended sentence from the Labour Court order.
4. As outlined in Chapter 6, it took some time for casuals to abandon hope in the CWU. However, by the end of 2011, this was almost complete and the CWU was largely reviled. The ANC, as a much larger and much more important organisation, was never as completely abandoned. While many Mabarete were part of the gradual drift away from the hegemonic support the ANC received among the African population (outside of KwaZulu-Natal) as a liberation movement, some remained loyal to the organisation.
5. The list reflected, at best, an approximation of who was on strike, given the fluidity of the strike at this point and the confusion generated. One striker was, for example, named three times in the list.
6. Or at least degrade it to a significant effect, possibly in combination with other negative outcomes, such as bad publicity for the company.
7. Though, even with picketing confined to these activities, what is written, chanted or sung can intimidate.
8. What is often overlooked, however, is the extent to which this is not only theatrically generated intimidation, but is also a co-production between strikers and those who wish to join the strike but are afraid to do so without having a reason that supervisors and managers cannot argue with. See Chapter 11.
9. Sewerage spills are not an uncommon occurrence in townships, which often suffer from inadequate infrastructure.
10. At least one group was accused of torture and murder in the Gauteng township of Tembisa (Chernick 2015). This rough justice was far from a monopoly of the Tactical Response Team. Regular policemen use the same tactics, if less frequently, as do community vigilante groups who, when patience snaps, will lynch suspected criminals.
11. Field notes, 13 January 2012.
12. Field notes, 31 March 2012.
13. A list of 411 was given to SAPO when the strike ended (see Chapter 15). This included those who had contributed in significant ways but not stayed the course, perhaps, for example, finding employment elsewhere.
14. Field notes, 15 November 2014.
15. Although the letter is dated mid-February, there was widespread knowledge that an offer was being made prior to this date. That this offer, which undermined the casuals' strike and their demand that all be converted to permanent positions, was made to CWU (the only recognised union in

SAPO) heightened the belief that CWU was working with management to maintain labour broking. The offer was overtaken by events.
16. The next two sections are drawn from a number of interviews with casuals who took part in the strike. All names are pseudonyms.

Notes to Chapter 14
1. Field notes, 31 March 2012.
2. A kasipolis is a conglomeration of adjacent townships. Another example would be Kathorus: the combined townships of Katlehong, Thokoza and Vosloorus on the East Rand. Arguably, Soweto is itself a kasipolis.
3. At the time of the Mabarete strike, few, if any, casuals could afford a smartphone. In later strikes, WhatsApp was used extensively to coordinate activity.
4. This did indeed happen and even though there were no convictions, it tied up individuals who were required to attend court hearings and put up bail money. Thus, being identified had to be avoided because there was the danger that a charge might stick, resulting in jail time, but also because charges, even if dropped later, weakened the capacity of the Mabarete. As the strike dragged on, this became an important concern for the Mabarete leadership. They urged caution. The standard rule was one beating or 'prayer' in an area before the entire hunting party should go to the nearest station and move on. On occasions, when 'officers' were unable to rein in more enthusiastic rank-and-file strikers eager to, say, search for a strike-breaker who had escaped and was hiding, leaders elsewhere would assist by being put on speaker phone while strikers huddled around. They would urge caution, sometimes using the Sesotho saying *E bona mahe, ha e bone leraba* (It sees the eggs [bait], it doesn't see the trap) (interview, Mosito).
5. Field notes, 9 June 2012.
6. Field notes, January and February 2012.
7. There were more complex mores when it came to the personal property of a captured scab. Early on in the strike, some captured strike-breakers had their cell phones smashed in front of them to add to their punishment. Theft would allow the victim to open a case with the police, while it would be much more difficult to explain why your phone had been smashed, without also revealing that you were strike-breaking. Later, as strikers faced dire financial situations, the personal property of scabs was stolen. Indeed, the severity of any beating might be increased if the scabs had nothing on them (field notes, 18 February 2012, 30 August 2014 and 24 June 2017).
8. Obviously, this argument ignores the fact that whoever needed the cheque or certificate was not going to get it while the strike was on.
9. Hence one reason for the widespread support for corporal punishment in schools, in conflict with the Constitutional ban on this practice.

10. The Mabarete songs were frequently adaptations of anti-apartheid songs, often sung in isiZulu, sometimes in Sesotho, often code-switched with different languages mixed in. Generally, the songs did not have names, but were part of a constantly adapted oral tradition. Usually, each song only has a few lines, but these can be almost endlessly repeated, as well as adapted, by singers in a call and response routine. The titles used here are my own.
11. The song is in Sesotho, other than 'usa', which is a Sesotho/Sekasi incorporation of the English verb 'use'.
12. I have found no evidence of it being submitted as an order of court.
13. Field notes, 19 January and 22 February 2013.
14. Field notes, 22 January 2012.
15. Field notes, 24 June 2017.
16. Much the same reluctance to press prosecutions and act as witnesses is reported in other strikes. See, for example, Angus (2014).
17. Field notes, 11 and 18 February 2012.
18. Gender likely also played a part here. The police and the Mabarete were men while the SAPO supervisor was a woman.
19. The material in this section derives from field notes, 22 and 28 January 2012.
20. *Pelo tse thata* can also be used to describe stubbornness as well as strength. It reflects strong feelings or determination.
21. Given high church membership in South Africa, the small congregations typical of some Christian denominations, such as African Independent Churches, and the predominance of men in leadership roles, it is not uncommon to find lay preachers, or at least those who can stand in for the role, among any group of African men.
22. Literally, patience gives birth to success.
23. The biblical verse describes the hardship mankind faces as a result of the fall from innocence in the Garden of Eden; here the Mabarete were using it differently: that it took effort to achieve what you wanted.
24. Field notes, 31 October 2014.
25. Field notes, 22 January and 20 March 2012.
26. Few Mabarete did not enjoy the hunting process. It set their wits against an adversary – a game of skill with a shot of adrenalin added. As previously discussed, however, there was a range of feelings towards the beating of a scab once caught.

Notes to Chapter 15

1. I am using the term disruptive power as outlined by Piven and Cloward (1977), although it should be noted that the Mabarete disruption was more violent than many of the examples of disruptive power provided by Piven and Cloward.
2. This was done at the Casual Workers Advice Office in Germiston.

3. The Public Protector was to produce a report on SAPO, 'Postponed Delivery', in early 2016. However, that report was in response to a letter from CWU, received almost a year earlier, complaining about corruption within SAPO around contracts, including those with labour brokers.
4. See https://www.sahistory.org.za/article/cosatu-timeline (accessed 10 December 2019).
5. Although the balance would be more complex in the townships (see Chapter 14).
6. Casuals sometimes had difficulty in differentiating CWU office-bearers from management. Indeed, one contemporary account I was given of the visit to Mervin's house reported that they had been visiting a manager's house (field notes, 25 February 2012).
7. And other casuals who subsequently joined with them, either within SAPAWU or then with their own union, the Democratic Postal and Communications Union, until the first DEPACU congress, which elected a national executive committee in May 2015.
8. An event linked to the internal power struggles within CWU (interview, Tutu Mokoena).
9. When agreement was finally reached after the 'second strike' (see Chapter 16), CWU's provincial secretary, Aubrey Tshabalala, explained, 'This is not an agreement between CWU and the Post Office. The Post Office has called workers to engage with them in negotiations. All bargaining matters in terms of the current agreement with the Post Office is that they must be discussed with labour [that is, CWU] . . . our view is that the Post Office is engaging on a Mafia style' (Sowetanlive 2012).
10. Although not all of them were on full-time contracts. The use of PPTEs (Permanent Part-Time Employees) continues to remain a point of contention between SAPO and unions at the time of writing this book.

Notes to Chapter 16
1. Field notes, 14 April 2012. A paraphrasing of Mark 10: 25: 'It is easier for a camel to go through the eye of a needle than for a rich person to enter the kingdom of God.' The same verse is also found in the gospels of Matthew and Luke.
2. Field notes, 22 September 2014.
3. Field notes, 31 March 2012.
4. There were eventually 411 names (see Chapter 15), although not all these 411 were given or took up offers.
5. Field notes, 24 and 31 March and 14 April 2012.
6. There were strong suspicions of corruption connected to the contracts (interview, Tutu Mokoena).

7. The attempt was heroic; the flow chart produced was some 3 metres long.
8. The Intelligent Information and Communications Union of South Africa (IICUSA), which emerged largely from the Second Strikers, adopted the slogan 'The Storm is Coming', which referenced this aspect of their heritage.
9. There has remained the category of Permanent Part-Time Employee. This category is paid at a pro-rata rate for part-time work. In depots they work a notional seven-hour day, alongside full-permanents in mail delivery who are paid for an eight-hour day, while in hubs hours of work are often less and a source of dispute.
10. In fact, initially the bulk of Second Strikers aligned with CWU following the Mabarete victory, but then broke away. Those who remained with CWU were those who had been closest to the attempt by the Democratic Socialist Movement to organise the casuals in 2010/2011 (see Chapter 10).
11. They were eventually re-employed after COSATU intervened directly in the dispute. See Chiwota (2013) for an account of the early stages of their dispute. A second, smaller group, nicknamed the Sliding Doors, subsequently tried the same move, but lost their fight to be reinstated.
12. Field notes, 21 April 2012.
13. See http://www.cnbcafrica.com/video/?bctid=3906733556001 (accessed 18 April 2016).
14. Field notes, 22–23 September 2014.
15. This had to be done at Witspos, where the records of the walks were kept. Until that happened, postmen were reduced to the much more laborious and inefficient method of sorting 'by tens'. This involves going through unsorted mail and placing it in piles of 100 addresses (such as for one street or block), then going through these piles and sorting each into piles of tens and then going through these piles and ordering them as they should be delivered, requiring that the postman sorting is familiar with the way in which the walk is most efficiently delivered.
16. Field notes, April and May 2014.
17. There is some truth to this assertion, although it is, in part, also a boast on the part of postmen. The increasing obsolescence of letters will likely render this advantage all but moot before long.
18. Field notes, 14 July 2014.
19. There was only one of the Top 9 leaders that I did not interview. This was Velapi Mabena, who called it a day saying, I was told, that he had achieved what he had set out to do and was content to be a permanent employee. My interviews snowballed to include other Mabarete leaders and the then SAPWU officials with whom they had partnered when negotiations had taken place. These were almost all also active in the disputes of 2014. Additionally, I was still receiving parallel, grassroots accounts of events from my continued visits to East Rand townships.

20. Field notes, 12 June 2014.
21. See Chapter 11 on 'mutual mobilisation' as a tactic to protect striking workers from dismissal during legally unprotected strikes.
22. It should be noted that this was before the enactment of the amendments to the Labour Relations Act regulating labour broking. But, even if the conversation were to take place as I write this in 2020, five years after the amendments came into law, my answer might be a bit longer, but not, in summary, very different.
23. This ideal-type account of a strike day in 2014 is based on my field notes: 14 July, 15 July, 16 July, 16 September, 19 September, 22 September, 23 September, 30 September, 2 October, 6 October, 8 October and 9 October 2014. However, I previously had intimate exposure to two strikes that assisted my understanding of what was happening. During 1998, while conducting my PhD research in the South African plastics industry, a national strike occurred. I was in the unusual position of having access to both unions and management in DPI Plastics, a company on the East Rand, as a result of them participating in NEDLAC's Workplace Challenge, to which I was attached as a researcher. Secondly, in 2012, as president of the Academic Staff Association of Wits University, I played a central role in a dispute with management, which involved two one-day strikes at the institution.
24. Tutu Mokoena from SAPAWU, though officially an observer, was the Mabarete's key negotiator, while E.T. Mpai was the SAPO manager who had, following the Mabarete visit to his home, finally broken SAPO resistance to opening negotiations.
25. Tumi Makgetla (2006) gives a figure of 57 fatalities during the strike.
26. I only heard one, hearsay, account of a worker being killed by being thrown from a moving train by the Mabarete. It was not corroborated by any other source. It is probable that this practice in urban/industrial lore was the source of this account.
27. In attempting to close this gap, SAIRR has, in at least five of its annual surveys, reported the then general secretary of COSATU telling the striking security guards in 2006 to *'mawagandwe amagundwane'* ('let the rats [scabs] be crushed'), arguing that this was incitement to attack non-strikers (SAIRR Surveys 2009/10, 2012, 2013, 2014/15 and 2016).
28. AMCU had been established when Joseph Mathunjwa was expelled as an NUM branch chairperson in 1999. See http://www.sahistory.org.za/people/joseph-mathunjwa (accessed 21 April 2018).
29. Field notes, 30 September 2014.
30. Field notes, 25 October 2014.
31. So, too, was SAPAWU and, because SAPO's subsidiary company, the Courier Freight Group, had been caught up in the strike, so were another

two unions: SATAWU and the Professional Transport and Allied Workers Union. Since the interdict cited only recognised unions and striking workers as respondents, IICUSA, despite striking, was not listed (though some of its members would have been in the appended list of 1 667 employees then deemed to be on strike) (Labour Court 2014).

Notes to Chapter 17
1. The minutes of the SAPO board meetings that would have recorded the discussions regarding this resolution no longer exist (Dawood Dada, SAPO Group Company Secretary, personal correspondence, 13 June 2018).
2. Primarily legitimate, limited-duration placements of longer than three months, as four-month cover for maternity leave or a limited-duration project of longer than three months.

References

African National Congress (ANC). 1996. 'Statement on the South African Foundation Document, "Growth for All"'. 12 March. http://www.hartford-hwp.com/archives/37a/024.html (accessed 8 January 2016).

———. 2004. 'Manifesto 2004: A People's Contract to Create Work and Fight Poverty'. https://cisp.cachefly.net/assets/articles/attachments/00952_manifesto2004.pdf (accessed 21 August 2018).

———. 2009. '2009 Manifesto Policy Framework: Working Together We Can Do More'. http://www.dhs.gov.za/sites/default/files/documents/outcome%208/Link2_ANC_2009_Election_Manifesto.pdf (accessed 21 August 2018).

Albright, Madeleine. 2003. *Madam Secretary: A Memoir*. New York: Miramax Books.

Anderson, Alistair. 2011. 'Research Shows Labour Brokers Help Not Hurt'. *Business Day*, 2 February.

Angus, Gordon. 2014. 'Law Won't Change Violent Character of Strikes'. *Business Day*, 24 October.

Barchiesi, Franco. 2007. 'Privatization and the Historical Trajectory of "Social Movement Unionism": A Case Study of Municipal Workers in Johannesburg, South Africa'. *International Labor and Working-Class History* 71(1): 50–69. https://doi.org/10.1017/S0147547907000336.

Barrientos, Stephanie. 2013. '"Labour Chains": Analysing the Role of Labour Contractors in Global Production Networks'. *Journal of Development Studies* 49(8): 1058–1071. https://doi.org/10.1080/00220388.2013.780040.

Benjamin, Paul. 2006. 'Beyond "Lean" Social Democracy: Labour Law and the Challenge of Social Protection'. *Transformation* 60: 32–57.

———. 2007. 'Friend or Foe? The Impact of Judicial Decisions on the Operation of the CCMA'. *Industrial Law Journal* 28: 1–43. http://www.commerciallaw.uct.ac.za/usr/commercial/downloads/10.pdf (accessed 28 January 2016).

———. 2012. 'To Regulate or to Ban? Controversies over Temporary Employment Agencies in South Africa and Namibia'. In *Labour Law into the Future: Essays* in *Honour of D'Arcy du Toit*, edited by Kitty Malherbe and Julia Sloth-Nielsen. Cape Town: Juta.

———. 2013. 'Law and Practice of Private Employment Agency Work in South Africa'. ILO Sector Working Paper No. 292, International Labour Organization, Geneva.

———. 2014. 'The Persistence of Unfree Labour: The Rise of Temporary Employment Agencies in South Africa and Namibia'. In *Temporary Work, Agencies and Unfree Labour: Insecurity in the New World of Work*, edited by Judy Fudge and Kendra Strauss. New York: Routledge.

Benjamin, Paul, Haroon Bhorat and Carlene van der Westhuizen. 2010. 'Regulatory Impact Assessment of Selected Provisions of the: Labour Relations Amendment Bill, 2010; Basic Conditions of Employment Amendment Bill, 2010; Employment Equity Amendment Bill, 2010; Employment Services Bill, 2010'. Report prepared for the Department of Labour and the Presidency. http://smegrowthindex.co.za/wp-content/uploads/2012/03/FINAL_RIA_PAPER_13Sept2010-1.pdf (accessed 6 January 2016).

Biko, Steve. [1978] 1996. *I Write What I Like*. Johannesburg: Ravan Press.

Bopape, Thabiso and Russel Mutavhatsindi. 2012. 'To the Communities of Gauteng: From the Striking Post Office Workers'. Leaflet.

Botes, Anri. 2014. 'Answers to the Questions? A Critical Analysis of the Amendments to the Labour Relations Act 66 of 1995 with Regard to Labour Brokers'. *SA Mercantile Law Journal* 26(1): 110–37.

Brown, Julian. 2015. *South Africa's Insurgent Citizens: On Dissent and the Possibility of Politics*. Johannesburg: Jacana.

Buhlungu, Sakhela. 2010. *A Paradox of Victory: COSATU and the Democratic Transformation in South Africa*. Pietermaritzburg: University of KwaZulu-Natal Press.

Burawoy, Michael. 1985. *The Politics of Production: Factory Regimes under Capitalism and Socialism*. London: Verso.

Business Unity South Africa (BUSA). 2012. 'Statement by Business Unity South Africa, on Amendments to Labour Bills'. *Polity*, 27 March. https://www.polity.org.za/article/busa-statement-by-business-unity-south-africa-on-amendments-to-labour-bills-27032012-2012-03-27 (accessed 25 April 2016).

Chernick, Ilanit. 2015. '10 Cops in Court for Murder'. *IOL*, 28 August. https://www.iol.co.za/news/10-cops-in-court-for-murder-1907048 (accessed 22 November 2017).

Chinguno, Crispen. 2015. 'The Unmaking and Remaking of Industrial Relations: The Case of Impala Platinum and the 2012–2013 Platinum Strike Wave'. *Review of African Political Economy* 42(146): 577–90. DOI: 10.1080/03056244.2015.1087396.

Chiwota, Elijah. 2013. 'Post Office Strike and Future Bargaining'. *South African Labour Bulletin* 37(2): 4-6.

Chun, Jennifer Jihye. 2009. *Organizing at the Margins: The Symbolic Politics of Labour in South Korea and the United States*. Ithaca, NY: Cornell University Press.

City Press. 2015. 'Amcu vs Gold Mines: Battle Lines Are Drawn'. *News24*, 27 April. https://www.news24.com/Archives/City-Press/Amcu-vs-gold-mines-Battle-lines-are-drawn-20150429 (accessed 23 April 2018).

Collins, Deanne and Matthew Ginsburg. 1996. '"The Way We Fight Is Very Important" - Ramateu "Lefty" Monyokolo'. *South African Labour Bulletin* 20(2): 86-8.

Commercial, Services and Allied Workers Union (COSAWU) and Labour Broker Workers Committee (LBWC). 2011. Response to offer by Marula Staffing on behalf of SAPO and TES Companies. 24 August.

Commission for Conciliation, Mediation & Arbitration (CCMA). 2008a. CCMA Case GAJB25271-08 [Marutha's case].

———. 2008b. CCMA Case GAJB25272-08 [Florida Mbageni's case].

———. 2009a. CCMA Case GAJB26778-09 [SAGWAWTU and TAS].

———. 2009b. CCMA Case GAJB41660-09 [Jabulani Mabena and ten others].

———. 2010a. CCMA Case GAJB13827-10. [Lepheane and TAS].

———. 2010b. CCMA Case GAJB28361-10 [Vaal Workers Committee and non-compliance with BCEA].

———. 2010c. CCMA Case GATW9539-10 [Raymond Efela/COSAWU case].

———. 2011. CCMA Case JB25003-11 [Marcus Makhura's dismissal].

———. 2012. CCMA Case HO884-12 [Membership Verification Report].

Communication Workers Union (CWU). 2009. 'CWU Emerge Victorious against SAPO Apartheid Wages'. Appendix MD7 to Labour Court Case J1905/09.

Congress of South African Trade Unions (COSATU). 1997. 'The Report of the September Commission on the Future of the Unions to the Congress of South African Trade Unions'. http://www.cosatu.org.za/docs/reports/1997/septcomm.htm (accessed 6 January 2016).

———. 2003. 'Restructuring and Job Losses'. In 'Resolutions of the COSATU 8th National Congress'. http://mediadon.co.za/wp-content/uploads/2018/12/8th-National-Congress-Resolutions.pdf (accessed 21 August 2018).

———. 2006. 'Labour Law and Labour Market Policy'. In 'Resolutions of the COSATU 9th National Congress'. http://mediadon.co.za/resolutions/ (accessed 21 August 2018).

———. 2010. 'COSATU Concerned at Zuma's Lack of Action on Labour Broking'. *Politicsweb*, 12 February. http://www.politicsweb.co.za/opinion/cosatu-concerned-at-zumas-lack-of-action-on-labour (accessed 21 April 2016).

———. 2012a. 'COSATU 10th National Congress'. 21–24 September. http://mediadon.co.za/resolutions/ (accessed 28 April 2016).

———. 2012b. 'Labour Brokers'. http://www.cosatu.org.za/docs/discussion/2012/discus0726.html (accessed 21 August 2018).

Congress of South African Trade Unions (COSATU), Food and Allied Workers Union (FAWU), National Education, Health and Allied Workers Union (NEHAWU), National Union of Mineworkers (NUM), National Union of Metalworkers of South Africa (NUMSA), South African Commercial, Catering and Allied Workers Union (SACCAWU) and South African Transport and Allied Workers Union (SATAWU). 2009. 'Submission on Labour Broking'. 26 August. http://www.cosatu.org.za/show.php?ID=2237 (accessed 21 August 2018).

Constitutional Court. 2018. *Assign Services (Pty) Limited v National Union of Metalworkers of South Africa and Others*. CC 194/17. http://www.saflii.org/za/cases/ZACC/2018/22.pdf (accessed 22 August 2018).

Countouris, Nicola, Simon Deakin, Mark Freedland, Aristea Koukiadaki and Jeremias Prassl. 2016. *Report on Temporary Employment Agencies and Temporary Agency Work*. Geneva: International Labour Organization.

Davies, Anne. 2013. 'Regulating Atypical Work: Beyond Equality'. In *Resocialising Europe in a Time of Crisis*, edited by Nicola Countouris and Mark Freedland. Cambridge: Cambridge University Press.

Davis, Dennis and Karl Klare. 2010. 'Transformative Constitutionalism and the Common and Customary Law'. *South African Journal on Human Rights* 26(3): 403–509. https://doi.org/10.1080/19962126.2010.11864997.

De Certeau, Michel. 1984. *The Practice of Everyday Life*. Berkeley: University of California Press.

Department of Labour (DoL). 2007. 'Ministerial Inquiry: Employees vs. Post Office G/S 8141'. Report, 9 March.

Dickinson, David. 2004. 'Research Report on Union Developments at "Flowco"'. Unpublished paper.

———. 2005. 'Beyond Marshmallow Mountain: Workplace Change in the New South Africa'. In *Beyond the Apartheid Workplace: Studies in Transition*, edited by Edward Webster and Karl von Holdt. Pietermaritzburg: University of KwaZulu-Natal Press.

———. 2015a. 'Fighting Their Own Battles: The Mabarete and the End of Labour Broking in the South African Post Office'. SWOP Working Paper 2. https://www.swop.org.za/working-papers (accessed 12 August 2016).

———. 2015b. '"In December We Are Rich, in January We Are Poor": Consumption, Saving, Stealing and Insecurity in the Kasi'. In *New South African Review 5*, edited by Gilbert Khadiagala, Prishani Naidoo, Devan Pillay and Roger Southall. Johannesburg: Wits University Press.

———. 2015c. 'Post Office Dispute Must Be Sorted'. *Business Day*, 2 October.

———. 2016. 'Kudos to Barnes's Ditching of Labour Broking'. *Business Day*, 4 August.

Eichhorst, Werner, Michela Braga, Andrea Broughton, An de Coen, Henri Culot, Filip Dorssemont, Ulrike Famira-Mühlberger, Maarten Gerard, Ulrike Huemer, Michael J. Kendzia, Jakob Louis Pedersen, Barbara Vandeweghe and Ewa Slezak. 2013. 'The Role and Activities of Employment Agencies'. IZA Research Report No. 57. http://ftp.iza.org/report_pdfs/iza_report_57.pdf (accessed 12 August 2017).

Ensor, Linda. 2013. 'SA Will Bleed Jobs if ANC Bans Labour Brokers, Says Busa'. *Businesslive*, 10 June. https://www.businesslive.co.za/bd/national/labour/2013-06-10-sa-will-bleed-jobs-if-anc-bans-labour-brokers-says-busa/ (accessed 25 April 2016).

Fantasia, Rick. 1989. *Cultures of Solidarity: Consciousness, Action, and Contemporary American Workers*. Berkeley: University of California Press.

Fin24. 2017. 'Company Snapshot: Adcorp Holdings'. http://www.fin24.com/Company/Adcorp-Holdings-Ltd (accessed 3 September 2017).

Forrest, Kally. 2015. 'Rustenburg's Labour Recruitment Regime: Shifts and New Meanings'. *Review of African Political Economy* 42(146): 508–25. DOI: 10.1080/03056244.2015.1085850.

Freeman, Richard and James Medoff. 1984. *What Do Unions Do?* Basic Books: New York.

Galtung, Johan. 1969. 'Violence, Peace, and Peace Research'. *Journal of Peace Research* 6(3): 167–91. http://www.jstor.org/stable/422690 (accessed 12 December 2018).

George, Dion. 2009. 'DA: Statement by Dion George, Democratic Alliance Shadow Minister of Finance, on Labour Brokers'. *Polity*, 12 October. http://m.polity.org.za/article/da-statement-by-dion-george-democratic-alliance-shadow-minister-of-finance-on-labour-brokers-12102009-2009-10-12 (accessed 21 August 2018).

Goba, Neo. 2016. 'Post Office Will Have Its Books in Order by 2018, Mark Barnes Says'. *Businesslive*, 1 September. https://www.businesslive.co.za/bd/companies/telecoms-and-technology/2016-09-01-post-office-will-have-its-books-in-order-by-2018-mark-barnes-says/ (accessed 9 July 2016).

Godfrey, Shane, Jan Theron and Margareet Visser. 2007. *The State of Collective Bargaining in South Africa: An Empirical and Conceptual Study of Collective Bargaining*. Cape Town: Development Policy Research Unit.

Hatton, Erin. 2011. *The Temp Economy: From Kelly Girls to Permatemps in Postwar America*. Philadelphia: Temple University Press.

Hirschman, Albert. 1970. *Exit, Voice, and Loyalty: Responses to Decline in Firms, Organizations, and States*. Cambridge, MA: Harvard University Press.

Hunter, Mark. 2010. *Love in the Time of AIDS: Inequality, Gender, and Rights in South Africa*. Bloomington, IN: Indiana University Press.

International Labour Organization (ILO). 1944. 'ILO Declaration of Philadelphia: Declaration Concerning the Aims and Purposes of the International Labour Organization'. https://www.ilo.org/legacy/english/inwork/cb-policy-guide/declarationofPhiladelphia1944.pdf (accessed 9 December 2019).

Jordhus-Lier, David. 2013. 'The Geographies of Community-oriented Unionism: Scales, Targets, Sites and Domains of Union Renewal in South Africa and Beyond'. *Transactions of the Institute of British Geographers* 38(1): 36–49. https://www.jstor.org/stable/24582439.

Kenny, Bridget and Edward Webster. 1998. 'Eroding the Core: Flexibility and the Re-segmentation of the South African Labour Market'. *Critical Sociology* 24(3): 216–43. https://doi.org/10.1177/089692059802400304 (accessed 8 September 2016).

Kunene, Sonqoba. 2008. 'Postal Workers Protest Poor Increase'. *Vaal Weekly*, 23–29 April.

Labour Appeal Court. 2006. *Security Services Employer Organisation (SSEO) and Others v South African Transport and Allied Workers Union (SATAWU) and Others*. Labour Appeal Court Case JA28/06 [Security services strike].

———. 2016. *CCMA v MBS Transport CC and Others, CCMA v Bheka Management Services (Pty) Ltd and Others*. Labour Appeal Court Case J1807/15.

Labour Broker Workers Committee (LBWC), Commercial, Services and Allied Workers Union (COSAWU) and Democratic Socialist Movement (DSM). 2011a. 'The Labour Broker Workers Committee says: Organise or Starve! Join COSAWU!' (Western Cape version). Leaflet.

———. 2011b. 'The Labour Broker Workers Committee says: Organise or Starve! Join COSAWU!' (Gauteng version). Leaflet.

Labour Broker Workers Committee (LBWC), Democratic Socialist Movement (DSM) and Commercial, Services and Allied Workers Union (COSAWU). n.d. 'Proposal for the Opening up of a Local Branch Account for the Gauteng SAPO COSAWU Branch'. Memo.

Labour Court. 2009a. Labour Court Case JR370/09 [Edenvale 18 case].

———. 2009b. *South African Post Office Ltd v Communication Workers Union and Others*. Labour Court Case J1905/09 [Ending of CWU's national strike].

———. 2010a. Labour Court Case JR1295/10 [Springs Depot case].

———. 2010b. Labour Court Case J1395/10 [Springs Depot case].

———. 2010c. Labour Court Case J1398/10 [Springs Depot case].

———. 2010d. Labour Court Case J1048/10 [Vaal Workers Committee appeal to the Labour Court].

———. 2011a. SAPO Founding Affidavit (Nyiko Magayisa, Senior Manager: Labour Law, SAPO) J1208/11 [First SAPO interdict against mid-2011 strike].

———. 2011b. Labour Court Case J1355/11 [Second SAPO interdict against mid-2011 strike].

———. 2011c. *South African Post Office Ltd v Nowosenetz NO and Others*. Labour Court Case JR663/11 [SAPAWU appeal against CCMA raising of recognition threshold for SAPAWU recognition in SAPO].

———. 2011d. Labour Court Case J1493/11 [Third SAPO interdict against mid-2011 strike].

———. 2012a. *TAS Appointment & Management Services v Mavuso and Others*. Labour Court Case J11/12 [Springs Depot case].

———. 2012b. *SA Post Office Ltd v TAS Appointment and Management Services CC and Others*. Labour Court Case J112/12 [SAPO interdict against the Mabarete strike].

———. 2012c. Labour Court Case J333/12 [CWU case regarding procedure over resignation of members in SAPO].

———. 2014. Labour Court Case J2558/14, Sections 47 and 48 [SAPO interdict against September/October 2014 strikes].

———. 2016. *CWAO & Others v CCMA & Others*. Labour Court Case J645/16 [CWAO case for workers to be represented by other than union officials at the CCMA].

Lee, Byoung-Hoon and Stephen Frenkel. 2004. 'Divided Workers: Social Relations between Contract and Regular Workers in a Korean Auto Company'. *Work, Employment and Society* 18(3): 507–30. https://doi.org/10.1177/0950017004045548.

Lee, Ching Kwan and Yelizavetta Kofman. 2012. 'The Politics of Precarity: Views beyond the United States'. *Work and Occupations* 39(4): 388–408. https://doi.org/10.1177/0730888412446710.

Lepheane, Moeketsi. 2010. 'Introduction and Organisational Rights'. Letter to TAS Appointment and Management Services, 29 April.

Louw, Andrew, Willie Madisha and Ian Ollis. 2009. 'Joint Statement: DA and COPE Withdraw from Labour Broking Public Hearings'. *Politicsweb*, 8 October. http://www.politicsweb.co.za/iservice/copeda-withdraw-from-labour-broker-hearings (accessed 21 August 2018).

Madonsela, Thuli. 2016. '"Postponed Delivery": Executive Summary of PP's SAPO Report'. *Politicsweb*, 24 February. https://www.politicsweb.co.za/documents/postponed-delivery-executive-summary-of-pps-sapo-r (accessed 10 November 2016).

Mail & Guardian. 2009a. 'DA to Boycott Labour-brokering Hearing'. *Mail & Guardian*, 8 October. https://mg.co.za/article/2009-10-08-da-to-boycott-labourbrokering-hearing (accessed 21 August 2018).

———. 2009b. 'Mdladlana Promises Drama over Labour Broking'. *Mail & Guardian*, 5 November. https://mg.co.za/article/2009-11-05-mdladlana-promises-drama-over-labour-broking (accessed 21 August 2018).

———. 2010. 'COSATU Prepares for the "Mother of all Battles"'. *Mail & Guardian*, 21 December. https://mg.co.za/article/2010-12-21-cosatu-prepares-for-the-mother-of-all-battles (accessed 24 July 2018).

———. 2012. 'Zuma: COSATU Was Part of Labour Brokerage Decision'. *Mail & Guardian*, 16 March. https://mg.co.za/article/2012-03-16-zuma-cosatu-was-part-of-labour-brokerage-decision (accessed 21 August 2018).

Majova, Zukile. 2009. 'Fight to Abolish Labour Brokers'. *Sowetanlive*, 12 October. https://www.sowetanlive.co.za/news/2009-10-12-fight-to-abolish-labour-brokers/ (accessed 21 August 2018).

Makhafola, Gertrude. 2016. '#Pikitup Strike: 19 Workers Arrested'. *IOL*, 29 March. https://www.iol.co.za/news/crime-courts/pikitup-strike-19-workers-arrested-2002287 (accessed 15 February 2018).

Makgetla, Neva and Saul Levin. 2016. 'A Perfect Storm: Migrancy and Mining in the North West Province'. Working paper, Trade & Industrial Policy Strategies. DOI: 10.13140/RG.2.1.3481.8328.

Makgetla, Tumi. 2006. 'Security Strike: Why the Violence?' *South African Labour Bulletin* 30(3): 4–9.

Manyatshe, Mandla. n.d. 'South African Post Office Presentation to Communications Portfolio Committee by Mr. M. Manyatshe, Group Chief Executive Officer'. https://www.slideserve.com/gerda/south-african-post-office-presentation-to-communications-portfolio-committee-by-mr-m-manyatshe-group-chief-execut (accessed 8 September 2018).

Markham, Coletane. 1987. 'Postal Strikes: Need for Unity'. *South African Labour Bulletin* 13(1): 16–21.

Marxist Workers Tendency (MWT). 1982. 'South Africa's Impending Socialist Revolution'. http://workerssocialistparty.co.za/mwt/south-africas-impending-socialist-revolution/ (accessed 8 September 2016).

Mataboge, Mmanaledi. 2013. 'Empowerment Arm Accuses Kelly of Creative Accounting'. *Mail & Guardian*, 31 May. https://mg.co.za/article/2013-05-31-00-empowerment-arm-accuses-kelly-of-creative-accounting/ (accessed 12 August 2016).

McParland, Robert. 2016. *Citizen Steinbeck: Giving Voice to the People*. Lanham, MD: Rowman & Littlefield.

Mdladlana, Membathisi. 2006. 'Labour Law in the Next Decade: Time for a Change?' Speech by the Minister of Labour, M. Mdladlana, at the 19th Annual Labour Law Conference, Sandton Convention Centre, 6 July. http://www.polity.org.za/article/mdladlana-labour-law-conference-06072006-2006-07-06 (accessed 19 July 2018).

Mhone, Guy. 1998. 'Atypical Forms of Work and Employment and Their Policy Implications'. *Industrial Law Journal* 19(2): 197–213.

Ministry for Posts, Telecommunications and Broadcasting. 1997. 'A Green Paper for Public Discussion: Postal Policy'. *Government Gazette* 18201, 11 August.

Mogane, Thabo. 2011. 'Declaration of a Dispute'. Letter to SAPO Human Resources Executive, 7 September.

Mutavhatsindi, Russel. 2009. 'Minute Book for West Rand Casual Workers Committee'. Meeting held 23 May.

National Economic Development and Labour Council (NEDLAC). 1998. 'Code of Good Practice: Picketing'. Issued in terms of Section 203(2) of the LRA. *Government Gazette* 18887, 15 May.

National Union of Mineworkers (NUM), Food and Allied Workers Union (FAWU), Chemical, Energy, Paper, Printing, Wood and Allied Workers Union (CEPPWAWU) and South African Municipal Workers Union (SAMWU). 2009. 'Labour Brokers'. In 'Final Draft Consolidated Resolutions to the COSATU 10th National Congress'. http://www.cosatu.org.za/docs/resolutions/2009/part1.pdf (accessed 21 August 2019).

Nemutudi, Mukhethuwa. 2011. 'Workers Strike for Permanent Jobs'. *The Tembisan*, 1 July.

News24. 2009. 'Mdladlana Slams Labour Brokers'. *News24*, 23 May. https://www.news24.com/SouthAfrica/News/Mdladlana-slams-labour-brokers-20090523 (accessed 21 August 2018).

Nicolson, Greg and Thapelo Lekgowa. 2014. 'Platinum Strikes: The Marikana Standoff Continues'. *Daily Maverick*, 15 May. https://www.dailymaverick.co.za/article/2014-05-15-platinum-strikes-the-marikana-standoff-continues/#.Wt5Hsm6FPX4 (accessed 23 April 2018).

Nkosi, Sechaba. 2015. 'SA Post Office to Appoint Board'. *Business Report*, 5 May. https://www.iol.co.za/business-report/economy/sa-post-office-to-appoint-board-1853660 (accessed 5 June 2015).

Ntsaluba, Sizwe. 2011. 'Factual Findings Report on the Independent Auditor to the South African Postal Services Limited in Terms of the Union Membership Verification Mandate Dated 2 August 2011'. October. Unpublished.

Oliphant, Mildred. 2011. 'Media Briefing on the Status of Labour Brokers and the NEDLAC Negotiations on Labour Law Amendments'. 19 July. https://www.politicsweb.co.za/party/labour-broking-will-be-dealt-with--mildred-oliphan (accessed 21 August 2018).

Ollis, Ian. 2010. 'Mdladlana Did Want to Ban Labour Brokers – DA' *Politicsweb*, 3 March. https://www.politicsweb.co.za/documents/mdladlana-did-want-to-ban-labour-brokers--da (accessed 23 January 2019).

Palmer, Greg. 2009. 'Labour Brokers under Threat'. *Polity*, 16 March. http://www.polity.org.za/article/labour-brokers-under-threat-2009-03-16 (accessed 21 August 2018).

Parkin, Frank. 1974. 'Strategies of Social Closure in Class Formation'. In *The Social Analysis of Class Structure*, edited by Frank Parkin. London: Tavistock Press.

Petersen, Charles. 2012. 'Appointment of 205 Permanent Postmen, by Converting 205 Labour Broker Employees to Permanent Postmen'. Letter to Gallant Roberts, General Secretary, CWU, 14 February.

Pike, Richard. 2012. 'Chief Executive's Report'. *Adcorp Integrated Annual Report 2012*. https://www.adcorpgroup.com/wp-content/uploads/2019/03/Adcorp-IAR-2012-final.pdf (accessed 22 January 2015).

Piven, Frances Fox and Richard A. Cloward. 1977. *Poor People's Movements: Why They Succeed, How They Fail*. New York: Pantheon Books.

Pongoma, Luzuko. 2009. 'Postal Strike On: Workers Defy Union Leadership'. *Sowetan*, 3 September.

Poplak, Richard, Diana Neille, Sumeya Gasa and Shaun Swingler. 2015. 'Casualties of Cola: Outsourcing, Exploitation and the New Reality of Work'. https://casualties-of-cola.com/ (accessed 19 July 2018).

Post & Parcel. 2014. 'Administrator to Lead Rescue Plan at Strike-hit SA Post Office'. *Post & Parcel*, 12 November. http://postandparcel.info/63325/news (accessed 24 November 2014).

Ramaphakela, Colleen. 2012. 'Re: TAS Appointment & Management Services/South African Post Office Limited'. 15 January. Response to letter from SAPO's lawyers, Eversheds Attorneys, of 13 January 2012. Labour Court Case J112/12, Annexure PM10.

Rantao, Jovial and Candice Bailey. 2011. 'Bheki Cele's Recipe for the Fight against Crime'. *The Star*, 15 September. www.iol.co.za/the-star/Bheki-celes-receipe-for-the-fight-against-crime-1137942 (accessed 22 November 2017).

Republic of South Africa (RSA). 1995. Labour Relations Act, 66 of 1995. Pretoria: Government Printer.

———. 1996. The Constitution of the Republic of South Africa, 108 of 1996. Pretoria: Government Printer.

———. 1997. Basic Conditions of Employment Act, 75 of 1997. Pretoria: Government Printer.

———. 1998a. Employment Equity Act, 55 of 1998. Pretoria: Government Printer.

———. 1998b. Postal Services Act, 124 of 1998. Pretoria: Government Printer.

———. 1998c. Skills Development Act, 97 of 1998. Pretoria: Government Printer.

———. 2013. *Hansard: Proceedings of the National Assembly*, 20 June 2013 and 20 August 2013.

———. 2014. Labour Relations Amendment Act, 6 of 2014. Pretoria: Government Printer.

Roberts, Gallant. 2009a. '2009/10 Substantive Negotiations Demands of the Communication Workers Union'.
———. 2009b. 'Consensus on Salary Anomalies and Salary Increment'. Letter to CWU Provincial Offices, from the General Secretary, 28 August.
Schloss, David. 1898. *Methods of Industrial Remuneration*. Third edition. London: Williams and Norgate.
Scott, James C. 1985. *Weapons of the Weak: Everyday Forms of Peasant Resistance*. New Haven, CT: Yale University Press.
Seale, Lebogang. 2009. 'Protesters Turn on Official over Unsettled Pay Deal'. *The Star*, 2 September.
Selota, Mashita Ignatius. 2012. 'The Burning Issue of Labour Brokers in the South African Post Office'. Reflective account of the Mabarete strike.
Shange, Liv. 2011. 'Equal Pay for Equal Work!' *Socialist World*. www.socialistworld. Net/print/5227 (accessed 1 June 2016).
Shilubana, Boitumelo. 2011. 'Empowered Women in Business'. *Voice of Hope* 9: 10.
Sinwell, Luke. 2015. '"AMCU by Day, Workers' Committee by Night": Insurgent Trade Unionism at Anglo Platinum (Amplats) Mine, 2012–2014'. *Review of African Political Economy* 42(146): 591–605. DOI: 10.1080/03056244.2015.1086325.
Sosibo, Kwanele. 2012. 'Mine Workers' Hope Lies in Mass Action'. *Mail & Guardian*, 19 October. https://mg.co.za/article/2012-10-19-mine-workers-hope-lies-in-mass-action/ (accessed 1 June 2016).
South Africa Foundation (SAF). 1996. *Growth for All: An Economic Strategy for South Africa*. Johannesburg: South Africa Foundation.
South African Institute of Race Relations (SAIRR). 2010. *2009/10 South Africa Survey*. Johannesburg: SAIRR.
———. 2017. *2016 South Africa Survey*. Johannesburg: SAIRR.
South African Post Office (SAPO). n.d. 'SAPO Group Strategy, 2012/13 to 2014/15'. https://static.pmg.org.za/docs/120426sapo.pdf (accessed 15 August 2016).
———. 2006. 'Take Note: Bonus Pay'. Internal memo, 5 September.
———. 2009. 'Touching Base Communication: Final Update on Protected Strike: End of Strike Action'. Communication on behalf of the chief operating officer, 28 August 2009.
———. 2010. 'Normal Rates for External Service Providers'. Pretoria.
———. 2012. *Integrated Annual Report 2012*. Pretoria: SAPO.
———. 2015. 'Findings Discussions with Organised Labour: March 2015'. Pretoria.
———. 2018. *Annual Report 2018*. Pretoria: SAPO.
South African Post Office (SAPO) and Communication Workers Union (CWU). 2009. 'Agreement on Salary Differential/Anomalies and Substantive Issues Pertaining to Employees in the Bargaining Unit'. Pretoria.

South African Post Office (SAPO) and Striking Casual Workers Delegates. 2012. 'Terms of Understanding between South African Post Office and Striking Casual Workers Delegates'. 5 June.

South Gauteng High Court. 2010. *Kelly Group Limited and Another v Solly Tshiki & Associates (SA) (Pty) Ltd and Others*. High Court Case 2010/5594 (GSJ), 11 March. http://www.saflii.org/za/cases/ZAGPJHC/2010/77.html (accessed 6 October 2012).

Sowetanlive. 2012. 'Post Office Strike Ends'. *Sowetanlive*, 7 June. https://www.sowetanlive.co.za/business/2012-06-07-post-office-strike-ends/ (accessed 6 October 2012).

Special Investigating Unit (SIU). 2017. 'Presentation to SCOPA'. 6 September, p. 21. http://pmg-assets.s3-website-eu-west-1.amazonaws.com/170906SIU.pdf (accessed 21 August 2018).

Spies, Derrick. 2017. 'Rubber Bullets Fly as Walmer Protesters Call for More Police'. *News24*, 21 November. https://www.news24.com/SouthAfrica/News/rubber-bullets-fly-as-walmer-protesters-call-for-more-police-20171121 (accessed 22 November 2017).

Standing, Guy. 2011. *The Precariat: The New Dangerous Class*. London: Bloomsbury.

Standing, Guy, John Sender and John Weeks. 1996. *Restructuring the Labour Market: The South African Challenge: An ILO Country Review*. Geneva: International Labour Office.

Statistics South Africa. 2015. *Quarterly Labour Force Survey: Quarter 4, 2014*. Pretoria: Statistics SA.

Steinberg, Jonny. 2008. *Three Letter Plague: A Young Man's Journey through a Great Epidemic*. New York: Vintage.

T&L Appointments (T&L). n.d. 'Attention: T&L Appointment Employees: All Depots'. Memo from T&L Management.

Telkom. 1991. 'Public Will Gain from Postal Services'. http://www.telkom.co.za/history/TelkomHistory/contentarticles/1991_Telkom_founded.pdf (accessed 19 August 2018).

Temporary Appointments and Management Services (TAS). n.d. 'General Terms and Conditions of Employment'.

———. 2011a. 'Notification of Disciplinary Hearing'. 31 March. Letter sent to Dennis Matsile.

———. 2011b. 'Notice to Attend a Disciplinary Hearing'. 22 August. Letter sent to Marcus Makhura.

Theron, Jan. 2009. 'Space for Organisation: Trade Unions in South Africa and the Prospects for Renewal'. In *New Forms of Organisation: Papers from the Annual ILRIG-Rosa Luxemburg Cape Partners Conference, 2009*, edited by Vaun Cornell. Cape Town: ILRIG.

———. 2010. 'Informalization from above, Informalization from below: The Options for Organization'. *African Studies Quarterly* 11(2 & 3): 87–105. https://asq.africa.ufl.edu/theron_spring10/.

———. 2015. 'What is Decent about "Decent Work"? An Argument for a Right to Decent Work in South Africa'. In *The Future Regulation of Work: New Concepts, New Paradigms*, edited by Nicole Busby, Douglas Brodie and Rebecca Zahn. London: Palgrave Macmillan.

Thompson, E.P. 1991. *Customs in Common: Studies in Traditional Popular Culture*. London: Merlin Press.

Venter, Robert and Andrew Levy (eds). 2011. *Labour Relations in South Africa*. Cape Town: Oxford University Press.

Von Holdt, Karl. 2003. *Transition from Below: Forging Trade Unionism and Workplace Change in South Africa*. Pietermaritzburg: University of Natal Press.

———. 2012. 'COSATU Members and Strike Violence: What We Learn from Quantitative and Qualitative Data'. In *COSATU's Contested Legacy: South African Trade Unions in the Second Decade of Democracy*, edited by Sakhela Buhlungu and Malehoko Tshoaedi. Cape Town: HSRC Press.

———. 2013. 'South Africa: The Transition to Violent Democracy'. *Review of African Political Economy* 40(138): 589–604. DOI: 10.1080/03056244.2013.854040.

Von Holdt, Karl, Malose Langa, Sepetla Molapo, Nomfundo Mogapi, Kindiza Ngubeni, Jacob Dlamini and Adèle Kirsten. 2011. *The Smoke that Calls: Insurgent Citizenship, Collective Violence and the Struggle for a Place in the New South Africa*. Johannesburg: Centre for the Study of Violence and Reconciliation and SWOP.

Von Holdt, Karl and Edward Webster. 2008. 'Organising on the Periphery: New Sources of Power in the South African Workplace'. *Employee Relations* 30(4): 333–54. DOI: 10.1108/01425450810879330.

Vosko, Leah F., Martha MacDonald and Iain Campbell. 2009. 'Introduction: Gender and the Concept of Precarious Employment'. In *Gender and the Contours of Precarious Employment*, edited by Leah Vosko, Martha MacDonald and Iain Campbell. Abingdon: Routledge.

Webster, Edward, Asanda Benya, Xoliswa Dilata, Katherine Joynt, Kholofelo Ngoepe and Mariane Tsoeu. 2008. *Making Visible the Invisible: Confronting South Africa's Decent Work Deficit*. Pretoria and Johannesburg: HSRC, DPRU and SWOP.

Webster, Edward, Deborah Budlender and Mark Orkin. 2015. 'Developing a Diagnostic Tool and Policy Instrument for the Realization of Decent Work'. *International Labour Review* 154(2): 123–45. DOI: 10.1111/j.1564-913X.2015.00017.x.

Whittles, Govan. 2014. 'Worker Hacked to Death on Platinum Belt'. *Eyewitness News*, 12 May. http://ewn.co.za/2014/05/12/Mine-strikes-mineworker-hacked-to-death (accessed 23 April 2018).

Wilderman, Jesse. 2015. 'From Flexible Work to Mass Uprising: The Western Cape Farm Workers' Struggle'. Working Paper 4, SWOP. https://www.global-labour-university.org/fileadmin/GLU_conference_2015/papers/Wilderman.pdf (accessed 8 September 2016).

Workers and Socialist Party (WASP). n.d. 'Brief History of the MWT'. http://workerssocialistparty.co.za/mwt/history-of-the-mwt/ (accessed 8 September 2016).

———. 2015. 'What We Stand For: Our Programme: Only Socialism Means Freedom'. http://workerssocialistparty.co.za/wp-content/uploads/2013/01/MES-No.1-Our-Programme-2014-03-28.pdf (accessed 8 September 2016).

Workforce Holdings. 2017. 'About Us'. http://www.workforce.co.za/overview/ (accessed 3 September 2017).

Zikalala, Snuki. 1993. 'Commercialisation of Post and Telecommunications: Racism and Retrenchments'. *South African Labour Bulletin* 17(1): 74–5. https://disa.ukzn.ac.za/sites/default/files/pdf_files/LaJan93.0377.5429.017.001.Jan1993.pdf (accessed 8 September 2017).

Zwane, Thuletho. 2014. 'Minister Delivers Post Office Ultimatum'. *Mail & Guardian*, 6 November. https://mg.co.za/article/2014-11-06-minister-delivers-post-office-ultimatum/ (accessed 24 November 2014).

Interviews (groups)

IICUSA office-bearers and members: Desmond Moeketsi, Gibson Ramotsi, Sibusiso Simelane, Prince Rampoti and Nkele Jele, 12 November 2014.

SAPO supervisors: Freddy Nkela, Bongani Nxumalo, Palesa Papi and two others, 25 November 2014.

Interviews (individuals)

Bokaba, Kodisang. 20 August 2015. APC executive member, union activist used the SAGWAWTU union to assist SAPO casuals, later employed as national organiser for DEPACU.

Bopape, Thabiso. 11, 14 and 18 February 2014; 7 March 2014. Postman, leader in the West Rand and member of the Mabarete 'Top 9' leadership structure, DEPACU national office-bearer.

Chauke, Caphus. 27 May 2014; 6 June 2014. Mail handler and then postman, leader on the West Rand and member of the Mabarete 'Top 9' leadership structure.

Choshi, Moraba. 15 April 2014; 9 and 29 May 2014. Postman, leader in the Tembisa Committee, member of the Mabarete 'Top 9' leadership structure and DEPACU national office-bearer.

Diane, Kenneth. 16 September 2014. Postman, Far East Rand.

Dlamini, Bheki. 3 July 2014. Postman, leader in the Tembisa Workers Committee and member of the Mabarete 'Top 9' leadership structure.

Hamilton, Weizmann. 1 October 2015. General Secretary of the Democratic Socialist Movement.

Hlekiso, Bazil. 18 April 2015. Postman, leader in the Vaal Casual Workers Committee.

John, Charles. 7 November 2014. SAPO Depot Controller on the West Rand, Gauteng provincial office-bearer in CWU, supporter of the casual workers organisation.

Khanye, Samuel. 13 September 2015. Postman, Vaal.

Khumalo, Eric. 18 August 2015. Mail handler, Far West Rand.

Kubheka, Siphiwe. 5, 8 and 11 August 2014. Postman, West Rand.

Lepheane, Moeketsi 'MP'. 9 March 2016. CWU provincial office-bearer, supported the casual workers organisation, later office-bearer for Information Communication Technology Union (ICTU).

Mabena, Jabulani. 11 March 2016. Postman, based at Springs Depot, engaged in a long legal fight against TAS after dismissal in 2009.

Mabulane, Mkwabe. 12, 24 and 27 June 2014. Postman, leader in the Tembisa Workers Committee and member of the Mabarete 'Top 9' leadership structure.

Maja, Jaqueline. 11 December 2018. Mail handler, leader in the Pretoria Workers Committee.

Makhura, Marcus. 5 December 2015. Postman, leader in the Tembisa Workers Committee, dismissed in 2011.

Mervin, Clyde (personal communication). 2 July 2014. SAPO manager, CWU regional and national office-bearer (president).

Moeketsi, Desmond. 12 November 2014. Postman, leader Far East Rand, IICUSA office-bearer.

Moeng, Zoleka. 20 August 2014. Mail handler, Free State Province.

Mofula, Peter. 28 August 2015. SAPO depot controller on the Vaal, CWU shop steward, supporter of the organisation of casual workers.

Mokhutsoane, Maja. Field notes. Postman, Elsburg and Germiston Depots, East Rand.

Mokoena, Justice. 18 January 2019. Hawker Germiston Station, supported the Mabarete strikers.

Mokoena, Papiki. 16 November 2014. Postman, leader in the Vaal Workers Committee.

Mokoena, Tutu. 25 and 27 November 2014; 4 and 12 December 2014. SAPO manager, CWU official, SAPAWU official, DEPACU official, assisted the Mabarete to negotiate with SAPO.

Molaza, Toto. 4 May 2015. Lecturer, Vaal University of Technology, supported the casual workers organisation.

Montoedi, Ernest 'Tovey'. 22 June 2015; 29 July 2015. Postman, Vaal.

Mosito, Alfred. 26 February 2014; 14 March 2014. Postman, leader in the Far West Rand Workers Committee and member of the Mabarete 'Top 9' leadership structure, later DEPACU office-bearer.

Mphuti, Mathapelo. 11 January 2016. SAPO manager, CWU national office-bearer, supporter of the casual workers organisation.

Mulaudzi, David 'City'. 30 September 2014. Postman, West Rand, leader West Rand Workers Committee.

Mutavhatsindi, Russel. 10 and 12 July 2014; 2 and 5 August 2014; 2 September 2016. Postman, leader in the West Rand Workers Committee and member of the Mabarete 'Top 9' leadership structure.

Petersen, Charles. 2 December 2014. CWU national office-bearer, SAPO HR manager.

Radebe, Malandela. 15 and 29 August 2014; 16 September 2014. SAPO manager, SAPAWU member, assisted the Mabarete to negotiate with SAPO, DEPACU national office-bearer.

Ramagaga, George. 16 November 2014. Postman, Vaal.

Ramotsi, Gibson. 12 November 2014. Postman, leader Far East Rand Workers Committee, leader of the second strikers, IICUSA office-bearer.

Schroeder, Ighsaan. 21 October 2014. Founder Casual Workers Advice Office, Germiston.

Sebei, Mametlwe. 2 December 2015. DSM organiser, used COSAWU in an attempt to organise casual workers.

Seema, Lerato. 19 and 22 September 2014. MCP mail sorter, Tembisa.

Sibiya, Themba. 2 October 2014. Postman, leader in the Tembisa Workers Committee.

Tseki, Phutas. 14 November 2014. NUMSA shop steward, COSATU official.

Tshabalala, Sean. 21 September 2014. SAPO manager, SAPAWU member, assisted DEPACU.

Vilakazi, Sifiso (personal communication). 20 January 2016. Postman in the Springs Depot, dismissed along with Jabulani Mabena.

Von Holdt, Karl. 13 August 2014. Past SAPO board member, academic.

Zwane, Levy. 27 June 2014; 3 and 14 July 2014. Postman, leader Vaal Workers Committee, member of the Mabarete 'Top 9' leadership structure, DEPACU national office-bearer.

Index

Adcorp 19-20, 43, 54
African National Congress (ANC) 22, 23, 33, 35, 36, 37-8, 40, 42, 106, 202, 282, 300n.4
African National Congress Youth League (ANCYL) 106
African People's Convention (APC) 106, 139-40, 295n.3
Amabarete *see* Mabarete
arbitration 192
Association of Mineworkers and Construction Union (AMCU) 271-2
A-Team 88, 89, 90, 141
atypical employment 16, 21-2, 23, 24, 32
Autemas Placements 115, 139

'bakkie brigade' 17, 19, 286n.8
Barchiesi, Franco 24
bargaining unit 80, 289n.1, 295nn.1, 4
Barnes, Mark 257
Basic Conditions of Employment Act 94, 112, 115, 116, 117
Basson, *Judge* 167-8
Benjamin, Paul 16, 38, 192
Biko, Steve 177
Bill of Rights on Labour Rights 104
Black Economic Empowerment (BEE) 18, 19, 53, 54

Bokaba, Kodisang 92, 99, 138, 139, 185, 186
Bopape, Thabiso 103, 106, 125, 169, 200, 239-40, 246, 253, 297n.11
Budlender, Deborah 26
Buhlungu, Sakhela 100
Burawoy, Michael 78
Business Unity South Africa (BUSA) 40

Casual Workers Advice Office (CWAO) 105
casualisation 17, 38-9, 43
casualisation in SAPO 1, 53, 56
casuals 1, 15
    types of companies supplying 18-19
    voice 121-2
    vulnerability 16, 20, 21, 32, 34, 36, 53, 75
    see also employment relationship model; workplace relationship model
casuals in SAPO
    conditions of work 71-5, 76, 78, 79, 112-13, 130
    constitutional and legal methods to end status 105-7, 110, 111-17, 199

323

conversion to permanent status 82, 86, 93, 158, 178-9, 184-5, 210, 249-50, 253, 255-6
corruption 69-70
exploitation of by permanent workers 77-8, 79
in the media 106, 108-10, 147, 240, 255
mobilising 134, 267, 294n.4
networking 134-5
number of 36, 53, 56
occupation of head office 268
organisational rights 99-100, 106, 138-44, 175-6, 182
organising 88, 106, 127, 131, 141, 143-4
pay 25, 53, 58, 64, 72, 123, 129, 173, 178, 181, 249, 289n.3, 298n.7
perks 73
petitions 110, 146, 147, 157, 240
race 71
reinstatement attempt 189-94
right to representation 88, 187, 189, 292n.4
seeking advice (extra-union) 105, 108, 114, 183
'victory' 8, 79, 112, 194, 250, 251
see also Mabarete; postman's work, description of; violence
Chauke, Caphus 123-4, 247
Chauke, Joe 96
Choshi, Moraba 73, 152-3, 201-2
Chun, Jennifer 110-11, 239
class 6, 28, 42-3, 146, 175, 198, 270
client company 15
use of multiple labour brokers 18
collective bargaining 21
casuals 20, 55, 85, 182
Commercial, Services and Allied Workers Union (COSAWU) 105, 138, 143, 144, 170, 171, 296n.7

Commission for Conciliation, Mediation and Arbitration (CCMA) 89, 99, 105, 107, 114-16, 130, 138, 140, 141, 142, 145, 180, 185-6, 190, 191-2, 194, 202, 203, 291n.16
Communication Workers Union (CWU) 8, 47, 51, 58, 59, 139, 174, 202
agency shop agreement 47, 80, 274
collective bargaining, casuals 85-6, 87, 88, 90, 91
corruption 91
decline in power 91, 100, 125, 273
divisions 81, 85, 91-2, 100, 141-2
and Mabarete 244-5, 249
and management 80, 85
membership 80, 91, 100, 125
protests 240-1
recognition agreement (casuals) 99-100, 138, 142
relationship to casuals in SAPO 86, 88, 92, 94-5, 97, 98-100, 104, 141-2, 157, 169, 300n.4
representation of casuals in disciplinary matters 81, 83, 87, 88-90, 98-100, 171, 172, 189, 191
and South African Postal Workers Union (SAPWU) 81, 91
violence 275
Congress of South African Trade Unions (COSATU) 31, 43, 105, 106, 202
affiliates 43
membership 32, 43
protests 39-40, 240-1
statements on labour broking ban 33, 34, 36-7, 40, 41, 42
Congress of the People 37
Constitution of South Africa 106, 110
Courier Freight Group 305n.31

De Certeau, Michel 196-7
decent work 26, 30, 282
Democratic Alliance 37, 40-1
Democratic Postal and Communications Union (DEPACU) 256, 262, 268-9, 272, 273, 274, 275
Democratic Socialist Movement (DSM) 106, 142-7, 168, 297n.12
Department of Labour 32, 33, 34, 37, 105, 106, 107
  investigation into labour broking 112-14
  Regulatory Impact Assessment 38
Dieho, John 210-13
disciplinary action 88, 176, 186-7, 188, 201
  statistics 87-8
disciplinary hearings 82, 83-4, 87, 109, 186-7, 188-9, 290n.5
disruptive power 207-8, 239, 242, 266, 268, 273, 282, 302n.1; *see also* insurgent unionism

East Rand 285n.1
East Rand Workers Committee 93, 102, 109, 135, 136, 144, 201; *see also* Tembisa Workers Committee
Efela, Raymond 143, 144, 145, 146
Employment Equity reports 56, 87-8, 290n.9
employment relationship 1, 15-16, 17-18, 20, 31, 180, 181, 195-6
employment relationship model 15-16, 17-18, 56, 194-6; *see also* workplace relationship model
externalisation 17, 23, 28, 283, 284

Far East Rand 292n.1
Far East Rand Workers Committee 135, 209

flexibility *see* labour flexibility
Forrest, Kally 78
Francis, *Judge* 171
Freeman, Richard 121
Frenkel, Stephen 77

Gauteng 10, 285n.1
  Premier 106, 110
Godfrey, Shane 21
Godi, Themba 139-40
Growth, Employment and Redistribution policy (GEAR) 23

Hamilton, Weizmann 168, 203, 297n.12
High Court (Namibia) 34
Hlekiso, Bazil 108, 116, 118, 119, 180-1
hunting *see* scab labour

industrial relations reform 3, 21
industrial relations system 30, 41, 257, 269, 274, 280; *see also* technologies of struggle
insurgent unionism 271, 272, 273; *see also* disruptive power
Intelligent Information and Communications Union of South Africa (IICUSA) 256, 261, 299n.10, 305n.31
Interim (company) 178, 179
International Labour Organization (ILO) 34
intimidation 154-5, 158, 206, 271, 300nn.7, 8; *see also* disruptive power

Jabangwe, Joshua 117, 191
John, Charles 129, 134, 291n.15
John, Quinton 129

Katlehong Township 4, 135
Kelly (company) 51, 53, 54
Kenny, Bridget 24, 32, 43
Kgodu, Jerry 215
Khayne, Samuel 103, 178
Kofman, Yelizavetta 27
Koto, Jaco 189
Kotsi, Janras 225
Kunene, Sonqoba 109
Kwata, Charles 89, 157

labour broker employees *see* casuals
Labour Broker Workers Committee (LBWC) 143-4, 145, 146-7, 172
labour brokers
  bribery among 54, 183
  categories of 18-20, 36
  competition between 18, 55, 175
  financial gain by 53-4, 130
  rates 55, 117
  and union recognition 99-100, 138-9, 140, 142
  see also lex loci
Labour Brokers Employees Committee 160
labour broking 1-2, 32-3, 278, 284, 197-8
  ban 33, 34, 35, 38, 40, 43, 81, 86, 101
  benefits 53-4, 198
  ending of in SAPO 40, 279, 282
  extent 34, 38-9, 278
  function 1-2, 15, 35-6
  maintenance of in SAPO 7-8, 176-7
  origins in SAPO 19-20, 25
  protests against 39-40
  public sector 24
  regulation 40, 41
  tactics (legal) 189-94
  tactics (organisational) 174-5, 176-7, 180-3, 186-9, 195
  tactics (psychological) 174-5, 176-80, 183-6, 21
labour costs 31, 32, 41
Labour Court
  arbitration 192
  casuals' use of 105, 117-19, 190-4
  pro-bono office 293n.13
  report-back to strikers 162-4
  SAPO's use of 96, 159-61, 167-8, 169-71, 172, 203, 275
  TAS's use of 141
Labour Equity General Workers Union of South Africa (LEWUSA) 105
labour flexibility 25, 32, 50
labour market 21, 22-3, 35
Labour Relations Act (LRA)
  amendments 3, 6, 31, 32, 36, 37, 38, 39, 40-1, 110, 282-3, 287n.9
  contesting of 'deemed' 3, 180
  'direct supervision' 38
  loophole 6, 20, 31
  permanent employee 3, 39
  on pickets 206
  Sections 11 to 16 99-100, 138
  Section 198 41
  temporary employment services 1, 15, 33, 38
  unintended consequences of 41
Lagrange, *Judge* 116-17
Lakey, Neal 84, 88, 89, 140, 189
Lee, Byoung-Hoon 77
Lee, Ching Kwan 27
legal recognition 7
Lepheane, Moeketsi 'MP' 89, 96, 97-9, 105, 135, 138, 141-2, 189, 191, 292n.25
lex loci 9, 223, 257, 266, 269-70, 273, 274, 275, 276, 281
Lushaba, Simo 260

Index

Mabarete
  activity, forms of 219-23, 244-5
  battle cry 222-3
  conceptualisation 231-4, 235, 237
  geographic distribution of
    operations 215-16
  home visits to management and
    union 244-5, 258
  increasing visibility 239-42
  informal nature 218, 236-7,
    244-5, 247, 258
  leadership 4, 134, 221-2, 247, 272,
    304n.19
  morality and township world view
    223-4, 227, 229, 258-60
  number 208, 218, 250
  organisational form 217-18, 219
  origin of name 207
  and police 225-6
  and religious beliefs and metaphors
    234-6
  songs 224, 233-4, 302n.10
  surviving the strike 238, 242-4
  see also under strikes; technologies
    of struggle
Mabaso, Mike 82, 83
Mabena, Jabulani 188, 190, 191, 192;
  see also Springs Eleven
Mabena, Velapi 304n.19
Mabulane, Mkwabe 152, 153, 161,
  263
Magayisa, Nyiko 160, 167
Mahomed, Imraan 160
mail delivery system 48, 304n.15
Maja, Jaqueline 131, 254, 296n.3
Makhura, Marcus 109, 136, 139, 152,
  153, 157, 160-1, 173, 186, 188,
  297n.13
Manamela, Johannes 136, 161, 173
Manyi, Jimmy 37
Marikana 270, 271

Marula Staffing and Workforce
  Management 20, 53, 82, 115,
  139, 160, 172-3, 175-6, 204,
  292n.24, 295n.4
Marutha, Freddie 83, 84-5, 89, 96,
  97, 135, 290n.6
Marxist Workers Tendency 143
Mashego, Booysen 168, 171, 172
Mashishini, Mike 211
Mathunjwa, Joseph 272
Matsile, Dennis 187
Mbangeni, Florida 81
Mail Collection Points (MCPs) 122,
  132
Mdladlana, Membathisi 33-4, 36,
  37, 38
Mdlungu, Mzwandile 161
Medoff, James 121
Mervin, Clyde 5, 82, 83, 84, 85, 93,
  95-6, 97, 100, 244-5, 291n.21
Metrorail, role in strikes 11, 154,
  155-6; *see also* rail commuting
Mhone, Guy 32
migrants 152
Minister of Communications 106,
  110
Moeketsi, Desmond 144, 146, 160,
  161, 209, 254, 260-1
Mofula, Peter 88-9
Mokhutsoane, Maja 150-2, 158, 162,
  296n.3
Mokoena, Justice 243-4
Mokoena, Papiki 118, 180
Mokoena, Tutu 168-9, 247-8,
  248-9, 267, 269, 305n.24
Molaza, Toto 107, 114, 183
Moloko Group 84, 140, 189, 290n.4
Montoedi, Ernest 'Tovey' 95, 103,
  121-3, 125, 177, 180-1, 183-5,
  210
'moral exclusion' 77-8

Morenamela, Petrus 136, 161, 173
Mosito, Alfred 134, 199, 200
Motlokoa, Michael 82
Mpai, E.T. 5, 109, 244, 245, 246, 248, 249, 267
Mphuti, Mathapelo 89, 94, 96
Mpolobosho, Moloko 139
Mutavhatsindi, Russel 93, 124, 126, 169, 200, 239-40, 246, 297n.11
Myburg, Susan 275

National Association of Bargaining Councils 38
National Communications and Allied Workers Union (NACAWU) 105, 106-7, 144-5, 170
National Council of the Provinces 41
National Council of Trade Unions 39
National Economic Development and Labour Council (NEDLAC) 33, 37, 38, 39, 40, 206
National Labour and Economic Development Institute 39
National Union of Mineworkers (NUM) 272
Ndumiso Voyi Incorporated: Attorneys 192
Nenjelele, Siphiwe 247
N.T. Ngidi (labour broker) 139, 160, 204

Oliphant, Mildred 38, 282
Orkin, Mark 26
outsourcing 17, 24, 31, 33, 35, 43, 283

Parkin, Frank 101
parliamentary hearings 36-7, 110
pay
   casual's take-home 53, 58, 64, 72, 123, 178

   flexible 129, 256
   increase 86, 93, 112, 115, 172-3, 181, 182, 249, 252
   permanent's take-home 53, 72-3
   rate set for labour brokers 55, 298n.7
   S32s 51, 178
permanent casuals 15, 51
permanent employee category 3, 39, 56, 71
Permanent Part-Time Employees (PPTEs) 85, 86, 303n.10, 304n.9
permanent workers in SAPO
   benefits 53, 55, 72-3, 74-5
   conditions of work 72, 74-5, 76
   exploitation of casuals 55, 77, 78-9
   pay 53, 55, 72-3, 93-4
   strike (2009) 93-7
Pike, Richard 43
placement agencies 51, 53
Portfolio Committee on Labour 36, 37, 40
Pos en Telekommunikasie Unie (PNL) 47
Post Office Employees Association 47
Post Office and Telecommunications Workers Association (POTWA) 46-7, 88
postal service
   commercialisation 47
   monopoly 45
   subsidisation 45-6
   universal 45, 46, 47-8
postman's work, description of 6, 48-9, 50, 57, 60-3, 64, 65-8, 69-70, 76, 79, 127-9; *see also* mail handlers; SAPO, depots; SAPO, hubs
precarious labour 3, 6, 28, 110-11
Professional Transport and Allied Workers Union 305n.31

Public Protector 106, 110

Quest Staffing Solutions 20, 51, 54, 288n.15, 292n.24

Radebe, Malandela 247
rail commuting 11-14
Ramaphakela, Colleen 5, 54, 176, 179, 182, 194, 203, 220, 244
Ramaphakela, Fulton 290n.4
Ramokgopa, Sello 252
Ramotsi, Gibson 187, 188, 299n.10
research
  methods 4, 5, 262
  sources 5, 298n.4, 304n.19
Roberts, Gallant 94, 96, 291n.21

S32 (form for SAPO contract employees) 51, 85, 86, 178, 249
salaries *see* pay
scab labour 151, 158, 164, 165-7, 170, 216, 221, 224-5, 226-9, 237, 245, 270-1, 301n.7
Schloss, David 283
Schroeder, Ighsaan 108
Scott, James 197
Sebei, Mametlwe 146, 168, 172, 296n.11
Seema, Lerato 132-4
Selota, Shitas 230-1
September Commission 31-2
Shange, Liv 142
Sibiya, Themba 153, 177
Skills Development Act of 1998 30
social reproduction 27-8
South Africa Foundation (SAF) 22, 23, 25, 29, 41
South African Communist Party (SACP) 40, 103-4, 106
South African Constitution 25, 28, 106, 120

South African Gaming, Waitron and Admin Workers Trade Union (SAGWAWTU) 92, 105, 138, 139-41, 185, 295nn.2, 4
South African Police Services (SAPS) 225-7, 228
South African Post Office (SAPO) 47
  board 257
  corruption 54-5, 82, 279, 303n.6
  depots 48, 81-2, 111, 123, 127-8, 135, 150, 152, 154, 159, 252, 255, 261, 264
  employment equity reporting 56
  hubs 48, 127-8, 216
  internal part-time and temporary workforce 46, 49, 51, 58, 86, 210
  Labour Court 5, 7, 96, 146, 159-60, 167, 275
  lawyers 160-1
  mail delivery process 48-9
  mail handlers 127-8
  management 46, 49, 53, 54, 74-5, 80, 84, 130, 158, 160, 179, 185, 198, 202, 244, 246, 248-9
  origins of labour broking in 2, 23-4, 25, 50, 51, 52
  profit 50
  structure and status 46
  supervisors 54, 55, 76-7, 134, 151, 174, 183-6, 187-8, 211, 220, 228
  and Telkom 46
  towards universal service 49-50
  voluntary severance packages 52
  workforce 1, 50, 51, 52-3, 55, 56, 260
  see also permanent workers in SAPO; postman's work, description of
South African Post Telecommunication Employees Association 47

South African Postal and Allied
  Workers Union (SAPAWU) 4, 8,
  81, 91, 247, 248, 249, 256, 267,
  273-4, 287nn.3, 4
South African Postal Workers Union
  (SAPWU) 47, 91, 105, 247, 256,
  273
South African Transport and Allied
  Workers Union (SATAWU) 270,
  305n.31
Springs Eleven 190-4
standard employee relationship 16
Steenkamp, *Judge* 161, 167, 168
strategies of casuals *see* technologies
  of struggle
strikes
  ambivalence about joining 184,
    209-13
  benefiting only permanent workers
    58-9
  definition and use of term 204-6
  dismissals following 84, 109, 134,
    173, 188
  involvement of women 131, 133-4
  Mabarete 4, 8, 40, 232, 258, 270,
    281
  Mabarete (phase I) 199, 200-4,
    207-13
  Mabarete (phase II) 215-16,
    218-19, 231-7
  Mabarete (phase III) 238, 244
  negotiations to end 94, 239,
    246-50, 265-6, 267, 268,
    303n.9
  partial 84, 107, 149
  platinum miners 270, 271, 272-3
  protected 20, 94, 105, 107, 140-1,
    153, 183, 184-5, 206, 263, 266,
    271
  right to 107, 199
  rotating 256, 262, 274

and SAPS 225-6, 236
'second' 253-5
security guard (2006) 270, 305n.25
surviving 242-4
'third' and beyond 255-7
in 2005 112, 149
in 2009 (CWU) 58, 91, 93-7,
  140-1, 149, 280
in 2011 (Tembisa Workers
  Committee) 4, 147, 150-2,
  153-73, 197, 223
in 2014 261, 264-6, 268, 273-4
unprotected 51, 150, 153-4, 176,
  203, 204, 254, 263, 266
unwritten agreement following
  249-50, 253, 255
wildcat 84, 132, 146, 168, 263, 271,
  281
subcontracting 17, 24, 35, 283-4
Swart, Pieter 246
'sweating system' 283-4
symbolic power 110-11, 239-42

Tabane, Richard 211
TAS Appointments and Management
  Services (TAS) 20, 54, 71, 289n.2
  disciplinary action 82, 83, 89, 176,
    187-8
  contracts 71-2, 112-14, 115,
    116-17
  Labour Court 141, 190-4, 203-4
  negotiating organisational rights
    with 99-100, 139-42
  pay increases 181-2
  Unemployment Insurance Fund
    (UIF) 115
T&L Appointments 122, 289n. 2
T&T Appointments 54, 139, 289n.2
technologies of struggle 257-8,
  261-2, 267, 269, 276,
Tembisa 152

Tembisa Workers Committee 7, 92, 109, 135, 136, 139, 144, 147, 169; see also East Rand Workers Committee
temporary employment services see under Labour Relations Act
Theron, Jan 21, 28, 119-20
Transman 51, 54, 288n.15
transport (Gauteng) 11-12; see also rail commuting
Tsotetsi, Daniel 141

unemployment 15, 175, 242
unionisation 18, 20, 256, 260, 274
University of South Africa (UNISA) 241-2

Vaal 111
Vaal University of Technology (VUT) staff member and students 105, 118, 183
Vaal Workers Committee 5, 106, 107, 111, 114, 115, 117-19, 144, 147, 170, 182, 183, 293n.9
Van den Berg, James 83
Vavi, Zwelinzima 98
Von Holdt, Karl 21, 28, 235
violence 206, 235, 261, 268, 269-70
  by casuals 2, 3, 164, 264-5, 265, 266, 268
  by CWU members 275
  by Mabarete casuals 8, 220, 221, 225, 232-3, 236, 246, 258-60, 281
  structural 3
  see also lex loci
Visser, Margaret 21
Voyi, Ndumiso 192-3, 194
vulnerable workers 16, 20, 32, 34, 53, 75

wages see pay
Weber, Max 162
Webster, Edward 21, 24, 25, 32, 43
West Rand Workers Committee 92, 93, 102, 130, 135, 136, 144, 147, 169, 170, 182, 188, 200, 201-2
women 13, 48, 51, 54, 82, 131-4, 209, 294n.4
Workers and Socialist Party (WASP) 143, 295n.6
workers committees, casuals 7, 105
  divisions and fragmentation 144, 147, 156, 169, 170, 201
  geographic spread 102, 135-6, 144
  leadership 123-6, 131, 136, 137, 144, 152
  nature of 102-4, 120, 125-6, 135
  see also under individual names; disruptive power
workers committees in platinum industry 271-2
Workforce Holdings 19
workplace order 175, 176, 177, 178, 184-7, 195; see also under labour broking
workplace relationship model 195-6; see also employment relationship model

Young Communist League (YCL) 106

Zondo, Tobias 212
Zuma, President 37-8
Zwane, Levy 135, 171

Printed and bound by CPI Group (UK) Ltd, Croydon, CR0 4YY
06/04/2026

14854926-0004